The Human Primate

Caricature of Darwin from *The Hornet* of 1871.

R. E. PASSINGHAM

THE HUMAN PRIMATE

W. H. FREEMAN AND COMPANY

Oxford and San Francisco

W. H. Freeman and Company Limited
20 Beaumont Street, Oxford, OX1 2NQ
660 Market Street, San Francisco, California 94104

Library of Congress Cataloging in Publication Data
Passingham, R. E., 1943-
The human primate.
Bibliography: p.
Includes index.
1. Psychology, Comparative.   2. Primates—Behavior.
3. Human behavior.   I. Title.
BF671.P4   156   81-5474
ISBN 0-7167-1356-X   AACR2
ISBN 0-7167-1357-8 (pbk.)

Typeset by Macmillan India Ltd., Bangalore
Printed in the United States of America

Ah! What is man? Wherefore does he why?
Whence did he whence? Whither is he withering?

DAN LENO

Contents

Preface

There are few who now deny that we share a common ancestry with the other primates. Yet it is little over a hundred years ago that Darwin (1871) published *The Descent of Man*, and was ridiculed by ignorant bishops and clever cartoonists (frontispiece). At the time there was little direct evidence from fossils, and Darwin was forced to rely on indirect evidence from similarities between the body of man and apes. By now the list of fossils is rapidly increasing, and we are starting to learn what our ancestors were really like.

But there is still controversy over the relevance of our ancestry to the understanding of the ways in which we behave. There are those who boldly assert that our genetic inheritance has little effect on our behaviour, and others who argue as if the proper study of man is not man but animals. Until now the issue has been discussed mainly in books written for a popular audience, and it is perhaps time for a more sober account.

Bertrand Russell once commented that 'whenever you happen to take your children to the Zoo you may observe in the eyes of the apes, when they are not performing gymnastic feats or cracking nuts, a strange strained sadness. One can almost imagine that they feel that they ought to become men, but cannot discover the secret of how to do it.' If ever apes learn to read I hope that they will find the secret in this book.

Acknowledgements

This book owes its origins to my teacher, George Ettlinger, who first introduced me to monkeys. It was he who fired my interest in the psychology and neurology of primates. I have worked with monkeys ever since.

The book ranges over many fields of interest and expertise. It was important that it be accessible to those who specialize in only one of the relevant disciplines. The physical anthropologist may know little psychology, the social scientist little neurology. I therefore chose to write at an elementary level; had I written a more technical account it would have differed in length but not in substance. I also tried to write in plain English and to avoid any jargon that might hinder understanding. I have shown particular chapters to experts in the relevant areas, in the hope of ensuring that the claims made in the text are scientifically accurate. I have been lucky to have received comments from Larry Weiskrantz, Alan Cowey and Peter Bryant (psychology), Richard Dawkins (sociobiology), Richard Wrangham and Alison Jolly (primatology), and Alan Walker and Bob Martin (physical anthropology). I am very grateful to them for the time they have given.

I have included a large number of photographs and diagrams. The purpose of these is not to entertain but to clarify the points made in the text by providing aids to the imagination. I thank Margaret Jones and Jenny Walker for producing the original diagrams and Jerry Broad and Paddy Summerfield for photographic help. The final artwork was supervised by Lawrence Fulbrook.

The manuscript has been through many changes. I am indebted to Sarah Bunney for the care with which she edited the text and for the many improvements she suggested. I am grateful to Judith Shingler who typed the final manuscript and to Cheryl Codling who typed an earlier draft.

I also thank Michael Rodgers of W. H. Freeman and Company for having faith in the manuscript and for convincing the author that it might be justified.

When I started to write the book I had supposed that I

knew how to write one. It was not until I had completed a draft that I realized that I did not. I would not have been able to summon up the morale to try again had it not been for the support given me by my wife, Clare. She has provided encouragement throughout, and has been ever tolerant of my enthusiasms. The book has had a long gestation period; that it was born is a testimony to her qualities as a midwife.

Oxford   R. E. PASSINGHAM
June 1981

Figure credits

For permission to reproduce illustrative material acknowledgement is made to the following: Figs 2.3, 3.1 and 4.20, The University of Chicago Press; Fig. 3.6, The Trustees of the British Museum (Natural History); Fig. 8.16, Grune and Stratton Inc.; Fig. 8.3 Sinauer Associates Inc.; Fig. 7.7, The Royal Anthropological Institute of Great Britain and Ireland; Fig. 8.4, MacMillan Publishing Co. Inc., copyright © 1975 by Philip Lieberman; Figs 10.3 and 10.4, MacMillan Publishing Co. Inc., copyright © 1972 by Alison Jolly; Fig. 10.5, David A. Hamburg and Elizabeth R. McGown, editors, *The Great Apes* (The Benjamin/Cummings Publishing Co. Inc., Menlo Park, 1979); Figs 2.11, 7.5, 8.14 and 8.15, copyright © by the American Association for the Advancement of Science; Figs 4.15, 8.10 and 10.6, copyright © by Scientific American, Inc., all rights reserved; Fig. 5.7 and Table 6.1, Oxford University Press; Figs 4.14, 5.8 and 8.1, The Zoological Society of London; Figs 8.5, 9.12 and 10.1, the New York Academy of Sciences; Figs 1.4 and 8.9, Erlbaum Associates; and Fig. 3.12, the British Psychological Society.

1 Relatives

Man has always considered himself to be set apart from animals. Ever since Linnaeus classified him as a primate in 1758 attempts have been made to put animals back in their proper place. Many differences have been claimed between man and the other primates. In the eighteenth century a Dutch anatomist called Petrus Camper thought that man should be reclassified because, unlike other primates, he lacked an intermaxillary bone or premaxilla in the upper jaw. In fact Camper was wrong, because this bone is indeed present during an early stage of man's development; but even had he been right such a trivial difference could hardly do much to bolster our pride. Others argued that man must be placed in an order of mammals of his own, because he cannot grasp with his feet (*Bimana*) like the other primates (*Quadrumana*), or because he is the only primate habitually to walk upright (*Erecta*) (Schultz 1950).

The nineteenth-century anatomist Richard Owen (1858) appreciated that differences in the brain would be of far greater significance. He put man in a separate subclass, set apart from another subclass containing all the other mammals. He called our subclass the Archencephela or 'ruling brains', claiming that there were three structures which were unique to the human brain. T. H. Huxley convincingly refuted these claims in a paper published in 1863 on 'the relations of man to the lower animals'; he demonstrated that all three structures, including the hippocampus minor, could be seen in the brains of other primates. He was rightly scornful of those who, as he put it, sought 'to base Man's dignity upon his great toe', or thought that 'we are lost if an Ape has a hippocampus minor'. The debate came to the notice of Charles Kingsley who parodied it in a famous passage in *The Water Babies*: 'You may think that there are important differences between you and an ape, such as being able to speak and make machines and know right from wrong, and say your prayers, and other little matters; but that is just a child's fancy, my dear. Nothing is to be depended on but the great hippopotamus test.' Understandably Kingsley felt that what mattered were not the minor details of anatomy but our many accomplishments.

The argument has continued into the twentieth century. There are still many, especially among the social scientists, who are not convinced of the relevance of Darwin's theory of evolution to the understanding of human behaviour. Wilson has been treated as a heretic for attempting in his book on sociobiology (1975) to treat man in the same way as other social species. The controversy continues (Ruse 1979); but the debate has the psychology of the Eskimo song duels in which the victor is judged by the ferocity of his insults. Science is not done in this way.

Man's image of himself has been much affected by advances in scientific understanding. When in 1872 Darwin wrote *The Expression of the Emotions in Man and Animals* he had to rely on anecdotal observations of monkeys and apes in zoos. It was only after 1930 that systematic studies began into the behaviour of the non-human primates in their natural surroundings, and it was not until the 1960s that knowledge began to accumulate fast (DeVore 1965; Altmann 1967). It was believed not so long ago that man was unique in making tools and transmitting cultural traditions. We now know that chimpanzees have a crude technology which they learn from each other. We are still the only animal that speaks; but we now find that we can teach chimpanzees to communicate with signs other than spoken language. Our pre-eminent position is clearly under attack, and it is time to take stock.

LIVING RELATIVES

That man is a primate is not now controversial. How closely we are related to other primates is an issue of more consequence.

Our nearest relatives are the African apes, the chimpanzee (*Pan troglodytes*) and the gorilla (*Gorilla gorilla*). Much of this account will dwell on the accomplishments of these marvellous creatures. The other primates are listed in Table 1.1, and Fig. 1.1 shows them in order of relatedness to man. The third great ape is the orang-utan (*Pongo pygmaeus*) from Borneo and Sumatra; this is nearer to our line than are the lesser apes—the gibbon (*Hylobates*) and the siamang (*Symphalangus syndactylus*). Of the monkeys we are closer to those that live in Africa and Asia, the Old World monkeys, than to those living in Central and South America, the monkeys of the New World.

Table 1.1 Classification of living primates

Order	Suborder	Infraorder	Superfamily	Family	Subfamily	Genus	Common name
Primates	Prosimii	Lemuriformes	Lemuroidea	Lemuridae	Lemurinae	*Lemur*	Common lemur
						Hapalemur	Gentle lemur
						Lepilemur	Sportive lemur
					Cheirogaleinae	*Cheirogaleus*	Dwarf lemur
						Microcebus	Mouse lemur
				Indridae		*Indri*	Indris
						Avahi	Avahi
						Propithecus	Sifaka
				Daubentoniidae		*Daubentonia*	Aye-aye
		Lorisiformes	Lorisoidea	Lorisidae		*Loris*	Slender loris
						Nycticebus	Slow loris
						Arctocebus	Angwantibo
						Perodicticus	Potto
				Galagidae		*Galago*	Bushbaby
		Tarsiiformes	Tarsioidea	Tarsiidae		*Tarsius*	Tarsier
	Anthropoidea	Platyrrhini	Ceboidea	Callithricidae	Callithricinae	*Callithrix*	Marmosets
						Leontideus	Tamarin
					Callimiconinae	*Callimico*	Goeldi's marmoset
				Cebidae	Aotinae	*Aotus*	Night monkey
						Callicebus	Titi
					Pithecinae	*Pithecia*	Saki
						Chiropotes	Saki
						Cacajao	Uakari
					Alouattinae	*Alouatta*	Howler
					Cebinae	*Cebus*	Capuchin
						Saimiri	Squirrel monkey
					Atelinae	*Ateles*	Spider monkey
						Brachyteles	Woolly spider monkey
						Lagothrix	Woolly monkey
		Catarrhini	Cercopithecoidea	Cercopithecidae	Cercopithecinae	*Macaca*	Macaque
						Cynopithecus	Black ape
						Cercocebus	Mangabey
						Papio	Baboon
						Theropithecus	Gelada
						Cercopithecus	Guenon
						Erythrocebus	Patas monkey
					Colobinae	*Presbytis*	Common langur
						Pygathrix	Douc langur
						Rhinopithecus	Snub-nosed langur
						Simias	Pagai Island langur
						Nasalis	Proboscis monkey
						Colobus	Guereza
			Hominoidea	Hylobatidae		*Hylobates*	Gibbon
						Symphalangus	Siamang
				Pongidae		*Pongo*	Orang-utan
						Pan	Chimpanzee
						Gorilla	Gorilla
				Hominidae		*Homo*	Man

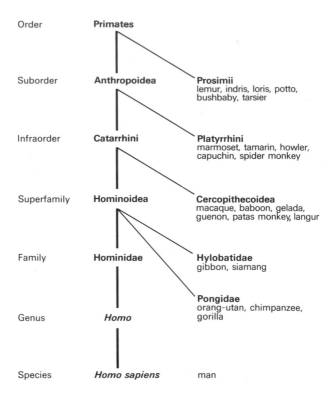

1.1 Relationship of man to the living non-human primates. Some of the genera are given. After Pilbeam (1970).

The monkeys, apes and man are sometimes referred to, perhaps arrogantly, as the 'higher' primates, and contrasted with the 'lower' primates. The latter are better referred to by the neutral term 'prosimians'; correspondingly the monkeys, apes and man are best called the 'simians'. The prosimians do not look like monkeys: some of them are strange-looking creatures; some are very beautiful. One odd little prosimian is portrayed in Fig. 1.2; this is the tarsier (*Tarsius*). This animal is important because it is more similar to the monkeys than to the other prosimians in some features of its anatomy. This has led some authorities to group the tarsier with the monkeys, apes and man as 'haplorhines', so as to distinguish it from the other prosimians, the 'strepsirhines' (Hill 1953; Luckett and Szalay 1975). This distinction is one that will be used in this book.

The genetic similarity between man and the other primates can be demonstrated in several ways: from the DNA of the genes themselves; from the proteins they specify; or from the bones and organs of the body they build. In the case of non-repeated sequences of DNA, the DNA of different species can be compared by fusing single strands from each species to form hybrid DNA. The

1.2 The tarsier (*Tarsius syrichta*). Courtesy of San Diego Zoo.

stability of the hybrid DNA gives a measure of the similarity of the two strands. Experiments of this sort suggest a startling conclusion: that the resemblance between the DNA of man and chimpanzee is greater than that between the DNA of mouse and rat (Kohne 1975). For non-repeated sequences over 98 per cent of the human and chimpanzee DNA is identical.

The proteins of different species can be compared in several ways. The sequence of amino acids has been worked out for some polypeptide chains, for example of the blood proteins. But the task of discovering the sequence is lengthy and impractical for large proteins. There are ways of demonstrating differences between proteins without the necessity for determining the sequence. These use electrophoretic or immunological techniques. The former make use of the fact that proteins vary in size and carry an electric charge; different proteins therefore migrate at different rates in an electric field. The immunological approach makes use of the fact that animals form antibodies to foreign proteins injected into them as antigens; the antibodies produced will differ according to the structure of the injected protein. If the proteins of different primates are injected into an animal such as a rabbit the similarity between the reactions caused provides an index of the extent to which the proteins are alike.

Whether the sequence of blood proteins is compared or immunological methods are used the result is the same. Man turns out to be closer to the chimpanzee and gorilla than they are to the other apes, the orang-utan and the gibbon (Goodman 1975). Forty-four proteins from man and chimpanzee have also been compared using electrophoresis, and again a remarkable similarity emerges (King and Wilson 1975). About half of the proteins surveyed react in the same way on the test. If we were to judge genetic distance on these grounds alone we would be forced to conclude that the relationship between man and chimpanzee is closer than that between different genera of rodents (Bruce and Ayala 1978).

Anatomists have long believed that we are most closely related to the chimpanzee and the gorilla; and it is reassuring that modern biochemical methods confirm this view. But there is a worrying disagreement. Anatomically we differ from these apes much more extensively than would have been supposed from the similarity in DNA and many proteins. The differences between the overall shape of the bodies of man and chimpanzee are many times greater than the differences in the structural genes (Cherry *et al.* 1978). Another striking example is provided by the brain. Even after the disparity in body size has been taken into account, the difference in size between the human and chimpanzee brain is greater than the difference between the brains of the chimpanzee and shrew. That this is true is demonstrated in Chapter 4.

How could such a vast difference arise if the genetic material is as similar as has been claimed? Our perplexity is almost certainly the result of our ignorance of the function of much of the DNA. By no means all the DNA codes for specific structural proteins; some of the genes are probably control genes, regulating the pace of development by turning processes on and off (Kohne 1975). Small changes in the regulating effects of such genes could have dramatic effects in altering the size and shape of the body's organs (Gould 1977). In Chapter 4 it is argued that the extraordinary development of the human brain is to be attributed to such a process.

ANCESTORS

We are closely related to the other primates. Placental mammals evolved around 100 million years ago, towards the end of the period geologists call the Cretaceous (Romer 1959). The primates diverged from the ancestral mammalian stock roughly 75 million years ago (Simons 1969). Fig. 1.3 shows the geological epochs during which

the primates have evolved, and also suggests the times at
which different primate groups diverged from the line
leading to modern man. Many details of the branching or
radiation have been omitted, for example the evolution of
the different subgroups of modern prosimians; the purpose is to emphasize man's lineage rather than to illustrate
the primate radiation as a whole.

It will be appreciated from Fig. 1.3 that we do not know
the exact time at which there was a separation between
man's family, the hominids, and the ape line, the pongids;
but it probably lies somewhere between 5 and 15 million
years ago (McHenry *et al.* 1980). The hominids have
therefore been evolving separately for between a tenth and
a fifth of the time during which primates have been on
Earth. But, as we shall see, our own species, *Homo sapiens*,
has been in existence for only 250 000 years or so; and our
subspecies, *Homo sapiens sapiens*, for a mere 35 000 years or
so. We are comparative newcomers.

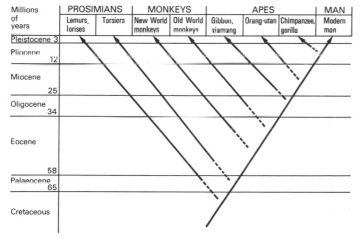

1.3 Primate radiation. The
geological timescale is given
on the left. The dates of
divergence from the line
leading to modern man are
only rough estimates; they
are based on figures given
by Simons (1969, 1972).

It will be apparent that there is much uncertainty about
the exact time at which our lineage separated from the
ancestral lines leading to other living primates. It is fossil
bones that provide the direct evidence for our ancestry,
but the sample of bones that we find is pathetically small;
of the creatures that have lived the bones of only a few
have survived and been found. When found it is rare for
the skeleton to be represented by more than one or two
bones. The fossil must then be dated, but our techniques
provide only very rough estimates. It is worth considering
each of these issues.

There are several crucial events during the evolution of
the primates for which we have evidence from very few

fossils indeed. One fundamental issue is the time at which the apes and monkeys separated. But the only fossil evidence for Old World primates during the first 15 million or so years of their radiation comes from the remains of a few genera found in the Fayum region of Egypt (Simons 1972). It is little wonder that there is still controversy.

But it is with the study of the evolution of the hominids that the poverty of our evidence is most disturbing. Most authorities believe that the ancestors of the hominids were the apes referred to as the dryopithecines, for which there is fossil evidence in Africa, Europe and Asia (Simons and Pilbeam 1972). The earliest dates for these apes are around 20 million years ago. The dryopithecine stock gave rise to several genera known collectively as the ramapithecids. One of these is *Ramapithecus*, a small primate known from both Africa and Asia (Pilbeam *et al.* 1977). Some authorities believe that *Ramapithecus* represents the earliest member of our family and should therefore be classified as a hominid (Simons 1977). Others accept that *Ramapithecus* may be ancestral to the hominids but have an open mind as to whether to regard it as an ape (Pilbeam *et al.* 1977). *Ramapithecus* is found in deposits dating from 14 to 8 or so million years ago. But there is then a gap of over 4 million years before good evidence is found of undisputed hominids in East Africa around 3.5 million years ago; and to fill this gap there are only one or two fragments (McHenry and Corrucini 1980).

The second problem in reconstructing our past is the preservation of only a few bones from any one individual. The task is made worse by the tendency for large bones to be fragmented, and by a bias in the sorts of bone that are preserved in the fossil record. The evolution of the early primates in the Palaeocene must be told mainly on the basis of teeth. McKenna (1976), an expert on the radiation of the early placental mammals, has delightfully carica-tured our efforts to reconstruct their appearance from the paltry evidence that we have: teeth, and bones from the ear and feet (see Fig. 1.4).

The problem becomes acute in discussions of our recent ancestry. The time at which the hominids diverged from the ancestral ape stock has been the subject of controversy (Pilbeam 1972). The matter could be settled if agreement could be reached on whether *Ramapithecus* can be re-garded as an early hominid; but almost all that remains of *Ramapithecus* are teeth and jaw fragments. This has not prevented attempts to give artistic impressions of what

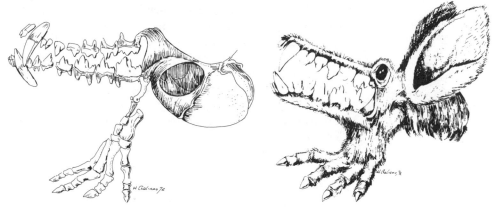

Ramapithecus was like, including details of the way it walked. Of course the teeth and jaw can be compared with those of undisputed hominids, but to classify on the basis of so few characteristics is not good practice in zoology. The palaeontologist must do his best given limited material, but we should remain sceptical of any dogmatic claims based on so little evidence.

We are understandably interested in when the genus *Homo* first appeared. Mary Leakey and co-workers (1976) have unearthed teeth and mandibles at Laetoli near Olduvai Gorge in Tanzania, and these are thought to be over 3.5 million years old. Other hominid fossils of around the same age have been found at Hadar in Ethiopia (Johanson and Taieb 1976; Johanson and Edey 1981). As yet there is no consensus about whether any of these finds represent *Homo* (Johanson and White 1979; Leakey, R. E. 1981; Tobias 1981). It is not until less than 2 million years ago that we find fully convincing evidence of the presence of *Homo*. At Lake Turkana in Kenya Richard Leakey's team have unearthed a skull referred to as KNM-ER 1470 (Leakey 1973a, b). The size of the braincase is impressive and it is very tempting to assign this skull to the genus *Homo*.

The story that can be told on the basis of fossil finds such as these is critically dependent on the accuracy of our techniques for dating fossils. In fact the fossil bones themselves cannot be dated; it is the deposits in which they are found that must provide the material that can be dated. There are several methods. Both potassium—argon and fission-track dating methods make use of the rate of decay of the radioactive isotopes to be found in volcanic ash. We can also use the direction of the magnetic field in the metals we find in sediments, as it reflects the direction of the Earth's magnetic field at the time that they were deposited.

1.4 McKenna's (1976) caricature of a fossil mammal as reconstructed from its bodily remains.

9

But where the deposits are not suitable for any of these methods indirect estimates must be made, for example from the type of fauna found in the same layers as the fossil to be dated.

Radiometric dates have been calculated for deposits at all the East African sites mentioned. But it is not possible to date directly the deposits in some caves in South Africa which have yielded some marvellous specimens of the australopithecines, an important group of early hominids. Tobias (1976) has reviewed the problem, and attempted to relate in time the finds from South and East Africa. Even where several methods can be used for dating, as at Lake Turkana, the margin of error is too wide for comfort. The site at which the skull KNM-ER 1470 was found has been given dates between 1.8 and 2.5 million years, although there is now general agreement that the correct date lies between 1.8 and 1.9 million years (Hay 1980; Curtis 1981). It is unsettling that it has proved so difficult to date a skull of this importance, as different interpretations of hominid evolution rest heavily on the dates attributed to the various fossils.

The most radical disagreement arises from the biochemical comparisons of man and other primates which have already been mentioned. Sarich and Cronin (1976) have calculated 'immunological distances' from the immunological reaction of the blood proteins of man and other primates. If the rate of evolutionary change of these proteins is known the 'immunological distances' provide an index of the time for which they have been separately evolving. Calculating dates of divergence in this way they estimate that man shared a common ancestry with the chimpanzee and gorilla as recently as 4 million years ago. This barely gives time for the evolution of so advanced a hominid as KNM-ER 1470 about 2 million years ago. The dates obtained for the divergence for the various other primate groups are also more recent than those estimated from potassium–argon dating (Simons 1969, 1981).

Several points require comment. The enterprise depends on first establishing the rate at which proteins change. This has been done by estimating the date at which the primates first evolved, and then comparing it with the immunological distance found between widely separated primates. If the date chosen is too late all the times calculated for the different primate groups will be too recent. Secondly, other biochemical methods for handling the antisera give dates earlier than those suggested by Sarich and his colleagues (Bauer 1974). The final point is that the rate of evolutionary change is affected by the length of the generations; the speed at which new mutations can become established in a population depends on the time it takes animals to become sexually mature. When a correction is made for generation length the dates of divergence are pushed back in time (Lovejoy *et al.* 1972; Kohne 1975). Until the 'clock' is better calibrated the results of molecular studies are not decisive.

It will be clear from what has been said that we can have little confidence in any particular story about the evolution of our hominid ancestors. This should not surprise us when we consider that there is still much uncertainty about the evolution of other mammalian groups such as the horses, for which there is a much more complete fossil record. There is not time in this book to go into the detail necessary when defending one story of hominid evolution or another. Two possible schemes are illustrated in Fig. 1.5, but there is disagreement amongst experts on many issues. The reader can consult the books by Wood

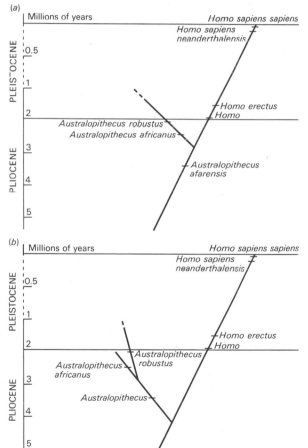

1.5 Two possible schemes for the evolution of the hominids. In scheme *a* the genus *Homo* is derived from an australopithecine stock (given the name *Australopithecus afarensis* by Johanson and White 1979). In scheme *b*, *Homo* is derived together with the australopithecines from a stock that is at present unknown. In scheme *b Homo* is regarded as having evolved separately for a longer period than in scheme *a*. The bar for *Homo* represents the skull KNM-ER 1470 and that for *Homo erectus* the skull KNM-ER 3733, both from Lake Turkana, Kenya.

(1978) and Kennedy (1980) for an up-to-date account.

Our more recent ancestry is less hotly disputed. Most authorities agree that *Homo erectus* lies on the direct line to modern man. The earliest skull comes from Lake Turkana in East Africa, and it is estimated to be 1.5 million years old (Leakey and Walker 1976). Later skulls have been found at Trinil in Java, and in caves at Choukoutien near Peking; the Trinil skulls are probably around 700 000 years old, the Peking skulls as recent as 400 000 years old (Day 1977).

Unfortunately we cannot be sure when *Homo sapiens* first appeared, as it is not possible to date the relevant fossils very accurately. A skull from Swanscombe in England and another from Steinheim in Germany both show some modern features, such as an expanded braincase. They may be over 250 000 years old (Oakley 1980). Campbell (1964) accepted these skulls as representing *Homo sapiens*, but placed them in their own subspecies *steinheimensis*, and many others agree with this proposal.

On this view modern man differs only in being another subspecies with the full title of *Homo sapiens sapiens*. He is found first in Europe around 35 000 years ago. The skeletons of the more rugged Neanderthal man (*Homo sapiens neanderthalensis*) are found in Europe from around 100 000 years on until they are suddenly replaced by the lighter *Homo sapiens sapiens*. Some believe the Neanderthals of Europe to be an offshoot from the main line leading to modern man. If this view is correct our more direct ancestors must be sought amongst peoples found outside Western Europe, perhaps in the Near East. What happened to the Neanderthals of Europe is unknown, and is the subject therefore of much controversy.

Our ignorance of our own ancestry should now be clear; it is apparent from the heat of the controversies that have raged. Where there is flimsy evidence opinions may be defended by dogmatic assertion in an effort to cover up the weak points in the tale. It is remarkable with what certainty claims have sometimes been made in the past, often on the basis of only a few fossil fragments.

We have evolved like any other species. It ought to be possible for us to view our evolution with the same scientific detachment that we cultivate when studying the history of other primates. The aim of the enterprise is no more to show that a man is nothing but an ape than that a chimpanzee is nothing but a shrew.

If species share a common ancestry they will have some characteristics which they share by virtue of their common ancestry, and others which have been separately derived in the different lines. The point is illustrated in the diagram (Fig. 1.6) which represents the characteristics of four living species, A1, A2, A3 and A4. Each has features which they all share, and which can be traced back in an unbroken line to the ancestral stock C. These shared features are indicated by the small squares. But all the four living species are also characterized by their own unique set of features. Some of these can be traced back to the intermediate stock B, as illustrated by the horizontal lines for A1 and A2, and the black squares for A3 and A4. Others are peculiar to the modern stock, for example the diagonal lines for A1 and the different set of diagonal lines for A4.

It is tempting to assume that wherever there are characteristics in common between two modern species they must have been inherited from the ancestral stock. But this does not follow, as can be seen from the hatched areas of A2 and A3: both share this feature, but it was not present in the ancestral or intermediate stocks; instead it must have been derived independently by A2 and A3.

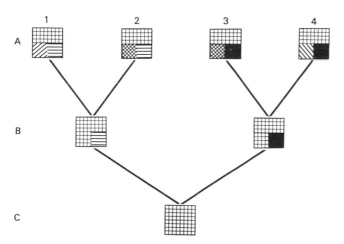

1.6 Schematic diagram of characteristics of modern (A) and ancestral (B and C) species. The different characteristics are shown by the different shadings.

This can happen if both move into similar environments to which they then adapt in similar ways. Whales, for example, look much like fishes although they are in fact mammals; in returning to the sea they have become streamlined, lost their hair and converted their limbs to flippers. The resemblance to fishes reflects the demands of underwater life. When the common adaptation occurs as a result of genetic change the two groups are said to undergo convergence or parallel evolution. But where the animals adapt by changing their behaviour they can also do so by parallel learning without any change in the genetic material.

The problems of interpretation are most intractable when considering the characteristics of mankind, and how they have been acquired. The reason is the hypertrophy of our brain, which endows us with such a proficiency at learning and in particular at handing on cultural traditions. It is not easy to see how to assess the relative contributions of the genes, the very rich cultural environment and the interaction between them.

The issue takes on more life if we consider claims that have actually been made. In his book on *The Expression of the Emotions in Man and Animals* Darwin (1872) compared the facial expressions of people with those of monkeys and apes. One reason for his interest was the hope that the theory of evolution might throw light on the origins of these expressions.

Let us take the human smile. It will become apparent that even for so simple a movement as this the task of seeking out its origins is formidable. Four distinct questions must be asked. Our attempts to answer them in this case will illustrate the logic of the way in which we might seek to discover the origins of any other aspects of human behaviour.

The first question is whether the smile is universal amongst mankind; that is whether all people smile. It is true, of course, that a trait need not be universal for it to be partly determined by genetic factors; it is only if these are the only factors affecting it that it must be universal. In spite of this proviso we might justifiably be impressed by any activity that was displayed by all peoples, and legitimately wonder whether it was not partly under the control of the genes.

There are two ways in which we might conduct the enquiry. One is to show photographs of various facial expressions to people from different cultures, asking them to interpret the emotions revealed. Ekman (1973) has done just this, and has found basic agreement between different peoples in the interpretation of expressions such as the smile; even isolated and preliterate people, such as the Fore of New Guinea, agree in their judgements with Americans. But there is no certainty that they have not learnt to interpret the faces of those Caucasians they have seen; they could do so even if their own expressions differed from those of other peoples.

This objection is partly answered by the alternative method of enquiry. This is to film the facial expressions used in different countries; and this has been done by Eibl-Eibesfeldt (1971, 1972) and by Morris (1977). These studies have been useful but they are not systematic. They certainly show similar expressions in people from a wide variety of cultures, but the context in which these are shown is not always adequately documented. Ekman (1973) has taken a more analytical approach. He chose his subjects from the Fore of New Guinea because he felt reasonably confident that they had not copied their expressions during the little contact they had had with Caucasians. The context for the expression was deliberately provided by reading them brief stories and asking them to pose the facial expressions that would be appropriate. On hearing that 'your friend has come and you are happy' they gave a convincing broad smile, as can be judged from the illustration (Fig. 1.7). The videotapes demonstrate that they have in their repertoire much the same expressions for happiness, sadness, anger and disgust as are seen the world over.

1.7 Smile posed by a man from the Fore of New Guinea. From Ekman (1973).

The second question is whether people learn to smile. To say that all people act in the same way is not to prove that they have not learnt to do so. While people might all independently learn a particular use of the smile, perhaps in polite greetings, it does not seem likely that they would all have independently learnt the same set of facial movements. However, there is only one way conclusively to prove that the basic pattern is not learnt, and that is to demonstrate that children still acquire the particular expression even if deprived of the opportunity to learn it.

Understandably we have qualms about intervening in the development of a child and depriving it of opportunities given to others. Experiments of this sort are conducted on animals, but even with animals they are technically difficult to perform. If we want to know if monkeys learn a particular facial expression we can deprive young monkeys of the company of their peers. If they still develop the expression they could not have done so by imitation of others. But if they fail to show it we cannot conclude that this expression is one which must be learnt; they may know how to produce it but be too emotionally disturbed to do so. A better experiment would deprive them not of the company of others but only of the opportunity to see their faces, perhaps by rearing them in the dark.

Nature has done this experiment for us. Some children are born blind, and therefore unable to see their parents' facial expressions. Eibl-Eibesfeldt (1973) has taken the opportunity to film the expressions of children born blind and deaf. There is no doubt that they smile, as can be seen from Fig. 1.8; and they do so in much the circumstances that elicit smiles from normal children, when they are patted or are playing with others. In rougher play or tickling games the smile turns into a laugh.

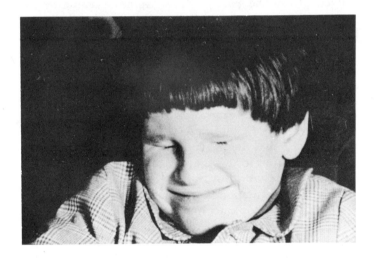

1.8 Smile shown by deaf and blind girl. From Eibl-Eibesfeldt (1973).

So far we have evidence that the smile is universal and that the basic expression is not learnt. This brings us to the third question. Can we identify in other primates facial expressions that look much like our smile? Van Hooff (1972) has drawn attention to the similarity between the human smile and the 'grin' or 'grimace' of monkeys and apes, and this can be appreciated in Fig. 1.9. The lips are drawn back and both sets of teeth exposed. Monkeys and apes 'grin' in this way when they are submissive in the presence of another animal; and this expression can also be seen in chimpanzees when they are trying to reassure a less dominant animal, as when a male approaches a mother with her infant. It is easily distinguished from the

1.9 'Grin' shown by chimpanzee. From van Hooff (1967).

'playface' in which the top teeth are covered and the jaw drops as seen in Fig. 1.10. This is shown by young monkeys and apes at play; tickling elicits the playface in chimpanzees, sometimes together with jerky grunts reminiscent of our laugh. Van Hooff (1972) proposes that the human smile is akin to the 'grin' and the laugh to the playface.

The last question is whether we have indeed inherited the smile from ancestral primates. But we have no way of answering this for certain, because all that remains of these ancestors is teeth and bones; the soft parts, the eye, brain and muscle are all irretrievably lost. It is true that we can reconstruct the probable appearance of ancestral species by analogy with living species which are built in a similar way. We can guess the diet from the teeth and the way they walked from the limb bones by making

1.10 'Playface' shown by chimpanzee. From van Hooff (1967).

comparisons with living species. We can determine the direction of gaze from the bony orbits and estimate the size of the brain from the cranial cavity. But what we will never be able to do is reconstruct the facial expressions from the skull. The bones themselves can never speak to us about the ways in which an animal communicated, or about other aspects of social living: the way the young were cared for, the social groups to which the animal was attached, or the fights in which it engaged. The fossil record is blank on such issues.

Our questions about communication, social organization and aggression can be answered only be appealing to indirect evidence, the behaviour of animals today. How fortunate we would be if there were some modern species which were 'living fossils', that had changed little in many millions of years, and had thus preserved for us the ways of a bygone age! It is very tempting to seize on some 'primitive' species in the vain hope that this animal is just such a 'fossil', enabling us to fill in the blank pages in the record. To take an example, the hedgehog (*Erinaceus europaeus*) is 'primitive' in some respects; that is it retains some of the characteristics that can be identified in fossils of early placental mammals. But that is no guarantee that it has not changed in other respects; we know, for instance, that its brain is larger than were the brains of early placentals (Jerison 1973). It would be dangerous to treat the hedgehog as if it were fully representative of the insect-eating mammals which lived 80 million years ago. Our problem is that all modern species differ in many respects from their ancestors, although it may be granted that some have changed more than others.

No one living species can provide the window through which we can observe our early ancestors in action. The gibbon, one of the apes, is not a copy of *Limnopithecus*, its probable ancestor of roughly 24 million years ago; the arms of *Limnopithecus* were not yet elongated and specialized for swinging through trees (Simons 1972). No more is the chimpanzee a copy of its early ancestor *Dryopithecus africanus* from 20 million or so years ago. If we wish to reconstruct the ancestral stock of living apes we will have to examine all the living apes and get clues from each. Each will have retained some ancestral characteristics and developed their own specializations; only by comparing them all can we sort out those features which they all possess. These common features may be reliable clues, evidence of retention from the ancestral stock, as illustrated by the squares in Fig. 1.6.

It is time to reconsider how we are to go about searching for the origins of behavioural characteristics such as the smile. If we find, when we examine other primates, that only a few of them exhibit the 'grin' we can have no confidence that the smile and the 'grin' are related; it could be that they have developed independently in several groups. But in fact we find the 'grin' and playface in most monkeys and apes (Jolly 1972) as well as in other mammals such as dogs (Fox 1971) and lions (Schaller 1972). The more widespread the trait the more likely that it is shared because of common inheritance from an ancestral stock.

Our hope was to establish whether the human smile is related to the 'grin' seen in other mammals. There is evidence that it is universal amongst mankind, need not be learnt, and has a resemblance to the 'grin' seen in many different mammal groups. Have we at last revealed the origins of the human smile? Van Hooff (1972) relates the smile to the 'grin' because both are used to reassure by appearing submissive. But young children smile when playing on their own as if the smile reflects a happy mood (Ames 1949). The smile posed by an adult from New Guinea in Fig. 1.7 was elicited by a story in which 'your friend has come and you are happy'. Perhaps the 'polite' smile on meeting strangers is forced or acted, the impression being artificially created that 'I am so happy to meet you'. That smiles grade into laughs is acknowledged by van Hooff (1972), and he therefore suggests that the origins of the smile may be complex, and that it is related not just to the 'grin' but also to the play face.

We can now appreciate that the task of tracing the origins of even such a simple movement as the smile is far from easy. There are four questions to consider. Is it universal? Is it influenced in any way by the genes? Can something like it be seen in other primates? And can it be attributed to inheritance from our ancestors? Even when an attempt has been made to give answers to these questions our conclusions can only be tentative. Issues such as these cannot be referred to the ultimate court of appeal, the fossil record.

But the claims that have caught the public imagination are not about the origins of simple movements such as our facial expressions. They encompass our whole social life. A series of popular books have been published on issues such as these. Why do we live in family groups (Morris 1967)? Why are all people not equal in social rank (Tiger and Fox

1972)? Why do we defend our property, and why do we go to war (Lorenz 1963; Ardrey 1967)?

Though the accounts given by these writers differ in many ways they are alike in sometimes naively assuming that where people and animals behave similarly they do so because of a common inheritance. We have seen that this assumption is dangerous. When comparing two related animal groups zoologists first consider whether similarities are due to parallel evolution. When comparing man and other primates we must follow the same scientific procedures; we must rule out not only parallel evolution but also parallel cultural change. Man may reach solutions by cultural adaptation to the same problems of living faced by other animals. This is not to deny the influence of genes on our abilities and our social life; only to point out that the influence of learning and culture are not always adequately considered in popular accounts comparing the social life of man and animals. Readers in search of an antidote can be prescribed the scepticism of Martin (1974) and Hinde (1974) and the sound judgement of Pfeiffer (1978).

Complex social traits are far removed from simple movements such as the smile which develops even under the most adverse environmental conditions. They are influenced by many factors and vary between different cultures. There are no practical ways of isolating the genetic factors; we cannot experimentally isolate a group of children from the society in which they live and see how they come to order their affairs as adults. Comparisons with other primates are not straightforward. What in human affairs are we to compare with the defence of its territory by a gibbon? Are we to equate this with people protecting their homes against robbery, or defending their country from invasion? Suppose we were satisfied that an analogy could be drawn, we must then examine other species to see how much the relevant social traits vary between and within species. We shall see in Chapter 10 that some primates defend territories and others do not, and that there are even species in which some members are territorial but others are not. In such circumstances how are we to limit our speculations?

The issue then is not the simple one that we might take it to be from popular accounts or indeed from some of the criticisms of these by social scientists. It is not the case that we know our inheritance to have an overriding effect on our social life, or, as others would have it, no effect at all. It is that we do not have adequate ways of assessing the contribution of our genetic inheritance. All we know is that we are specialized for learning, as attested by the size of our brain. Remember that the gap between man and chimpanzee in the development of the brain is wider than the gap between chimpanzee and shrew. What would we find out about the social life of a chimpanzee by watching a shrew?

HUMAN SPECIALIZATIONS

We have established that we are very closely related to the chimpanzee; and that we may have shared a common ancestor as recently as 5 to 15 million years ago. In that time our hominid ancestors acquired their own specializations as we can see from their remains; the relative size and pattern of the teeth, the shape of the pelvis, the orientation of the big toe for striding. But, as Huxley advised us, it is not on our big toe that we should rest our dignity. Our most important specialization is the growth of our brain. It is in our abilities and our way of life that we are most specialized, and about these we can pick only a few scraps of information from fossil and archaeological remains.

Those who tried to set us apart from animals had a point. We are unique in a way that makes it reasonable to separate animals from men. It is not just that we are so successful and have adapted to so many different environments. The dinosaurs too were successful, for 130 million years. Our species is unique because, in only 35 000 years or so, we have revolutionized the face of the Earth. We have created totally new environments for ourselves, have changed the lives of animals, and have the power to threaten the existence of life on our planet.

Here then is the paradox: on the one hand we are closely related to other primates; on the other we are not to be compared with them. Let us take first the degree of relationship. Taxonomists do not agree on the principles that should govern the classification of animals (Simpson 1975). But one point of view is that the classification should be based only on the number of branching points in the ancestral tree, irrespective of the degree of change in any of the lines. On such a view man and his direct ancestors may merit only a subfamily of their own, the Homininae, to be included with the great apes in the family of Hominidae (Delson and Andrews 1975). Goodman (1975) has supported this proposal because of the marked similarities between human and ape proteins.

A 'cladistic' tree of this sort pays no attention to notions of advancement or the degree of difference between species. But we may legitimately concern ourselves with the level reached by different species, that is with the 'grade' attained (Gould, S. J. 1976). We can ask how well they do what they do. If they are fish we might compare them in the efficiency of swimming; if they are mammals we could compare them in intelligence, for example the dolphin with the chimpanzee. The same grade can be achieved by animals that are only distantly related. Though man is very closely related to other primates he has reached a totally different grade.

That he has done so is the result of the dramatic increase in the relative size of the brain. It is on our brain that our accomplishments rest. Much of this book will be concerned with the consequences of this remarkable human specialization.

It is tempting to suppose that our own extraordinary abilities must be the result of specializations unique to our brain. The argument in the nineteenth century between Owen and Huxley was over just this. The evidence discussed in Chapter 4, indicates that in the main Huxley was right; our brain is a larger version of the chimpanzee brain, except for some specialization for speech. It is not unreasonable that our accomplishments should depend mainly on the size of our brain; after all a large general-purpose computer has capacities quite outside the range of a small computer. It will be argued here that, in the main, our brains follow the primate pattern, and that our achievements have been made possible by specialization in relative brain size.

The account starts by considering the way we are built; Chapters 2, 3 and 4 document our anatomical specializations. Chapter 5 argues that our intelligence can be attributed in the main to the relative size of our brain. The next three chapters review the accomplishments of our ancestors in technology, culture and language. Only by considering these can we understand the selection pressures that led to an increase in the size of the brain and thus in the intelligence of our ancestors. The last two chapters illustrate the effect of this selection for intelligence on the social order: the way the young are reared, the social groups, and the regulation of competition for resources. It becomes apparent that social disorder is not to be explained by regarding us as a 'territorial' or 'imperial' animal (Ardrey 1967; Tiger and Fox 1972). Both our strengths and our problems have the same source. If a catch phrase is needed it is that we are the 'brainy' animal.

2 Senses

Our senses determine the way in which the world appears to us. Information about it is received through the senses, and from this an internal representation or model of the world is constructed in the brain. This model allows the prediction of events so that they can be controlled. The world will therefore take on a different appearance to those animals which make much use of senses which are poorly developed in us; the dog, for instance, which has a highly developed sense of smell, or the bat which hears high frequencies to which we are deaf.

The senses differ in the aspects of the world about which they provide information. Animals need to be able to detect, localize and identify things. The senses of smell and hearing can be used to detect objects and events, but they are usually of less value in localizing them and judging their distance. The position of something can only be roughly determined from the strength of smells or from the difference in the time at which sounds reach the two ears; sight, on the other hand, can pinpoint the source of stimulation very accurately. Things cannot be as precisely identified from smells and sounds as they can from their appearance to the eye, their brightness, colour and shape. Sight is superior to the other senses in the detail it can provide about the nature of things and the relations between them.

There are three issues of special interest concerning the human senses. Why is our sense of smell so poor when it is so good in most other mammals? For, if it is of such value to them it is not obvious why it should be of less value to us. The second question arises from the observation of the crucial importance to us of sounds; all day we listen to and respond to the sounds of speech. Is our hearing, then, in any way specialized for the perception of speech? The final issue is over the sense we make of the world as we examine it with our eyes and hands. Is the world as we see and feel it different from the world as perceived by a chimpanzee? To find answers to these questions we must consider the evolution of our primate ancestors.

SMELL

Let us take first the question of our poor sensitivity to smells. Comparisons with other species will establish the extent to which we are unusual in this respect. We can then ask why our ancestors came to depend so little on smell.

Strangely it has been so widely assumed that we are less sensitive to smells than are other mammals that there have been few experiments to demonstrate the fact. Dogs have been shown to be around 100 times more sensitive than people to the smell of butyric acid (Moulton *et al.* 1960). Both rats and people have been tested for their ability to detect fine differences in concentration between solutions of amyl acetate; rats prove to be very much more sensitive than we are (Slotnick and Ptak 1977). Our nose is clearly not one of our strong points.

Because tests of this sort have not been conducted on many mammals we are forced to rely on studies of the olfactory apparatus itself. The nose or snout contains the turbinal system, a set of folded membranes on which there are sensory receptors for smell. The nerve fibres from the nose terminate in the olfactory bulbs of the brain. Some indication of the sensitivity of smell is therefore given by the number of olfactory fibres or the size of the olfactory bulbs. But the size of the bulbs is also affected by the size of the animal; larger animals tend to have bigger olfactory bulbs than smaller animals (Jerison 1973). Obviously we need some index which takes account of the size of the animal. The measure used here (Fig. 2.1) relates the size of the olfactory bulbs to the size of the medulla. This is a part of the brain which closely reflects the size of the animal's body, as will be explained in Chapter 4.

Our lack of sensitivity to smell is shown in the very poor development of our olfactory bulbs compared with other mammals. This can be seen in Fig. 2.1 where we are compared with insectivores and with other primates. Several other points emerge. The olfactory bulbs are smaller in insectivores that swim than in those that do not; they are smaller in primates than in those insectivores that live on land; and the bulbs are smaller in haplorhine primates (the tarsier, monkeys and apes) than in strepsirhine primates (prosimians other than the tarsier).

There is another respect in which the haplorhine primates differ from the strepsirhine primates and from other mammals; they lack the wet nose or 'rhinarium' that can be seen in animals such as cats or dogs. In mammals

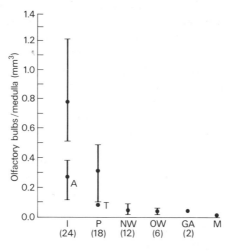

with a rhinarium the nose is attached to the upper gum by a strip of naked skin (Fig. 2.2). The moisture of the nose picks up minute samples of food and other things that make contact with the nose; these are then conveyed to a small olfactory organ, called Jacobsen's organ, at the base of the nasal septum. As can be seen in Fig. 2.2 in the tarsier as in monkeys, apes and man the nose is not connected to the upper gum in this way (Hill 1972). Jacobsen's organ has been identified in some monkeys (Starck 1975), but it is vestigial in adult man (Moulton 1978).

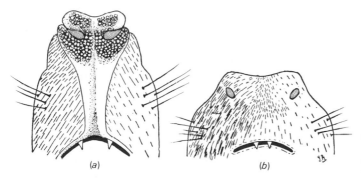

2.2 Rhinarium of a strepsirhine primate (lemur) (a); snout of a haplorhine primate (tarsier) (b). From Hill (1972).

It is now evident that we are not alone in having a poor sense of smell; so too have the monkeys and apes. To understand how this came about we must go back to the early evolution of the primates.

The early placental mammals appear to have fed mainly on insects, as far as can be told from their teeth. The skull of one of them, *Zalamdalestes* from the late Cretaceous, is shown in Fig. 2.3; it can be seen that its head was probably

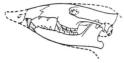

2.3 Skull of *Zalamdalestes* from the late Cretaceous of Mongolia and suggested reconstruction. From Romer (1959).

not unlike that of the hedgehog in appearance. Creatures such as this nosed around looking for insects. We do not know for certain whether they hunted on the ground in the undergrowth like the hedgehog, or whether they also ran on small branches like some of the tree shrews (*Tupaia*) of today; this issue will be taken up in the next chapter. What we do know is that the earliest primates were tree dwellers, able to move about efficiently in the trees by grasping branches with hand and foot. Of the primates today most still live and move in trees; and all prosimians do so except for the ring-tailed lemur, *Lemur catta*, which spends some of its day on the ground (Jolly 1972).

We need to know how the olfactory bulbs of early prosimians compared in size with those of other mammals of the time. We can get a rough estimate of the size of the olfactory bulbs in fossil species from the size of the hollow in the cranial cavity in which they rest. The bulbs of early prosimians do not seem to have been radically different in size from those of some modern prosimians (Radinsky 1970; Martin 1973). Relating the cast of the olfactory bulbs to the rest of the brain cast Radinsky (1970) points out that in prosimians of the Eocene the bulbs appear relatively smaller than in other contemporary mammals. But it is not clear to what extent this impression is given because of a reduction in the size of the bulbs or an increase in the size of the rest of the brain.

It is unfortunate that we also lack measurements of the olfactory bulbs in modern non-primate mammals other than the insectivores. Although the bulbs of modern prosimians are clearly smaller than those of some rodents or carnivores we do not know whether there are other mammals in which they are also as poorly developed.

There is no doubt, however, that the olfactory bulbs of simian primates are smaller than those of most other mammals. It is natural to seek for an explanation in their adaptation to life in the trees; birds which nest in trees also have reduced olfactory bulbs (Cobb 1960). Smells may be more quickly dispersed in trees than on the ground where they are better protected from air currents. But this effect should not be exaggerated; smell is clearly still of importance to the prosimians. They have specialized scent glands with which they mark both branches and other animals; and the members of the loris family also mark with their own urine, after washing their hands and feet in it to impart their scent (Doyle 1974).

The sense of smell may be thought to be of particular use to animals which are active in the evening or at night, when detailed vision becomes difficult. Only a minority of mammals are active by day. In one census only 20 per cent of the mammals in a region of forest in Gabon in equatorial Africa were found to be completely diurnal in their habits, and only 9.5 per cent of the mammals on Barro Colorado Island off Panama (Charles-Dominique 1975). There is reason for thinking that the ancestors of placental mammals may also have been active mainly during the evening or at night (Crompton *et al.* 1978). In this way they could have exploited niches not open to the reptiles. The latter would have been less active when the air was cool, as they lacked the efficient mechanism for regulating body temperature that was developed by birds and mammals.

Most of the living prosimians come out only in the evening or at night, and they probably evolved from ancestors which were nocturnal (Martin 1973). The best evidence for this is the existence in the eye of all modern strepsirhines of a light-reflecting membrane called a 'tapetum'. It is the presence of the tapetum which gives the characteristic shine to the eye of the cat. The tapetum increases the amount of light caught by the light-sensitive elements of the eye. The tapetum lies behind the layer containing these receptors so that light reaching it through this layer can be reflected back again across the receptors. It is of great value at night when light levels are low, and it is usually found only in the eyes of nocturnal animals; but it is not of value for vision in daylight. The presence of this membrane in the eyes of day-living prosimians such as the ring-tailed lemur, is best explained by supposing it to have been inherited from ancestors which were nocturnal.

By contrast all but one of the monkeys and apes are only active by day. The exception is the night monkey, *Aotus trivirgatus*, which, like the tarsier, probably evolved from diurnal ancestors (Noback 1975). Thus the olfactory bulbs are particularly small in those primates which live by day, as they are in birds, almost all of which are diurnal.

But this cannot be the full answer. Most squirrels are also diurnal and like primates are fully adapted to an arboreal life; but their olfactory bulbs are larger. We need to bring in one further factor: it is not just living in a tree and feeding by day that is crucial; it also matters how food is picked up. Squirrels and tree shrews usually pick food up with their mouth, whereas primates typically use their hands. For animals that forage with their mouths the nose provides direct information about the things that are about to make contact with the mouth. But an animal using its hand has the opportunity thoroughly to examine each object with its eye and hand before putting it in its mouth. It appears that within the monkeys and apes there has been selection for an improvement in detailed vision, and that they have become less dependent on the relatively crude information provided by smell.

We started by asking why people have such a poor sense of smell and we have found some clues. The ancestral primates took to the trees. The ability to grasp with the hand allowed them to examine things closely with eye and hand and not simply with nose and mouth. The ancestral monkeys and apes exploited daytime niches, and their detailed vision became much improved. We shall have more to say about all these aspects of primate evolution.

HEARING

The next question was whether our hearing is in any way specialized, and in particular for the perception of speech. We shall consider first the ability to detect sounds, and then the ability to interpret patterns of sounds, as in speech.

Detection

We can ask people if they can hear a tone. Although we cannot ask animals, there are other ways of finding the answer. We can, for instance, teach an animal to press a lever to work for its food; then we teach it that if it hears a tone an electric shock is imminent. If we now play the warning tone while the animal is pressing the lever we can observe whether the animal stops pressing the bar. Only if it hears the tone can it have cause for alarm; so that if it stops pressing the bar we may be confident that it heard the tone.

Whether an animal or person can detect a tone depends on its pitch, that is on the frequency of the sound waves. The characteristics of the hearing of a species can be systematically examined by playing sounds of different frequencies, and finding how loud a tone of any particular frequency must be if it is to be heard. The results may be plotted in the form of an audiogram, in which the frequency of the tone is plotted against the intensity needed for the tone to be reliably heard (Fig. 2.4). It can be seen from Fig 2.4 that the audiogram will show how

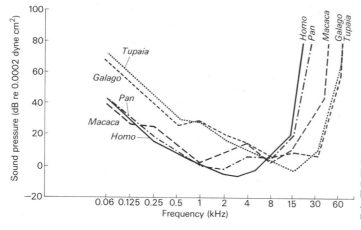

2.4 Audiograms of man, three non-human primates and tree shrew. The intensity of sound is plotted in decibels (dB) and the frequency of sound in kilohertz (kHz). *Tupaia*, tree shrew; *Galago*, bushbaby; *Macaca*, macaque; *Pan*, chimpanzee; *Homo*, man. After Stebbins (1978).

low or high a tone must be for the animal to be deaf to it, however loudly it is played.

Mammals have a more efficient mechanism than other vertebrates for the transmission of sounds from the eardrum to the inner ear; it works by a chain of three bony ossicles. As a result mammals can hear much higher frequencies than reptiles (Stebbins 1976). Many mammals can detect frequencies of 50 or more kilohertz (that is of 50 000 cycles per second); and bats and dolphins are sensitive to very much higher frequencies than that (Fig. 2.5).

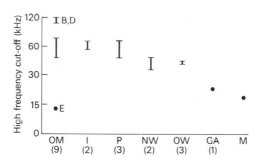

2.5 High-frequency cut-off in man and other mammals. High-frequency cut-off is a measure of the highest frequency in kilohertz (kHz) that can be detected. OM, other mammals; I, insectivores; P, prosimians; NW, New World monkeys; OW, Old World monkeys; GA, great ape; M, man. The upper range for other mammals is for bats (B) and the dolphin (D). E, elephant. The figures along the bottom give the number of species represented. Data from Masterton *et al.* (1969) and Heffner and Heffner (1980).

But people do less well: we can only detect frequencies up to 20 kilohertz or so (Figs 2.4 and 2.5). The apparent inferiority of our hearing remained a puzzle until studies were made of mammals that were larger than ourselves. It turns out that the elephant (*Elephas maximus*) can hear no higher than 12 kilohertz even if the sound is very intense (Heffner and Heffner 1980). It is a general rule in mammals that the larger the distance between the two ears the poorer is the higher frequency hearing. The most plausible explanation for this relationship is that it results from selective pressures for sound localization (Heffner and Heffner 1980). One cue to the direction from which a sound comes is given by the difference in the time at which it reaches the two ears; the greater the distance between the ears the more salient will be this cue. Animals with small heads compensate by making more use of other cues which are available only if the animal can hear high frequencies. It is not that man is aberrant; our high-frequency hearing is as would be expected for our size. Indeed the chimpanzee can hear only a little higher (Figs 2.4 and 2.5).

Our sensitivity to low frequencies is within the range of mammals that have been tested; Fig. 2.6 shows the sensitivity to sounds of 1 kilohertz. Like the monkeys and apes we are as acute in our hearing at this frequency as are the carnivores that have been tested. The prosimians are less sensitive, although no less so than other mammals.

2.6 Sensitivity at 1 kilohertz (kHz) measured in decibels. This is a measure of how loud a 1-kHz tone must be played in order to be heard. OM, other mammals; I, insectivores; P, prosimians; NW, New World monkeys; OW, Old World monkeys; GA, great ape; M, man. The figures along the bottom give the number of species represented. Data from Masterton *et al.* (1969).

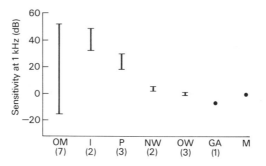

So far we have enquired only whether we can hear an isolated tone of any particular frequency; but this is only one measure of the sensitivity of our hearing. In real life we are often called upon to make comparisons between sounds that we can hear. Our ability to do this can be measured in the laboratory by presenting a standard tone, and then seeing how close a comparison tone must be to be judged as the same. With monkeys the same procedure can be followed, the monkey being required to lift its hand from a key when it hears a change in a tone that is presented repetitively (Stebbins 1973).

These judgements can be made for differences in pitch or loudness. In Fig. 2.7 we are compared with monkeys in our ability to resolve fine differences in frequency. Although, as we have seen, the range of frequencies we can hear extends less high than in monkeys, we appear to be better at detecting differences in pitch within that range

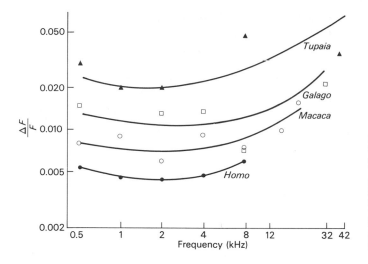

2.7 Change in frequency that can be detected plotted over a range of frequencies. The graph shows the difference detected (ΔF) as a function of the frequency of the standard stimulus (F). *Tupaia*, tree shrew; *Galago*, bushbaby; *Macaca*, macaque; *Homo*, man. After Stebbins (1971).

(Stebbins 1976). The ability of monkeys to judge a change in intensity has also been tested; and again we turn out to be slightly more sensitive (Stebbins 1978). But in neither of these experiments have chimpanzees been tested, and it is possible that they too might perform better than a monkey.

Speech perception

We have no solid evidence of any specialization in human hearing for the detection of sounds, or for the resolution of fine differences in frequency or intensity. We have next to examine our ability to perceive patterns of sounds. We are so dependent in particular on the comprehension of speech that it is not implausible that we might have specialized perceptual mechanisms for this purpose.

As before we can compare animals with people only if we can devise methods for finding out from the animal what sounds it thinks it has heard. The tasks that have been used have not always been well designed. Monkeys have, for example, been trained to reach to the left given one sound and to the right given another, although it is known that an animal attends better to a stimulus if required to reach towards it (Cowey 1968). Difficulties in training monkeys in this way to discriminate between sounds led, at one time, to speculations that primates might be less attentive to sounds than carnivores such as cats (Wegener 1964); we now know that monkeys are as efficient at making these discriminations as cats if they are tested in identical ways (Wegener 1976).

31

Given that an animal can be shown to tell the difference between two sounds it is natural to ask whether it can recognize other examples of the same sound. The point is most clearly made by considering human speech; we recognize the sounds of speech as being the same when produced by different speakers. This requires that the differences in intensity, pitch and quality of the voice be ignored when identifying the sound. It could be that this ability is restricted to people.

In fact it is not. Chinchillas (*Chinchilla laniger*) can tell the difference between the sounds [a] and [i], and continue to do so even when they hear the vowels spoken by different people or hear vowels which have been artificially synthesized (Burdick and Miller 1975). Cats trained to tell the difference between [i] and [u] as spoken by a man recognize them when spoken by a woman (Dewson 1964). Old World monkeys trained to make a discrimination between [ba] and [da] can then recognize new examples from the same speaker or the same sounds synthesized (Sinnott *et al.* 1976). There is no reason to assume that animals are naturally less proficient than people in this respect, especially considering the vast amount of practice that people have at listening to the sounds of speech.

It has been suggested that we might differ from other animals in the way in which we categorize speech sounds. Lieberman (1975) has claimed for us the ability for 'categorical perception'. He gives the example of [b] and [p]: these differ in the time that elapses between the start of the consonant and the onset of 'voicing', that is the production by the vocal cords of a periodic sound source. If voicing starts with only a short delay the sound is categorized as a [b], and if with a long delay it is categorized as a [p]. Examples of [b] and [p] can be synthesized which vary in the time of onset of voicing. People exposed to these find it relatively easy to assign them to the one category or the other, [b] or [p]. Within either category they treat examples differing in time of voicing as much alike, although they can certainly tell the difference between them. The claim is, then, that we impose categories on the speech sounds we hear (Pisoni 1979).

But it is not obvious that animals behave differently. There have been several studies of the ability of animals to discriminate phonemes, that is the basic units of significant sound in a language. Chinchillas appear to draw the distinction between [da] and [ta] in much the same way as

English-speaking subjects (Kuhl and Miller 1975; Kuhl 1979). Rhesus monkeys (*Macaca mulatta*) are better at making discriminations between phonemes than they are at distinguishing examples from within one category of phoneme (Morse and Snowdon 1975; Waters and Wilson 1976; Snowdon 1979). In one study Old World monkeys and people were tested on the same task in the same apparatus (Sinnott *et al.* 1976). People took longer to make judgements about examples if they came from the same rather than different categories. This was not found for the monkeys; but this could be because they lack not the capacity but our long experience of listening to speech. It would be rash to conclude on this evidence alone that we possess special mechanisms for the perception of speech.

TOUCH

The last question posed was whether the world feels and looks the same to another primate as it does to us. There are three issues to discuss: how the world appears to our touch; the aspects of the world revealed to us by our vision; and the way in which we construct a three-dimensional world of objects by combining information provided by our hands and eyes. Each of these will be treated in turn.

Most mammals use their mouth to pick up objects. They need information about things that are near the muzzle, and this is given to them by facial hairs or vibrissae. Many mammals have vibrissae on their brows, cheeks, chin and lips, and a further set on the wrists of their forelimbs. Although lemurs have a full complement of vibrissae there are fewer in lorises and tarsiers. While the monkeys retain some vibrissae they have been entirely lost by apes and by man (Le Gros Clark 1971; Hill 1972).

The reduction in vibrissae reflects the lesser importance of sensory receptors on the face in animals which make more use of their hands than of their face and muzzle in exploring the world and obtaining food. Almost all primates have nails rather than claws on all their fingers (see Chapter 3). Nails provide mechanical support for the ridged touch pads at the ends of their fingers and thus permit the development of pads which are very large and sensitive.

Some of the nerve endings in the hands and feet of primates differ from the end organs found in the hairless skin of other mammals; these are the balls of neurofibrils, referred to as Meissnerform corpuscles (Winkelmann 1963). Even racoons (*Procyon*), which have grasping hands rather than paws, lack these particular nerve endings. The corpuscles in our hands are more complex with several convolutions. This might suggest a greater sensitivity to light touch; but no one has carried out experiments to compare directly the sensitivity of our hands and those of another primate such as a chimpanzee.

Information from touch receptors is relayed in sensory fibres to the neocortex of the brain. The area in which it is first analysed is shown in Fig. 2.8. By recording the electrical activity of cells in this area we can see which groups of cells respond when a particular part of the body is touched. We find that there is a 'map' representing the body surface; cells respond in different parts of the area according to where the body is stimulated. But the map is distorted, some parts being represented by more tissue than is warranted by their size. The extent of the representation is related to the importance to the animal of information from that region of the body.

In small mammals such as the hedgehog, tree shrew or rat the sensory representation of the muzzle, lips and vibrissae is very extensive (Woolsey 1958; Lende and Sadler 1967; Lende 1970). In the rat the vibrissae account for 20 per cent of the map of the body, and the head and neck a further 46 per cent; the limbs take up only 27 per cent of the representation, and the trunk and tail a mere 7 per cent (Welker 1971). To primates it matters more what they feel with their hands, and the area devoted to the hand is proportionately larger than in a rodent or carnivore (Fig. 2.8). The North American racoon (*Procyon lotor*), which can grasp with its hand like primates, also has a large sensory representation for the hand (Welker and Seidenstein 1959). Some New World monkeys can use their tails as a fifth limb for grasping, and have at the end of their tails a patch of bare ridged skin which is very sensitive to touch. In one such monkey, the spider monkey (*Ateles*), the part of the map devoted to the tail is five times as large as the corresponding area in a macaque (Radinsky 1975a).

The area devoted to the hand appears to be relatively larger in squirrel monkeys (*Saimiri sciureus*) than in marmosets which have claws rather than nails on their hands and feet. In the squirrel monkey the area for the hand is so enlarged that it separates the areas for the face and neck, and thus distorts the sequence in the map; the same is true for rhesus monkeys, chimpanzees and man (Woolsey 1958). In man the area representing the hand is

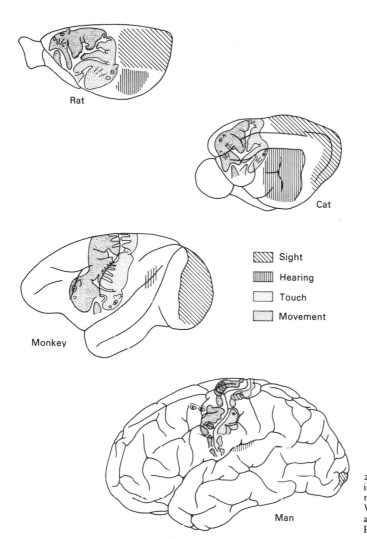

2.8 Sensory and motor areas in the brains of rat, cat, monkey and man. After Woolsey (1958) and Penfield and Jaspar (1954). From Passingham (1981c).

very large as in the rhesus monkey and chimpanzee; it forms roughly a quarter of the total representation of the body as in the rhesus monkey. But the foot is represented by an area roughly half that given over to the hand, whereas in the rhesus monkey the foot and hand are equally represented (Passingham 1973). In the human brain, then, the representation of the foot is relatively small. This probably reflects our loss of the ability to manipulate things with our feet, as a result of specializations of the foot for walking upright.

We owe the great sensitivity of our hands to the early adaptation by the ancestral primates to life in the trees. The same hands that were able to grasp branches when moving

35

in the trees could be used to grasp objects such as food. The hands became of great value in exploring the world and there was selection for greater sensitivity. But there is no good evidence that our own hands are more sensitive than those of, let us say, a chimpanzee.

SIGHT

For our detailed knowledge of the world we are crucially dependent on sight. Our vision is excellent: we can detect fine detail, we are sensitive to colour, and we can make accurate judgements of distance. In each of these aspects of our vision we are indebted to our primate ancestry.

Detail

The ability to resolve fine detail is partly determined by the structure of the retina. A schematic cross-section through the human retina is shown in Fig. 2.9. There are two light-sensitive elements, the rods and the cones; the rods are most efficient in dim light, as in twilight, and the cones in bright light, as in daylight. These receptor elements are connected to 'bipolar' cells, and these in turn to 'ganglion' cells which send their nerve fibres or axons through the optic nerve.

There are two respects in which the eyes of nocturnal and diurnal mammals differ (Glickstein 1976). The retinae of nocturnal species tend to contain mostly rods; the retinae of some strongly diurnal species, such as the common tree shrew (*Tupaia glis*), have cones but no rods. There are other species which are active by day in whose retinae both rods and cones can be found; this is true, for instance, of monkeys and apes.

The other difference lies in the way in which the receptor cells are connected via the bipolar cells to the ganglion cells (Glickstein 1976). In nocturnal species any one ganglion cell may receive information directly or indirectly from very many receptor cells. High sensitivity to light is achieved by this arrangement; a single ganglion cell can pool information from many receptors. But this can be done only by sacrificing the ability to tell exactly where on the retina the light falls; the ganglion cell does not know which of the many receptors to which it is connected have been stimulated. For animals that live by

LIGHT

nerve fibres

ganglion cells

bipolar cells

cone

rods

2.9 Schematic diagram of a section through the retina. From Gregory (1966).

day the detection of light is not at a premium; they can afford to gain greater resolving power at the expense of lesser sensitivity. This can be achieved by arranging that a single ganglion cell will receive information from rather few receptor cells.

We should expect to find that diurnal animals can see finer detail than nocturnal ones. To test the animal's ability we can teach it to choose between a pattern of vertical lines and a blank field, and arrange that choice of the vertical lines wins the animal food. If the width of the lines is then decreased by stages we can determine the point at which the animal can no longer choose the lines consistently, because it no longer reliably sees them. This point is a measure of the acuity of the animal's vision.

The results of such tests are clear-cut. Nocturnal

mammals such as rats and cats have poor visual acuity, whereas acuity is good in the common tree shrew, a diurnal mammal (Walls 1967; Ordy and Samorajski 1968). Diurnal primates, such as the ring-tailed lemur or squirrel monkey, are roughly three times as good at resolving fine lines as two nocturnal primates, the thick-tailed bushbaby (*Galago crassicaudatus*) and the night monkey (Ordy and Samorajski 1968) (Fig. 2.10).

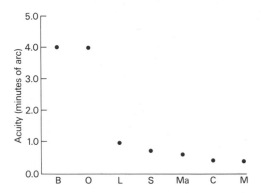

2.10 Visual acuity in minutes of arc as measured in man and some other primates. B, bushbaby; O, owl monkey or night monkey; L, lemur; S, squirrel monkey; Ma, macaque; C, cebus monkey; M, man. Data from Ordy and Samorajski (1968) and DeValois and Jacobs (1971).

The retina of monkeys, apes and man has a further specialization which is thought to improve the resolving power of the eye. In many day-living mammals there is a central area of the retina, referred to as the area centralis, in which the ratio of receptors to ganglion cells is lower than it is at the periphery of the retina. This is a local area which is capable of higher resolution than the surrounding tissue of the retina. In haplorhine primates, that is in the tarsier, monkeys and apes, this area contains a pit or fovea, in which the cell layers overlying the receptor elements are pushed to one side (Wolin and Massopust 1970). No other mammalian retina possesses a fovea, but a fovea can be identified in the retinae of some fish, reptiles and birds (Walls 1967). Why the fovea is shaped as it is we cannot be certain; there are several rival views (Walls 1967; Glickstein 1976).

Here we need consider only the assumption that it acts to improve visual resolution, however it is supposed to do so. There is no question that this is the region of highest resolution in the retina. It may be entirely free of rods, as in the chimpanzee and man. In our retina there are $1 : 1.3$ receptors per ganglion cell near the fovea compared with $1 : 32$ in the extreme periphery (Wolin and Massopust 1970). Using rhesus monkeys it has been shown that destruction of tissue within the fovea leads to a decrease in visual acuity (Weiskrantz and Cowey 1967).

But it remains to be shown that an animal with a fovea is better equipped than one without; this can be demonstrated only by comparing the abilities of different species. Neither the common tree shrew nor the ring-tailed lemur has a fovea; yet they appear to be able to see lines which subtend an angle of only 1.0 minute of arc at the retina, and can probably do slightly better (Ordy and Samorajski 1968) (Fig. 2.10). Though the values for monkey, ape and man differ slightly from each other the resolving power of their eyes is probably much the same when account is taken of differences between the size of their eyes. The visual acuity of monkey, ape and man is nearly twice as good as that of the lemur, and this represents a valuable improvement.

We have inherited an eye that is very acute. We can detect detail 10 times finer than anything a cat can resolve, and over 40 times finer than the smallest stimuli a rat can see (Hughes 1977). We owe this ability to an important event in the history of our ancestors, the time when they were able to leave the refuge of a nocturnal life. Although it is now nocturnal the tarsier too probably had diurnal ancestors; it is not easy to explain in any other way how it came to possess a fovea in its retina (Noback 1975). But the eyes of our haplorhine ancestors did not become totally specialized for daytime vision. The retina of monkeys, apes and man contains a mixture of rods and cones; by contrast the retina of tree shrews, squirrels and most birds contains only cones (Walls 1967). The human eye, like that of the monkeys and apes, is a compromise. The rods tend to be distributed towards the periphery of the eye, and our peripheral vision is very sensitive to light; owls are only two and a half times as sensitive as we are (Martin 1978). At the same time we can resolve very fine detail with our foveal vision, even if we cannot match the eye of the hawk (Walls 1967). If our eye is a compromise it is a good one.

Colour

There are many mammals which do not see colours; and of those that do there are some that do not see them exactly as we do. The ability to see colour depends on pigments contained in the cones but not in the rods. Those nocturnal mammals which have no cones in their retina, such as rats, are blind to all colours.

We cannot be sure from the presence of cones in the retina that an animal has colour vision. We can prove this only by giving tests in which the animal is presented with a choice between coloured patches, and must consistently pick out one colour rather than the other if it is to obtain food. It is not easy to set up tests which conclusively prove that the animal can distinguish colours. We must be sure that it is not basing its choice on differences in brightness between the colours; even a colour-blind animal may tell colours apart by their subjective brightness. Either the pairs of colours must be equal in brightness to the animal, or the brightness of each must be varied randomly from trial to trial, so that brightness could not form the basis for a consistent choice of one of the colours.

If our animal passes a test of this sort, and can distinguish, let us say, blue from green whatever their brightness, our next task is to try it on colours from other parts of the spectrum. People with one form of colour-blindness are unable to distinguish wavelengths over one part of the spectrum, in some cases green and red; these people are referred to as dichromats. A person with normal colour vision is called a trichromat; three colours must be mixed in order to match any colour he sees. An animal can only be shown to be a trichromat if its colour vision is assessed at several points on the spectrum.

The ability to see colours has been demonstrated in fish, reptiles and birds (Hess 1973). We may assume that it was present in the reptilian ancestors of the mammals, but it has been argued that it may have been lost by the early mammals (Walls 1967). The structure of the cone in the mammalian retina differs in some details from the cone of other vertebrates, and this might be explained by supposing that the early mammals were nocturnal and had eyes which only contained rods, and that the cone was later independently redeveloped from the rods. But we cannot be sure that the early mammals were active only at night; if some were active in twilight they could have retained some form of colour vision like the cat. The cat is crepuscular in its habits; its eye possesses some cones and it can distinguish colours at various points along the spectrum, although it prefers to depend on differences in brightness (Mello 1968).

Not many mammals have been adequately tested for colour vision. We may assume that it is absent in nocturnal species where there are few or no cones in the retina, as in most of the prosimians (Wolin and Massopust 1970); the thick-tailed bushbaby, for example, is unable to distinguish red from green (Ehrlich and Calvin 1967), although it has not been tried on other pairs, such as blue and red. In day-living mammals some form of colour vision has been shown in the common tree shrew and European squirrel (*Sciurus vulgaris*), as well as in ungulates such as horses and pigs (Walls 1967; DeValois and Jacobs 1971; Hess 1973). All the monkeys that have been tested, apart from the night monkey, can see colours (DeValois and Jacobs 1971). Some squirrel monkeys and cebus monkeys (*Cebus*), both from the New World, are trichromats, but are poorer than normal human subjects at making discriminations within the longer wavelengths, that is towards the red end of the spectrum. This can be seen from Fig.2.11, which plots the minimum discriminable difference in

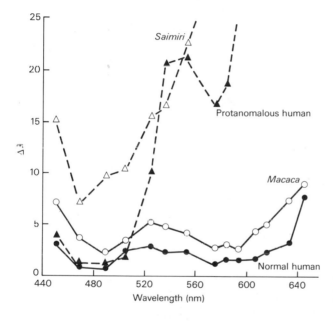

2.11 Hue discrimination in normal trichromats (macaques and man) and protonomalous trichromats (squirrel monkeys and man). The graph shows the minimum discriminable difference in wavelength ($\Delta\lambda$) and the wavelengths at which measurements were taken. Note that the squirrel monkeys and protonomalous human subjects have good hue discrimination only in the shorter wavelengths. After DeValois and Jacobs (1968).

wavelength for each of 14 wavelengths. These monkeys are like those people who are classified as 'protanomalous' trichromats; that is, compared with a person with normal trichromatic vision they require more red to be mixed with green if they are to see yellow. The rhesus monkey, an Old World monkey, is a normal trichromat (Fig.2.11) and so is the chimpanzee. There is no significant difference between the colour vision of these primates and a normal human subject, except that people are slightly more sensitive to differences in colour at all wavelengths.

We owe our colour vision to the adaptation of our simian ancestors to daytime activity. Like other diurnal mammals they took advantage of the information that was given by wavelength. To an animal with colour vision objects stand out much more effectively from their background than they do to an animal judging on the basis of contrast in brightness alone. The advantages to an animal searching for fruit amongst leaves or jumping in the branches are obvious. Why the primates of the Old World developed a more refined colour vision than those of the New World is less obvious. Whatever the reasons we have benefited in inheriting efficient colour vision over a wide range of the spectrum.

Depth

The third aspect of our vision that is of especial interest is our ability to use stereoscopic cues to depth. There are several ways in which we can judge distance. The further away an object is in space the less coarse is the apparent texture; parallel lines appear to come together as they go into the distance; and if the head is moved distant objects appear to move more slowly than objects which are close, an effect referred to as motion parallax. All these cues can be used by each eye separately, but there are two cues which depend on the use of both eyes, convergence and stereopsis. If the eyes converge on an object its distance can in theory be estimated from the degree of convergence of the two eyes, so long as the object is relatively close.

Stereopsis works by comparing the different views of the world provided by the two eyes. You can convince yourself that the views are not the same if you look at a nearby object first through one eye and then through the other. For the brain to be able to compare the two views information from the two eyes must come together in some part of the brain. Fig.2.12 shows one way in which this is arranged in the brain of a primate. If the gaze is directed forward the field of view to the left (shaded) falls on the right half of each retina; from here fibres pass to the right hemisphere, those from the left eye crossing to the other side at the optic chiasm, and those from the right remaining on the same side; these fibres then terminate in the lateral geniculate nucleus, which in turn sends fibres to the visual area of the neocortex of the right hemisphere (shaded). This area is thus provided with information about the view of the world to the left as seen by each eye.

We cannot prove that an animal can or cannot use stereoscopic cues to depth by indirect arguments from its anatomy; we need direct tests in which the animal is required to make judgements about depth. It is a requirement

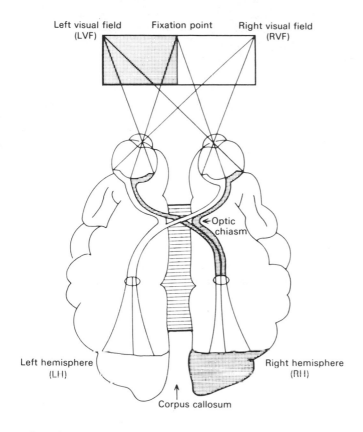

Left visual field (LVF)   Fixation point   Right visual field (RVF)

←Optic chiasm

Left hemisphere (LH)   Right hemisphere (RH)

Corpus callosum

2.12 Schematic diagram of the arrangement of the visual pathways in a typical primate. It will be seen that information from the left field of view reaches the visual areas of the neocortex of the right hemisphere. This happens because the optic fibres from the right half of the left retina cross at the optic chiasm while those from the right half of the right retina remain uncrossed. After Cohen (1977).

of such tests that the animal be unable to make use of cues to depth other than those provided by stereopsis; it must not be possible to solve the problem by using motion parallax or convergence. One elegant test has been devised by Julesz (1971). In this the subject is shown two patterns of randomly distributed dots, one to each eye; the patterns are identical except that a central group of dots in one pattern is shifted slightly to one side compared with its position in the other pattern. The two eyes get an identical view of the two patterns, except for the central section of dots which is viewed differently by the two eyes. The subjective impression is that the central section appears to stand out in depth from the other dots surrounding it; but this impression is created only if the subject has the ability to use stereoscopic cues to depth. Using these patterns stereoscopic vision has been convincingly demonstrated in the falcon (*Falco sparverius*) (Fox *et al.* 1977) and in the rhesus monkey (Cowey *et al.* 1975).

An alternative test is to show the animal rods and require it to judge which is the closer. Bushbabies have been reported to pass this test, but the experimental conditions were such that the animals could have been using motion parallax (Treff 1967). Under conditions in which the only available cues were those of stereopsis cats have been shown to be able to make judgements of depth (Fox and Blake 1971). By using thin needles, one above the other, it is possible to measure how accurately monkeys can make fine judgements of depth; it turns out that a rhesus monkey can perform as well as human subjects (Sarmiento 1975).

There is another, though less direct, way in which we can establish whether an animal can make use of stereoscopic cues for depth. This is to record the electrical activity of cells in the visual areas of the brain, and thus to determine whether the relevant mechanisms for analysing depth can be found in the brain. In monkeys and cats cells have been found which alter their activity according to the apparent depth of an object (Pettigrew 1972). Cells with the same properties have also been reported in the visual areas of the sheep brain (Clarke *et al.* 1976). Thus stereoscopic depth vision is not confined to primates and carnivores.

Stereoscopic cues to depth are available only for that part of the field of view for which information is available from both eyes. The size of this binocular area can be estimated from experiments in which electrical recordings are taken from the visual areas of the brain. For each position in the animal's field of view we can determine whether a visual stimulus causes a cell to fire whichever eye is allowed to see it. We find that even in those mammals with eyes placed to the side of the head the area of binocular overlap is by no means negligible: it measures around 50° in the European hedgehog and around 60° in the common tree shrew and grey squirrel (*Sciurus carolinensis*) (Kaas *et al.* 1970, 1972). Whether these animals are able to make use of stereoscopic depth cues in this region we do not yet know, as the relevant experiments have not yet been carried out. But the lateral position of the eyes cannot be used as evidence that these animals lack stereopsis.

If we cannot tell whether an animal has stereopsis from the size of the area of binocular overlap we cannot do so either from the position of the eyes in a fossil species. Yet the changing position of the eyes during primate evolution has often been used as evidence for the evolution within the primates of the mechanism for stereoscopic depth vision. In primates of the Palaeocene, such as *Palaechthon* (Kay and Cartmill 1974), the orbits were placed towards the side of the head; in prosimians of the Eocene they were positioned frontally, as in *Tetonius* and *Notharctus*; and in monkeys of the Oligocene, such as *Apidum* and *Tremacebus* (Hershkovitz 1974), the orbits were placed well forwards as in living monkeys (Simons 1962) (Fig. 2.13). This trend is impressive, and needs explaining.

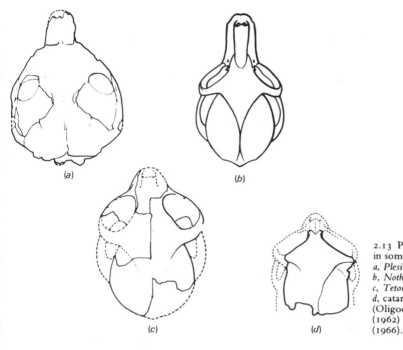

(a)

(b)

(c)

(d)

2.13 Position of the orbits in some fossil primates. *a, Plesiadapis* (Palaeocene); *b, Notharctus* (Eocene); *c, Tetonius* (Eocene); *d*, catarrhine monkey (Oligocene). After Simons (1962) and Buettner-Janusch (1966).

We may hope to get hints by looking at the position of the eyes in living mammals (Walls 1967). Many small mammals—insectivores, rodents, rabbits—have their eyes placed well to the side of their head; the area of binocular overlap is small, but each eye has a wide view to the side and to the back of the animal. This is illustrated for the grey squirrel in Fig. 2.14. In carnivores the eyes tend to be placed more frontally, giving in the cat an area of binocular overlap of 90° (Fig. 2.14). The eyes are placed even more to the front in monkeys and apes; the illustration shows the night monkey which has roughly 150° of binocular overlap (Fig. 2.14).

There is no problem in seeing why some small mammals have laterally placed eyes. An animal such as a rabbit must keep watch for predators over a wide area; a panoramic view can be achieved if the eyes are placed to the side of the head. It is more of a problem to explain why

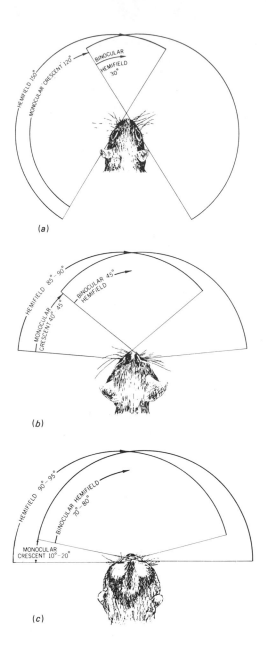

2.14 Visual fields in the squirrel (*a*), cat (*b*) and owl monkey (night monkey) (*c*). These have been estimated on the basis of electrophysiological experiments in which records are taken of the activity of nerve cells in the lateral geniculate nuclei while visual stimuli are presented to each eye in turn. After Kaas *et al.* (1972).

in some animals the advantages of panoramic vision have been sacrificed by the placement of the eyes towards the front. Clearly there must be advantages to having the eyes at the front, and they must be ones which are valued by carnivores and simian primates.

There may be optical advantages. Light may be

distorted less if it passes straight through a lens rather than at an angle; if the eye is to the side light from the front of the animal must pass sideways through the lens. Any distortion so caused cannot be great, because the tree shrew has laterally placed eyes but nonetheless has good visual acuity.

A second possibility is that things may be seen more clearly with two eyes than with one; that is visual acuity might be better when viewing with both eyes than with just one. This has been found to be true for people (Tommila 1974; Hughes 1977). But the effect is too small to provide much of an advantage in having the eyes facing to the front rather than to the side.

We are left with the idea that the advantage of having a large area of binocular overlap is related to stereopsis. If, for the moment, we assume that many mammals are able to use stereoscopic cues to depth, then those animals with eyes placed to the front are helped because they can use these cues over a wide area of their field of view. This might be of advantage in two ways, in finding food and in moving about.

Hunters, such as the cats, must be able to detect prey which are camouflaged, and stereoscopic cues to depth would be of great help in seeing the prey stand out in space against the background. Furthermore, when they are stalking the exact position of the prey could be determined without moving the head or eyes, as would be necessary if relying on motion parallax. Many prosimians hunt insects which they stalk and then catch with their hands; presumably they would be aided in detecting camouflaged insects and in catching them if they could use stereoscopic cues over a wide field. Fruit-eating primates may also benefit in the same way, as they need to detect and reach for fruit which can sometimes be difficult to pick out against a background of leaves.

It is tempting to suppose that in primates there is a further reason why it might pay them to maximize the degree of binocular overlap. They move in trees on a discontinuous surface, and must often jump from branch to branch. A wide stereoscopic field may enable them to judge with accuracy the distance to be jumped. On this view tree-living mammals would be expected to have eyes placed further to the front than ground-living mammals; but this is not always the case (Cartmill 1974). Squirrels and tree shrews move about and jump efficiently in trees, even though their eyes are directed well to the side. But they jump on relatively thick branches, landing with their whole body and gripping with their claws; whereas small primates such as the bushbabies can jump from one thin vertical support to another, grasping the branch with their hands and feet. It could be, therefore, that stereoscopic cues are more crucial for an animal which grasps with its hands and feet to get a purchase.

We have pointed to hunting and tree-living in trying to explain why there is a large area of binocular overlap in many carnivores and primates. But a more general answer can be given. Neither carnivores nor tree-living primates are usually in such danger from predators as are small mammals which live in the open, such as rabbits. It is less important that they keep watch all round, and they can therefore afford to sacrifice a wide panoramic view and to concentrate their attention more on what lies ahead. Both have a particular interest in what lies ahead, carnivores in the prey they are hunting, primates in the insects they are catching or the fruit they are plucking by hand. There are many activities carried out under the guidance of central vision which will be more efficiently performed if judgements can be made about distance on the basis of stereopsis (Hughes 1977).

We share the primate characteristics discussed here. Our eyes are directed well to the front, and we can use stereoscopic cues to depth. In general our sight is much like that of Old World primates; we can resolve fine detail, have trichromatic colour vision, and are capable of stereoscopic depth vision. It is true that we appear to be more sensitive than monkeys to fine differences in colour, just as we appear more sensitive to fine differences in the pitch or intensity of sounds. But this apparent superiority could be due to an ability to concentrate harder on a task. Until chimpanzees have been tested we should be wary of claiming that our senses differ in any way from the senses of our closest primate relatives.

PERCEPTION

We are very similar to monkeys and apes in our sensory capacities; and like them we examine the world with our hand and eye. But does the world take on the same appearance to us as it does to them? Do we classify what we see and feel in the same way as they do?

Like us animals must classify the information provided by their senses. They need to be able to recognize what they see as being a member of a class of similar things they have come across before. To give one example: having learnt that one member of a species of predator is dangerous it pays to avoid other members in the future, even though they may differ from the first in some respects.

We attach words to the categories we use; so we can easily study the way in which a child classifies the world by asking it what something is, let us say a chair. Although we cannot ask animals in the same way tests can be devised along much the same lines as those used for examining sensory capacities. We can first collect a series of pictures that depict the same object, for example a tree; each picture shows a different tree, which may vary from the others in species, size, or the angle from which it is viewed. We also need a further set of pictures which are alike only in that they do not show trees. The animal is now taught that it will get food only if it picks a picture with a tree in it, and not if it picks a picture in which there is no tree. If it can do this we know that it treats different trees as being in some ways similar, that is it classifies them in the same way. By such means pigeons have been successfully taught to distinguish pictures of people from pictures of objects or animals (Hernstein and Loveland 1964) and to recognize pictures of trees, water, or a particular person (Hernstein *et al.* 1976; Hernstein 1979). Similar tests were carried out on Viki, a chimpanzee brought up in a human household. She could discriminate animals from inanimate objects, and children from adults at a level comparable with that attained by three children between the ages of $4\frac{1}{2}$ and $5\frac{1}{2}$ (Hayes and Nissen 1971).

A different and ingenious method for studying concepts in animals has been devised by Humphrey (1974a). Rhesus monkeys were allowed to control a projector which showed pictures on a screen in the monkey's cubicle. They could decide by pressing a button whether to keep a picture on the screen or to turn it off. Monkeys shown pictures of domestic animals quickly lost interest in them after being shown several pictures of one species, treating them as much the same and not therefore worthy of attention. But, if they were exposed to a large series of animals, they began to treat domestic animals as being of interest, since they were now much better at telling them apart. The experiment shows both that they initially classified the animals as being the same, and that with experience they learnt to see the differences.

The concepts of chimpanzees can be studied in another way. Chimpanzees, but not monkeys, can be induced to sort objects or pictures into consistent piles (Garcha and Ettlinger 1979). The most impressive demonstration is that carried out on Viki, the home-reared chimpanzee (Hayes and Nissen 1971). Viki could separate spoons and forks or buttons and screws, and put pictures of people into one pile and pictures of animals into another. She could also sort objects differing in shape, size and colour into piles on the basis of one of these properties, say size; and then sort them the next time round into piles based on another property such as colour. This clearly shows her ability to abstract the relevant features.

It is intriguing that other primates can make sense of pictures and photographs, since there has long been a controversy about whether peoples from primitive cultures can do this if they have not seen pictures or photographs before (Segal *et al.* 1966; Deregowski 1972). The best way of testing this ability in animals is to use the procedure referred to as 'matching'. In this the animal is shown a sample object, and then required to pick which of two others is identical with the sample object in order to obtain food. Chimpanzees can do this even when they have to match an object with a picture of that object. They can choose which of two photographs depicts the sample object (Hayes and Hayes 1952), or which of two objects is shown in a photograph or line drawing (Davenport and Rogers 1971; Davenport *et al.* 1975).

It is not entirely clear whether chimpanzees must learn to make sense of photographs. In one study chimpanzees with little experience of them failed to appreciate that they represented objects (Winner and Ettlinger 1979). It may be that chimpanzees must learn that photographs are representational if they are to recognize what is illustrated in any new photograph that they are shown. Children, so it seems, do not require such experience; a child prevented from seeing pictures or photographs could at 19 months correctly interpret them on first viewing (Hochberg and Brooks 1962). The 'inability' of people in certain cultures to recognize photographs should not be exaggerated. The children may have little problem, and even the adults may be able to identify people in certain poses (Forge 1970).

Like other mammals primates can recognize their image in a mirror as the image of an animal; monkeys always behave as if they regarded it as another animal to be threatened or appeased (Gallup 1975). But it is a remarkable fact that chimpanzees and orang-utans can learn to recognize the image as their own (Gallup 1975; Suarez and Gallup 1981). If a spot of dye is placed on their forehead while they are anaesthetized they will later try to remove it when they see it in a mirror. We do not know at what age children first recognize themselves in mirrors. In one study were children marked in the same way; 65 per cent of the children between 20 and 24 months tried to remove the spot when they saw themselves in a mirror (Amsterdam 1972). But insufficient care was taken to ensure that they did not know where they had been marked even without the use of the mirror.

The last issue of importance is how information from the several senses is put together to form a single representation of the world. We will confine the discussion here to the ability to recognize an object as being the same whether it is felt or seen. Associations between sounds and sights, as in naming things, will be treated later in the chapter on language (Chapter 8).

The matching technique can be used to investigate whether animals are able to perceive an object as equivalent whether felt or seen. We can show an object to the animal as a sample, and then require it to pick out by feel alone the one of two objects which matches the sample. But a problem of interpretation arises. The animal could learn an arbitrary rule, that A as seen goes with A^1 as felt, and that B as seen goes with B^1 as felt; to do this it would not need to appreciate that A is identical with A^1 and B with B^1. Clearly we need to find conditions under which the animal has no opportunity to learn such arbitrary associations and can succeed only if it can recognize equivalence.

The problem is best solved by giving a series of critical problems in which all the objects are novel to the animal, and in which it is only given one trial with any one sample object. Under these conditions the animal cannot learn arbitrary pairings of the objects, because each object appears only once as a sample. This technique has been used with great apes; they were first trained on a series of problems to teach them what they had to do, and they were then given a series of critical problems with new objects. It was found that chimpanzees and orang-utans can pick out by feel the one of two objects that matches a sample object they can see (Davenport and Rogers 1970); chimpanzees can also tell which of two objects they see is the same as a sample object they have felt (Davenport et al. 1973).

It has proved more difficult to find convincing evidence that monkeys can do the same (Ettlinger 1977). Ingenious techniques have been needed to show that monkeys can indeed recognize things that they see and feel as equivalent. One of these makes use of pieces of food which differ in shape, the shape of the food being a guide to whether it is edible or inedible. The animal is given an opportunity in the dark to discover which of two shapes of food is edible, and is then shown one example of each in the light and allowed to choose between them. Both rhesus monkeys and cebus monkeys can choose correctly, basing their choice on their previous experience of feeling the shapes in the dark (Cowey and Weiskrantz 1975; Elliott 1977).

An alternative procedure has been developed for use with monkeys; it has a formal similarity but differs in that objects rather than pieces of food are used. The monkey is taught to feel two objects in the dark, under one of which there is food. When it has learnt reliably to pick that object it is presented with two objects once in the light, and given the choice as before; this is repeated for a series of pairs of objects. On test trials rhesus monkeys, like chimpanzees, can choose the object which conceals food, showing that they can use the knowledge they gained about the object when they felt it in the dark (Jarvis and Ettlinger 1977).

These experiments show one thing clearly; our own ability to recognize objects as being the same when seen and felt does not depend on our possession of language. We might have supposed that our ability to recognize in this way comes about because we apply the same name to an object irrespective of the sense with which we perceive it. If further demonstration were needed there are the elegant studies of Bryant et al. (1972) on children between the ages of 6 and 11 months who had not yet learnt to speak. They were given an object to feel which made an attractive sound when moved, and then shown this object and one other. They tended to pick the object they had previously found to make a sound, recognizing it as the same one when they saw it. Later studies have shown that even babies of 26 to 33 days old can recognize by sight a shape they have explored with their mouths (Meltzoff and Borton 1979). But though it is not necessary to have language to be able to recognize in this way, it is quite possible that the names that language provides may facilitate this ability.

We must conclude that the world as we perceive it probably differs little from the world as perceived by an ape. Our sensory capacities are remarkably similar (Prestrude 1970). Like chimpanzees we have a poor sense of smell, are deaf to high frequencies and have very sensitive pads to our fingers. Like them we have eyes which are not as specialized as those of the squirrel or the hawk; eyes which are sensitive to light at night-time and able to resolve fine detail by day. We share with chimpanzees excellent trichromatic colour vision and the ability to use stereoscopic cues to depth.

Chimpanzees appear to classify the world in much the same way as we do, can learn to interpret pictures and photographs, and to make sense of mirrors. They examine the world as we do, mainly with their eye and hand, and they can recognize the equivalence of things as they see and feel them.

The primate inheritance that we share with chimpanzees has equipped us well for dealing intelligently with the world. Information is needed about things in the world and about the relations between them, so that we can construct inside the head a model of the world. Our senses are superior in two ways to those of, let us say, a shrew enabling us to build a much more accurate picture of the world. First, the hand is a very much better instrument for exploring things than is the paw or the mouth. Secondly, we have the advantage of living by day, so that our sight is sharper. With eye and hand we obtain detailed information on just those properties of things about which we must learn if we are to use them to our ends: their shape, size, weight and so on. Our senses make possible an intelligent understanding of the world.

3 Limbs

The physical resemblance between a person and a chimpanzee is very striking. Our skeleton clearly identifies us as a primate, and not, say, a member of the cat family.

It is no coincidence that it was a primate that came to dominate the world. However big-brained a cat it would have only a paw with which to influence its environment. The hand is one of the most valuable parts of the legacy we have been left by our primate ancestors. We should have had little success without this marvellous all-purpose tool with which we have shaped the world to our ends.

In primates, including man, the skeleton is relatively unspecialized (Le Gros Clark 1971). We retain many features of the skeleton of early mammals—the collarbone or clavicle, a separate tibia and fibula in the leg, and radius and ulna in the forearm. But, most important of all, we still have five independent digits on hand and foot. In many other mammals some of these features have been lost; for example, most carnivores lack a proper collarbone, and the ungulates have hooves instead of paws or hands (Wood Jones 1926).

It is true that there is one important respect in which our skeleton has become specialized; unlike other primates we are built for walking upright, as can be easily appreciated by examining our foot or hip. But we are not so specialized that we can no longer move about in other ways. We have kept a flexibility lost by the horse, which is built for speed and pays the price in being capable of only a restricted range of movements. As Haldane (1956) observed, only a man can swim a mile, walk 20 miles, and then climb a tree.

This is not an anatomy textbook. Readers wanting a detailed account of our skeletal structure and of how it evolved can find one in the authoritative accounts by Le Gros Clark (1971) and Campbell (1974). We shall concern ourselves here mainly with the use of the hand. We have first to appreciate why it is that the primates have hands and not paws. Then we must consider how it happened that our hominid ancestors came to walk upright, and thus left their hands free at all times for manipulating the world, as when carrying and using tools. This had the consequence that there was much advantage to be gained from developing greater manual skill. Our last concern will be to enquire why the right hand came to be particularly favoured when tackling skilled tasks.

LOCOMOTION

The bones of our foot and hand are remarkably like those of the mammal-like reptiles of over 150 million years ago (Fig. 3.1). Like some living reptiles, such as turtles and tortoises, they had five digits; and the first digit was distinguished from the others by possessing two rather than three phalanges, just as in the human hand (Romer 1966). Why, then, have our hands and feet been so little modified?

Climbing

The answer is that the primitive structure of the front and back feet proved well adapted for movement in trees. There is no agreement about whether the ancestral placental mammals moved on the ground, in trees, or in both settings (Jenkins 1974). Our only evidence is the structure of the foot and ankle. The early Tertiary mammals had the first digit set at an angle to the rest of the foot, and it might be supposed that they were able to grasp branches between the first digit and the others (Matthew 1904). But the fact that the first digit diverges from the others does not prove that it can be opposed to them in this way (Gidley 1919). It has been claimed that the thumb of *Claenodon*, a mammal from the Palaeocene, could be opposed to the other digits (Matthew 1937); but it has not proved possible to confirm that the joints are capable of the necessary movements (Haines 1958). The ankle joints have been preserved from two late Cretaceous mammals, *Procerberus* and *Protungulatum*; and they do not appear to permit the full range of movements typically found in those living mammals which are able to climb (Szalay and Decker 1974). But it would be absurd to conclude on the basis of material from so few species that all early placental mammals must have been confined to the ground. We must simply admit our ignorance.

The early primates were built for climbing. In

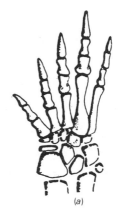

(a)

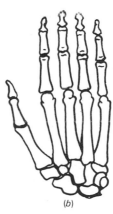

(b)

3.1 Hands of advanced mammal-like reptile (a) and modern man (b). From Romer (1966) and Campbell (1974).

Notharctus, a primate from the Eocene, the ankle joint is flexible, allowing the same degree of rotation as we find in modern prosimians such as the sifaka (*Propithecus*) (Decker and Szalay 1974; Szalay and Decker 1974). We are fortunate to have relatively complete skeletons of *Notharctus* and of the related Eocene primate *Smilodectes* (Simons 1972), and these leave no doubt that the hands and feet could be used for grasping trees. These prosimians also lacked claws; almost all living primates have nails instead of claws, although some prosimians have a toilet claw on one toe (Fig. 3.2).

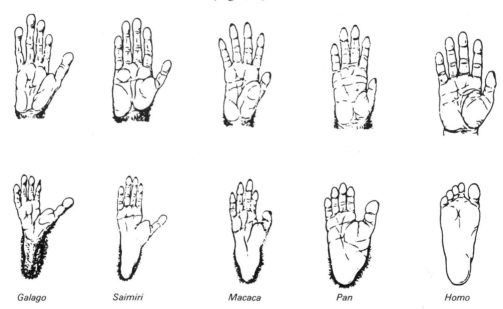

Galago　　Saimiri　　Macaca　　Pan　　Homo

3.2 Hands and feet of bushbaby (*Galago*), squirrel monkey (*Saimiri*), macaque (*Macaca*), chimpanzee (*Pan*) and man (*Homo*). After Schultz (1956).

The absence of claws is very significant. Those placental mammals that can climb, such as squirrels and cats, do so by digging their claws into the bark and thus getting a purchase. Primates climb in quite a different manner, grasping the branch by gripping it between the thumb and fingers and between the big toe and the rest of the foot. How they do this can be illustrated by taking one primate, say the bushbaby; it can be seen from Fig. 3.2 that its thumb and big toe are set at an angle; and Fig. 3.3 shows how the bushbaby uses its hand and foot to clutch a thin vertical support.

Primates are therefore well equipped for moving in trees. Of the 189 living species 166 spend most or all of their time in trees (Napier 1971). All non-human primates sleep in trees, except for some gorillas, and the hamadryas baboon (*Papio hamadryas*) and gelada (*Theropithecus*

3.3 Bushbaby clinging to vertical support. Courtesy of A. Walker.

gelada), which live in desert; most feed in trees although there are some, such as the macaques and baboons, which also feed on the ground; and all primates, other than the patas monkey (*Erythrocebus patas*), typically escape by climbing into the safety of the trees. The ability of all primates to climb by grasping may be regarded as the most basic primate adaptation. It has required little modification of the hand and foot they inherited from the ancestral mammals.

There has been another very important consequence of the way in which primates climb; they tend to keep their trunk upright more than other mammals. This is apparent in three situations. (1) They are upright when they climb trees. Some prosimians, such as the bushbaby shown in Fig. 3.3, often cling to vertical supports, and travel in trees by leaping from one such support to another. There is some argument about whether the early prosimians in the Eocene also moved in this way, but it has not been satisfactorily resolved; we lack fossil evidence on more than one or two of the anatomical features that are diagnostic of this pattern of clinging and leaping (Oxnard 1973). But we can be confident that the early primates were able to cling to upright trunks and branches. (2) Primates also hold themselves upright when hanging by their arms from branches. A few primates such as the spider monkey and gibbon often feed while hanging in this way, and travel by swinging from their arms (Fig. 3.4). (3) Primates, unlike most other mammals, tend to keep their back upright when sitting, whether on branches or on the ground. If they sit upright, without relying on their arms for support, they can use their hands to feed or for some other purpose, such as grooming (Fig. 3.5). Monkeys may spend up to three-quarters of the daytime sitting (Jolly 1972).

3.4 Gibbon jumping through the trees. Courtesy of D. Chivers.

The upright posture is reflected in the way in which the head is carried. When a mammal such as a dog walks on all fours it looks forwards, with its head extended. But when a primate clings to a vertical branch (Figs. 1.2 and 3.3), hangs from a horizontal one (Fig. 3.4), or sits upright (Fig. 3.5) it must flex its head forwards to view its surroundings. In the dog the spinal cord enters the skull through an opening at the back; this opening is called the foramen magnum, and it is flanked by the occipital condyles, the surfaces which articulate with the vertebral column (Fig. 3.6). But in monkeys and apes the foramen magnum is situated on the base of the skull, partly because of an

upright posture and partly because of the expansion of the braincase. The foramen magnum lies further forwards in man than in the chimpanzee (Fig. 3.6). The way in which the head is carried on the vertebral column is illustrated in Fig. 3.7 which shows a tarsier clinging, a gibbon hanging and a man standing upright.

3.5 Gelada sitting while grooming. Courtesy of San Diego Zoo.

Walking

Although non-human primates often hold their trunk upright they do not habitually walk upright, that is on two legs. We are the only primate that does this. When walking on branches or on the ground monkeys and apes typically walk on all fours; monkeys walk with the palms of their hands pressed on the ground, chimpanzees and gorillas supporting themselves on their knuckles.

But there are occasions when some primates do stand or walk for short distances on two feet (Hewes 1964). By standing on two legs they can increase their height; the patas monkey sometimes gets up to look over long grass, and baboons (*Papio anubis*) have been seen standing to reach a branch from the ground (Hall 1965; Rose 1976). If the animal holds itself up on two legs its hands are freed for

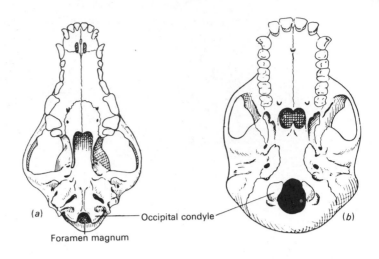

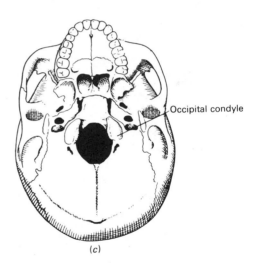

(a)

Occipital condyle

Foramen magnum

(b)

Occipital condyle

3.6 Foramen magnum in dog (a), chimpanzee (b) and man (c). From Le Gros Clark (1970).

(c)

uses other than supporting the weight of the body. Chimpanzees tend to stand upright in several situations (van Lawick-Goodall 1970), as when throwing sticks or stones (Fig. 6.5), and when brandishing sticks or using them as clubs (Fig. 6.6). Food is also sometimes carried in this way. A group of Japanese macaques (*Macaca fuscata*)that were fed potatoes on a sandy beach were seen to carry them to the water while waddling on two feet (Hewes 1964). And chimpanzees presented with a large quantity of bananas can solve the problem of transporting them by carrying them off in armfuls (Fig. 3.8), running upright for as much as 50 yards or so (van Lawick-Goodall

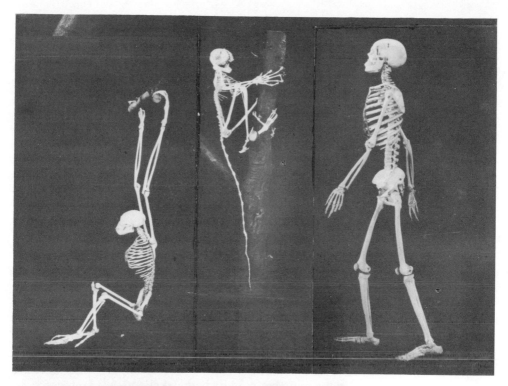

3.7 Skeleton of the gibbon (left), tarsier (centre) and man (right). From Napier and Napier (1967).

3.8 Chimpanzee walking upright so as to carry bunches of bananas. Courtesy of A. Kortlandt.

1968a). Chimpanzees have also been seen walking upright when carrying meat (Suzuki 1975).

But it is still true that the great apes most commonly walk on all fours. And our best evidence is that the apes of the Oligocene and Miocene were also quadrupeds (Fleagle and Simons 1978; Aiello 1981). That is not to say that they were like the living great apes. We are lucky to possess most of the forelimb of a Miocene ape of perhaps 20 million years ago; this is the ape *Dryopithecus africanus*, sometimes referred to as *'Proconsul' africanus* (Simons 1972). There is a resemblance to the limb structure of the modern howler monkey (*Alouatta*), which climbs with great mobility of the limbs and is capable of hanging underneath branches as it feeds (Aiello and Day in press).

Let us suppose that this fossil ape provides some clues as to the appearance and gait of the common ancestors of man and the great apes in the Miocene. If we do so we gain a valuable insight into the crucial question of how it happened that our hominid ancestors came to adopt upright walking as their usual way of moving around. For those primates which can feed by hanging from branches are built in such a way that they may be said to he 'pre-adapted' for upright walking. The notion of 'pre-adaptation' is that in evolution an anatomical specialization for one function may turn out to serve as a useful stepping-stone towards a new and different usage. In those New World monkeys, such as the howler monkey, which climb slowly and can suspend themselves by their fore-limbs or hindlimbs, the musculature of the hip and thigh resembles the human pattern (Stern 1971). And there are many respects in which the skeleton is adapted for an upright posture in those primates which feed while suspending themselves from branches by their arms, for example in the spider monkey and the gibbon (Tuttle 1975; Aiello 1981). Furthermore whether they are on branches or on the ground the spider monkey, gibbon and orang-utan sometimes walk on two feet, even though they are not carrying things (Stern 1971; MacKinnon 1974; Tuttle 1975). In other words, the adaptations for climbing that we see in these living primates make upright walking feasible. If the ancestors of the hominids were of a similar build then the hominids inherited a skeletal structure that would give them a good start when the pressures grew to adopt a bipedal gait.

We do not know when the crucial change took place. But we do know for certain that as long as 3.5 million years ago there were hominids which were walking upright; and not only that but doing so efficiently. At Laetoli in Tanzania Mary Leakey has found an astonishing series of footprints made by hominids around that time, with many prints of three individuals in the main track (Leakey and Hay 1979; Leakey, M. D. 1981). There is no question that these hominids were striding by pushing off with the big toe (Day and Wickens 1980); the prints show that the big toe was aligned with the rest of the toes, as is true in man but not apes (Fig. 3.3). Most of the bones of a foot have also been found at Olduvai in Tanzania, and these are roughly 1.8 million years old. Here too the big toe is clearly set in alignment with the rest of the toes, and not at an angle (Day 1977).

For upright walking further adjustments had also to be made to the hip and thigh. Compare the pelvis in the chimpanzee and modern man as illustrated in Fig. 3.9. They differ in many respects: the most obvious is the broader iliac blade in man, which provides a more extensive attachment for the muscles used in holding the trunk upright (Le Gros Clark 1971). A pelvic bone has been found at Hadar in Ethiopia, dating from over 3 million years ago; it was discovered together with much of the rest of the skeleton of the same individual. The pelvis shows clear adaptations for bipedal walking (Johanson and White 1979). We are also fortunate to possess an almost complete pelvis from a later hominid, a gracile australopithecine from South Africa (Fig. 3.9). This too betrays specializations for upright walking; the iliac blade, for instance, is broader than in the chimpanzee (Robinson 1972).

Modifications had also to be made to the leg, and particularly to the thigh bone or femur. In chimpanzees

3.9 Pelvic bone of chimpanzee (left), *Australopithecus* (centre) and modern man (right). From Rosen (1974).

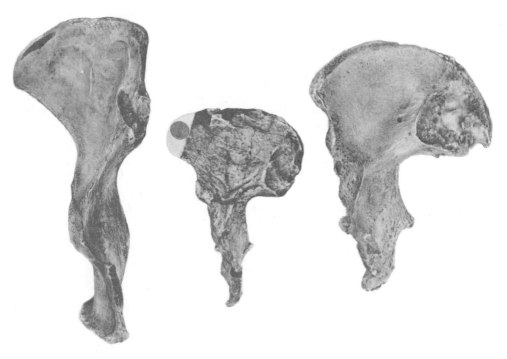

the femur is held upright; whereas in man it is held at an angle, the two femora being further apart at the pelvis than they are at the knee (Pilbeam 1972). When chimpanzees walk upright they roll from side to side in an ungainly fashion so as to bring their centre of gravity over the weight-bearing leg (Jenkins 1972). But when we stand or walk our knees are close together and near the line through the centre of gravity. A complete femur has been found at Lake Turkana of the same age as the skull KNM-ER 1470, around 1.8 million years (Leakey 1973a). It is very modern in form (Day *et al.* 1975).

Thus all the evidence, from the footprints and skeletal remains, suggests that the hominids were walking on two legs at a much earlier date than we had once supposed. But why did they, alone of all the primates, turn to walking upright? We should not pretend that we know exactly what all the pressures were that led to this innovation and which of the possible advantages were the first to prove decisive. We can be confident only that a crucial factor must have been the movement of the hominids from forests into woodlands and more open savannah (see Chapter 6).

The hominids were walking at a time well before we have evidence of their activities from archaeological remains. All we can say is that by the time we have such evidence they were clearly using their hands to carry things. At even the earliest sites at which stone tools are found there are indications that some of them were not made on the spot; they must have been carried there (Isaac 1978a). And both at Olduvai and at the Koobi Fora site at Lake Turkana we have evidence that carcasses were probably brought to particular places to be dissected and eaten (Isaac 1978a). As we have seen there are reports that chimpanzees too may walk on two feet if they have to carry large quantities of fruit or meat. In general, upright walking has the effect that the hands are relieved of their duties as supports and are thus freed for many other purposes. The achievements of man and his hominid ancestors would not have been possible had we not adopted the new stance.

MANIPULATION

The hand that can be used for climbing can serve other purposes. If it can grasp a branch it can also grasp and manipulate other objects.

Most mammals must use their mouth to pick things up. Their paws can push or pull but not grasp. There are only a few exceptions: the racoon has a hand with which it can take hold of things; and tree shrews can pick up meal worms in one paw, although in general they use their mouths when dealing with objects (Jolly 1964). Some rodents, such as the squirrels, can hold things in their paws, but only by gripping them between both paws at once.

All primates are able to pick up food and other objects with their hand. Some prosimians still occasionally use their mouth for gripping things; the lemur (*Lemur*) sometimes picks food up in its mouth and peels fruit with its teeth while holding it in the hands (Bishop 1964). The prosimians also groom themselves with their lower teeth, though some part the fur with their hands (Buettner-Janusch and Andrew 1962). But in the main prosimians pick fruit by hand, and those that feed mainly on insects, such as the bushbabies, catch them in the air or on branches by reaching out with their hand (Charles-Dominique 1972; Martin 1972). All monkeys use their hand in feeding, and in parting the fur when grooming themselves or others; this is true even of the marmosets which have developed claws rather than nails on their fingers (Bishop 1964). In general, most primates have a relatively short snout compared with many other mammals. We may suppose that this partly reflects the much greater use they make of their hands rather than their mouths for manipulating objects in the world around them.

Objects differ in their size and shape. It would therefore be most efficient if the grip used in holding them could be varied according to the properties of the object being manipulated, such as its size. The prosimians grasp all objects in the same way, by closing their whole hand around them (Bishop 1964); bushbabies catch small insects in the air with a stereotyped lunge of the arm and closure of the hand (Charles-Dominique 1975). Most New World monkeys also grasp objects with their whole hand, irrespective of the size of the object. But a few hold small objects with their fingers; the spider monkey and woolly monkey (*Lagothrix*), for instance, grip them between two fingers or tuck them under the thumb (Bishop 1964). All Old World monkeys and apes are able to pick up and hold small objects delicately at the finger tips. This sort of grip is referred to as 'precision grip', and contrasted with a whole hand grip or 'power grip' (Napier 1961).

Old World monkeys and apes can grip with their

fingers in a way not possible for any New World monkey, that is by opposing the thumb to one of the other fingers, usually the forefinger. Some New World monkeys can hold things between the sides of the thumb and first finger. But Old World monkeys and apes can rotate the thumb at the base to bring the ball of the thumb in contact with the pulp of the finger (Napier 1961). The efficiency with which the finger and thumb can be opposed in this way is partly determined by the relative proportion of the thumb to the index finger; the relation between them can be expressed as an index, higher indices indicating a greater degree of opposition. The hands of a few primates are illustrated in Fig. 3.2. The ground-living primates such as the macaques tend to have higher indices than the apes, for example the chimpanzee; and our hand has the highest index of all (Napier 1971). The different degree to which the chimpanzee and man can oppose thumb and forefinger can be clearly appreciated from the photograph (Fig. 3.10).

The ability to adapt the grip to the object being handled is of the greatest importance when using or making tools. The chimpanzee uses a precision grip when poking twigs or grasses down termite holes so that it can eat the termites that cling to the end (Fig. 6.7); this use of tools is described in Chapter 6. Both power and precision grips are called for in the making and use of stone tools. The chopper tools could have been made using the power grip alone (Napier 1962), but the fine tools of the Upper Pleistocene required much more delicacy of workmanship. The skill and precision of the human hand is without doubt the result of selection for greater dexterity in the use and manufacture of tools.

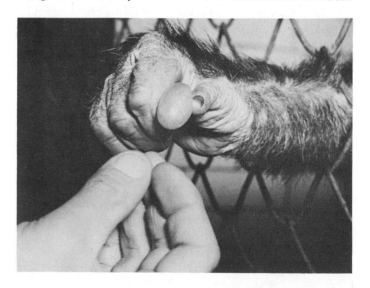

3.10 Chimpanzee gripping a grape between thumb and forefinger. From Napier and Napier (1967).

Our manual skill is so manifest that there have been no thorough studies comparing our dexterity with the skill of other primates. We do not need studies to tell us that a chimpanzee could not move the keys of a piano with the speed and finesse of which we are capable.

There have been three studies comparing the manual skills of different primates. The first measured the speed and accuracy of reaching in different prosimians, but did not make formal comparisons with monkeys (Bishop 1964). In the second study tests were devised to examine the ability to reach from different angles, to rotate the wrist when picking up food, and to push one or more fingers through narrow openings to retrieve a grape (Welles 1975). Man and chimpanzee were better than Old or New World monkeys on two of the conditions: when required to reach into a box through a hole on the other side, and when the grape had to be retrieved through a hole with a single finger.

The third comparative study used a test referred to as the bent-wire problem (Davis 1974). A sweet or candy with a hole in the middle is threaded on a wire, and the animal's task is to take it off. The problem is made more difficult by the use of a series of wires which are bent in different ways so that the sweet cannot be pulled straight off but must first be manoeuvred along the bends in the wire. The North American racoon can solve simple versions of this puzzle. Among the primates the only prosimian that has been tested is the ring-tailed lemur, which is as competent as New World monkeys; but Old World monkeys prove superior. The chimpanzee is the most efficient of any of the primates tested; its performance is roughly equivalent to that of 2-year-old children. But although we have systematic information on how well different species perform on this test the results are not easy to interpret. The bent-wire problem certainly requires manual dexterity; but it also requires the intelligence to appreciate the means by which the sweet can be removed, and to see that the various detours of the wire must be followed if success is to be achieved. Indeed it was as a test of intelligence that the puzzle was originally devised.

We are left with no good estimate of the relative degree of skill of man and chimpanzee. We know that chimpanzees brought up in human households prove skilful in their use of such household objects as cups, spoons, light switches, door knobs and so on; and that they can build with blocks or make a pot of tea (Kellogg and Kellogg 1933; Hayes 1951; Kellogg 1968; Fleming 1974). But their skills have yet to be properly evaluated.

The manual skills of primates depend partly on specializations of the area of the neocortex of the brain which directly controls movements. We saw in the last chapter that there is a representation of the body in the area of the brain analysing information from the body surface (Fig. 2.8). In front of this sensory map lies the area directing the movements of the limbs, usually referred to as the 'motor area'. Electrical stimulation of points within this area produces discrete movements of different parts of the body, and a map can be constructed on the basis of the parts that move when each point is stimulated. Fig. 2.8 shows that this map is distorted in the same way as the sensory map; the larger the representation of any part of the body the more complex the control exerted over that part. In primates the hand and foot take up a large proportion of the total map (Woolsey et al. 1952) but in man the area controlling the foot is less well developed than in the rhesus monkey (Penfield and Rasmussen 1950). Presumably this is because we differ from monkeys in being unable to use our foot for grasping.

The motor area issues its commands via the pyramidal tract, the main bundle of motor fibres; and these fibres directly or indirectly influence the nerve cells in the spinal cord that control the muscles. The number of fibres in the pyramidal tract reflects the complexity of the direction of the movements of the limbs. We have information on the number of pyramidal fibres in ungulates, rodents, carnivores and primates (Towe 1973; Heffner and Masterton 1975). When allowance has been made for differences in the size of the body we find an orderly relationship (Passingham 1981a). There are fewest pyramidal fibres in ungulates, which have hooves; more in rodents and carnivores, which have paws; and most in primates, which have hands. The number of fibres is greater the more the use made of the forelimbs for manipulation. When matched for body size man has no more fibres in the pyramidal tract than a non-human primate, but twice as many as a carnivore or rodent and 4.2 times as many as an ungulate.

There is reason for thinking that the greatest skill can only be achieved if the motor area sends pyramidal fibres that directly connect to the nerve cells in the spinal cord which control the movements of the muscles, that is the 'motorneurones'. The course of the pyramidal fibres is known in several different mammals (Petras 1969; Philips 1971). In mammals such as cats the pyramidal fibres influence the motorneurones only indirectly via other intervening nerve cells, but in the racoon, which is skilful with its hands, a few fibres appear to terminate on the motorneurones themselves. In New World monkeys direct pyramidal connections are found in the woolly monkey and spider monkey which have a form of precision grip, but not in the squirrel monkey which can only grasp with the whole hand (Harting and Noback 1970). Old World monkeys and apes can all oppose their thumb to their other fingers, and all have direct connections from the pyramidal tract to the motorneurones. In chimpanzees, which are particularly skilful, there are more than in monkeys. In spite of our superior skill, however, we differ little from chimpanzees in the proportion of fibres in the pyramidal tract which terminate directly on the motorneurones (Kuypers 1964).

The pyramidal fibres that influence the motorneurones directly in primates come from the parts of the motor area that control the movements of the hand and foot (Kuypers and Brinkman 1970). If the pyramidal tract is cut or if the motor area itself is removed a rhesus monkey recovers in general remarkably well; the only striking symptom is an inability to move the fingers independently of each other (Lawrence and Kuypers 1968). This is easily revealed by requiring the animal to use its thumb and forefinger in opposition to remove food from a slot. Normally a rhesus monkey can place the thumb and forefinger in the groove and tuck the other fingers out of the way, but if the cortical area controlling the hand is removed the monkey can attempt only to grasp the food in its whole hand (Passingham *et al.* 1978) (see Fig. 3.11).

Thus in primates the motor area is particularly concerned with the control of finger movements, and it exercises this control via fibres in the pyramidal tract which connect directly to the motorneurones of the spinal cord. But there is no specialization in this system which is peculiar to man. Our hand does not differ greatly from a chimpanzee's; the pyramidal tract has no more fibres than would be expected for a primate of our size; and the part of the motor area representing the hand is not obviously larger than in a rhesus monkey. Yet our superior manual skill is not in doubt; consider only the ease with which we move the fingers independently when typing. We must look for an explanation to higher mechanisms in the brain which influence the motor area (see Chapter 5).

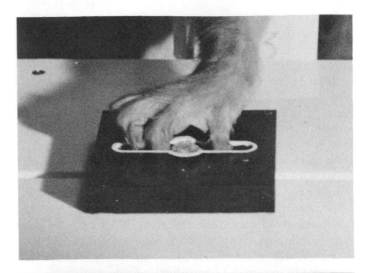

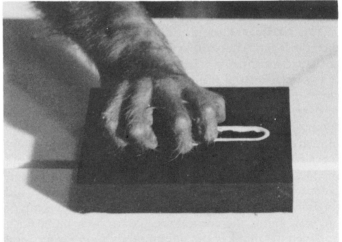

3.11 *a*, Precision grip of a rhesus monkey. *b*, The crude grasp of a rhesus monkey after removal of motor cortex. From Passingham *et al.* (1978).

Handedness

Our two hands are not equally skilful. Take a relatively simple task: the person is asked to move a number of pegs from one set of holes to another, and to do so as quickly as he can. Most people are faster at doing this with their right than with their left hand (Annett 1972). There are a variety of other tasks, both practised and unpractised, which most people have been found to perform more proficiently with their right than their left hand (Barnsley and Rabinovitch 1970). Even children as young as three to five are usually quicker at tapping with the fingers of their right hand (Ingram 1975). The left hand tends to be superior to the right only in making isolated movements, such as flexing individual fingers; whenever sequences of movements are required the right is usually the better hand (Kimura 1976).

Most people also prefer to use their right hand to their left, not just when writing but also when performing other tasks. In one study people were asked which hand they would use for tackling each of 12 tasks; 66 per cent said they would use their right hand on all of them, 30 per cent that they would use their left hand for some of them, and only 4 per cent that they would use their left hand for all tasks (Annett 1972) (Fig. 3.12).

Handedness would not be of so much interest to us here if it were the case that children learn which hand to use. Handedness tends to run in families; 28 per cent of the children of left-handed mothers are themselves left-handed, and so are roughly 50 per cent of the children of two left-handed parents (Annett 1973). But, of course, the children might have copied their parents. One way to find out is to look at the hand preference of children brought up away from one or both of their own parents, and to see if they tend to use the same hand as their parents, in spite of being deprived of the opportunity to copy them. There is one study of this sort, and it found that the handedness of adults was related to the handedness of their true parents rather than their foster parents (Hicks and Kinsbourne 1976a). But, although there is no good evidence that people acquire their hand preference by learning we have yet to establish the mode of inheritance of handedness (Hicks and Kinsbourne 1976b; Morgan and Corballis 1978).

Hand preferences can be looked for in animals on a single task or over a series of tasks. Japanese macaques have been studied in the wild to see with which hand they picked up peanuts; out of 504 monkeys 39 per cent tended to use their left hand, 28 per cent their right, and 33 per cent either hand (Tokuda 1969). In a similar experiment carried out in the laboratory 171 rhesus monkeys were observed retrieving peanuts; on average the monkeys used the same hand to pick up peanuts on all but 15 per cent or so of trials, but as many used their left as their right hand to do this (Lehman 1978).

The consistency of hand use across different tasks is of more interest, because it is in this way that handedness is usually assessed in people. A small group of 10 stump-tailed macaques (*Macaca arctoides*) have been tested on 17 different tasks but there was no evidence of any tendency

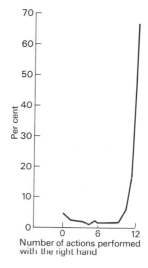

3.12 Percentage of 241 recruits preferring the right hand for 0–12 actions. After Annett (1972).

to right-handedness; two preferred their left hand for manipulation, four their right, and four used either (Beck and Barton 1972). In a very thorough investigation 81 rhesus monkeys were given five tasks: they had to reach for peanuts, slide food along a trough, remove rings of food from a length of wire, insert their hand into a bottle to get food, and take a raisin or peanut from an upright glass (Warren *et al.* 1967). The data for 33 of these animals are analysed and plotted in Fig. 3.13. The distribution of hand preference across the five tasks is clearly a symmetrical one; as many monkeys are left- as right-handed, and the majority, 45.5 per cent of them, are ambidextrous. Chimpanzees are no more likely to prefer the right hand; of 40 chimpanzees tested on four unrelated tasks 30 per cent used their right hand on 90 per cent or more of the trials on all tasks, and 30 per cent used their left (Finch 1941). It seems that although other primates often have hand preferences they are no more inclined to prefer the right hand than the left. In this they differ completely from people, since we show a very marked bias towards right-handedness.

In general people are consistent across their lifetime in the hand they prefer to use; but rhesus monkeys are not nearly so consistent. When tested on reaching for food and then retested two years later they are nearly as likely to change their hand preference as to maintain it (Warren *et al.* 1967; Warren 1977). Where they are required to manipulate things, to displace blocks, pull handles and so on they are only moderately consistent in the hand they use over a two-year period. Of course it might be that their hand preference might become more stable with more experience and practice. But clearly handedness in monkeys is not like handedness in people for whom it is a consistent trait, determined in the main by the time of birth.

There are two things to explain: how it came about that people tend to use the same hand consistently and for most tasks, and why it is the right hand that is preferred by most people. The key to the first question must lie in the nature of the cerebral organization of the movements of the hands. Each hand is primarily controlled by a single hemisphere of the brain, the right hand by the left hemisphere and the left hand by the right hemisphere. Skills are acquired initially by the hemisphere directing the hand that is used, and the other hemisphere has only indirect access to the information by way of the fibres of the corpus callosum that connect the two hemispheres.

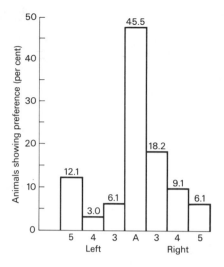

3.13 Handedness in rhesus monkeys. A, ambidextrous. The numbers 3, 4 and 5 along the bottom refer to animals showing the same hand preferences on 3, 4 and 5 tasks. From Passingham (1979a). Data from Warren et al. (1967).

This means that if the same hand is used throughout skills acquired on previous tasks will be immediately accessible when new but related tasks are tackled.

To the apes there would be little advantage in training one hand in this way; in their natural life they are not faced with a series of related tasks on which the relevant skills must be perfected through practice. Even in the laboratory the tests used to assess handedness in non-human primates make minimal demands on manual skill; it matters little if the block is pushed with the left hand and the handle pulled with the right. To the hominids, on the other hand, much was to be gained from improvements in the manufacture of tools. The techniques of toolmaking demand that one hand steadies while the other strikes or cuts or chips; only one hand need develop the necessary skills (Frost 1980). In this situation it pays that the same hand be used to carry out the basic repertoire of skilled manipulations.

But this argument carries no implication that the practised hemisphere should be the same for most people, nor that it should be the left hemisphere. There is little to say on this issue other than to note that there are quite a few cases in the animal kingdom where organs are not symmetrical, and in most instances it is the left side that is the better developed (Morgan 1977). This is true, for example, of the vertebrate heart and the brain region called the habenula in amphibians. It is as if there is some tendency for the left side to develop earlier or more rapidly than the right (Corballis and Morgan 1978).

It is not just in the case of manual skills that the left hemisphere has assumed a dominant role. In right-handers it is the left hemisphere that directs vocal skill, that is the production of speech. It is time to consider the specializations of the human brain.

4 Brain

Our claim to pre-eminence rests not on our senses or limbs but on our brain. Of all our organs it is the brain that is the most radically specialized. Each organ of the body has its own function—the heart, the liver and so on—and the brain may be regarded as the organ of behaviour. It is in what we are able to do that our distinction lies.

There are three ways in which an organ such as the brain may be specialized. It can be distinctive in its overall size; it can be unusual in shape, that is in the relative proportions of its parts; and it can possess some specialized area not to be found in other brains. So we have first to consider the size of the human brain, and the relative size of each of its functional areas. Then we must try to establish whether there are any areas peculiar to the human brain, areas which, like Owen's hippocampus minor (see page 1), might serve to reassure us of our unique position in the animal kingdom. But comparisons with the brains of our primate relatives will not tell us how and when our brain became so specialized; to find out we will have to examine the fossil remains of our ancestors.

SIZE

It is not of the absolute size of our brain that we should boast. It is true that our brain is very much bigger than a monkey's or a chimpanzee's, as can be appreciated from Fig. 4.1. But elephants have brains four times as large as ours, and there are whales with brains five times greater than our own. The absolute weight of our brain would hardly be a flattering guide to our relative intelligence.

The reason that elephants and whales have such large brains is, of course, that they are enormous creatures. The bigger the animal the larger each of its organs must be if they are to carry out their functions with equal efficiency. This is as true for the brain as it is for the heart or the lung (Stahl 1965). The brain must analyse information from the senses and issue commands for the contractions of the

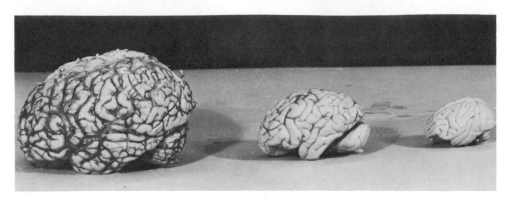

4.1 Brains of man (left), chimpanzee (centre) and rhesus monkey (right). From Rosen (1974).

muscles. The number of the sensory receptors and muscle fibres increases with the size of the body, and thus bigger bodies demand bigger brains.

It is tempting, therefore, to relate the size of the brain to the size of the body in the form of a simple ratio, brain weight/body weight, hoping in this way to derive a measure on which we could be validly compared with other animals. The result is disappointment. We are now outstripped by such little animals as the squirrel monkey, which has a brain/body ratio of roughly 1/31 compared with the ratio of 1/49 for man (Stephan *et al.* 1970). Where we previously compared unfavourably with larger creatures we are now bettered by smaller ones.

To understand why this should be so we must look at a graph on which the brain and body weights of different species are plotted. Fig. 4.2 gives the values for 39 primates including man. As we move from small to large species it will be seen that as body size increases the brain also enlarges, but not at the same rate. If the rate was the same, the slope of the line through the points would be 1, that is the line would be at 45°. But in fact it rises less steeply, indicating a slower rate of increase for the brain. It follows that, all other things being equal, the larger the animal the smaller the brain/body ratio, which is why we come out poorly from comparisons based on this index. Comparisons are only valid between species that are alike in size.

There are two ways out of the impasse. The first is to find some ratio which is not open to the same objection. The most attractive ratio is that relating the size of the brain to the size of the spinal cord (Krompecher and Lipák 1966). Intelligence might be thought to depend, in part, on the amount of brain tissue in excess of that needed for analysing incoming sensory information and for controlling the muscles of the body. The most direct

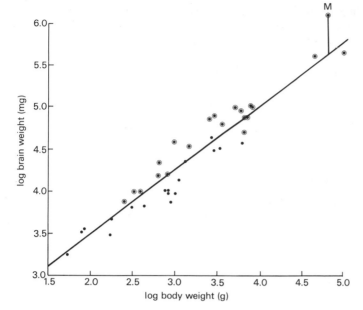

4.2 Brain and body weight of 38 non-human primates and man (M). The regression line is fitted through the points for the non-human primates. The vertical line shows the difference between the value of brain size predicted for man and the actual value. The human brain is 3.1 times as big as expected for a non-human primate of the same weight. •, Prosimians; ⊚, simians. After Passingham and Ettlinger (1974). Data from Stephan *et al.* (1970).

measure of the inputs and outputs of the brain is the size of the spinal cord together with the cranial nerves; all the nerves to and from the body connect to the spinal cord, other than the cranial nerves which innervate the head. A less direct measure is the size of the medulla, the region forming the lower part of the brain stem, adjacent to the spinal cord (see Fig. 4.6); the fibres passing between the spinal cord and the brain all pass through this region. If we are interested in the amount of the brain tissue over and above that required for sensory analysis and for the direction of movements it will make sense to compare the brain with the size of the spinal cord or medulla (Passingham 1975a, 1978).

But we do not possess information on the size of these areas in more than a few animals; and so we are forced back on comparisons with the size of the body. In so far as it reflects the number of sensory receptors and muscle fibres, body size gives an indirect measure of the information the brain must handle. We have, therefore, to find a way of making valid comparisons of brain to body ratio across species differing in the size of their body. Fortunately there is a way of doing this. The procedure is as follows: first study the relation between the size of the brain and the weight of the body in the group of species in which you are interested. For primates the relation is illustrated in Fig. 4.2. Each point represents the brain and body weights of a different species of primate; the logarithms of these values are used as the points will then tend to fall along a straight line. A 'regression' line can then be fitted through these points so as best to represent the trend to be found in the data. The regression line for non-human primates is the one that best describes the relation between brain and body size in this group.

We now have the solution. We have already seen that it would not be valid to compare, let us say, the human brain with the brain of another primate lighter than ourselves. But we can now compare our brain with the brain of a *hypothetical* primate which weighs the same as us. We do this by reading off from the regression line the brain size which we would predict for a non-human primate which was matched with us in weight. In the diagram a vertical line connects the point representing man to the point on the line representing this hypothetical primate. It is immediately obvious that our brain is much larger than we would expect of a primate of our weight.

We are now able to make a valid comparison between the human brain and the brains of other primates, and can make the relevant calculations (Passingham and Ettlinger 1974). Fig. 4.2 illustrates perhaps the single most important fact about mankind. *Our brain is three times as large as we would expect for a primate of our build.*

We can appreciate what a staggering difference this is by looking at the brains of other primates. Fig. 4.3 gives the size of the brain relative to the medulla in primates. The gap between man and a great ape, such as the chimpanzee, is greater than the gap between the chimpanzee and an insectivore, such as the shrew (*Sorex*). We are indeed special creatures.

But we should not look down too severely on our closest relatives, the monkeys and apes; for they have the biggest brains, relative to their weight, of any mammals that live on land. Jerison (1973) has compared the brains of a variety of mammals. He calculates an 'encephalization quotient', EQ for short, by relating the brain size of each species to the size expected for an average mammal of the same body weight. By definition the average mammal has an EQ of 1.0; if the brain is smaller than average the EQ will have a value less than 1.0, and if larger a value of more than 1.0. The values for some of the mammalian groups are given in Fig. 4.4. Three broad classes can be distinguished: insectivores and rodents with small brains for their weight; carnivores, ungulates and prosimians with brains of a moderate size; and monkeys and apes with large brains. Though the elephant has a brain many times

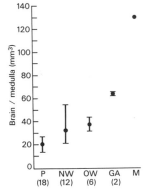

4.3 Volume of the brain (mm³) relative to the volume of the medulla (mm³) in primates. The mean is shown by a dot and the range by the vertical line. P, prosimians; NW, New World monkeys; OW, Old World monkeys; GA, great apes; M, man. The figures along the bottom give the number of species represented. Data from Stephan *et al.* (1970).

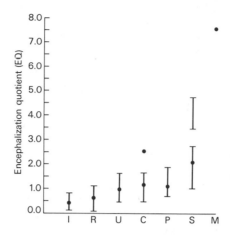

4.4 Encephalization quotient (EQ) in a variety of mammals. The mean is given by the dot and the range by the vertical lines. The dot above the carnivore range gives the value for a single carnivore. The upper range for the simian primates gives the values for two cebus monkeys. I, insectivores; R, rodents; U, ungulates; C, carnivores; P, prosimians; S, simians; M, man. After Passingham (1981a). Data from Jerison (1973).

larger than that of a monkey or ape its EQ is well within the range for carnivores and ungulates. The superiority of the monkeys and apes is impressive: if we discount one suspiciously low value given for a langur (*Presbytis cristatus*), we find that only 3 out of 25 ungulates have an EQ within the range for 48 monkeys and apes, and only 2 out of 15 carnivores (Jerison 1973).

Within the primates comparisons of the different groups produce anomalous results when they are based on encephalization indices using brain and body weight. For example, some small monkeys such as the cebus monkey are placed well above all other primates, as in Fig. 4.4; and the largest apes, the orang-utan and the gorilla, are ranked below many of the monkeys (Stephan 1972). The picture becomes more orderly when the brain is related not to the size of the body but to a more direct measure of the inputs and outputs of the brain, such as the size of the medulla (Passingham 1975a). The great apes are now established at the top of the hierarchy (Fig. 4.3).

These enquiries have shown that the animals to which we are most closely related are specialized in being equipped with brains which are large for their build. The brain is the only organ which is better developed in monkeys and apes than in other land mammals; their hearts, lungs and other organs are in no way special as regards their relative size (Stahl 1965). The same feature that sets us apart from monkeys and apes sets them apart from other animals. Our large brain testifies to our primate ancestry.

There is one potentially embarrassing anomaly. There are some sea mammals, seals, toothed whales and dolphins, which can boast brains which are larger than ape brains, even when account has been taken of the fact that they are very big creatures (Mangold-Wirz 1966; Stephan 1972). This might be taken to indicate that they are more intelligent than apes, and indeed dolphins are noted for their circus tricks in captivity.

But there may be less interesting explanations. Some of the brains of sea mammals that have been studied have been taken from juvenile animals, and it is known that the brain is larger relative to the size of the body in juveniles than in adults. We should also be suspicious of comparisons between land and sea mammals; the design of their bodies is very different, and we cannot assume that bodies of equal size make equal demands on the brain. We know that in one sea mammal, the seal (*Callorhinus ursinus*), there are more fibres in the pyramidal tract than we would expect of an ape of the same weight; yet the seal has minimal digital dexterity and the ape is capable of great manual skill (Passingham 1981a). So when the seal is matched for body weight with a land mammal, the size of its pyramidal system is a poor guide to its dexterity; perhaps the size of the whole brain, when assessed in the same way, gives an inflated estimate of an animal's intelligence. It would be better to relate the size of the brain in sea mammals to the size of the spinal cord, since the latter gives a more direct measure than body weight of the inputs and outputs of the brain. Comparisons between land and sea mammals have not yet been made using this measure, and we must therefore accept that the issue of the relative brain size of sea mammals has yet to be settled.

PROPORTIONS

Is our brain, then, just an expanded version of the brain of another primate such as the chimpanzee? In asking this question we are not, of course, suggesting that the human brain evolved from the chimpanzee brain. But, given that our brain is so much larger, there is good reason to be curious as to whether it follows basically the same plan. To find out we need to know the relative proportions of its various parts.

This is not the place for a detailed description of the various structures in the vertebrate brain. The reader who is interested can consult the book by Sarnat and Netsky (1974) for a short account and the volume written by Pearson and Pearson (1976) for a longer one. We need concern ourselves here only with the major subdivisions of the brain.

The brain is made up of nerve cells, each cell having a cell body and a fibre or 'axon' along which small electrical impulses are conducted. Bundles of the fibres of many cells are said to form a nerve when they run to and from the brain or spinal cord, and a tract when they run within these structures. Congregations of cell bodies are referred to as nuclei. When the cell bodies aggregate in layered sheets around the outside of the brain they create what we call 'cortex', the Latin word for bark. The cortex is what we refer to in common speech as the 'grey matter' on the outside of the brain; it covers the 'white matter' below, that is the fibres passing to and from the cortex. This can best be visualized from a cross-section through a primate brain, as shown in the photograph (Fig. 4.5).

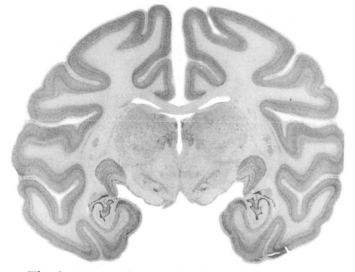

4.5 Cross section through the brain of a rhesus monkey. The neocortex is stained dark and can be seen on the outside of the brain whether exposed or in the fissures.

The brain may be grossly divided into three main sections, the hindbrain, midbrain and forebrain. Table 4.1 shows the allocation of some of the more important areas of the brain to each of these divisions. The hindbrain comprises not only the pons and medulla but also the cerebellum which is covered with cortex, the cerebellar cortex (Fig. 4.6). At the base of the forebrain lies the thalamus, an important group of nuclei which relay sensory information to the neocortex. It is the neocortex, sometimes loosely referred to as the cortex, which covers most of the outside of the cerebral hemispheres or cerebrum (Fig. 4.6). It is so called to distinguish it from other cortical areas of the forebrain, the piriform cortex (or palaeocortex) and the hippocampal cortex (or archicortex). It is with the neocortex that we will be primarily concerned, because we know it to play a crucial

Table 4.1 Subdivisions of the brain

Hindbrain (Rhombencephalon)		Cerebellum, pons, medulla
Midbrain (Mesencephalon)		Colliculi, tegmentum
Forebrain (Prosencephalon)	Inter-brain (Diencephalon)	Thalamus, hypothalamus
	Endbrain (Telencephalon)	Olfactory bulbs, striatum, piriform cortex (palaeocortex), hippocampal cortex (archicortex), neocortex

role in some higher forms of learning (see Chapter 5).

There are many claims in the literature that this or that part of the human brain is much better developed than in the brains of other primates. Most of these claims are worthless. It has not been until recently that adequate

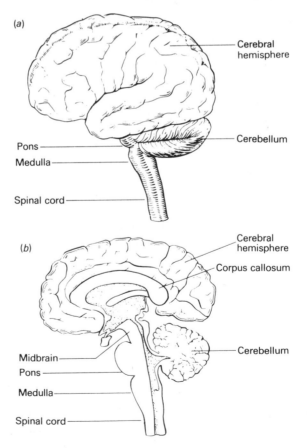

4.6 Cerebral hemispheres of the human brain as seen from the side (a) and from a medial view (b). The pons, medulla and cerebellum are also labelled. After Thompson (1967).

material for such comparisons has been made available. Stephan and his colleagues (Stephan *et al.* 1970) have published invaluable data on the size of the various parts of the brain in 39 primates of known body size, including man. We have already compared the weight of the whole human brain with that expected for a primate of our build; we can now do the same for each of the parts of the brain, using the same methods. The procedure is to take any part of the brain and predict how large it would be in a primate of the same body weight as man. The difference between the predicted value and the actual value for the human brain gives an index of how many times larger that area is in man than would be expected in a primate our size.

Comparing the indices for each of the parts of the brain, as given in Fig. 4.7, we discover an orderly and interesting pattern (Stephan and Andy 1969; Passingham 1975b). In the human brain the pons and medulla of the hindbrain are no greater than we would expect for a primate our size. Compared with other primates there is a moderate enlargement of the midbrain (mesencephalon), and of the interbrain (diencephalon) and the striatum in the forebrain. But the greatest difference is in the areas of cortex, the piriform cortex (palaeocortex), hippocampal cortex (archicortex), cerebellar cortex and neocortex. It is in the extraordinary development of the cerebellum and the neocortex that the human brain is most specialized. These two are closely interconnected, the cerebellum sending fibres to the neocortex via the thalamus, and the neocortex returning fibres to the cerebellum via the pons

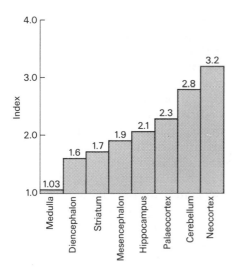

4.7 Indices showing the difference in size of each area of man's brain compared with the values predicted for non-human primates of the same body weight. The index is the obtained value/the predicted value. After Passingham (1975b). Data from Stephan *et al.* (1970).

(Eccles 1973). Both the cerebellum and the neocortex play a critical role in learning, as we shall see in the next chapter.

Different areas of the neocortex have their own specialized functions. There are the areas which receive information from the senses via the thalamus, and there is the area which controls movements; these are the sensory and motor areas which have already been illustrated in Fig. 2.8. The areas of neocortex other than the sensory and motor areas are loosely termed the 'association areas'; in Fig. 2.8 they are the areas that are not shaded. The next chapter will demonstrate that it is these areas that contribute most to learning (Fig. 5.2).

What we require are good estimates of the amount of tissue in each of these areas, that is the sensory, motor and association areas. To obtain such estimates the areas must first be identified; and fortunately there is a very rough correspondence between the function of an area and its appearance when viewed down a microscope. The types of cell and the look of the cell layers serve to identify the areas, giving them their characteristic cellular arrangement or 'cytoarchitecture'. On this basis a crude division can be made between three types of area, 'koniocortex' as seen in the sensory areas, 'agranular' cortex as seen in the motor area and in the 'premotor' area in front of it, and 'eulaminate' cortex as seen in the association areas (von Bonin and Bailey 1961). There is information on the extent of each of these divisions of neocortex in five primates including man (Shariff 1953). Analysing the data in the same way as before, we find that for a primate of our build our brain is distinguished by the extent of agranular (motor plus premotor) cortex and of the association areas (Fig. 4.8), but that the amount of sensory cortex is much as would be expected (Passingham 1975b). From other data it looks as if it is premotor cortex rather than motor cortex which is particularly large in the human brain (von Bonin 1944; Blinkov and Gleser 1968).

The association cortex can in turn be subdivided into different association areas according to their position in the different lobes of the brain. Each lobe is identified in Fig. 4.9. The association areas of the frontal, temporal and parietal lobes are each specialized for performing different tasks (see Chapter 5). Unfortunately the extent of each of these has not yet been separately measured, but there is an indirect way in which we can form some estimate. We can make use of the fact that different nuclei of the thalamus send fibres to separate regions of association cortex, the dorsomedial nucleus to frontal association cortex and the

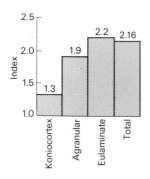

4.8 Indices showing the difference in each area of the neocortex of the human brain compared with the values predicted for non-human primates of the same body weight. The index is the obtained value/the predicted value. After Passingham (1975b). Data from Stephan *et al.* (1970).

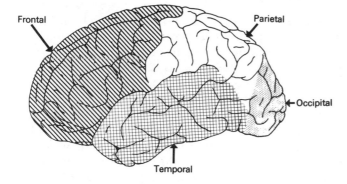

Frontal

Parietal

←Occipital

Temporal

4.9 Lobes of the human brain.

pulvinar to temporal and parietal association cortex. Data are available for the size of the various nuclei of the thalamus in man and three other primates (Hopf 1965). So we can estimate for each nucleus the size we would expect it to be in a primate as large as man. Both the dorsomedial nucleus and the pulvinar are found to be unusually large in the human brain, even when account is taken of our weight; but there is no evidence that the one is better developed than the other (Passingham 1979a). In other words until we have better data we must assume that the different areas of association cortex are equally well developed in the human brain.

We started out by asking whether the human brain is an expanded version of the brain of a monkey or ape. We have discovered that it is not simply a bigger version if that is taken to mean one which is larger but retains its relative proportions unaltered. Some parts are more expanded than others; in particular the cerebellum and neocortex are proportionately much larger than in the brain of, let us say, a chimpanzee. The extent to which the cerebellum and neocortex are enlarged in the human brain can be visualized from Figs 4.10 and 4.11 in which the values for the other primates are given for comparison.

Are we to conclude that the human brain is not just a large primate brain? To do so would be to assume that primate brains of different size maintain roughly similar internal proportions, and we should first check to see if this is so. In fact it is not, as is immediately obvious if we take, for purposes of illustration, the size of the neocortex, including the white matter underlying it. Fig. 4.12 shows that the neocortex forms a smaller percentage of the total brain in prosimians than in other primates, and in monkeys than in apes. In general the proportion of neocortex to total brain increases in primates as brain size increases (Passingham 1975a).

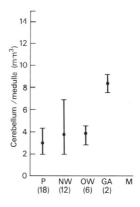

4.10 Volume of the cerebellum (mm³) relative to the volume of the medulla (mm³) in primates. The mean is shown by the dot and the range by the vertical line. P, prosimians; NW, New World monkeys; OW, Old World monkeys; GA, great apes; M, man. The figures along the bottom give the number of species represented. Data from Stephan *et al.* (1970).

85

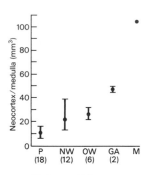

4.11 Volume of the neocortex (mm³) relative to the volume of the medulla (mm³) in primates. The mean is shown by the dot and the range by the vertical line. P. prosimians; NW, New World monkeys; OW, Old World monkeys; GA, great apes; M, man. The figures along the bottom give the number of species represented. Data from Stephan *et al.* (1970).

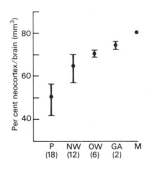

4.12 Volume of the neocortex (mm³) as a percentage of the volume of the brain (mm³) in primates. The mean is shown by the dot and the vertical line. P, prosimians; NW, New World monkeys; OW, Old World monkeys; GA, great apes; M, man. The figures along the bottom give the number of species represented. After Passingham (1975a). Data from Stephan *et al.* (1970).

This means that we would have expected a brain larger than that of an ape to differ also in its proportions; and thus to possess for example, proportionately more neocortex than a smaller primate brain. But, given the size of the human brain, what proportions would we expect it to have? The relevant calculations can be done by using the same methods that we have just adopted to predict the size of any part of the brain for a primate of our body weight. The difference is that now we base our predictions not on the weight of the *body* but on the size of the *brain*, and so estimate how large any part of the brain should be for a primate with a *brain* as large as ours.

This exercise is carried out in Fig. 4.13 for the neocortex (Passingham 1975b). The volumes of the brain and neocortex are plotted for each species of primate, and a regression line is fitted to the data for the non-human primates. Reading from this line it is possible to work out the size of neocortex that would be expected for a hypothetical primate with a brain matched in size with the human brain. The answer is striking: the point for man falls very close to this line (Fig. 4.13). In other words our brain has no more neocortex than we would predict for such a primate.

If the extent of the neocortex in the human brain is predictable in this way, is the same true for the association cortex that makes up much of the neocortex? If association cortex is identified on the basis of cytoarchitectonic criteria as before then data are available to answer this question. It turns out that man has no more association cortex than we would expect given the size of his neocortex (Passingham 1973). There is another way of tackling the question, by comparing the volumes of the nuclei of the thalamus which send fibres to the association areas. The relevant nuclei, the dorsomedial nucleus and the pulvinar, are no greater in the human brain than would be expected for a primate with a thalamus that was as large as it is in man (Passingham 1979a).

Like all scientific conclusions these claims are provisional. There is uncertainty in the data and in their interpretation. Reliable data exist on the extent of the major subdivisions of the brain in a large series of primates, but the studies conducted so far on the subdivisions of the neocortex are not of this quality. It would be a massive undertaking indeed to measure each of the functional subareas of the human neocortex and to make comparisons with a large number of other primate species. This account has of necessity relied on preliminary studies of a more limited scope.

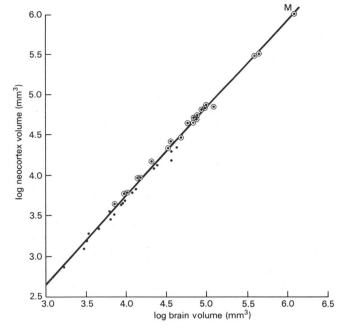

4.13 Volume of neocortex (mm³) as a function of the volume of the brain (mm³) in primates. •, Prosimians; ⊚, simians; M, man. After Passingham (1975b).

The interpretation given here accounts for much of the data, but there are findings that have still to be satisfactorily explained. Emphasis has been placed on those cases in which it proves possible to predict the size of an area of the human brain given knowledge of how the same area varies in size in primate brains of differing weight. However, as Holloway (1979) has pointed out, there are instances in which data for the human brain do not fit the predictions well. In some of the cases that he cites the reason is a simple one: the prediction is made on the basis of information on only a few primates and is therefore prone to considerable error. Furthermore the available data are not always consistent. For example, one study suggests that the frontal association cortex of the human brain may be more extensive than expected on the basis of the size of the neocortex (Brodmann 1912); but the values given for frontal association cortex in the human brain are not consistent with those reported in other studies (Passingham 1973). There is at present only one reliable finding which suggests that the human brain may not be as fully predictable as this account has maintained. It appears that the neocortical area which first processes visual information, the striate cortex, is smaller than the size of the whole neocortex would lead us to expect (Passingham and Ettlinger 1974). But it would surely be premature to use this result as the basis for any large claims about reorganization of the neocortex in the human brain.

It is time to take stock. The human brain is unique for its overall size when account is taken of the weight of the body. But, knowing its size we can in many instances predict the relative development of its parts, using data on the proportions of the brain in other primates. In other words the human brain seems to fit the primate pattern.

But could it also be regarded as an expanded rat or cat brain? Let us take the example of the neocortex again. Fig. 4.14 plots data for the size of brain and neocortex (not including the white matter) in a series of mammals (Passingham 1981a). Different regression lines have been fitted, one for monkeys and apes, one for carnivores and prosimians, and one for rodents. It is plain that the rule relating the size of the neocortex to the size of the brain is not the same in these groups. A brain of the same size would have proportionately more neocortex in a monkey or ape than in a prosimian or carnivore, and the same would be true in a comparison between a prosimian or carnivore with a rodent. The magnitude of the difference between monkeys and apes and other advanced mammals can be illustrated by taking the example of the cebus monkey. We can estimate from Fig. 4.14 that the neocortex would form 39.6 per cent of the brain in a carnivore with a brain of the same size as the cebus monkey. This is appreciably less than the value of 53 per cent which is found for the monkey. Analysis of other data on mammals confirms this general finding (Passingham 1981a). Clearly it is not adequate simply to state that the human brain is a large one. Its proportions are those we would expect for a brain after the pattern of a monkey or ape but not of a rat or a cat.

It may fairly be objected that the comparisons between the brains of man and of monkey and ape have, so far, used very crude measures, the size of particular areas. Perhaps a finer examination of the human brain would reveal crucial differences. But if we look to the number of the nerve cells and their density we come across yet another example of the predictability of the structure of the human brain given its size. The number of cells in the human neocortex is much as would be expected for so extensive a neocortex (Passingham 1973). The spacing of the cells is of especial interest because the less densely they are packed the greater the number of interconnections that can be made between the cells (Bok 1959; Holloway 1968; Jerison 1973). In mammals the density of cells decreases as the brain increases in size. A single rule governs the density of cells in the brains of mammals varying in size from mouse to elephant

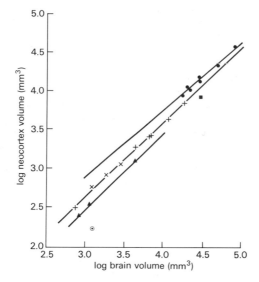

4.14 Volume of the neocortex (mm³) as a function of the volume of the brain (mm³) in mammals. ⊙, Marsupial; ▲, rodents; ■, ungulate; +, carnivores; ×, prosimians; ●, simians not including man. After Passingham (1981a). Data from Harman (1947).

and whale; and the human brain obeys that rule (Tower 1954). The density of the nerve cells in the human neocortex is as predicted for a brain as large as ours.

There is an even more extraordinary case where the human brain can be shown to be constructed according to principles that apply to the brains of other mammals. In a variety of mammals thin sections have been taken at various points in the neocortex, and the number of cells counted through the thickness of the cortex, from the surface down through all the layers (Rockel *et al.* 1980). Surprisingly the number of cells in sections of the same width is the same in all mammals. This can be so because if large brains are compared with small ones the lesser density of cells in the large brains is compensated for by an increase in the depth of the neocortex. The human brain has the same number of cells in a cylinder of cortex as have other mammals. It is apparent that our brains are constructed with the same building blocks as in other mammals.

The survey is now complete. We find the human brain to differ in its proportions from the brain of an ape, but to differ in a predictable way. That is to say that our brain seems to be a large brain after the primate pattern. But to say that differences are predictable is not to say that they are unimportant. The human brain has more neocortex to total brain volume than the chimpanzee brain, the ape has more than a monkey, and the monkey more than a prosimian (Fig. 4.12). The fact that this proportion is closely related to brain size in a lawful way does not imply that differences in this proportion between species are of no significance in determining intellectual capacities.

LANGUAGE

The capacity of which we are most proud is our ability to speak. Can we account for this in terms of the matters we have discussed so far—the size and gross proportions of the brain? Or must we assume that there are specialized areas which evolved in our brains but not in those of other primates, so allowing us to understand and produce speech?

Brain size

It is tempting to suppose that the extraordinary size of the human brain must be responsible in part for our possessing the capacity for language. It is not difficult to see how, when a brain reaches a certain size, new capacities might become available. A chimpanzee has a brain roughly three times as large as a small prosimian such as the mouse lemur (*Microcebus murinus*), even when account has been taken of the disparity in size between the two animals (Stephan 1972) (Fig. 4.3). The neocortex, including the white matter, forms 76 per cent of the total brain in the chimpanzee compared with only 46 per cent in the mouse lemur (Passingham 1975a). Yet the chimpanzee not only learns more quickly, but can master things of which the mouse lemur is not capable, such as the use and manufacture of tools. The difference between the relative size of our brain and the chimpanzee's is as great as that between chimpanzee and mouse lemur (Fig. 4.3); so that this difference could well account for capacities which we alone possess. The obvious analogy is that of the computer, in which the number of logic elements, as well as the storage space, is one of the determinants of what the machine can and cannot do.

Is there then a Rubicon, a size the brain must reach if language is to be possible? Jerison (1976b) has argued that indeed there is. He first estimates the amount of neocortical tissue which processes language in the human brain, and then calculates that a brain must be at least 600 to 1000 grams in weight if the neocortex is to possess enough tissue to handle language.

Lenneberg (1967), on the other hand, argued that there was no such Rubicon. He drew attention to the small brains of the dwarfs referred to as nanocephalic or 'bird–

headed' dwarfs, some of whom could speak. The most convincing case is that of a man whose speech was good even though at the age of 22 he had a brain weighing only 517 grams (Seckel 1960); a brain, that is, which is smaller than the brains of some gorillas (Tobias 1971). But it is not irrelevant that he was a dwarf, weighing only 18 kilograms, and when account is taken of his small size it turns out that his brain is larger than would be expected for a great ape of the same weight (Passingham and Ettlinger 1974).

Having said this it must be admitted that there are other microcephalic or small-headed people who are not dwarfed, and there are reports that some of them can nonetheless speak (Holloway 1968). This clearly shows that the mechanisms for *speaking* do not require a brain that is larger, whether in absolute or relative terms, than that with which a gorilla may be endowed. But all these microcephalic people are profoundly retarded mentally, and the complexity of the language which they can produce is not impressive (Holloway 1968). They can name, but so can chimpanzees and gorillas using the gestures of sign language, as we shall see in Chapter 8. In other words it has yet to be shown that the *language* capacity of these people is significantly more impressive than that which has been documented in apes. We may conclude that it is not the relative size of their brains that forbids apes to speak; they probably lack the relevant neural mechanisms. But this is not to say that relative brain size is unimportant for the understanding and use of language. Indeed it is highly plausible that the amount of tissue available to some extent determines the complexity of linguistic processing that can be carried out.

Cerebral dominance

What evidence is there, then, that our brains are specialized in ways other than mere size? There are two specializations usually taken to be unique to the human brain. The first is cerebral dominance: this refers to the greater role played by the left than the right hemisphere in controlling speech. The second is the existence of 'speech areas' in the neocortex, that is areas which direct the comprehension and production of speech. Each of these possible specializations will be examined in turn.

Cerebral dominance was first demonstrated in patients with damage to the left or right hemisphere. In right-handers damage to the right hemisphere rarely causes any disruption of speech, whereas damage to the left hemisphere often does so (Hécaen and Albert 1978). The best evidence for cerebral dominance for speech is provided by the effects of temporarily inactivating one hemisphere by injecting sodium amytal into its blood supply. This has been done as part of a series of tests carried out on epileptic patients referred to the neurological clinic for possible surgery (Milner 1975). In 96 per cent of right-handed patients the temporary inactivation of the left hemisphere disrupted speech, but in only 4 per cent of such patients was speech affected by inactivation of the right hemisphere. In left-handers the situation was more complicated. Speech was found to be controlled by the left hemisphere in 70 per cent of patients, the right in 15 per cent and by both hemispheres in a further 15 per cent. In by far the majority of people, then, only one of the two hemispheres directs speech, and this is usually the left hemisphere.

Although this is true in the normal course of events we know that the right hemisphere is nonetheless capable of learning and controlling speech (Passingham 1979a). If the left hemisphere is damaged in early childhood the right hemisphere can assume the direction of speech; in such cases the pattern of dominance is shifted to the right hemisphere as assessed by injecting sodium amytal (Rasmussen and Milner 1977). Indeed the whole of the left hemisphere can later be removed without affecting the understanding or production of speech (Basser 1962). In adults the right hemisphere is less efficient at taking over language functions after damage to the left hemisphere. Presumably this is because it is already committed to the execution of other functions; given that it is anatomically equipped for the control of speech in young children there is no reason to suppose that it loses the relevant fine circuitry in adulthood.

The language capacities of the right hemisphere can be established in adults by studying two groups of patients. There are a few people in whom the left hemisphere had to be removed in adulthood so as to excise a tumour. In such cases their understanding of speech can be tested directly by asking them to pick out the pictures that correspond to the words they hear. There are also patients in whom the surgeon has cut the corpus callosum and the other forebrain commissures connecting the two hemispheres in an effort to contain severe and long-standing epilepsy. In these patients it is possible to interrogate the right hemisphere only by asking the patients to choose between pictures that are shown to that hemisphere alone. This can be done by presenting stimuli only to the left or to the right field of view (see Fig. 2.12).

We find that with the right hemisphere alone patients can understand the meaning of some spoken words as evidenced by their ability to pick out the relevant pictures (Smith 1966; Zaidel 1977). But in one study patients were unable to understand a simple grammatical rule when their right hemisphere alone was tested (Gazzaniga and Hillyard 1971). They could not, for example, distinguish between the spoken sentence 'the boy kisses the girl' and 'the girl kisses the boy'. The right hemisphere of an adult also appears to be incapable of evoking the sounds of words. With their right hemisphere alone patients with section of the commissures cannot match pictures on the basis of a correspondence in sound between the names of the objects shown in the two sets of pictures (Levy and Trevarthen 1977). If, for instance, they are shown a picture of a bee, they have to pick out a picture of a key. The right hemisphere in such patients appears to be inarticulate, unable even to repeat words silently. By the time we reach adulthood our right hemisphere has given up much of its claim on language, and devoted itself to other things.

Anatomical asymmetry

Recently it has been discovered that the two cerebral hemispheres of the human brain are not entirely symmetrical. The asymmetries of most interest to us are those involving one of the areas processing language, often referred to as Wernicke's area. This area is discussed in the next section, and its location is shown in Fig. 4.16. Part of this area is situated in the temporal lobe of the neocortex, in and below the sylvian fissure (Fig. 4.15). If the brain is cut along this fissure, as shown in Fig. 4.15, an area is exposed which is referred to as the planum temporale, part of Wernicke's area. Both in adults and babies the planum temporale tends to be larger in the left than the right hemisphere (Geschwind and Levitsky 1968; Witelson 1977). The cortex in this region can be subdivided into several different sub-areas on the basis of cytoarchitecture. These sub-areas have been studied in detail in four human brains, and in three of them the area designated Tpt was found to be larger on the left than on the right (Galaburda et al. 1978). In the same laboratory measurements have been taken in 10 brains of the area referred to as Broca's

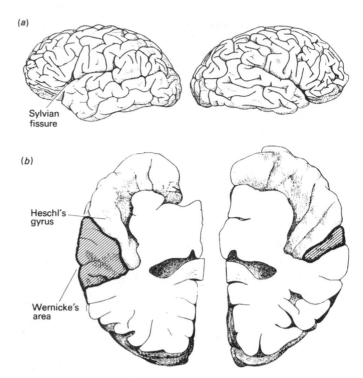

(a)

Sylvian
fissure

(b)

Heschl's
gyrus

Wernicke's
area

4.15 Planum temporale in
the human brain. *a* shows
the sylvian fissure; *b* shows a
brain sectioned in the plane
of the sylvian fissure. The
planum temporale is
outlined in black. After
Geschwind (1972).

area (Fig. 4.16); it was larger on the left in six brains and on the right in only one (Galaburda 1980). The results of both studies are intriguing, but they require confirmation with larger samples.

There are two other asymmetries in the sylvian fissure that are related to those already described. The left sylvian fissure tends to be longer than the right (Rubens 1977); and the back of this fissure also tends to run lower on the left than on the right (LeMay 1976).

The interest of these asymmetries would be much enhanced if it could be shown that they are related to cerebral dominance for speech. There is only one study that has looked into the matter directly. In 58 patients the hemisphere controlling speech was identified by injecting sodium amytal into the blood supply in the way that has been described above. In the same patients X-ray pictures were also taken which allowed an estimate of the height of the back of the sylvian fissure in the left and right hemispheres as judged from the disposition of the blood vessels. The study found that in patients with left hemisphere dominance for speech the sylvian fissure ran lower on the left than the right, and that this tendency was less marked in patients in which speech was controlled by

the right hemisphere or by both (Ratcliff *et al.* 1980). But
on this evidence the relationship between brain asymmetry and speech dominance is a very loose one; the
asymmetry was as well developed in many of those
patients with atypical speech dominance as in those with
the typical representation of speech in the left hemisphere.

A more indirect way of approaching the same problem
is to try to relate brain asymmetry to handedness, but so
far this has only been done for the height of the sylvian
fissure. In one study the end of the sylvian fissure was
found to run lower in the left hemisphere of 67 per cent of
right-handed people compared with only 21.4 per cent of
left-handers (LeMay 1976). By contrast it was higher on
the left in only 7.5 per cent of the right-handers and 7.2 per
cent of the left-handers.

But we should be cautious in interpreting these results.
Asymmetries in the length and height of the sylvian fissure
have also been found in great apes. The length of the
sylvian fissure has been measured in rhesus monkeys,
chimpanzees and people (Yeni-Komshian and Benson
1976). There was no difference between the two sides in
the monkeys, but there was in the chimpanzees, as in
people. The left fissure was longer than the right in 80 per
cent of the chimpanzees and 84 per cent of the people; and
the right longer in 8 per cent of the chimpanzees compared
with 16 per cent of the people. A similar result has been
found for the height of the sylvian fissure at the back; again
asymmetries have been demonstrated for great apes and
people, but not for monkeys of various species (LeMay
1976). In 57.1 per cent of the apes the right fissure was
higher; and the left ran higher in only 3.5 per cent of the
apes. The correspondence between the figures for apes and
people is very striking.

These results should make us hesitate before concluding
that all these anatomical asymmetries are related to
cerebral dominance for speech in man. We have already
seen that there is no tendency for other primates to be
right-handed, and it would appear to follow that these
asymmetries cannot relate to handedness in apes. Either
these asymmetries are not in fact connected with cerebral
dominance in people, or we must suppose that the apes
also exhibit some form of cerebral dominance. Chimpanzees and gorillas can master some aspects of language, as
will be described in Chapter 8; but we do not know if
these capacities depend on the one hemisphere more than
the other.

Wernicke's area

We must now examine in more detail the areas within the dominant hemisphere of the human brain that are specialized for language. There are two 'speech areas' in this hemisphere, Broca's area in frontal cortex and Wernicke's area in temporal and parietal cortex (Fig. 4.16). They have been identified as speech areas by the effects of damage caused by war wounds, accidents or strokes. If tissue is disrupted within a wide area of temporal and parietal cortex the person will have difficulty in understanding speech; whereas if the lesion is in or around the region of Broca's area the person will suffer from a poverty of speech and a loss of fluency (Hécaen and Albert 1978).

There is another way in which these two regions can be identified. When patients are undergoing neurosurgery on the dominant hemisphere it may be important to locate the speech areas so as to avoid them when excising pathological tissue. If the operations are performed under local anaesthesia this can be done by electrically stimulating points on the cortex while asking the patient to speak. A site is taken as lying within the speech areas if stimulation at that point causes the patient to be unable to find words, to misname, or to confuse numbers while counting. The map of the speech areas that is obtained by this method agrees roughly with that shown in Fig. 4.16 (Penfield and Roberts 1959). It should be emphasized that this figure gives only a rough indication of the extent of areas that are critical for speech, and that damage to tissue lying outside these boundaries can lead to problems in understanding or producing speech (Luria 1970; Mohr 1976; Bogen and Bogen 1976).

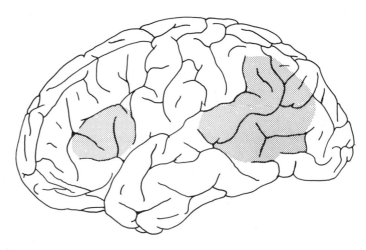

4.16 Speech areas (stippled) of the human brain. The extent of the two areas is based on lesion and stimulation data reviewed by Penfield and Roberts (1959).

Are these areas unlike anything to be found in the brains of other primates? To take Wernicke's area first, the different anatomical sub-regions have been given labels according to their cytoarchitecture, that is the types of cell and the pattern of cell layering. In the human brain the temporal cortex within Wernicke's area has been labelled TA, and the parietal cortex PF and PG (von Economo 1929). Similar regions have also been identified in the brains of the rhesus monkey and the chimpanzee (von Bonin and Bailey 1947; Bailey *et al.* 1950). But on the temporal plane in the human brain there is an area which has been called the 'magnopyramidal region' because there are large pyramidal cells in the third layer of the cortex; and this area cannot be identified in the brain of a monkey (Braak 1978). It would clearly be worth investigating whether this area can be detected in the brain of a chimpanzee. Until this is done we cannot be certain that this area is unique to the human brain.

The most critical experiment is to remove in monkeys or apes any area that is thought to be analogous to the speech area of the human brain. In this way we can establish whether the areas perform the same functions as in man. One such region is the area of superior temporal cortex labelled TA (Fig. 4.17). Removal of this area in rhesus monkeys impairs their ability to tell the difference between sounds, even though they can still hear them; for example, the monkeys are poor at identifying which of two speech sounds they have heard, the sound [i] or the sound [u] (Dewson *et al.* 1969). But the monkeys have a further disability: even when they have been trained to distinguish adequately between two

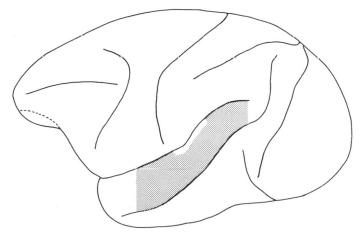

4.17 Area TA (stippled) of the superior temporal gyrus in a rhesus monkey. Based on von Bonin and Bailey (1947).

sounds, a tone and a hiss, they are bad at telling in what order the two sounds are played, tone followed by hiss or hiss followed by tone (Cowey and Weiskrantz 1976). In rhesus monkeys, then, this area of temporal cortex plays a role in the identification of sounds and in the perception of the sequence of sounds. We also know from studies of the electrical activity of cells in this region that it contains the physiological apparatus for the recognition of the different calls in the repertoire of the species (Newman 1979). The sub-area Tpt, which has been described as part of Wernicke's area in the human brain, can also be identified in the monkey brain (Galaburda and Sanides 1980). Many nerve cells in this region change their pattern of activity when the monkey hears sounds, and some even do so when consonants are played to the animal (Leinonen *et al.* 1980). It is reasonable to conclude that the temporal cortex of monkeys may be equipped with at least some of the mechanisms needed for the perception of speech.

But in people the understanding of speech is disrupted by damage to the left hemisphere but not to the right. This raises the question of whether removal of temporal cortex from one hemisphere alone would lead to any impairment in monkeys, and if so whether it matters which hemisphere is damaged. Certainly rhesus monkeys are poor at reporting sequences of sounds even when the removal is made on one side alone (Dewson *et al.* 1970). There is also preliminary evidence suggesting that it may make a difference whether the tissue is removed from the left or right hemisphere (Dewson 1977). Rhesus monkeys were tested for their ability to tell a tone from a hiss. Removal of the superior temporal cortex, TA, from the right hemisphere had no effect in two animals; but similar removals on the left led to an impairment in four others. This preliminary finding is intriguing, but confirmation is required with more animals.

There is another way in which we can try to establish whether or not there is cerebral dominance for the appreciation of sounds in monkeys. One test used with people is the dichotic listening task, on which two different digits or words are played simultaneously to the two ears. The subject is required to report the words he hears, and if he gives mainly the words played to the right ear it is assumed that his left hemisphere is dominant for speech. The assumption is that it is the hemisphere opposite an ear that is primarily responsible for analysing sounds played to that ear. The task has been adapted for monkeys by testing their ability to make difficult discriminations between monkey calls, and comparing the performance of the animals when the calls are played to the right or left ear alone (Petersen *et al.* 1978; Beecher *et al.* 1979). Japanese macaques turn out to be better at making discriminations between calls of their own species when they hear them through their right rather than their left ears. In other words in these animals the left hemisphere may play a larger role than the right in analysing the sounds these monkeys use to communicate.

What are we to conclude? Many processes are involved in the understanding of speech: the sounds must be analysed, their meanings must be identified, and the rules must be appreciated by which the words are ordered. As we shall see in Chapter 8 apes are capable of understanding the meanings of words, and their brains must therefore be equipped with mechanisms that can perform this task. It is controversial whether apes can learn to understand the grammatical rules that determine the meaning of even the simplest sentences. There may well be specialized mechanisms that are required for understanding speech and that are lacking in the brains of monkeys and apes. But we have yet to identify them.

Broca's area

In the human brain Broca's area lies on the inferior surface of the frontal lobe (Fig. 4.16). It can be identified on the basis of its characteristic cytoarchitecture as viewed down the microscope (von Economo 1929). It can also be delineated in patients by electrical stimulation of the cortex during surgery; as explained above stimulation of this region interferes with speech.

There has been no general agreement about whether Broca's area can be identified in the brains of monkeys and apes. In their early studies von Bonin and Bailey believed that they could identify an area with a similar microscopic structure in the brains of both rhesus monkeys and chimpanzees (von Bonin and Bailey 1947; Bailey *et al.* 1950). The area they proposed lies within premotor cortex, that is the region immediately in front of motor cortex; in Fig. 4.18 it is marked with hatching. But on reconsidering the material these authors were less confident that they could make out a specialized area within the premotor cortex (von Bonin and Bailey 1961). More recently Galaburda and Pandya have claimed that in the monkey brain there is indeed an area which is like Broca's area in cytoarchitecture (Galaburda 1980; Galaburda and

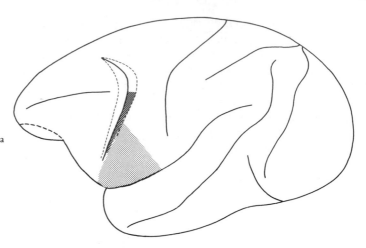

4.18 Rhesus monkey brain showing cortical larynx area (stippled) and proposed Broca's area (hatched). Larynx area based on von Bonin and Bailey (1947) and Hast *et al.* (1974); Broca's area as proposed by Galaburda and Pandya (1981).

Pandya 1981). They point to an area of premotor cortex that lies within the posterior bank of the arcuate sulcus as indicated by the dark hatching in Fig. 4.18. This region shares a further similarity with Broca's area in that it receives anatomical connections from the auditory areas of the temporal lobe (Galaburda and Pandya 1981).

The issue cannot be decided on the basis of anatomical data alone. We need to be convinced that an area not only looks like Broca's area but also plays a functional role in vocalization. Electrical stimulation of the area indicated by stippling in Fig. 4.18 elicits movements of the vocal cords in monkeys (Hast *et al.* 1974). But this very demonstration casts doubt on the suggestion that this area is functionally similar to Broca's area. In the human brain Broca's area lies in front of the cortical area which directly controls the vocal cords as shown by the effects of electrical stimulation (Penfield and Rasmussen 1950; Penfield and Roberts 1959). It is in front of the region controlling the larynx that we should look for a candidate for Broca's area in monkeys or apes (Jürgens 1979). But as yet no study has been carried out to discover whether it is possible to interfere with vocalization in monkeys by stimulating the tissue in the posterior bank of the arcuate sulcus (dark hatching in Fig. 4.18).

An alternative method is to investigate the effects of cortical damage on vocalization. Incomplete removal of the area of premotor cortex that controls the larynx has no discernible effect on the spontaneous calling of monkeys; and they can still make a call to a signal as taught to do before the operation (Sutton *et al.* 1974; Sutton 1979). If the area of motor cortex representing the face is also removed the monkeys have a feeble and low-pitched voice (Green and Walker 1938); but this could result from the general facial paralysis. A better parallel for the loss of fluency that results from damage to Broca's area is provided by the marked decrease in spontaneous calling that follows the removal of prefrontal cortex in monkeys, that is of the area in front of premotor cortex (Myers 1976). But no one has yet investigated the effects of removing the area in the arcuate sulcus shown in Fig. 4.18. This must be done before we can be certain that this region of the monkey brain corresponds to Broca's area.

Something is known of the functions of other parts of premotor cortex in monkeys. If tissue is removed in and around the upper limb of the arcuate sulcus monkeys have difficulty in making sequences of movements with their hand. This can be shown by requiring them to operate three catches in the right order so as to open a box. Though they can still make the individual movements they now make mistakes in the order in which they tackle them (Deuel 1977). In another experiment the lesion was confined to premotor cortex; the monkeys were poor at a task which required them to make one movement of the hand or another, depending on which visual cue was presented (Halsband and Passingham, to be published). This suggests that premotor cortex plays a role in ensuring that actions are appropriate to the context.

By analogy it is tempting to suggest that the primary function of Broca's area is to direct the sequencing of the movements of the vocal cords, and to direct them according to context (Passingham 1981b). Meaning is conveyed in speech by the serial ordering of the phonemes and morphemes, and a high order of vocal skill is demanded (MacNeilage 1970). Patients with large anterior cerebral lesions have difficulties in sequencing sounds. In one study of such patients they were found to be able to say 'ba-ba-ba', but unable to repeat the sequence 'ba-da-ga' (Mateer and Kimura 1977). The lesions encroach on tissue controlling movements of the face, since the same patients have difficulties with copying simple facial movements or with repeating sequences such as retracting the lips, putting out the tongue and biting the lower lip (Mateer and Kimura 1977). It is possible to demonstrate a defect in reproducing the sequence without a corresponding difficulty in copying each oral movement on its own. This has been done by electrically stimulating anterior points in the left cerebral hemisphere of patients undergoing neurosurgery under local anaesthesia. On three occasions stimulation of inferior frontal sites well forward of the motor area has rendered the patient unable to copy a sequence of oral movements although the ability to copy each one on its own was preserved (Ojemann and Mateer 1979a,b).

Why should it be the case that Broca's area in the left hemisphere is more important for speech than the corresponding area in the right hemisphere? It has been common to suppose that the key to cerebral dominance for speech must lie in handedness, since there is a close link between the hand that a person prefers to use and the hemisphere in which speech is represented. But cerebral dominance for vocalization can be present without handedness, as is shown by the existence of some birds in which there is an asymmetry in the neural control of song. In canaries (*Serinus canarius*), chaffinches (*Fringilla coelebs*) and white-crowned sparrows (*Zonotrichia leucophrys*) section of the nerve innervating the left syrinx markedly impairs singing, whereas section of the nerve innervating the right syrinx has little or no effect (Nottebohm 1977). Left dominance has also been demonstrated in canaries for the central controlling area, the hyperstriatum ventrale pars caudale; the number of syllables of song that the bird loses is much greater if lesions are made on the left rather than on the right (Nottebohm 1977).

This example suggests that there may be reasons why cerebral dominance is of advantage for the production of sounds. Perhaps the key to dominance lies not in handedness but in the way in which the brain innervates the vocal cords. The hand is controlled mainly by the opposite hemisphere. If the motor area of, say, the left hemisphere is damaged the right motor cortex is unable to direct the normal range of movements of the right hand. This is true in monkeys even if the damage occurs very early in life (Passingham *et al.* 1978).

The arrangement is quite different for central organs of the body such as the tongue and jaw. If the motor cortex is electrically stimulated in people the limb which moves is always the one opposite the hemisphere stimulated; but movements of the tongue and jaw can be elicited from either hemisphere (Penfield and Roberts 1959). If the hypoglossal nerve, which innervates the tongue, is cut on one side in monkeys, stimulation of the motor area on the other side still elicits most tongue movements (Walker and Green 1938). This indicates that there are paths from each hemisphere to both sides of the tongue. If, therefore, the motor area is removed in one hemisphere, a monkey can still rotate and deviate its tongue to either side; and it remains able to rotate its tongue either way even if the hypoglossal nerve is sectioned on the same side as the cortical lesion (Green and Walker 1938).

It has been demonstrated in monkeys that the vocal cords also receive a bilateral innervation from the neocortex; the cords can be excited by electrical stimulation of the cortical larynx area in either hemisphere (Hast et al. 1974). Vocalization can be induced in patients by stimulating the left or the right hemisphere (Penfield and Roberts 1959). This bilateral organization permits considerable recovery of function. It has traditionally been believed that lesions of Broca's area in people give rise to a long-lasting aphasia, but more careful analysis indicates that where the lesion can be shown to be confined to Broca's area and the adjacent larynx area the patients recover their speech remarkably well (Mohr 1976; Mohr et al. 1978). This improvement may occur partly because the corresponding areas in the contralateral hemisphere can take over the relevant function.

It does not necessarily follow that because an organ can be controlled by either hemisphere it would be most efficient for one hemisphere to assume the dominant role. The movements of the tongue, for example, are relatively simple, and there is no reason why the relevant cortical areas cannot co-ordinate their instructions without loss of proficiency. But such an arrangement would not be optimal for the execution of complex sequences of movement as in the production of speech. In such a case we would surely expect the highest skill to be achieved if the sequence was directed by one central programme, located in a single hemisphere, rather than by two separate programmes which must use the long commissural pathways between the hemispheres to co-ordinate their instructions. The same reasoning applies to the production of intricate songs by birds which, like canaries, learn a new song each season (Nottebohm 1977, 1979).

If there is an advantage to be gained from programming speech from one area rather than two it follows that those people in whom speech is controlled by both hemispheres should be at a disadvantage. There is suggestive evidence that this is so. Stutterers have difficulty in speaking fluently, and there are indications that speech is more likely to be under the control of both hemispheres in people who stutter than in those who do not (Rosenfield 1980; Rosenfield and Goodglass 1980).

Thus we may reasonably entertain the notion that where complex sequences must be programmed it will be more efficient to set up one programme rather than two.

But there is an additional consideration. Those song birds that produce sequences of sounds also learn their songs by listening to the songs of adults of their species (Thorpe 1961; Marler 1976a). There might be reasons why it is more efficient to analyse complex sounds in a single hemisphere, or to rely on a single mechanism for imitating sounds by adjusting the sounds that are produced so that they match those that are heard.

But how are we to account for the link between cerebral dominance for speech and handedness? If plans of action are to be formulated in words it will be more efficient if they are executed by the same hemisphere that is specialized for language. In fact we know that the left hemisphere also has some influence over the actions performed by the left hand. Damage to the left parietal lobe in people sometimes produces a syndrome called 'apraxia' in which the patient has great difficulty in carrying out actions which pose no problems to other people (Hécaen and Albert 1978). For example, they may be unable to carry out the simple sequence involved in striking a match and lighting a cigarette. Even those patients who are less severely handicapped may be poor at copying a series of hand movements or at learning a sequence of movements as in pushing a button, pulling a handle, and pressing a lever; and they are impaired whichever hand they use (Kimura 1979; Kolb and Milner 1981). While it is not being suggested that these patients are having problems because they have difficulties with language, it is not unreasonable to suppose that it is because the left hemisphere is dominant for vocal skill that it has assumed the direction of manual skill.

It could, of course, be claimed that the opposite is the case. As we shall see in Chapter 8 it has been argued that our hominid ancestors might first have communicated with gestures of hand, presumably using the same hand they preferred to use when handling implements. If one hemisphere had become specialized for the direction of manual gestures the later development of vocal communication might have proceeded most efficiently if the same hemisphere assumed a dominant role for speech. Some such sequence of events has been suggested by Kimura (1976, 1979). It might be thought that this idea derives support from the fact that damage to the left hemisphere in deaf people impairs their ability to communicate by making the gestures used in the formal system of sign language (Kimura 1976). But in fact this observation can be accounted for on either view, whether we suppose that it was manual gestures or speech that first required the specialization of the left hemisphere. That the primary constraint may have been vocal skill and not handedness is suggested by the evidence for cerebral dominance for vocalization in some song birds.

For whatever reason cerebral dominance became established in the human brain the re-organization had a very important consequence. It has been pointed out by Levy (1977) that in the brains of other primates there appears to be an unnecessary duplication between the tasks performed by each hemisphere. Removal of an area of association cortex from either hemisphere may have only a small effect in disrupting a monkey's ability to cope with particular tasks; the consequences of removing tissue from both sides are usually much more severe (Ettlinger and Gautrin 1971; Warren and Nonnemann 1976). If one hemisphere is totally removed monkeys can still learn a complicated task with apparently normal facility (Nakamura and Gazzaniga 1978). That is not to say that there are no instances where one hemisphere contributes more than the others; and indeed evidence has already been quoted suggesting that even in rhesus monkeys the two hemispheres may not be completely equal in the functions that they perform. Nonetheless the degree of duplication is in general such that we might doubt that it is of great benefit to a monkey to have two hemispheres rather than one.

The human brain is organized in what seems to be a more efficient way. In each association area, whether of frontal, temporal or parietal cortex, different though related functions are assigned to the two hemispheres (Kolb and Whishaw 1980). If patients are examined with damage to one of these areas of association cortex patients with lesions on the left will typically do poorly on tasks using verbal material and patients with right-sided lesions will be impaired with spatial and pictorial material (Milner 1973). The specialization of the left hemisphere for language has led to a consequent re-organization with the assignment of different roles to the two hemispheres.

There is a very important implication of this. We cannot validly compare the size of the human brain with the brain of other primates on the assumption that processing power is simply a function of total brain size. If the brains of a person and a chimpanzee are not organized with equal efficiency comparisons of this sort will greatly underestimate the disparity between the cognitive capacity of the two brains. The gap between man and chimpanzee is probably much greater than we earlier supposed.

EVOLUTION

Now that we know something of the differences between the brains of man and other primates we are ready to ask how those differences came about. There are two issues to which we must address ourselves, the rate at which the human brain evolved, and the mechanism by which the changes occurred.

We immediately face a problem: there are no fossil brains. We have to be content with examining the cranial cavity itself and taking casts of the impression that the brain makes on it. These 'endocasts' often reproduce the pattern of the major blood vessels and fissures, although less well with large than with small brains. They can be very impressive, as in the case of the cast taken from the brain case of the early hominid KNM-ER 1470 (Fig. 4.19). But, however ingenious the investigator, casts can tell us no more about a brain than can be inferred from its size and the pattern of the fissures. Although it is fortunately true that fissures often bound areas that are different in cytoarchitecture and function, there are many areas in the brains of the fossil hominids the boundaries of which cannot be detected by inspecting a cast.

We found earlier that we lack adequate data on the

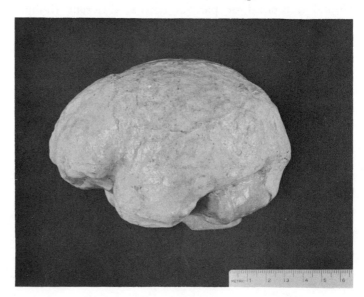

4.19 Cast taken from the skull of KMN-ER 1470 from Lake Turkana, Kenya. Courtesy of R. Holloway.

extent of the association areas in modern man. This should warn us to treat with suspicion any claims to have measured the extent of these areas in fossil man. The limits of each of the association areas as indicated by cytoarchitecture are not to be seen on a cast of the inside of the skull. Yet attempts have been made to measure the size of them from such casts (von Bonin 1963; Kochetkova 1978). We should be wary until it has been shown that the same measures, when made on casts from modern skulls, do indeed correspond to anatomically distinct regions as judged when viewing the brain down a microscope (Passingham 1973). The only sophisticated analysis that has been made is that being pursued by Holloway (1981). The overall shape of the endocast is described by taking measurements from 171 points on the surface of each side. These measurements have been taken on endocasts from fossil hominids and modern apes. The preliminary analysis points to a development of frontal and parietal association cortex in the hominid endocasts (Holloway 1981).

When making comparisons between the brains of living primates it is necessary to take account of the size of the body; it is as important to do so when examining casts from fossil primates. Estimates of the size of fossil species must be derived from measurements of the long bones of the arm and leg, the vertebrae or the teeth. It is not a matter of mere academic quibbling that an attempt be made to form an impression of the size of the animal; important issues may hang on the estimates at which we arrive. To give one example, Jerison (1973, 1976a) has calculated the brain and body weights of a series of fossil mammals. He finds that, when changes in body size are taken into account by calculating the encephalization quotient (EQ), there was little advance in the size of the brain for 100 million or so years of mammalian evolution; but that during the last 50 million years there has been a four- to fivefold increase in the relative weight of the brain. The calculations are crucially dependent on the body weights assigned to these animals; if they were lighter than suggested the relative brain size or EQ would have been correspondingly greater. Radinsky (1975b, 1976) has argued that some of the mammals of 50 or so million years ago may have had brains which were relatively larger than had been supposed.

The first issue of importance for the present account is how early there were primates which were specialized as large-brained creatures. We are lucky enough to have seven skulls, from the Eocene, Oligocene and Miocene, which are complete enough to allow endocasts to be taken, and for which estimates of the size of the body can be made (Radinsky 1974, 1977). An EQ can therefore be computed for each of these animals: as explained earlier this index relates the size of the brain to the size expected for an average mammal of the same body weight.

But there is a snag. Different workers have arrived at different estimates of the size of the body in these fossils. In general Jerison (1973, 1979a) believes the primates to have been lighter and the other mammals heavier than does Radinsky (1977, 1978). On the first view (Jerison 1979a) three of the early prosimians have an EQ outside the range of the other mammals that were contemporary; these are prosimians with some affiliation to the tarsiers, *Tetonius* and *Necrolemur* from the Eocene, and *Rooneyia* from the Oligocene. The other two prosimians, *Adapis* and *Smilodectes* from the Eocene, are both related to the lemurs, and their EQ lies within the range for other mammals. But if we assume that these primates were heavier than has been supposed in these calculations and the other mammals lighter, then the picture changes. All these Eocene and Oligocene prosimians then fall within the upper part of the range for mammals of the time (Radinsky 1978).

Clearly we can reach no conclusion until agreement can be reached on the probable sizes of these fossil animals. But we may note that modern prosimians do not have EQs which are greater than those of many carnivores and ungulates; it is only the monkeys and apes that excel (Fig. 4.4). There is, therefore, no special reason why we should suppose a priori that the early primates should have been distinguished by the relative development of their brains.

The earliest apes for which we have evidence date from roughly 28 million years ago in the Oligocene (Simons 1972). They have been identified as apes mainly on the basis of jaws and teeth, but the skull of one of them, *Aegyptopithecus*, is well-enough preserved to allow an estimate of the cranial capacity (Radinsky 1973). The figure of 27 cubic centimetres has been proposed (Radinsky 1977); and the size of the teeth suggests an animal of around 5.6 kilograms (Gingerich 1977). These estimates would give an EQ of 0.71, which is not widely discrepant from the value of 0.97 which has been calculated using other estimates of brain and body weight (Jerison 1979a). In either case the relative brain size of this ape places it towards the top of the range of Oligocene mammals (Jerison 1973; Radinsky 1978).

It would be of especial interest if we could form some estimate of the relative brain size of the dryopithecine apes of around 20 million years ago, since we believe that it was from this stock that both pongids and hominids were derived. We have a skull of *Dryopithecus africanus* (Fig. 4.20a), but unfortunately it is very badly crushed (Le Gros Clark and Leakey 1951). Radinsky (1974) suggested a very rough figure of 150 cubic centimetres, and he calculated that this would give an estimate for relative brain size that was within the range of modern apes. But he has since commented that he has very little faith in the figure he gave for cranial capacity (Radinsky 1979). The truth is that the specimen is too damaged to permit confidence in any estimate.

Of the brain size of the earliest hominids we know nothing. We have fossil remains of *Ramapithecus* which date from between 14 and 8 or so million years ago, but it is controversial whether these represent a hominid (Pilbeam *et al.* 1977). So far we have no bones from the cranium; all that we possess of the skull are jaw bones and teeth (Fig. 4.20b).

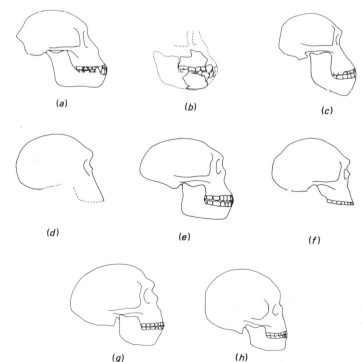

(a)

(b)

(c)

(d)

(e)

(f)

(g)

(h)

4.20 Skulls of eight hominids and one pongid. a, *Dryopithecus africanus*; b, *Ramapithecus*; c, *Australopithecus africanus*; d, KNM-ER 1470; e, *Homo erectus*; f, Steinheim skull; g, *Homo sapiens neanderthalensis*; h, Cro-Magnon skull. After Le Gros Clark (1964) and Campbell (1974).

It is not until around 3 million years ago that there is solid evidence of the shape and size of the cranium in the hominids. Parts of the cranium of two individuals have been found at Hadar in Ethiopia (Johanson and White 1979); and the larger of these is thought to have a cranial capacity of around 500 cubic centimetres (Holloway, personal communication). This is within the range for the australopithecines found at later dates in South and East Africa (Table 4.2).

To establish relative brain size we require some estimate of body weight. The size of the vertebrae and femora provide some basis for such a judgement, and values for body size have been suggested for the australopithecines and for early *Homo* from East Africa (McHenry 1976). These are given in Table 4.2 together with the most reliable estimates of the cranial capacities of the relevant hominids (Holloway 1978). The table also provides EQs that have been calculated using these data.

The brain is smaller in absolute terms in the lighter *Australopithecus africanus* (Fig. 4.20c) than in the more rugged *Australopithecus robustus*. But this difference vanishes when account is taken of their different build (Leutenegger 1973a); the mean EQs for the two groups are very similar—3.42 and 3.39 (Table 4.2). Both values are above the EQs obtained for modern chimpanzees: Table 4.2 gives a mean EQ of 2.63 for 23 chimpanzees (5 *Pan paniscus*, 18 *Pan troglodytes*); the values for individuals range from 2.11 to 3.34.

Table 4.2 Cranial capacity, body weight and encephalization quotient (EQ) in hominids and chimpanzee

Genus	Site	Brain (cm³)			Body (kg)			EQ
		n	Mean	Range	*n*	Mean	Range	
Australopithecus africanus	SA	6	442.0	428−485	2	35.3	27.6−43.0	3.42
Australopithecus robustus	SA and EA	4	517.5	500−530	5	45.4	36.1−52.7	3.39
Homo (KNM-ER 1470)	EA	1	752.0	—	2	52.8	51.3−54.3	4.45
Homo erectus	Java	4	895.7	815−943	—	55.0	—	5.16
Homo erectus	Peking	5	1043.0	915−1225	—	55.0	—	6.01
Homo sapiens (modern)	—	1039	1395.1	870−2150	1039	68.7	30.0−134.0	6.5 }
Pan	—	23	366.4	309−423	23	39.9	27.1−54.0	2.63

SA, South Africa; EA, East Africa.
Data on cranial capacity in fossil hominids from Holloway (1976, 1978) for australopithecines, *Homo* (KNM-ER 1470) and *Homo erectus* (Java), and from Tobias (1976) for *Homo erectus* (Peking). Data on brain size and body weight in modern man from Pakkenberg (personal communication) and in chimpanzees (*Pan*) from Schultz (personal communication). Estimates of hominid body size from McHenry (1976) for australopithecines and *Homo* (KNM-ER 1470).

The brain is further advanced in the earliest representatives of the genus *Homo*. The skull KNM-ER 1470 (Fig. 4.20*d*) from Lake Turkana in Kenya is thought to be between 1.8 and 1.9 million years old (Hay 1980). It has an impressive cranial capacity of 752 cubic centimetres (Holloway 1978), and on the basis of two femora found at the same site a body weight of 52.8 kilograms has been suggested (McHenry 1976) (Table 4.2). These figures give an EQ of 4.45, much higher than the EQs of the australopithecines. Three large crania have also been found at Olduvai in Tanzania at sites which are slightly more recent, and these are usually classified as *Homo habilis* (Leakey *et al.* 1964). These have cranial capacities which are greater than those of the australopithecines. Estimates have been given of 590 cubic centimetres for OH 24, 650 cubic centimetres for OH 12, and of between 700 and 750 cubic centimetres for OH 7 (Holloway 1978, 1980).

The earliest skull of *Homo erectus* that we possess comes from Lake Turkana at a site that is around 1.3 to 1.6 million years old. As yet the cranial capacity has not been formally estimated, but it is clearly greater than in the earlier specimens of *Homo* and may be of the order of 800 to 900 cubic centimetres (Leakey and Walker 1976). However, the cranial capacity had been established for another *Homo erectus* skull that was found at Olduvai and is dated at over a million years ago (Day 1977). The estimate for this skull, referred to as OH 9, is 1097 cubic centimetres (Holloway 1978).

Most of our evidence for *Homo erectus* comes from the later finds in Java and Peking (Fig. 4.20*c*). The range of cranial capacities is given in Table 4.2 (Tobias 1975; Holloway 1978). But no proper calculations have yet been published to suggest the likely size of these hominids. For present purposes a very rough figure of 55 kilograms will be used, but with no pretence that this figure represents other than guesswork. Using these estimates we arrive at an EQ of 5.16 for the Java finds which are somewhere over 700 000 years old, and an EQ of 6.01 for the skulls from Peking which are later, perhaps 400 000 years old. This represents a further increase on the relative brain size of early *Homo*.

We have established that there was a dramatic increase in the relative size of the hominid brain in the last 3 million years. This can best be appreciated from Fig. 4.21 which plots the EQs suggested for the various hominids and the times at which the hominids are believed to have lived. Clearly all these values for EQ are to be treated with

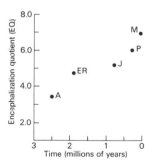

4.21 Encephalization quotient (EQ) in hominids plotted against time in millions of years. A, *Australopithecus africanus*; ER, KNM-ER 1470; J, *Homo erectus erectus* from Java; P. *Homo erectus pekinensis* from Peking; M, modern man. Data from Table 4.2.

scepticism given the many errors involved in estimating cranial capacity and body size (Holloway 1978; Falk 1980). For each group there is a wide range of possible EQs, as the individuals in the group vary in brain size and body size. But the general impression that the figure gives is surely to be trusted, that even when changes in body size have been accounted for there was a dramatic increase in the size of the brain in the evolution of the hominids in the last few million years.

The speed at which the change in brain size occurred can be assessed by making use of the unit proposed by Haldane (1949) as a measure of the rate of evolutionary change. This unit, which he called the 'darwin', corresponds to a change of 1/1000 in 1000 years. When measured in this way the period of fastest growth in the absolute size of the brain is that from late *Homo erectus* to early *Homo sapiens* (Bilsborough 1973; Blumenberg 1978). The rate of change during this time is faster than any other evolutionary changes that we know of during the Tertiary period, that is from the Palaeocene to the Pliocene (Kurtén 1960). But if we consider the body size of European mammals during the Ice Ages and during the immediate postglacial period we find that some of them, such as the bears, underwent an even more rapid evolutionary change (Kurtén 1960). During the Ice Ages the selection pressures for adaptive change were high. Whereas some mammals coped by enlarging their body our ancestors survived by enlarging their brains.

Though impressive in its speed this process could have occurred through the operation of relatively simple mechanisms. Evolution acts partly through changes in the pattern of developmental growth. The rates of development are under the direction of control genes, and small changes in these rates and in the timing of development could have very marked effects.

The most significant clue is that compared with other primates we are born at a time when our brain is relatively small compared with its size in adulthood (Sacher and Staffeldt 1974). In a newborn macaque the brain has reached 60 per cent of its adult weight, and in the chimpanzee the corresponding figure is 46 per cent; but in a baby the brain is only 25 per cent of the size it will reach in the adult (Blackfan 1933; Schultz 1941; Holt *et al.* 1975). At birth the brain of a human baby is much the size that we would expect of a newborn monkey or ape of the same body weight (Passingham 1975b). Before birth the increase in the size of the brain relative to the body occurs at the same rate in man, chimpanzee and macaque (Holt *et al.* 1975). The rate then slows down markedly just before birth in the macaque and just after in the chimpanzee; but in man the brain continues to grow at the foetal rate for two years or so after birth (Holt *et al.* 1975). The rapid growth in the absolute size of the human brain after birth is documented in Fig. 4.22. In other words the increase in the relative size of the brain in hominid evolution could have been achieved by lengthening the developmental period after birth for which the brain continues to grow at the rate characteristic of the foetus.

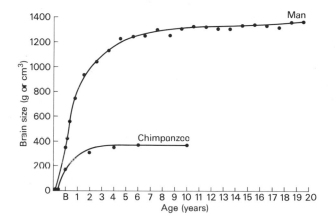

4.22 Growth of the brain in man and chimpanzee. The figures for chimpanzee are for cranial capacity (cm³) and those for man for brain weight (grams). After Passingham (1975b). Data from Blackfan (1933) for man and Schultz (1940) for chimpanzee.

This chapter has documented the ways in which the human brain is specialized and has described what is known of the evolution of the brain in our ancestors. It remains to ask why the brain increased in relative size so markedly in hominid evolution, and to try to specify the selective advantage in terms of technology, culture and language. This is the task of the rest of the book.

5 Intelligence

Our survey of man's physical characteristics is complete. In many respects we are built in much the same way as the monkeys and apes, possessing an acute eye and agile hands, although we differ in that we take an upright stance. The monkeys and apes are distinguished from other mammals in the development of only one organ of the body, that is the brain. And it is in the further development of the brain that man is most obviously specialized.

This being so, it is tempting to summarize matters as follows: man is equipped by nature not so much with unique skeletal adaptations as with an enhanced ability to adapt and to deal intelligently with the world. But in saying this we are assuming that there is an association between intelligence and the relative size of the brain, and we have yet to show that this is the case.

There are two methods by which we can attempt to relate intelligence to the development of the brain. The first is experimentally to interfere with the workings of the brain and discover how this disrupts normal intellectual functioning. When comparing the performance of the intact and damaged brain we may attribute any decline in ability to the damage or lesion. The second method at our disposal is comparative: it makes use of the fact that nature has arranged that the brains of different species vary in size and complexity. By comparing the abilities of these various species we observe that the variation in the brains is reflected in differences in ability. The two methods are alike in that the capabilities of different brains are compared; in the one case it is we who arrange the variation in the brains by altering them, and in the other it is nature.

BRAIN LESIONS

It is understandable that many experimenters have chosen to work with monkeys when studying the functions of the different areas of the neocortex. In people, the damage caused by wounds, tumours or strokes is rarely confined to specific areas; but in monkeys the different regions can be removed selectively by operation. Whether we are studying people or monkeys we investigate the function of the areas of the neocortex in much the same way, devising tests of perception, memory and so on, and attempting to interpret the reasons for failure on these tests when the brain is damaged. By these means we try to isolate the contribution to intellectual performance made by the different areas.

In the last chapter it was established that the human brain is characterized by the extensive development of the cerebellum and of the association areas of the neocortex. We must now try to establish what this means in terms of the abilities that depend on these structures.

Consider first the ability to interpret the world as observed by the various senses. A simple test, already mentioned, is the discrimination task, often given to animals such as monkeys. It can be illustrated by taking the visual version of the test. On this the monkey is repeatedly shown two objects, and must learn under which of the two the food is always hidden; it demonstrates its knowledge by always choosing that object, as in Fig. 5.1. To be able to learn to do this the monkey must be capable of recognizing the objects and remembering under which one it has previously found the food; that is it must interpret the present state of the world in terms of what it remembers of previous situations. Other versions of the task test the monkey's ability to choose between objects which it can feel but not see, or to choose between two sounds.

5.1 Rhesus monkey performing on visual discrimination task. It has just pushed one of the objects to uncover the food well underneath. Courtesy of Wisconsin Regional Primate Center.

We have discovered two facts of importance about the mechanisms in the monkey brain that enable them to succeed on these tasks. The first is that removal of parietal and temporal association cortex disrupts the ability to solve these tasks, whereas removal of frontal association cortex does not (see Fig. 5.2). The second is that within parietal and temporal association cortex the effect is different depending exactly where the tissue is removed. Damage to the lower region of temporal cortex interferes with discriminations made by sight; removal of the upper region has a similar effect for sounds; if the removal is confined to parietal cortex the monkey will be poor only when required to tell objects apart by feeling them (Butter 1968). Each of these three regions is specialized for interpreting information presented to a particular sense. That is not, of course, to say that there are no areas wich consider the world as perceived through all the senses; only that for the present we know little about them.

While we know that these various regions of association cortex play a role in learning their exact function is difficult to specify. When asked to choose between two objects the monkeys might have trouble for several reasons: they might, for instance, be unable to recognize the objects; or alternatively they might recognize them but forget under which they had previously seen the food. It has proved to be time-consuming to devise and administer tests which will clarify these issues.

With people this task is simpler, because it is easy to give them instructions, and they can be directly asked what they see or remember. In patients, as in monkeys, damage to parietal and temporal association cortex leads to problems with recognition and recall (Milner and Teuber 1968). The crucial difference is that with people it usually matters which of the two hemispheres is damaged. The ability to remember lists of words or letters is impaired after damage to the left temporal lobe; but the ability to remember simple drawings or tunes is disrupted by lesions in the right temporal lobe (Milner 1971). Patients with lesions of right parietal association cortex may have difficulty in recognizing what they see; they may be poor at interpreting photographs and drawings, and are sometimes at a loss when required to recognize an object as shown in a photograph from an unusual angle (Warrington and Taylor 1973). Very occasionally patients are seen who are unable to recognize real objects and say what they are; though able to describe these objects they appear not to appreciate their meaning

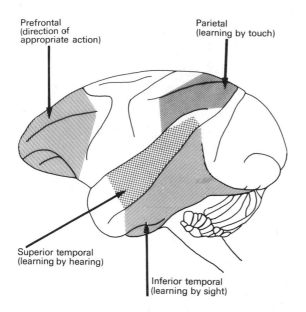

Prefrontal
(direction of
appropriate action)

Parietal
(learning by touch)

Superior temporal
(learning by hearing)

Inferior temporal
(learning by sight)

5.2 Role of association areas
in learning in the brain of a
rhesus monkey.

(Hécaen and Albert 1978). To summarize the evidence from monkeys and people we are justified in concluding that the ability to interpret the world depends on mechanisms in parietal and temporal association cortex.

But neither animals nor people simply observe their world passively; they also act on it. Mechanisms of two sorts are required: to ensure that actions are well directed and skilfully performed; and to guarantee that only those actions are selected which are appropriate in the circumstances. We think that control of the first sort is exercised by the cerebellum and by the motor and premotor areas of the neocortex (Fig. 5.3). The final control over movements is without doubt exerted by motor cortex (Philips and Porter 1977); in monkeys damage in this region causes a temporary paralysis and a permanent loss of manual dexterity (Passingham *et al.* 1978).

This area is in turn influenced by the premotor area directly in front of it and by the cerebellum. If premotor cortex is damaged monkeys are poor at orienting their arm and hand correctly when picking up food (Moll and Kuypers 1975, 1977). They are also poor at a task which requires them to make one movement or another depending on which sensory cue they are shown (Halsband and Passingham, to be published). Damage to the cerebellum disrupts basic skills as in walking or reaching; the movements are clumsy and lack finesse (Brodal 1981). It has been plausibly suggested that the cerebellum plays an important role in the learning of automatic skills, ensuring

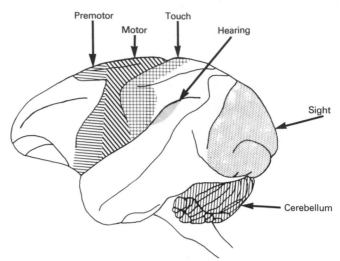

Premotor Motor Touch Hearing Sight Cerebellum

5.3 Sensory and motor areas
in the brain of a rhesus
monkey.

that they are practised with smoothness and accuracy
(Eccles 1973).

The direction of the appropriate action appears to be
partly the responsibility of frontal association cortex, the
area lying in front of premotor cortex (see Fig. 5.2). There
are various opinions about the exact functions of this area,
but everybody agrees that lesions of frontal association
cortex render a monkey less flexible in the actions it
performs. The animal does well on a simple discrimination
task on which it must consistently choose one of two
objects. But it has trouble when it is required to unlearn
this habit, and to learn that the food is now to be found
under the other object (Mishkin 1964). A 'reversal' task of
this sort is illustrated in Fig. 5.7b. A monkey without
frontal association cortex will persist in its previous choice,
apparently unaware of the consequences of its actions. The
disability will be most marked if the animal is required to
learn a sequence, as in alternating between choosing the
object on its left on one occasion and the object on the
right on the next, repeatedly doing the opposite of what it
has just done (Fuster 1980). Such inflexibility would serve
it poorly in the real world, where circumstances are often
changing and old habits must be unlearnt if the actions
appropriate to the new situation are to be performed.

Patients with damage to frontal association cortex show
a similar rigidity in their behaviour. This can be revealed
by testing them on problems which they must solve, and
then changing the correct solution without warning.
These patients tend to persist with the original solution,
and to be poorer at coming up with alternatives (Milner
1964).

Unlike animals people live in a world full of artefacts with particular uses, matchboxes, keys, scissors, and so on. We have to learn how to use a wide range of such tools, since we are dependent on our technology for survival. We must recognize what each of these is, and appreciate what can be done with it. The ability to do this is sometimes disrupted by lesions of the left hemisphere. In mild cases the patient may have problems only in copying gestures and other movements; in severe cases the patient may be unable to demonstrate the use of even simple objects such as a matchbox (Hécaen and Albert 1978). There is reason to think that the ability to use objects appropriately involves mechanisms of both parietal and frontal cortex (Kimura 1979; Kolb and Milner 1981).

From the evidence cited above we are entitled to draw the following conclusions. First, neocortex and especially association cortex play a crucial role in learning. Secondly, different areas of association cortex are specialized for particular functions. Finally, parietal and temporal cortex are concerned in general with the interpretation of the world, and frontal cortex with the modification of actions upon the world according to their consequences. It is on these neocortical mechanisms that the intelligent under-standing and manipulation of the world depends.

We can now return to our original question, which was how we should interpret in terms of abilities the difference between the brains of man and other primates. We are clearly justified in attributing our impressive manual skill and dexterity to the notable development of the human cerebellum and of the premotor area in the human neocortex. The apparently equal development of all association areas points to an increase in all intellectual abilities, and not in some at the expense of others. Our brain equips us such that we have a unique grasp of the world and of how to act on it.

HUMAN INTELLIGENCE

We have attributed man's intellectual pre-eminence to the development of his brain, and in particular of the neocortex. Our confidence in this conclusion would be strengthened if we could show that, in general, the better the brain is developed in primates the better they perform on cognitive tasks. We should be able to relate natural variation in the brain to differences in intelligence. The brain varies both within species and between species, and it will be worth our while to consider variation of both sorts.

Variation within a species can readily be examined in people. Human brains vary considerably in size, but it is important not to exaggerate this variation; it is no greater than the variation found in fossil hominids, chimpanzees or cats (Jerison 1979b). The variation in a typical sample of 1039 people is shown in Figs. 5.4 and 5.5. All but 5 per cent of men were found to lie within a range of 524 grams, from 1180—1704 grams; and all but 5 per cent of women within a range of 500 grams, from 1033—1533 grams (Passingham 1979b).

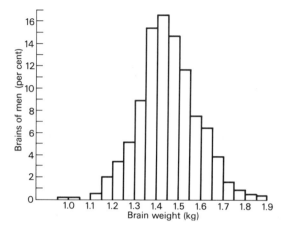

5.4 Distribution of brain weights (kilograms) in a sample of men. One brain weighing 2150 grams is not shown as it had very marked oedema. After Passingham (1979b). Data from Pakkenberg (personal communication).

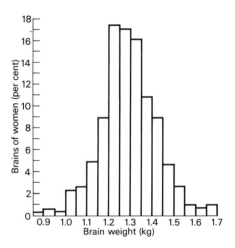

5.5 Distribution of brain weights (kilograms) in a sample of women. After Passingham (1979b). Data from Pakkenberg (personal communication).

Are people with larger brains more intelligent? It has often been denied that they are. The reason given is usually that there are people with small brains but normal intelligence, and that there have been others who have reached distinction even though their brains are reputed to have been small (Cobb 1965; Tobias 1970). These arguments are not sound, for three reasons.

The first is that the size of the body must be taken into account. The Pygmies, for example, have been reported to have an average cranial capacity of around 1108 cubic centimetres (Dart 1956). But they are, of course, very short; and their relative brain size is probably in no way abnormal.

The second point is that the values of brain size which are quoted are usually those reported for famous historical figures. The worthlessness of many of these values was exhaustively documented over 40 years ago (Hamilton 1936); but this has not prevented continued use being made of them. The values of well over 2000 grams given for the brains of Cromwell and Byron should not be trusted: the figure given for Cromwell comes from a commentary written 42 years after his death; and the figure for Byron varies by 400 grams according to whether it is supposed that Neopolitan, Venetian or English pounds were being used. The very low figures of little over a 1000 cubic centimetres for Gall and Anatole France are also suspect, as the brain decreases considerably in weight with age, and the weight after death varies greatly with the causes of death (Pakkenberg and Voigt 1964).

Finally, it must be emphasized that one does not disprove a relation between brain size and intelligence by citing single cases. Unless the relation is very close we would expect that there would be some highly intelligent individuals with brains less heavy than those of lesser ability. This would show only that the relationship was less than a perfect one.

Any study of relative brain size and intelligence in people is faced with a problem. Data on intelligence are easily acquired, but as long as the people live the size of their brain can only be estimated indirectly from the size of the head. Post-mortem data on the brains of people are also available, but in such cases records of intelligence are difficult to obtain, although occupation provides an indirect measure of intelligence.

It is possible to demonstrate a very loose relation between cranial capacity, as measured from outside the skull, and intelligence as assessed on IQ tests in a modern population (Murdock and Sullivan 1923; Van Valen 1974; Passingham 1979b). But this effect disappears when account is taken of differences in height (Passingham 1979b). We should not be surprised at this negative result, since the relation between cranial capacity as measured from outside the skull and from inside the skull is not at all close (Hoadley and Pearson 1929). The lack of a close correspondence between external measurements and internal cranial capacity, and therefore brain size, could well mask any small, but genuine, relation between brain size and intelligence.

The best series of brain that are available is that already illustrated in Figs 5.4 and 5.5; for in this case we also have information on the heights of the people, their age and the cause of death (Pakkenberg and Voigt 1964). Unfortunately there are no records of intelligence as assessed on proper tests, and we must make do with the occupations in which the people engaged in their lifetime, on the assumption that these give some indication of abilities. When differences in height are allowed for we find that there is indeed a relation, though slight, between occupation and the weight of the brain (Passingham 1979b). In this sample relative brain size is marginally bigger in professional people than in semi-skilled and unskilled workers. But the effect is very small, and there is very considerable overlap between the groups. We should be very cautious in interpreting this finding. It is possible that it reflects some relation between brain size and intelligence, but to prove it would require a full-scale study where adequate data on IQ were available. Nonetheless it would be foolish to rule out a priori the possibility that the effect is a genuine one.

So far we have looked at variation between the brains of different people. But the brain decreases in weight with age, and we might therefore also wonder whether this variation is reflected in changes in intelligence. The change in the weight of the brain with increasing age is documented in Fig. 5.6a (Pakkenberg and Voigt 1964). With the passing years nerve cells in the brain break up and die and they are not replaced: the loss in the neocortex becomes marked from the age of 50 or so on (Brody 1970; Scheibel et al. 1975) (Fig. 5.6b). There is also an intellectual decline with ageing as measured on a variety of tests (Horn and Donaldson 1976). It is tempting to assume that there is indeed some relation between the number of nerve cells in the neocortex and intellectual performance.

There are indications, then, that brain size may be related to intelligence in the human population. But we have no evidence which would persuade us that the relationship is close. Theoretically there is no reason to suppose that it should be, since the advantage conferred by

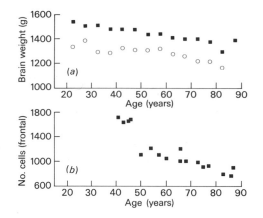

5.6 *a*, Brain weight (grams) for men and women of different ages. *b*, Number of nerve cells in superior frontal gyrus-frontal pole of brains of people of various ages. Data on brain weight from Pakkenberg and Voigt (1964) and on nerve cells from Brody (1970).

a larger brain need only be slight for the rapid evolution of the human brain to be adequately explained (Van Valen 1974).

ANIMAL INTELLIGENCE

We can attempt to relate brain size to intelligence in other primates only if we can show that we have tests which do indeed measure their intelligence. When IQ tests are devised for people, it is required that they be proved to be reliable, valid and fair. If they are reliable they will give much the same answer if administered to the same person twice, or if alternative versions of the test are used. If they are valid they will test what they are supposed to test; this can be demonstrated by showing that performance on the test is a good predictor of future intellectual achievements. If the tests are fair they will not be biased in their contents such that they are easier for people in some cultures than others.

The merits of tests of animal intelligence must be assessed in just the same way. We have to admit that the worth of many of these tests is in serious doubt (Warren 1973). There are cases of poor reliability, where the results of apparently the same test differ according to the type of apparatus in which they are carried out. More worrying is the apparent bias in many of the tests, favouring some species and not others. The usefulness of a test is challenged if it can be shown to be biased in this way. To give one example: many tests require the animals to choose between objects they can see; this may be very much easier for a monkey which has excellent vision than for a rat which has not. The disparity in their performance may reflect the difference between their sense organs rather than differences in intelligence. In so far as we can confine our attention to primates we may hope that differences of this sort are minimized.

What, then, of the validity of tests of animal intelligence? A test is valid if it measures what it purports to measure. We might make our task simpler if we first ascertained what is measured by IQ tests for people. These tests typically consist of a series of subtests tapping a range of abilities; but in so far as these measure anything in common that is usually referred to as general intelligence, sometimes called 'g' (Vernon 1961). Typical tests used to measure this factor are those which provide a series of items, whether diagrams, numbers or letters, and then require the person to generate the next item in the series. To solve such problems it is necessary to discover the rule that is obeyed in the series and then to apply it. In general these tests may be said to measure the ability to appreciate rules and make valid inferences.

Rules

We require, then, tests which will measure these same abilities in animals. One such test was devised by Harlow (1949), who noted that up till that time animals such as monkeys had usually been presented only with single problems, such as the object discrimination problem illustrated in Fig. 5.7a. Instead he gave a series of such problems; the monkey would try one for a few trials, and would then be given another one with a new pair of objects, and then another and so on. All the problems in the series obey the same rule: the food is under one of the two objects and remains under that one throughout the problem. If the monkey could detect this rule it would be able to solve later problems more rapidly than the initial ones; and if it does so it is said to have achieved a 'learning set'. The degree of improvement over the series thus provides a measure of the animal's ability to perceive and apply rules.

By modelling a test on a human IQ test one might hope to produce a valid measure of animal intelligence. But is the attempt successful? Luckily in this case there is an answer, because the same test has been given to children whose IQ was independently measured (Harter 1965). The children were given a series of pairs of objects, and required to find the marble which, for any pair of objects, always lay under the same object. The more intelligent children, as assessed on the IQ test, showed greater

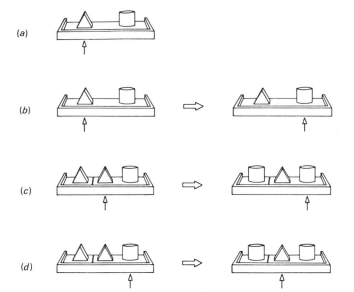

5.7 Tasks used with animals.
a, Visual discrimination;
b, visual discrimination
reversal; *c*, matching;
d, oddity or non–matching.
From Passingham (1981c).

improvement over the series. When asked what the solution was some children correctly described the rule: 'it's always under the same one', or 'you stick to the same thing all the time'. The rule may be simple, but nonetheless it requires intelligence to appreciate it.

The original question was whether there is any relation between intelligence as measured on such a test and the development of the neocortex in primates. On limited evidence it appears that indeed there is. Primates can be ranked according to the amount of neocortex in relation to the medulla as in Fig. 4.11. Their rank on this measure turns out to give a reliable prediction of how much improvement they show over a series of discrimination problems (Passingham 1975a).

But do monkeys and apes perform better on this task than other mammals? In answering this question care must be taken to compare the performance of monkeys and apes with that of other mammals only where the conditions of training were equivalent. There is information on the degree of success achieved by a wide variety of mammals (Hodos 1970; Warren 1973, 1974). But when the methods used in each of the studies are closely examined it turns out that the procedures used vary greatly (Kintz *et al.* 1969). Some present each discrimination problem to the animal for six trials only, some give more trials on each problem, and yet others train the animal on each discrimination until it has reached a high level of performance and only then proceed with the next problem (Passingham

1981a). Yet the efficiency with which monkeys improve over a series of problems is determined more by the total number of trials it receives than by the number of problems given (Miles 1965). It will not, therefore, be valid to make comparisons between two species over a fixed number of problems if they are not matched in the number of trials for which they were presented with each problem. The species which has more experience on each problem will have an unfair advantage. Claims that there are mammals and even birds which rival the monkeys and apes in their performance (Hodos 1970) can be shown to be invalid once this point of methodology has been appreciated (Passingham 1981a).

There are only a few studies which have used a standard procedure, presenting the animals with six trials on each problem. The results are plotted in Fig. 5.8 which shows the performance of the animals on the second trial (T2) of each problem. The three species of monkey out-perform the four species of non-primate mammal; on the last 400 problems there is no overlap in performance between the marmosets (*Callithrix jacchus*) and the cats. The three rodents perform less well than the cat, the only carnivore for which there are comparable data.

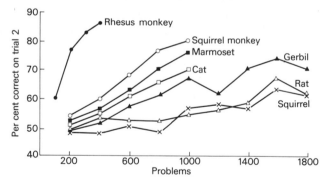

5.8 Visual discrimination learning set in mammals. Per cent correct on the second trial of each problem (T2) is plotted against the number of problems given. Each problem was given for six trials. After Passingham (1981a).

These results are as we might expect given the relative brain size of rodents, carnivores and simian primates. Data on a few other primates can be added to the comparison. In one study squirrel monkeys were found to be inferior to the spider monkey (*Ateles geofroyi*) and cebus monkey (*Cebus albifrons*), and chimpanzees can out-class rhesus monkeys (Hayes *et al.* 1953; Shell and Riopelle 1958). When these primates and other mammals are ranked in terms of their rate of improvement over a series of problems their rank proves to be well predicted by an index of brain development (Riddell 1979). This index estimates the number of nerve cells in the brain over and above those needed for controlling bodily functions (Jerison 1973).

The learning set task described is a relatively simple one. The problems in the series are identical except for the material used; only the pairs of objects change from problem to problem. We can stretch the animal more severely if we decrease the similarity between problems, although retaining some rule that is common to them all. One way this has been done is to divide the task into two sections. In the first the animal is given a series of reversal problems. This task is illustrated in Fig. 5.7b; the animal learns to choose one object of a pair, and when it does so consistently the position of the food is then changed, now being placed under the other object. When the animal has reversed its choice the position of the food is again changed back to the original object, and so on. When a series of such reversals has been learnt the second section of the test is presented; the animal is now given a series of object discriminations. The two types of problem, reversal and object discrimination, are alike, in that it pays the animal to stick to the same object so long as it finds food there, but to change to the other object when it fails to find food.

Chimpanzees and rhesus monkeys improve more rapidly on a series of object discrimination problems if they have previously been trained on a series of reversals; but cats trained under the same conditions do not show this effect (Warren 1974). It is not even necessary that in their initial training rhesus monkeys be required to learn to reverse their choice between objects. They derive as much benefit from the opportunity to find food now on the left, now on the right, and so on reversing between the two positions (Warren 1966). It is fair to conclude that both chimpanzees and rhesus monkeys can transfer strategies from a series of one type of problem to a series of related, though different, problems. They can make use of the fact that there are common principles which apply to the two series.

There is another type of problem which tests the animal's ability to appreciate a general rule or principle. There are alternative versions: on the matching task the animal must decide which of two objects is the same as a sample object (Fig. 5.7c); on the 'oddity' task it must pick the one that is different (Fig. 5.7d). These are much like one class of item that is commonly included in intelligence tests devised for people: this asks the person to state in what way two things are alike, or alternatively to pick the odd one out from a series of words or pictures. A test of this sort taps the ability to classify things and to appreciate the relationship between them.

If the animal is presented with a series of such problems, each with new objects, it will become apparent whether it can recognize that the problems can all be solved by application of the same principle. If the rule is grasped the animal will be able to solve new problems with increasing ease. If we give a single oddity problem, with one set of objects, rats and cats can solve it; but if we give a series of such problems almost all cats fail to improve their performance as the series progresses (Warren 1965). In other words animals that can learn to pick the odd one out, given each new problem, may nonetheless fail to see that all the problems are basically the same.

All the primates that have been tested improve over a series of oddity problems, indicating that they have grasped the relevant principle. Rhesus monkeys and chimpanzees have been shown to be able to learn the rule under conditions when racoons and cats fail to do so (Strong and Hedges 1966). Of the primates lemurs and squirrel monkeys show less improvement than cebus monkeys (*Cebus apella*) or rhesus monkeys (Davis *et al.* 1967). Chimpanzees show their superiority on this as on other tests, mastering the oddity principle with relative ease, and transferring their knowledge rapidly to new situations in much the same way as young children do (Strong 1967).

In the discussion so far of the abilities of different mammals no mention has been made of the dolphin and other sea mammals. This neglect might seem unwarranted, since dolphins are widely regarded as very clever animals. Indeed claims are sometimes made on their behalf which are so lacking in sobriety as to be of very dubious scientific worth. There is an obligation to attempt to assess the intelligence of dolphins, and to compare them in this respect with apes and monkeys.

How have dolphins come to acquire a reputation that would be envied by a chimpanzee? They are easily tamed, but so are dogs; they are ready performers in shows of public entertainment, but so are many circus animals; they help their fellows, but so do wild dogs (*Lycaon pictus*) or baboons (Wilson 1975). Indirect evidence such as this is hardly convincing.

We need proper standardized tests which the dolphin can be given, so that the scores can be compared with those obtained by monkeys and apes. Appropriate tests are difficult to devise because land and sea mammals are built in such different ways. One dolphin (*Tursiops truncatus*) has been given a series of formal tests in which it was required to choose between sounds rather than objects. In a study of its ability to form a learning set the conditions of training were especially devised to promote rapid learning, and valid comparisons cannot be made with the performance of monkeys and apes (Herman and Arbett 1973; Passingham 1981a). On the matching task the dolphin performed accurately and improved in proficiency over a series of new problems; it clearly mastered the general principle (Herman and Gordon 1974). That the dolphin is a clever animal was never in doubt; but, for the present, it is possible to say no more than that their abilities may be comparable with those of some of the advanced simian primates (Herman 1980).

The rank assigned here to monkeys and apes is based on their performance as judged by proper comparative studies. They can be demoted not by force of enthusiastic anecdote but only by well-designed experiments. The credentials of the monkeys and apes, our closest relatives, have yet to be successfully challenged. We may reasonably attribute their superior abilities to their specialization as creatures with brains which are very large for their build.

Tools

The approach so far has been to compare primates on a variety of tests in which the animal must discover under which object food is hidden. By looking for the food the animal learns the principles governing where it is to be found. There is a different type of problem, one on which the animal must learn not where food is but what actions to perform in order to secure it. On tests of this sort intelligence is tested by observing the ways the animal tries to get round the problem. In the simplest case the animal can see the food, but there is some physical barrier preventing access; it must take a detour and find a way round. In more complicated versions the only way round is to use some implement with which to reach for the food.

It was Thorndike (1911), an American psychologist, who was the first to attempt to measure the intelligence of animals in this way. Cats, dogs and monkeys were placed in boxes from which they had to learn to escape by moving pedals, or tripping some other mechanism. But these tasks were hardly fair to the animals, because they were unable to see the workings of the catch that locked the door. Little more could be expected of them other than relatively random attempts.

During the First World War Köhler (1925) had an opportunity to study some chimpanzees on the island of Tenerife. He designed a set of problems that would give them a greater opportunity to show their intelligence. Food was put in full view of the chimpanzee, but out of reach. To obtain it the animal had to use sticks if it was beyond bars and stack boxes if it was hanging from the ceiling; the tools served to increase the reach of the animals. All the equipment necessary for the solution of the problem was visible.

The chimpanzees could solve these problems (Köhler 1925). They used sticks to rake in food, and one of the chimpanzees, Sultan, even learnt to join one stick to another to increase the length of his reach. Sultan was also the first to attempt to stack boxes, but the others quickly learnt the trick by watching him at work (Fig. 5.9). These tasks were later used in more systematic studies at the laboratory set up by Yerkes (1943) in America for the study of apes. There chimpanzees which had already mastered the stacking of two boxes were able to pile them three and even four high (Bingham 1929).

These observations prompt two questions: what is the nature of the ability that enables these animals to solve such problems, and can it be related to the development of the brain? The first of these questions has often been phrased by asking whether the animals are capable of insight, but this way of putting it is unhelpful because the concept of insight is ill defined. We would do better to tackle two simpler issues, the origin of the attempts the animal makes and the process by which it can select between different possible solutions.

The attempts at a solution might originate in the animal's natural repertoire or in its past history. That the first may be true is indicated by the observation that chimpanzees without experience on these problems will join sticks together, and will stack and climb on boxes even when there is no food to be won by these means (Schiller 1952). That the second may also be true is shown by study of chimpanzees reared in the laboratory (Birch 1945). Those chimpanzees that at first failed to learn to use sticks to pull in food were later able to do so after they had been given sticks with which to play in a large enclosure. Wildborn chimpanzees use objects in a more varied way than those reared on their own in the laboratory, and are

5.9 Box stacking by chimpanzees. From a photograph in Köhler (1927).

much quicker at learning that sticks can serve as a rake (Menzel *et al.* 1970). Problems of this sort are more easily solved if the animal has already had experience with the properties of sticks, and knows that they can be used to move things at a distance.

We assume, then, that the animal comes to the task with a set of solutions that it will try. Its task is not to produce a solution 'out of the blue', but rather to 'put two and two together' by drawing on relevant areas of previous experience. When it sees food outside the cage it may first attempt to reach it through the bars, then try to tear the bars open, and finally perhaps, if a stick is in sight, may experiment with that.

But does it have to try out each solution in turn to test whether it works, or can the animal select in its head the solution most likely to work. The question is whether it knows in advance which actions are the most appropriate, and what can be done with particular objects. We can find out by directly asking the animal which of a variety of objects would prove useful in solving a problem. This has been done by showing video films to a chimpanzee in which a person struggles to achieve some particular goal; for example the person might be trying to reach for bananas hanging from the ceiling, or to retrieve them from under a partition, or to escape from a locked cage, and so on (Premack and Woodruff 1978). The chimpanzee was then shown photographs of the equipment that might be used to solve the problem, a box, rod, key, and various other objects. On viewing each problem for the first time the chimpanzee was able to pick out the correct implement on all but one of the eight situations it was shown. In other words it knew from its previous experience of the uses of the objects which would be of value when solving particular problems.

So chimpanzees can compare present situations with past ones, and select those actions that worked in conditions thought to be relevantly similar to those that now hold. In doing this the animals are learning the principles that govern actions, just as they can learn the principles governing the location of food. We may take it to be a mark of intelligence that the animal can transfer its knowledge about one situation to another that is similar in some respects. Köhler's chimpanzees would, if no boxes were available, turn stones, blocks of wood, iron grills and a miscellany of other objects to use as ladders (Köhler 1925). They could do so because they knew that the properties of these objects were relevantly similar to those of a box. We have already noted that the ability to appreciate the similarity between the properties of things is one that is measured on some items in IQ tests for people.

The ability of chimpanzees to master these problems gives some indication of their general intelligence. But what of other animals? Can we demonstrate that the capacity to solve puzzles and use tools in this way relates to the development of the brain? The question is not one that can be easily answered, because of the obvious difficulties in setting up problems which are equally fair to all the animals tested. Tools are most readily used in the hand; neither the paw nor the mouth is as efficient.

Even if we confine our attention to the primates comparisons may be biased, because the hands of prosimians and New World monkeys are less dextrous than those of the monkeys of the Old World. This complicates our interpretation of the results on tasks such as the bent-wire problem already described in Chapter 3. The animal must unthread a sweet or candy from a piece of wire, and since the wire is bent into different shapes the animal may have to push the sweet away from itself in negotiating particular bends (Davis 1974). The animal will at first attempt to pull the sweet, and must learn with experience that a detour is required if the sweet is to be taken off the wire. On this task macaques are more successful than squirrel monkeys or the ring-tailed lemur (Davis and Leary 1968). But it is not clear to what extent the greater success of the macaques reflects their dexterity or their intelligence.

It would be of more value if we had information on the relative ability of different primates to use sticks as a rake or to pile boxes to reach food. But unfortunately we have little information. Cebus monkeys, Guinea baboons (*Papio papio*) and macaques have all been reported to rake in food with sticks in captivity; and cebus monkeys have been seen to pile boxes (Beck 1975, 1980). Those who have worked with cebus monkeys in the laboratory or in the wild are impressed by their propensity for fiddling with objects, and their persistence in manipulating them; they are superior to rhesus monkeys in opening difficult latches (Elliott 1976). As yet no formal comparison has been made of the ability of great apes and monkeys to manipulate and use tools in captivity. However, as we shall see in the next chapter no monkey rivals the chimpanzee in the variety of uses to which it puts tools in the wild (Table 6.2).

The lack of much evidence on tool use in the laboratory forces us to cast our net wider, and to compare animals in their reactions to objects and what they spontaneously do with them. A wide variety of different mammals have been watched in zoos to see how they react when shown novel objects such as steel chains and wooden dowels (Glickman and Sroges 1966). The primates and carnivores were much more responsive than rodents, insectivores or marsupials, showing a much greater interest in the objects presented (Fig. 5.10). Of the primates it was the chimpanzees and gorillas that devoted the most attention to the objects, although it must be admitted that these were in their youth when curiosity is most marked. A chimpanzee brought up in a household may rival a young child in the intensity of its interest in and exploration of its rich surroundings (Kellogg and Kellogg 1933).

If we consider the data on the primates in zoos we can rank the animals on their responsiveness to objects. This allows us to relate their rank to the development of their brains as indicated by the size of the neocortex relative to the medulla. We find that this measure gives a fair prediction of their relative performance on the task (Passingham 1952a).

So far we have confined our attention to the degree of curiosity exhibited towards objects. It is more enlightening to consider what is done with the object. In the study

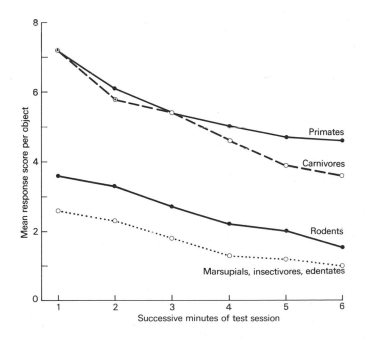

5.10 Responsiveness of a variety of zoo animals to novel objects. The figure plots the mean number of times that animals oriented to or made contact with each of four novel objects. The data are presented separately for each of the six minutes of a trial. After Glickman and Sroges (1966).

of zoo animals it was noted that the primates and carnivores differed in the way they treated the objects (Glickman and Sroges 1966). The carnivores tended to mouth and chew the objects and to bat at them with their paw; the primates often held the objects in their hands, examined them by eye, and picked at them, twisted them, rubbed them and so on. We know from other studies that a monkey such as a rhesus monkey will happily play with simple mechanical puzzles for hours on end, and will fiddle with them for the single motive of working out how they can be opened (Butler 1965).

A formal test of the capacity to use objects inventively can be devised by presenting a series of primates with an object such as a piece of rope. The degree of invention can then be measured by noting the number of different parts of the body used, the parts of the object touched, and the various actions performed. A number of zoo primates have been studied in this way (Parker 1974). A great variety of actions could be carried out with the rope: pulling, mouthing, waving, twisting, rubbing and so on. The chimpanzee, gorilla and orang-utan performed roughly four times as many different actions as did the monkeys that were tested. An index was also calculated which combined the information given by the three measures recorded; and on this index too the great apes far excelled the other primates. This test is reminiscent of one of the tests used to measure creativity in people in which they are asked to give as many uses as they can of a single object such as a brick (Getzels and Jackson 1962). It is reasonable to conclude that the great apes are creative in their response to objects.

It is the inventiveness of their behaviour, as seen in play, that partly accounts for the superiority of chimpanzees on tests involving the use of tools. This is well illustrated by a study of one group of chimpanzees that were kept in a large enclosure (Menzel 1973). They learnt spontaneously to stand loose branches vertically on the ground and then to climb up them or vault with them. This later led to the discovery that the branch could be leaned against a tree or wall (Fig. 7.3), and that they could make their escape from the enclosure by means of this crude ladder (Fig. 7.4). Chimpanzees solve problems well not just because they are efficient in their use of past experience, but also because they try a great variety of approaches.

The great apes can even learn to modify objects so that they can serve as tools. In a Russian study a captive chimpanzee was set to solve a problem in which food is placed is in a pipe or tube, and the animal must use a rod to push it out (Krustov 1970) (Fig. 5.11). When the solution had been learnt the task was made more difficult by putting crossbars on the rod, providing rectangular strips which were too wide, or by supplying a disc. Each of these had to be modified by breaking it and shaping it until it fitted into the tube; and the chimpanzee was able to learn to do this.

5.11 Chimpanzee Viki solving the stick-and-tunnel problem. From a photograph in Hayes and Hayes (1952). Drawing from Riopelle (1967).

What it did not learn was to use a stone tool rather than its teeth to cut the wood; but the experimenter was perhaps not patient or artful enough, because another ape has since succeeded on much the same problem. This was an orang-utan called Abang, which was taught to use a sharp flint to cut the string holding a box closed and thus to get at the food contained inside (Wright 1972). It was then shown by demonstration how to strike flakes from a large piece of flint (Fig. 5.12); and after a few sessions it mastered the technique and used the flakes for cutting the string (Fig. 5.13). It is, then, within the capacity of a great ape to use one tool to produce another, if, that is, it is taught how to do so. That it could invent this technique is less likely. The ability to devise such a technology must require a much greater degree of intelligence than the capacity to copy it when it is demonstrated by others.

We have been considering practical abilities, the use to which intelligence is put in changing the world. Primates start with a great advantage, as the hand is such a versatile instrument. We might speculate that the hand gives greater scope for intelligent action, and thus promotes selection for the intelligence with which to use it. However, it has not been possible to make any formal assessment of the relation between the development of the brain and the intelligent use of tools. Nonetheless it is impressive how inventive the great apes are in putting objects to various uses, and it can hardly be a coincidence

5.12 Orang-utan Abang
with hammer-stone and
core. Courtesy of R.V.S.
Wright.

that they also excel in the development of their brain. If
the direct ancestors of the hominids were blessed with half
the intelligence of modern apes we would be some way
towards explaining the evolution of human intelligence.

INTELLIGENT ANIMALS

The previous sections have documented the relationship between the development of the brain and
intelligence; we now draw attention to other relations of
great significance. There are a cluster of features which
tend to go with brains which are large relative to body
weight. At the centre of this complex are the length of life
and the number of young to which an animal gives birth.

If we want to predict how long mammals of a particular
species live we can do so with considerable accuracy if we
have information on four characteristics: these are body

weight, brain weight, metabolic rate and body temperature (Sacher 1976). When we take into account the relations between brain size and body weight and between metabolic rate and body temperature we can simplify the prediction by basing it on just two factors, relative brain size and a metabolic factor (Sacher 1976). The greater the relative brain size and the lower the metabolic rate the longer the animal will live. Of the structures in the brain it is the neocortex which is the best predictor; the larger the neocortex in relation to the rest of the forebrain the longer the lifespan (Sacher 1975).

5.13 Orang-utan Abang using a flake to cut string. Courtesy of R.V.S. Wright.

There is great variation in the maximum length of the life of different mammals (Sacher 1972). Rodents and insectivores tend to live less long than carnivores or ungulates. Monkeys and apes are as long-lived as most creatures other than the elephants and whales; in a zoo a chimpanzee has lived to the age of 41 years (Napier and Napier 1967). The average lifespan of a person is around 70 years, and people can, of course, live to be over 100 years old (Deevey 1950). But the human lifespan is no greater than we would expect for a primate with a brain that was as large in relation to body size (Passingham 1975b).

In general the longer a species lives the longer are the periods of gestation and development (Passingham 1975b). How long gestation lasts is primarily determined by the absolute size of the brain that has to be built. This can be shown in two ways: in mammals the larger the brain at birth the longer is the period of gestation; and this period is also more extended the more advanced the brain at birth as indicated by its size relative to the weight of the adult brain (Sacher and Staffeldt 1974).

The human brain is much less advanced at birth than the brains of the monkeys and apes. As already mentioned in a newborn chimpanzee the brain forms around 46 per cent of its adult weight, but in a human baby it is only 25 per cent of that weight (Blackfan 1933; Schultz 1941). Using these proportions as an indication of maturity we can calculate that our brain is not as mature as the brain of a neonatal chimpanzee until we are 6 months old or so (Passingham 1975b). By that time the human brain weighs well over 600 grams (Fig. 4.22), and would be much too large to be safely delivered through the birth canal. Babies must therefore be born at a time when their brains are relatively immature, and as a result they are peculiarly helpless in the months after birth. There are also other respects in which a baby is less mature than an infant monkey or ape: to cite just one instance, the wrist bones of the macaque are fully ossified at birth and are largely so in apes; but in a baby they are not completely ossified until long after birth (Gould 1977).

The length of postnatal development can be measured in two ways, either as the time during which the animal continues to grow or as the time before it is sexually mature. In primates the larger the relative size of the brain the longer the life they lead, and also the longer the period before the animal is sexually mature (Passingham 1975b). A lemur reaches sexual maturity in around $2\frac{1}{2}$ years, a macaque in from $3\frac{1}{2}$ to $4\frac{1}{2}$ years, and a chimpanzee in 8 to 9 years (Napier and Napier 1967). In people development is slower still: girls are not usually sexually mature until they are 13 or so, and growth continues until the age of 18 (Tanner 1961). But although development takes longer than in other primates the length of this period is no greater than would be expected for a primate that lived as long as we do (Passingham 1975b). The slowing down of our development has occurred according to the rules governing the life periods in other primates.

Now consider the animal's reproductive strategy, and in particular the number of young to which it gives birth.

This too is predictable if we know the absolute size of the animal's brain. In mammals the larger the brain and the more advanced it is at birth the fewer the offspring that are produced (Sacher and Staffeldt 1974). At the same time the period of gestation becomes longer. Rodents and insectivores tend to have large litters; typically the Norway rat has 8 offspring, the hedgehog 4 or 5 and the tenrec (*Tenrec ecaudatus*) over 30 (Sacher and Staffeldt 1974; Eisenberg 1975). Many carnivores have multiple births, but most ungulates give birth to only one offspring. There are only a few primates that give birth to more than one infant, such as the mouse lemur, some bushbabies and the marmosets (Leutenegger 1973a).

Brain size, then, can be used to predict a complex set of features relating to life periods, and reproduction. We can impose order on this network of relationships by contrasting two different reproductive strategies that an animal can adopt. The first is to give birth to many young after only a short period of gestation, and for the young to reach sexual maturity early so that they can themselves reproduce as soon as possible. Since many young are produced the chances of at least some of them surviving to reproduce are good, even if the parents can provide only limited care to each one. Though the life of each individual is relatively short fecundity is high. The second strategy is to produce few young and after a more extended period of gestation. The offspring have a longer period of immaturity during which the parents invest considerable time in their care. The survival of the offspring over a long life is made more certain by selecting for those features that promote intelligence.

The first strategy puts a premium on numbers, the second on the development of the brain so that each individual has the maximum chance of surviving. It has been suggested that which strategy is adopted will depend on the number of animals that any particular environment can take, that is on its carrying capacity. Where this capacity is high there will be selection for fecundity; where it is low there will be selection for the better care of fewer offspring. The technical literature draws a distinction between r selection, where r is fecundity, and K selection where K is the carrying capacity (Wilson 1975).

Different animal groups vary in the degree to which they adopt one or other of these strategies (Pianka 1970). In general the insects which live less than a year adopt the first, and mammals which are longer lived the second. But within the mammals we can discern groups which rely more or less heavily on the development of the brain. As we have seen the rodents and insectivores, most of them small creatures, tend to have brains which are relatively small, to have large litters and to reach reproductive age early. Monkeys and apes form a complete contrast; they are large brained for their size, long-lived, and slow to reach sexual maturity. There is hardly any need to point out that these characteristics are most highly developed in man.

Lovejoy (1981) has argued that the key to the evolution of the hominids may lie in a shift in reproductive strategy. He suggests that an improvement in the quality of parental care would have been of great advantage as the young took longer to reach adulthood. This view is attractive, but it is difficult to find the sort of evidence in the record of the early hominids that would confirm it. The relative brain size of the hominids gives some indication of the length of their life-periods (Sacher 1975); but at present we have no fossil crania from the earliest stages of human evolution.

It is worth asking why it should be that a long life demands a relatively large brain. Consider why an animal should be able to learn at all. We know that nature can build into the brains of animals the circuits which, if development is normal, can direct elaborate sequences of actions. In any environment in which the animal finds itself it must sleep, eat, drink and reproduce, and there is often no need for the animal to have to learn how to do so. In insects which are very short-lived the actions that will be appropriate can usually be predicted, and their brains can therefore be programmed to perform them. But environmental conditions are not always predictable, especially in animals that are long-lived. If conditions vary over life the animal must depend also on mechanisms that allow it to learn during its lifetime. By its experience of local conditions it can predict those that it is most likely to come across in the future; where conditions change it can adapt to meet them. If the behaviour that is adaptive can be foreseen the mechanisms that direct it can be built into the brain; where it cannot the animal must learn what is adaptive by relying on brain mechanisms which promote adaptability. The longer the life the greater the possibility that conditions will change, and the longer the time for learning. This may be one reason why large brains and long lives tend to go together.

Just as conditions may be less stable the longer time passes so they may be more variable the larger the area over which an animal moves. In primates, and also in other mammals, large animals tend to range over wider areas than smaller ones, presumably because they cover ground more efficiently (Schmidt-Nielsen 1972; Clutton-Brock and Harvey 1977b). It is also true that day-living mammals tend to be heavier than nocturnal ones, and thus that in primates the monkeys and apes tend to be larger than the nocturnal prosimians and also to live in more extended ranges (Charles-Dominique 1975; Clutton-Brock and Harvey 1977a,b). But the size of a primate's range is also related to the relative size of its brain, the range being more extensive the larger the relative brain size (Clutton-Brock and Harvey 1980). We could account for this by supposing that the larger the animal, and thus the further it ranges, the greater is the selection pressure on brain size, if the animal is to learn to cope with all the varied contingencies it will meet. The specialization of the monkeys and apes for a large relative brain size might not have occurred had their ancestors remained night-dwellers. The move into daytime niches appears to have set in motion the extraordinary development of the brain in these primates.

This chapter has documented the relation between the development of the brain and general intelligence. It has shown the monkeys and apes to be specialized as intelligent creatures. Their intelligence equips them for survival in a wide variety of environments; so that these animals are characterized not so much by specific adaptations as by their general adaptability (Le Gros Clark 1971). In man it is just those characteristics which are most typical of monkeys and apes that have been exaggerated. The human strategy for survival is basically the same as that of his close relatives. The next chapters show how the intelligence in which we have specialized has enabled us to outstrip our relatives in colonizing the world.

6 Technology

Why has mankind come to depend on technical mastery?
The answer must be that it was environmental conditions
that led the hominids to adapt in this way, and we shall
have something to say about these conditions. When did
the hominids become specialists in technology? The early
hominids will be compared with other primates in the use
they made of tools, and the stages will be described by
which they came to rely more and more on invention.
How was this technical expertise made possible? A crude
account will be given of the relation between technical
achievements and the rapid increase in the relative size of
the hominid brain.

HABITAT

New adaptations arise in response to new environmental
conditions. Conditions may alter either through a change
in the habitat, perhaps as a result of a shift in climate, or
through migration into new habitats. In the history of our
ancestors we can discern three such events of major
importance. The first was the movement of our ancestors
from the woodlands into more open country. The second
event was the migration of members of the genus *Homo*
out of Africa and into Europe and Asia. The last was the
very unstable climatic conditions during the Ice Ages,
which put a premium on technology as a means for
ensuring survival.

Savannah

Primates are basically tree dwellers; they are to be found
where there is tropical and subtropical forest. In the late
Cretaceous there was a widespread radiation of flowering
plants or angiosperms, and trees covered a much wider
area than is true today. During the Palaeocene and Eocene
the mean annual temperature was higher than it is now,
and hot climates could be found well to the north and

south of their present bounds (Napier 1970) (Fig. 6.1). Tropical and subtropical forests flourished not only in South America, Africa and Eurasia but also in North America. It is in North America and in Europe, to which it was then connected, that the earliest primates have been found (Simons 1972).

But since the Eocene the temperature has fallen, and the tropical forests have contracted towards the Equator (Fig. 6.1); and there has also been a change in the relative positions of the continents as a result of continental drift (Napier 1970). The non-human primates are now restricted to South and Central America, Africa and Asia; their present confines are illustrated in Fig. 6.2. Of the prosimians the members of the loris family are to be found in Asia and mainland Africa; members of the lemur family are restricted to the island of Madagascar, where they have been isolated for many millions of years. Monkeys of the New World range through the forests of South and Central America, but there are no longer any primates in North America. In the Old World the monkeys are spread throughout much of Africa, India and South East Asia. Two of the apes, the chimpanzee and gorilla, are confined to equatorial Africa; the gibbons live in tropical forests in South East Asia; and in Borneo and Sumatra the orangutan faces possible extinction, due to destruction by man of the rain forests on which it depends.

Trees provide the non-human primates with all they need—food, shelter and a refuge (Jolly 1972). They sleep in the trees, and if they venture into the open on the ground they run back up into the trees when in danger. The smaller prosimians protect themselves by coming out

6.1 Limits of tropical and subtropical forest during the Eocene (continuous line) and today (dotted line). After Napier (1971).

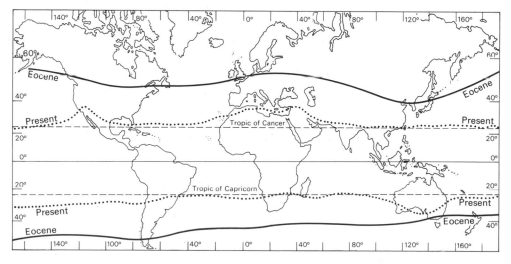

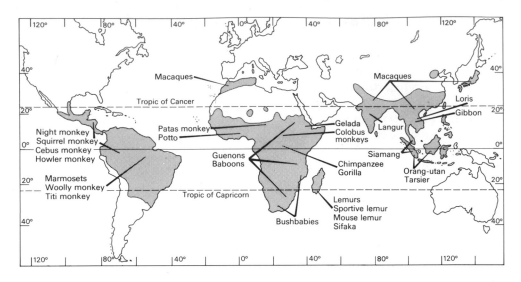

6.2 Distribution of living non-human primates (shown by shading). The arrows indicate the location of those primate species that are mentioned in the text.

only at night and living secretive and relatively solitary lives (Charles-Dominique 1975).

The trees also supply a wide variety of foods: fruit, seeds, leaves, gum and insects. The primates vary in their preference for these items, and they can roughly be divided into three groups according to the amounts of fruit, leaves, and insects that they eat (Clutton-Brock and Harvey 1977a,b). Some of the smaller prosimians, such as the bushbabies, rely on insects for much of their diet (Charles-Dominique 1974a). Some larger primates, such as the howler monkey, the langurs and the colobus monkeys (*Colobus*), have digestive tracts which are specialized for the digestion of leaves. The gibbon and orangutan feed mainly, though not entirely, on fruit. But the majority of primates will eat both fruit and leaves, and many supplement their diet with insects (Jolly 1972). In general monkeys and apes accept a wide variety of foods and avoid narrow specialization.

Not all primates confine their search for food to the trees; some have come to the ground and forage in the grass. In Africa the savannah expanded during the Miocene (Napier 1970); the larger ungulates moved into this new niche, and so later, in the Pliocene, did the baboons, gelada and patas monkey (Jolly 1967). Unlike the ungulates with their clumsy hooves, these primates could use their hands to dig up tubers and rhizomes, detecting their presence by wisps above the ground (Altmann and Altmann 1970). The gelada, for instance, survives mainly on grasses, eating the blades, seeds and roots, digging with its fingers, and plucking seeds and grass blades with its thumb and

forefinger (Jolly 1970; Dunbar 1976). The hamadryas
baboon, like the gelada, is able to eke out a living even in
arid semi-desert in Ethiopia (Kummer 1968). In Asia too
the open country has been exploited by the macaques,
which are closely related to the baboons (Simonds 1974).

During the Miocene the dryopithecine apes, relatives of
the living great apes, were spread not only through Africa
and Asia but also over much of Europe, as can be seen from
Fig. 6.3. They lived in a wide variety of habitats (Simons
and Pilbeam 1972). A related group, the ramapithecines,
are known to have lived in East Africa, Hungary, Greece,
Turkey, Pakistan, India and China between 14 and 8 or so
million years ago (Pilbeam *et al.* 1977) (Fig. 6.3). As
already mentioned, they are of great importance, because
their teeth and jaws are in some respects like those of
hominids. At least in some areas, as in the Siwalik Hills in
Pakistan, they appear to have lived, not in dense forests,
but in regions of woodland or bush (Pilbeam *et al.* 1977).

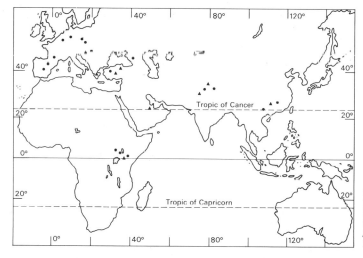

6.3 Sites at which advanced
primates from the Oligocene
and Eocene have been
found. ●, Ramapithecines;
▲, dryopithecines. After R.
E. Leakey (1981).

Irrespective of whether we accept the ramapithecines as
ancestral hominids we suppose that at some time our
ancestors moved from woodland on to more open
savannah (Simons and Ettel 1969). This crucial transition
seems to have occurred in East Africa. In this region the
climate has long been unstable and major geological
rifting occurred in the Miocene and Pliocene, producing a
very wide variety of different habitats (Kortlandt 1980a).
An area such as this presents a great challenge, stimulating
its inhabitants to adapt to new environments. Here the
baboons have spread on to the savannah, and the
chimpanzee can be found in open woodlands (Kortlandt

and van Zon 1969; Itani 1979). It is here too that we know for certain that hominids were living several million years ago. Their remains have been found at Hadar in Ethiopia, Lake Turkana in Kenya, and Olduvai and Laetoli in Tanzania (Day 1977); these areas can be located on the map (Fig. 6.4). Australopithecines have also been discovered in cave deposits in South Africa (Fig. 6.4), but the dates of these fossils have yet to be firmly established (Tobias 1976). The fossil finds from East Africa come from lake or river deposits, and reconstructions of these areas suggest a mosaic of different habitats: beaches, swamps, grassland, bush and so on (Isaac 1978b). In general the environments both here and at the South African sites can be characterized as being in the broad sense savannah country (Isaac 1978b).

To survive in more open country these hominids had to alter their diet and exploit new foods. We can learn only a little about the plants they ate from archaeological traces, and so we must be guided instead by the ways in which the

6.4 Sites at which the fossil hominids mentioned in the text have been found. ●, Australopithecines; □, *Homo habilis*; ■, *Homo erectus*; △, Neanderthal; ×, early *Homo sapiens*; ○ *Homo sapiens sapiens*. Based on Johanson and Edey (1981).

hunter−gatherers of South and East Africa today earn a subsistence on the savannah. The means by which they support themselves have been well documented (Lee and DeVore 1968). To take the !Kung Bushmen or San as an example: in one study (Lee 1968)they were reported to eat 85 food plants, including a nut very rich in proteins, 29

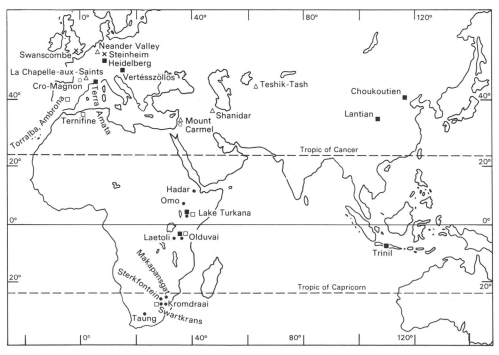

species of fruits, berries and melons, and 30 species of roots and bulbs; 90 per cent of their vegetable diet comes from only 23 species. But they supplement this with meat, which forms 33 per cent of their total diet; amongst other animals they hunt warthogs, antelopes, duikers and hares. The Hadza of Tanzania also obtain roughly 80 per cent of their diet by gathering plant foods, the rest being contributed by the meat from hunts (Woodburn 1968).

It is intriguing that both baboons and chimpanzees sometimes supplement their vegetarian diet with meat (Fig. 9.15). By 1975 reports could be collected from the literature of 182 kills or attempted kills by baboons and of 184 by chimpanzees (Teleki 1975). The baboons preyed on two species of primate, eight species of ungulate and two species of small mammal; 41 per cent of the kills of identified species were of hares. The chimpanzees also preyed on a variety of species: seven primates, four ungulates and two small mammals; but of the prey that could be identified 63 per cent were primates. Some of the prey killed by baboons and chimpanzees are also hunted by human hunter—gatherers living in South and East Africa. While these non-human primates sometimes kill after accidentally stumbling on prey there are also occasions on which, like people, they deliberately hunt, stalking and pursuing their quarry (Harding 1973; Teleki 1973a).

Chimpanzees have been found to eat meat in all the areas in which they have been properly studied— Tanzania, Uganda, Equatorial Guinea and Senegal (McGrew in press). In some of these areas the chimpanzees are deliberately provided with food by the human observers, and these conditions could encourage hunting for several reasons: the animals may be stressed through competition for the food, they may have more time for hunting, and they may be more likely to come into contact with other species at the feeding sites (Reynolds 1975; Gaulin and Kurland 1976). But it is not possible to explain away all instances of meat eating by reference to these effects. Chimpanzees eat meat even in areas where the animals are not artificially fed; one such area is Mount Assirik in Senegal (McGrew et al. 1979a; McGrew in press).

Many of the reports of hunting by baboons and chimpanzees have come from East and South Africa. The areas lie broadly within the Great Rift Valley running down through East Africa and into South Africa, and it is in the same general region that most of the contemporary

African hunter – gatherers live, the San, Pygmies, the Hadza and others (Teleki 1975). And it is in this varied environment that we find evidence of the activities of early hominids around 2 million years ago (Isaac 1978b). Here there were opportunities not only to gather plant foods but also to supplement this diet with meat from the many animals living on the savannah.

The evidence that these hominids probably hunted comes from the accumulations of bones found in association with stone tools. For example, at Olduvai in Tanzania and at Lake Turkana in Kenya tools have been found either with the bones of a single large animal, or with the bones of several different species (Isaac 1978b, 1981). Of course, some of the meat was probably obtained by scavenging; at the Koobi Fora site at Lake Turkana the bones of a hippopotamus have been found along with some tools, and it seems most likely that the hominids simply butchered an animal which they found dead (Isaac 1978a). But it is implausible that all the meat, including that of small animals such as hares, was won in this way (Isaac and Crader 1981). While carnivores such as lions and hyenas scavenge a proportion of the meat they eat, most of the meat eaten by baboons and chimpanzees comes from kills made by themselves. Chimpanzees will seize prey from baboons (Morris and van Lawick-Goodall 1977), but they show little interest in meat or dead animals left on the ground (Teleki 1975). Until we have better evidence we may assume that the early hominids hunted as well as scavenged, killing the young and the sick where they could and the healthy when necessary (Schaller and Lowther 1969).

If we accept that these hominids supplemented a vegetarian diet by hunting they appear to have been better hunters than other primates. Neither baboons nor chimpanzees have ever been seen capturing a prey over 10 kilograms in weight (Teleki 1975). In contrast living hunter – gatherers kill not only small game but also much larger mammals; in one bushman group, the G/wi, the proportion of kills yielding 16 kilograms of meat has been found to be as much as 65 per cent of the total meat eaten (Teleki 1975). Both at Olduvai and at the Koobi Fora site at Lake Turkana a great variety of mammal species appear to have been eaten by the early hominids—pigs, hares, porcupines, waterbuck, gazelles and even giraffes; the most common animals are the medium-sized antelopes (Isaac 1976a, 1978b). Even if they had only primitive weapons the hominids would probably have been able to kill animals up to 30 kilograms or so (Isaac 1978a).

On the supposition that, like the African hunter— gatherers of today, they depended both on foraging and on hunting we must admit that we have no direct information on the proportion of food contributed by each of these activities. Meat contributes roughly a quarter to a third of the diet of living hunter—gatherers in Africa, but only between 1 and 5 per cent of the diet of baboons and chimpanzees (Teleki 1975). Evidence from the but- chering sites at Olduvai and Koobi Fora suggests that the hominids there were more dependent on meat than are these non-human primates (Isaac 1978a) but they were probably less so than living hunter — gatherers whose technology is more sophisticated. As with these peoples, but not the baboons and chimpanzees, hunting was probably more than simply an occasional activity.

Migration

In considering the activities of the early hominids in East and South Africa no attempt has been made to distinguish between the hominids of the genus *Australopithecus*, and those whom some authorities assign to the genus *Homo* (Walker and Leakey 1978). By 1.5 million years ago, however, there was in East Africa a hominid more advanced than those we have discussed so far. Two skulls have been found from around this time at Lake Turkana which have been classified as *Homo erectus* (Leakey and Walker 1976; Walker and Leakey 1978). They come from hominids which were contemporary with hominids of another species, members of the group of robust australopithecines. The presence of *Homo erectus* is also attested at Olduvai over a million years ago (Day 1977).

But though originating, as it appears, in East Africa *Homo erectus* spread not only through the continent of Africa but also into Eurasia. We know that by 700 000 years ago at least he had reached Trinil in Java where several skulls have been found; and he had reached China too by this time as attested by a skull found at Lantian. Skulls discovered in caves at Choukoutien in China indicate his presence there around 400 000 years ago (Day 1977). The Javan and Chinese sites are shown in Fig. 6.4 (page 146), which also illustrates the presence of *Homo erectus* in Europe. A jaw discovered at Heidelberg in Germany is thought to be over 500 000 years old (Oakley 1969), and a skull bone from Vertésszöllös in Hungary has been estimated to have a date of around 350 000 years (Day

1977). There are many other areas in Europe at which *Homo erectus* is known to have been present from the tools that have been unearthed, and some of these are shown on the map.

Sometime before 100 000 years ago the place of *Homo erectus* was taken in Africa and Eurasia by Neanderthal man, usually referred to as *Homo sapiens neanderthalensis*. His presence is documented by tools, skulls and other skeletal remains; a few of the more important sites are shown in Fig. 6.4. It will be seen from this figure that Neanderthal man spread from Western Europe through Asia to China. He in turn was replaced, some 35 000 years ago, by modern man *Homo sapiens sapiens*; spreading perhaps from the Middle East modern man moved into Europe and Asia (Oakley 1969; Pilbeam 1972). We know from the tools they left that, before the end of the Ice Ages, some people had migrated far to the north in Central and Eastern Europe; many tool sites have been unearthed in the USSR (Bordes 1968). At some time before the end of the glaciations people must have migrated as far north as the Bering Strait, crossing into North America while the sea level was low enough to permit their passage (Dumond 1980). Others reached Australia at least 40 000 years ago, some crossing by the Timor Straits (Kirk 1981). By the end of the Pleistocene man had colonized all the continents of the world other than Antarctica.

Ice Ages

There were members of the genus *Homo* in Europe and Asia at least 750 000 years ago, and they may have arrived long before that. Throughout this time there have been marked fluctuations in temperature. Measurements of the temperature in Europe over this period show four major depressions, referred to as the Ice Ages and known as the Günz, Mindel, Riss and Würm glaciations (Kurtén 1971) (Table 6.1). During these glaciations the ice sheets advanced southwards, so that glaciers covered regions which are now temperate. In the periods between the glaciations the temperatures were little lower than today, but during the glacial periods they were as much as 15° lower. In Africa there were related fluctuations in rainfall (Table 6.1).

Conditions such as these put a premium on adaptability. The expansion of zones with an Arctic climate led to the evolution of many species adapted to life on the tundra, and particularly to giant forms such as the woolly

PROVISIONAL TIME SCALE (YEARS)	GEOLOGICAL PERIODS EUROPE	Africa	CULTURAL PERIODS EUROPE	AFRICA
	Postglacial		METAL AGES NEOLITHIC MESOLITHIC	
10 000				
50 000	Fourth glaciation (Würm)	W D W Drier	MAGDALENIAN, SOLUTREAN, AURIGNACIAN MOUSTERIAN	
115 000	Last interglacial			
	Third glaciation (Riss)	Wetter		
250 000	Middle interglacial period	Drier	ACHEULEAN	
	Second glaciation (Mindel)	Wetter		
500 000	First interglacial period	Drier		ACHEULEAN
	First glaciation (Günz)	Wetter Dry		
1 000 000	Villafranchian			
2 000 000	PLIOCENE			OLDOWAN

(Europe geological column marked: NEOCENE / PLEISTOCENE subdivisions; Europe cultural bracket: PALAEOLITHIC)

Table 6.1 Geological and cultural periods during the Ice Ages. After Harrison, Weiner and Reynolds (1977).

mammoth (*Elephas trogontherii*), the woolly rhinoceros (*Coelodonta*) and the great European cave bear (*Ursus spelaneus*) (Kurtén 1971). With the passing of the Ice Ages many of these species have become extinct. During the same period *Homo erectus* and Neanderthal man, *Homo sapiens neanderthalensis*, also became extinct; the only hominid that survived the Ice Ages was modern man. He owed his survival to the adaptability he achieved through the use of a sophisticated technology.

So long as the hominids remained in Africa there is no reason to suppose that they were more dependent on meat than hunter—gatherers living there today. But as they moved to the North, and as weather conditions deteriorated, they would have been able to find fewer plant foods, and would therefore have been forced to include more meat in their diet. Data have been analysed for 58 present-day societies of hunter–gatherers (Lee 1968). In tropical, subtropical and warm-temperate latitudes, 0° to 39° up from the Equator, 25 out of 28 of the societies rely predominantly on gathering plant foods; in cold-temperate to cool climates, 40° to 59° from the Equator, 14 out of the 22 societies rely most on fishing and 4 on hunting; but in the highest latitudes, 50° to 59° from the Equator, of the 8 societies 6 rely on hunting and 2 on fishing. A similar picture emerges if the societies are classed according to the severity of the winter. When the hominids migrated northwards into Europe we find them hunting big game; at Torralba and Ambrona in Spain *Homo erectus* hunted deer, aurochs, horses, elephants and other large mammals (Butzer 1972). Associated with the remains of Neanderthal man in Europe are mammoths, the woolly rhinoceros, bears, reindeer and horses (Butzer 1972). The harsh climate forced the hominids to become professional rather than casual hunters; and in doing so it also increased the reliance they placed on their technology.

TOOLS

The hominids became meat eaters without the natural equipment of the carnivores. In canids and felids, for example, the canines are very large, and a pair of premolar teeth on either side, the carnassials, are specialized for shearing. The teeth of the hominids, on the other hand, are less specialized and are only of modest size; the canines are relatively smaller than those of other primates (Le Gros Clark 1971). Such teeth are not adequate for the task of cutting up and skinning large animals; to do this requires the assistance of tools.

A tool may be thought of as a substitute for a particular anatomical specialization. The woodpecker finch (*Cactospiza pallida*) of the Galapagos Islands lacks the long bill of the woodpecker, but it compensates by gripping cactus spines in its bill and using these to probe for insects in the crevices of bark (Bowman 1961). The cactus spine proves a useful substitute for a long bill. The Ya̧namamö, a group of South American Indians, use as a knife the lower incisor of a rodent, the agouti (Chagnon 1968). Here the tooth is used as a tool for the same purpose for which it serves the agouti; people lack teeth as sharp as those of rodents, but can easily make up for this deficiency by using rodent teeth as substitutes. To cite one final example, the Eskimoes are not naturally endowed with the thick coats that are necessary for survival in Arctic conditions; instead they equip themselves with the furry hides of the caribou that are ideally suited to provide insulation against extreme cold (Balikci 1970). Tools extend the range of activities for which the user is fitted by adding artificial to natural equipment.

There is an advantage that follows from using a tool rather than adopting the relevant anatomical special-izations: the amateur retains an adaptability lost by the professional. The professional carnivores are commit-ted to one particular way of life, and can survive only for as long as prey continues to be available. Since they used weapons and prepared their meat with knives and scoops the hominids were less committed. When, during the last glaciation, big game were plentiful in Europe modern man could hunt them; when the ice finally receded and the big game either became extinct or moved northwards the people could exploit other resources, for example by fishing with the harpoon; and finally they turned their hand to tilling the soil (Binford 1968). If environmental conditions change it takes very many generations to change specializations in anatomy; but tools can be picked up and discarded at will. The tool user has a variety of specializations at his finger tips.

Non-human primates

Man was once thought to be the only user of tools; we now know this belief to have been unfounded. There are reports of tool use both in birds and mammals. Our present concern is not with the isolated instances in which particular animals have been observed to make use of tools in captivity (see Chapter 5), but with those species which are known to use them in their natural habitat.

Tool use has been reported to occur in the wild in 17 genera of monkeys and apes (Beck 1975, 1980). But no prosimians use tools. Furthermore there is only one non-primate mammal that regularly does so in the wild. This is the sea otter (*Enhydra lutrus*) which cracks mussels against stones which they hold on their chest as an anvil (Beck 1980).

It is true that the primates have an unfair advantage in possessing hands; the mouth or paw is less efficient for wielding tools. But this is not to say that non-primate mammals are barred from making use of objects. Indeed there are isolated reports of horses, bears, dolphins and others using tools in captivity (Beck 1980). There are also birds that use their beaks to handle tools in the wild. The Egyptian vulture (*Neophron percnopterus*) drops stones on large eggs to crack them (van Lawick-Goodall 1970); the woodpecker finch breaks off cactus spines and uses them to dislodge insects from the crevices of bark (Alcock 1972); and there are several other such instances (Beck 1980).

It is not the number of occasions on which monkeys and apes use tools that should impress us, but rather the variety of purposes to which they are put. We can best consider these by first dividing the cases into three groups according to the purpose for which the tools are used, in threat or attack, for obtaining food, and for the care of the body.

All the apes, and many Old and New World monkeys have been seen dropping twigs or branches from the trees to scare off intruders. It is not difficult to imagine how they might learn to do this. They need only notice the effect on the intruder of any falling branches which they accidentally break off when disturbed. It is more difficult to assess to what extent the missiles are deliberately aimed. Chacma baboons (*Papio ursinus*) have been reported to bombard human observers from a cliff top with stones (Hamilton *et al.* 1975). The stones were aimed in the sense that they were dislodged only at the point above the observer, and not to either side; but they were still dropped when the observer was too far away from the cliff side to be struck. There are also primates which, when on the ground, will throw objects to enhance aggressive displays: the gorilla, for instance, tears off branches and throws vegetation about as part of its chest-beating display (Schaller 1963). Several primates learn to throw with reasonable aim in captivity (Kortland and Kooij 1963). In the wild chimpanzees which live in relatively open woodland can aim stones as missiles in the right general direction, sometimes achieving a direct hit (van Lawick-Goodall 1970) (Fig. 6.5). Wild chimpanzees have been presented with a stuffed leopard; they have been seen not only to brandish and throw sticks left by the experimenters but even to use them to club the dummy animal (Kortlandt 1972) (Fig.6.6). Unlike other animals, then, monkeys and apes are capable of making use of weapons, in threat and even in attack.

The second purpose for which tools are used is obtaining and preparing food (Teleki 1974). Some baboons in the wild have been reported to open hard fruit by smashing it

6.5 Chimpanzee throwing a stone over-arm. From a photograph in van Lawick-Goodall (1970).

with stones on a rock, and macaques in Singapore have been seen to clean their food with leaves (Chiang 1967; Marais 1969). Chimpanzees are also known to pound nuts and hard-shelled fruit with stones (Teleki 1974). At the Gombe National Park in Tanzania chimpanzees make use of several other objects when feeding (van Lawick-Goodall 1970). Sticks are occasionally used to force open an ant nest, and even to prize open the lid of boxes in which bananas have been placed by the scientists observing the animals (Fig. 7.8). They have not been seen digging with sticks for edible roots, although chimpanzees can learn to do this in captivity (Köhler 1925). They use grasses, bark and twigs as probes to poke down the holes in termite nests, pulling out and eating the insects that cling to the probe (Fig.6.7). They take the task seriously, and on average work at it for 25 minutes or so (McGrew *et al.* 1979b). The chimpanzees in this region also put leaves to use: remnants of brain tissue may be scooped out of the skull of a dead animal by wiping the inside of the skull with leaves (Teleki 1973a,b); and since leaves soak up water they prove useful as a sponge with which to collect it when it is not otherwise accessible (van Lawick-Goodall 1970). In no case, however, have tools such as sticks or stones been used to kill or dismember prey on the occasions when the animals hunt (Teleki 1974).

6.6 Chimpanzee brandishing a stick when displaying at a stuffed leopard. Courtesy of A. Kortlandt.

155

6.7 Chimpanzee 'fishing' for termites. Courtesy of G. Teleki.

There are other miscellaneous uses to which objects are put by monkeys and apes. Perhaps the most important of these is care of the body. A baboon in the Gombe National Park has been observed to wipe fruit juice off its mouth with a stone, and another to wipe blood from its face with a maize kernel (van Lawick-Goodall *et al.* 1973). In captivity chimpanzees have been seen to pick their teeth with stones and in the wild to wipe blood or faeces from their fur with leaves (van Lawick-Goodall 1970; McGrew and Tutin 1973). However, in spite of their facility with tools chimpanzees have never been reported to protect themselves from the rain by constructing any form of shelter, although orang-utans do construct crude shelters for this purpose (MacKinnon 1974).

Is the ability to use tools in the wild a mark of intelligence? The monkeys and apes outclass all other animal groups not only in the number of recorded instances of tool use but also in the variety of purposes to which they put them (Beck 1980). The evidence for this claim is set out in Table 6.2, which gives the purposes for which tools are used and the means by which these ends are achieved. It lists 14 different actions performed by monkeys and apes, of which 12 have been seen in the wild and the remaining 2 only in captivity. The most impressive feature is the variety of the actions which are carried out with tools by chimpanzees, baboons, macaques and cebus monkeys. The chimpanzee has a repertoire of 11 actions in the wild, quite outclassing a bird with just one relatively stereotyped performance. Furthermore, monkeys and apes are capable of using the same object for several different purposes. Stones can be used as missiles, for cracking hard fruit or for wiping blood; and sticks serve in clubbing, digging and probing into the nests of insects. We might summarize by saying that monkeys and apes can put objects to intelligent use.

If tool use is to be taken to reflect intelligence we must

Table 6.2 Tool use in primates*

Action	Tool	Aim	Chimpanzee	Baboon	Macaque	Cebus	Other apes	Other monkeys
Drop	Branches, etc.	Hit or scare intruder	W	W	W	W	2W	6W
Throw	Stones, etc	Hit or scare intruder	W	W	C	W	2C	2W, 2C
Club	Sticks	Hit or scare intruder	W			C	1C	
Pound	Stones	Open fruit, nuts	W	W	W	W		
Dig	Sticks	Open nests, dig up roots	WC	W				2W
Lever	Sticks	Open container (of food)	W	C			1C	
Insert	Twigs, grasses	Probe for insects, honey	W				1C	
Sponge up	Leaves, rope	Take up water to drink	W				2C	
Wipe	Stones, leaves	Clean self	W	W	W		1W	
Wash	In water	Clean food			W			
Reach out	Sticks	Touch object to investigate	W					
Rake in	Sticks	Reach and draw in	W	C	C	C	2C	1C
Prop up	Branches	Reach by climb 'ladder'	C				1C	
Stack	Boxes	Reach by mount boxes	C					

W, observed in the wild; C, observed only in captivity.
* Data from Beck (1975, 1980) and Warren (1976).

be satisfied that it is learnt. Unfortunately we lack the relevant evidence for many of the cases reported in the literature. A fledgling woodpecker finch has been reared on its own, and it was found that it naturally poked about with twigs in its beak; but it appears to have needed to learn the value of the twig in probing for insects (Eibl-Eibesfeldt 1967). Similar studies have not been carried out on other tool-using birds. In the case of primates our confidence that they must learn to use tools comes partly from studies of their behaviour in captivity, where, as described in the previous chapter, they will acquire skills they do not exhibit in their natural environment (Warren 1976). The distribution of tool use in the wild provides supporting evidence; the next chapter will describe the different repertoires that chimpanzees possess in different areas, and will document the evidence that these are acquired as cultural traditions.

There is one further consideration. There are a few animals that not only use tools but make them. No bird makes tools in the wild; the woodpecker finch has only to pluck a cactus spine to obtain a tool. In captivity, on the other hand, blue jays (*Cyanocitta cristata*) have been seen to tear strips of paper, crumple them and then poke them through the side of the cage so as to agitate food pellets outside and thus bring them nearer (Jones and Kamil 1973).

The only convincing cases of toolmaking in non-human primates come from studies of chimpanzees (van Lawick-Goodall 1970). When using sticks to lever open the lids of boxes containing bananas chimpanzees of the Gombe National Park sometimes stripped off the leaves and even bit pieces off the end, thus making them more suitable as levers. Similarly the twigs they use to probe for termites are sometimes modified by stripping off the bark or leaves (McGrew *et al.* 1979b). The modifications made when crushing leaves for use as a sponge are perhaps less impressive. The chimpanzee's capacity to make a tool has also been well demonstrated in captivity. We have already referred to two studies: a chimpanzee learnt to modify pieces of wood to use as rods, breaking off a cross-bar, biting pieces off and so on (Krustov 1970); and an orang-utan learnt to chip sharp pieces off a flint for use as a knife (Wright 1972) (Figs 5.12 and 5.13). The ability of chimpanzees to modify tools in a variety of ways testifies to their general level of intelligence.

Why was it that hominids turned tool-using from a hobby into a profession? In answering this question we face the same problem we met when considering the advantages of walking upright: there are many possible advantages, but it is extremely difficult to demonstrate which of them proved to be critical. There are innumerable ways in which the use of tools could have improved efficiency in defence and in the acquisition and preparation of food. Among the earliest stone tools found, roughly 1.8 million years old, some were almost certainly used for cutting up meat (Bunn 1981; Potts and Shipman 1981). The tools found in East Africa at Lake Turkana and Olduvai are often associated with the bones of animals, and many of these tools are small sharp flakes that make excellent knives for slicing meat (Isaac 1978b). Artifacts have been found amongst the remains of large mammals such as the hippopotamus, and it is unlikely that the carcasses could have been dismembered without the aid of cutting tools (Isaac 1978a). If the survival of the hominids was in part dependent on obtaining meat it would have been of selective advantage to develop even a crude technology.

But unfortunately we have no record of the earliest tools, since we may reasonably assume that materials other than stone were also used; wood, for example, has many uses, but is not preserved. Sticks could have been used to dig up roots, as they were by Köhler's (1925) chimpanzees, and as they are today by hunter — gatherers such as the Hadza in Tanzania (Woodburn 1970). Pieces of bark would have served as convenient tools for carrying food and other things (Isaac 1978a); and thorn branches would have proved to be effective weapons for scaring off predators and warding off competitors (Kortlandt 1980b). All these could have been put to use without any further modification.

Bone too would have provided a suitable material; but it is difficult to prove that it was so used. A large number of animal bones have been found in the caves at Makapansgat and Swartkrans in South Africa, in which australopithecine skulls have also been discovered (Wolberg 1970). Dart (1957) argued that some of the bones had been used as tools; as some types of bone were much more common than others he believed that hominids must have selected those which were most suitable as tools: jaws as saws, distal humeri as clubs, and so on. But it has since been demonstrated that at Swartkrans carnivores such as leopards were probably responsible for the bone collections, and that at Makapansgat the selective nature of the remains is just what one would expect from the different durability of the various bones of the body (Brain 1978). This is not to say that some of the bones were not used as tools, only that further evidence is needed to prove this. There are only a few cases where there are clear indications of use; at Sterkfontein in South Africa a bone has been found which is pointed and worn smooth in the way that would be expected if it had been used (Wolberg 1970): and at Olduvai a few long bones have had flakes stripped off them or their ends split in a way that is not characteristic of the remains from carnivore kills (Leakey 1976).

The literature concentrates on stone tools only because they are the most durable, and because we can easily verify that they were put to use by examining the pattern of wear on the edges. Presumably the hominids used stone long before they learnt how to modify it deliberately so as to better suit their purposes. Stones would have proved serviceable: they could be thrown to ward off predators or competitors, to smash nuts and open hard-skinned fruit, and to cut up meat. Experience with the use of stone would bring the opportunity to learn the properties of stone, what can and cannot be done with it; and this knowledge would aid in selecting those stones most suited to the task in hand. There are many agencies in nature which cause stone to be suitably chipped or flaked; indeed the archaeologist is sometimes hard put to it to distinguish stones flaked by nature from the crude tools manufactured by the early hominids (Oakley 1972).

We will never know exactly how our ancestors first discovered that they themselves were capable of modifying stones so as to copy those chipped by nature. But there is no reason to suppose that the achievement required abilities different in kind from those known to be possessed by chimpanzees. We have seen that if a stick or a twig is ill-suited to its purpose, whether to lever, to push or to probe, chimpanzees are quite capable of modifying it to make it more suitable. The initial discovery may be accidental: an apt illustration is provided by the achievements of one of Köhler's (1925) chimpanzees called Sultan. When the animal had learnt to use a stick to rake in food Köhler provided it with two sticks neither of which was long enough to reach the food, to see if the chimpanzee would learn to nest the sticks together to make a longer rake. It tried to reach the food in vain, and when its efforts proved useless started to play with the sticks. By chance it discovered that one could be inserted into the end of the other, and immediately the chimpanzee raked in the food. The animal saw the significance of its chance observation, and set out to repeat the find by deliberate experiment, successfully reproducing the performance on many occasions.

The history of science testifies to the contribution of chance observations when made by the prepared mind (Koestler 1964). Perhaps chance played a part also in the origins of the making of stone tools; if a stone is seen to fall and chip, or to break when thrown, it requires only that the natural experiment be repeated artificially for the crucial discovery to be made. Once it is known that stone fractures and flakes on striking stone the process can be deliberately copied by hitting one stone with another. Some of the small flakes produced in this way, however crude the technique, would have proved to have been very serviceable as knives (Isaac 1978b).

This brings us to a crucial question. We are assuming that the ability to make tools reflects high intelligence and, as previously argued in Chapter 5, that intelligence depends in part on the relative size of the brain. But can we show a relationship between the toolmaking abilities of the hominids and the development of their brains?

The earliest stone tools that we have come from the Hadar region of Ethiopia (Roche and Tiercelin 1980; Johanson and Edey 1981); present estimates of their age suggest somewhere between 2.5 and 2.7 million years (Lewin 1981). Tools ranging in date from around 1.8 million to 2.1 million years have also been found at three other sites in East Africa, the Omo valley, Lake Turkana and Olduvai (Merrick 1976; Isaac 1978b). Two broad classes can be distinguished—core tools from which flakes have been struck so as to produce a sharpened edge, and the flakes themselves. An example of the first is the 'chopper' which is made by deliberately sharpening one end by removing flakes from either side of the edge; a chopper from Olduvai is illustrated in Fig. 6.8. If the flakes have been further modified by trimming they are classified as tools, and it is often possible to tell that they have been used by the patterns of wear (Leakey 1976; Isaac 1978b); Fig. 6.9 shows a flake trimmed along one edge.

We know that stone must have been transported on occasion, whether unworked or already modified, because tools are sometimes found which are made of types of stone not available at these particular locations. At the

6.8 Drawing of a chopper tool from Olduvai Gorge, Tanzania. From Leakey (1979).

6.9 Drawing of a flake tool from Olduvai Gorge, Tanzania. The flake is trimmed along one edge. From Leakey (1979).

Koobi Fora site at Lake Turkana stone must have been carried for 3 or 4 kilometres in some instances (Isaac 1976a); and at Olduvai some of the raw materials were also brought some distance to the area where they were worked (Leakey 1976). That tools should be transported should not surprise us, since chimpanzees are also known to carry them on occasion (van Lawick-Goodall 1968a; Nishida 1973). Probes for working termite mounds are occasionally selected from up to 100 metres or more away from the mound, and there are cases in which they have been carried for more than an hour and over a distance of more than 1 kilometre (Teleki 1974).

What was the relative size of the brain of the early toolmakers? The fact is that we cannot be sure; we have no means of deciding for certain which of the species of early hominid was responsible for the tools we discover. Tools are often unearthed in layers which contain no hominid bones, and even where hominid bones and tools are found together there is no guarantee that the tools were not the work of some other hominid whose remains are not preserved in those layers. Faced with this problem archaeologists and anthropologists have tended to be conservative. When tools are found at sites where two species of hominid are known to have been present they are usually attributed to the hominid with the more impressive relative brain size (Tobias 1971). Hughes and Tobias (1977) argue that the tools from Sterkfontein in South Africa were made by a hominid of the genus *Homo* which was larger brained than the gracile australopithecines also found at this site. Mary Leakey (1967) suggests that the tools of Bed I at Olduvai were the work not of the robust australopithecines but of a larger brained hominid, *Homo* (Leakey *et al.* 1964) (see Table 4.2). At Lake Turkana australopithecines were also contemporary with *Homo habilis* as represented by the cranium KMN-ER 1470 (Leakey 1973a). However, it is parsimony alone that dictates that the tools be taken to be associated with *Homo*. Unfortunately no hominids have yet been found at the site at Hadar which yielded the earliest known stone tools; further exploration here may resolve the issue. For the present we remain ignorant of the relative brain size of the first hominids to fashion tools from stone.

The best record of the advances in the accomplishments of the early hominids comes from Olduvai. Here the layers of Beds I to IV provide archaeological evidence over a period of roughly a million years starting over 1.8 million years ago. Mary Leakey (1976) has compared the materials from the various layers, and two important conclusions can be drawn from her analysis. The first is that the number of the different types of tool increased with time. In Bed I, containing the earliest layers, the average number of tool types is seven; and of these the chopper makes up 64.5 per cent and scrapers a further 19 per cent. This tool industry is referred to as Oldowan (Table 6.1). In Bed II a similar industry is found that can be regarded as deriving from the first, and this is called Developed Oldowan; in this assemblage the average size of the toolkit is over 10. For the present we have no reason to suppose that the hominids responsible for the Developed Oldowan were of a different species from those responsible for the earlier Oldowan. There is no evidence of any crucial change in the relative size of the brain over this period.

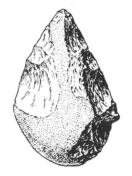

More important than the change in number of tools was the invention of a new type of tool, the bifacial handaxe (Leakey 1976). This can be made from a core or a large flake. Instead of working only one edge, as when making a chopper, further flakes are removed from two faces so as to produce a pointed tool with curved sides that fits comfortably into the hand (Fig. 6.10). The handaxe is more efficient than a flake for butchering animals (Jones 1981). Small and primitive versions or 'proto-bifaces' are found in Bed I at Olduvai and in the earlier Developed Oldowan sites of Bed II. True handaxes occur in small numbers in the later Developed Oldowan sites of Bed II; but they form as much as 54 per cent of the tools found in the industries of Bed II that are referred to as Lower Acheulean (Leakey 1976) (Table 6.1). The handaxes from Bed IV at Olduvai are associated with the remains of *Homo erectus* (Leakey 1976); and a *Homo erectus* skull has also been discovered in Bed II, though not in the same layers as the tools (Day 1977). It seems likely that it was *Homo erectus* who was responsible for the full development of the handaxe, although it has been suggested that it might have been hominids that were more advanced yet (Leakey, L.S.B. 1973).

6.10 Drawing of a handaxe from Olduvai Gorge, Tanzania. After Leakey (1979).

The next major advance was the development of a technique for preparing cores in such a way that flakes of known size and shape could be struck off them, as illustrated in Fig. 6.11 (Isaac 1976c). Flakes can be produced economically in this way. The different flake tools produced had their particular uses, for boring, cutting, scraping, skinning and so on. This so-called Levallois technique first appears in late Acheulean

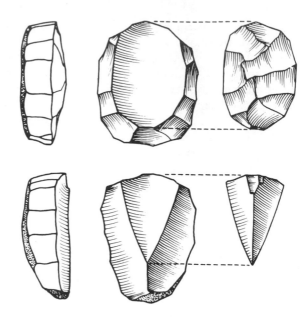

6.11 Levallois technique of striking a flake from a prepared core. From Bordes (1968).

industries, but it was more fully exploited in the Mousterian industries that followed (Bordes 1968; Oakley 1972) (Table 6.1). These are associated with Neanderthal man. The absolute cranial capacity of Neanderthal man was comparable with that of modern populations (Olivier 1973).

While neurological advances may manifest themselves in improvements in technology, there is, of course, no need for alterations in the relative size of the brain if technical advances are to occur. The Upper Palaeolithic industries of Cro–Magnon or *Homo sapiens sapiens* appear in Europe around 35 000 years ago; and they testify to a process of rapid cultural change (Oakley 1972). Flakes were removed by pressure with a piece of bone, and fine workmanship was possible with this method; the tools of the Solutrean culture are, perhaps, the finest examples of the delicate shaping that can be achieved in this way (Bordes 1968) (Fig. 6.12). The technique of hafting may have been invented earlier (Isaac 1976c), but it was certainly the peoples of the Upper Palaeolithic who utilized it most fully; spears, for example, were made by hafting points on to wood (Fig. 6.12). The peoples of the Magdalenian culture also made harpoons with antler for spearing fish (Oakley 1972).

We have concentrated on tools of stone or bone because the record is detailed, and we have therefore dealt only with the use of tools for obtaining and preparing food. But technology was used for other purposes, as in the

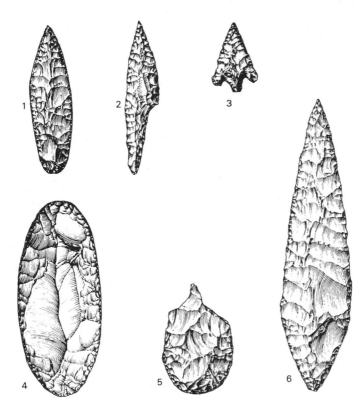

6.12 Drawings of Solutrean tools. 1, Leaf-shaped point; 2, shouldered point; 3, arrowhead; 4, end-scraper, 5, borer; 6, laurel leaf. After Bordes (1968).

provision of shelter and warmth (Campbell 1972). The first evidence of any artificial construction is a circle of loosely piled blocks of lava which has been unearthed in Bed I at Olduvai; this may have been designed as a wind-break (Leakey 1976). But the earliest known huts are very much later: at Terra Amata near Nice in France imprints of a series of stakes and lines of stones have been discovered together with the impressions of thick posts (de Lumley 1969). It appears that oval huts were constructed with stakes for walls and large central posts. These are thought to be around 300 000 years old, the work of *Homo erectus*. Fire was probably used for warmth long before the discovery of how it could be ignited. The earliest evidence for the controlled use of fires comes from around 350 000 years ago: at Vertésszöllös in Hungary charred bones have been discovered, and hearths are found in the caves at Choukoutien near Peking in association with the remains of *Homo erectus* (Butzer 1972). We cannot be sure when clothes were first made to keep out the cold. Neanderthal man had boring tools and scrapers that could have been used in preparing skins, but it is not until the Upper Palaeolithic and the coming of modern man that we find the bone and ivory needles that are an adequate testimony that clothes were sewn (Oakley 1972).

INVENTION

A brief outline has been given of some of the landmarks in the development of technology by our hominid ancestors. Were these advances in any way responsible for the rapid evolution of the brain? It is not yet possible to give any detailed account of the relationship between invention and neurological advance; but a few very general remarks can be made.

The relative size of the brain increased very rapidly in the last 2 million years of hominid evolution. Chapter 4 presents the relevant data, and these are summarized in Fig. 4.21 and Table 4.2. For present purposes there is no need to assert that the rate of change was faster than in any other known evolutionary event; indeed this was probably not the case (see Chapter 5). It is enough to claim that the pace was very fast.

We assume at the outset that intellectual competence depends to some extent on the relative size of the brain. The previous chapter described the evidence supporting this assumption. Though this relationship may be slight within a species, as in modern man, it is more substantial if we make comparisons between different species; and it is comparisons of this sort that are made when considering the evolution of the hominids.

We also assume that evolution usually proceeds in response to environmental change, whether through migration into new habitats or ecological change. It is reasonable, therefore, to expect the most rapid evolutionary transformations where environmental conditions are the least stable. The Ice Ages provided such conditions.

But was any process at work in the evolutionary development of the hominids which has no parallel in the evolution of other species? Several authors have pointed out that we could cite the advances in the hominid brain as a special case of the operation of 'positive feedback' (Holloway 1967; Bielicki 1969; Darlington 1969; Tobias 1971). The notion of positive feedback is that small deviations may set up conditions that favour further deviations in the same direction; in this way the initial deviation is amplified (Maruyama 1963).

Positive feedback probably operates in many of the

major changes in evolution (Szarski 1971). One example is the evolutionary development of birds from arboreal reptiles (Romer 1966). Each change in the size and shape of the scales would increase the tendency to attempt jumps through the air; and the more the experience of flight the greater the selection pressure for a further transformation of the scales into feathers (Szarski 1971). Adaptation to a new ecological niche occurs because morphological changes increasingly tempt the animals into a new environment, and that environment then promotes a further change in the same direction.

How, then, are we to account for what has rightly been called the 'human revolution' (Hockett and Ascher 1964)? The basic mechanism at work in the evolution of the hominids was probably no different, but there may be a special reason why the increase in the relative size of the brain proceeded so rapidly. The following account can be given (Bielicki 1969). (1) An increase in the relative size of the brain allowed an increase in mental capacity, and thus proved its worth in technological advance. (2) New technical inventions generated new selection pressures for the intelligence with which to capitalize on these advances. (3) This led to a further increase in the relative size of the brain. Thus there was a cycle of positive feedback, neurological advance promoting technical invention and invention in turn promoting the continued development of the brain.

This account makes one plausible assumption. That is that new technology presents challenges which are met more effectively by the more than the less intelligent. To put this in other words, it is assumed that those individuals who are endowed with the greater mental capacity are the more likely to see the point of taking over an invention and to appreciate the directions in which it may be further applied and developed (Staddon 1980).

In what way does this account differ from accounts of other evolutionary changes which also result from a process of positive feedback? The key difference is that the hominids were not just moving into a new environment or reacting to changes in the natural world; they were also creating a new artificial environment of their own through cultural advance. This technical environment could change rapidly, because technology is passed from generation to generation by cultural and not by genetic transmission; advances in one generation make possible further progress in the next (see Chapter 7). Given that the hominids were not only creating a technical environment but also reacting to it, they were living in an environment that was rapidly changing. Such conditions would set up a high selection pressure for the neurological changes that would allow the capacity to cope with this cultural environment.

This is not to claim that the evolution of the brain in hominids is to be accounted for only by reference to its selection pressures induced by technology. Demands are also made by language, by the organization of group endeavours such as hunting, and in general by the intelligent ordering of society (Holloway 1969, 1970). The social and linguistic environment must have had an influence quite as great as that of the physical world of technology (Tobias 1981). The latter is stressed here only because the artefacts provide concrete evidence which can be dated. As Chapter 8 will make clear we have little idea as to when spoken language was invented, or when other forms of communication, as by gesture, were first used. It is fair to assume that technology can advance most rapidly when there is a language with which to teach it to future generations. By speeding cultural change language would add considerably to the selection pressures on the brain.

It has been argued that the key to the rapid evolution of the hominid brain may have been cultural advance. But the final result has been that man has increasingly protected himself from further genetic change through continued natural selection. This is because he has come to assume almost total control over his environment, such that it is now of his own making. He combats climatic change with clothing and housing; he controls the food supply by agriculture; and he protects himself from disease by medicine (Campbell 1972). Whereas animals change to suit their environment man changes his environment to suit him.

7 Culture

If each generation had to re-invent the technology of the previous one little progress would be made. The ability to pass on cultural traditions allows information and skills to accumulate; instead of having to start out afresh sons can inherit the knowledge and technology of their fathers. This legacy is not one that can be handed on by genetic inheritance. It is a dogma of modern genetics that characteristics acquired during a lifetime cannot modify the genes and so be transmitted to future generations (Maynard Smith 1975). Lamarck believed that inheritance of this sort could occur (Darlington 1964), and we might regard it as a serious limitation in the genetic process that it does not. But it is a limitation that can be overcome, by transmitting by means of learning rather than genetics.

The study of culture has traditionally been the concern of the historian and social anthropologist. It has tacitly been assumed that cultural traditions are unique to man; indeed they have often been defined in such a way that they could only be handed on by word of mouth. Tylor (1881), one of the founding fathers of social anthropology, regarded culture as 'that complex whole which includes knowledge, belief, art, morals, law, custom, and any other capabilities or habits acquired by man as a member of societies'. He did not envisage that animals might acquire cultural traditions, lacking as they do the language with which to express beliefs or encode laws. Social anthropologists have spent many words trying to improve on this definition, and most of the suggestions have deliberately used terms which can be applied to man alone (Kroeber and Kluckhold 1952). One of the most influential proposals is that submitted by White (1959): 'culture is a class of things and events, dependent upon symboling, considered in an extrasomatic context.' Apart from the decline in the standard of clarity of expression, this definition differs from Tylor's in expressly stating that cultural traditions depend on the possession of language.

It would be more profitable if we chose to define culture in a way that did not pre-judge the issue of whether human beings have the sole rights to culture. We can identify as cultural traditions those patterns of behaviour which are passed from generation to generation by means of social learning. The term 'social learning' refers to cases in which individuals acquire information or skills from others; we shall have more to say about it in the next section.

A more formal proposal has been made by McGrew and Tutin (1978) who require that six criteria be met: these are innovation, dissemination, standardization, durability, tradition and diffusion. These can be expanded as follows. (1) The tradition must start with an innovation. (2) It must pass from one individual to another. (3) Different individuals must behave in much the same way. (4) Individuals must continue to behave in this way even when the demonstrator is not present. (5) The custom must be passed from generation to generation. (6) It must also pass from area to area. Of these criteria the first five spell out the implications of the definition given above. The sixth is not essential, since, although cultural traditions may spread by diffusion, there is nothing in the meaning of the word that specifies that they must.

McGrew and Tutin (1978) argue that there may be reason to add two further criteria, but these are not included in the definition proposed here. First, they suggest that subsistence activities be excluded; the reason is that it is often difficult to be sure that group differences in, let us say, food preferences reflect cultural tradition as opposed to differences in the distribution of local resources. But, though it may be practically difficult to arrive at a proper judgement in such cases, in principle there is no reason why there should not be cultural traditions which involve subsistence activities. The other requirement is that the behaviour pattern in question should adapt the individuals to their natural environment rather than to novel conditions resulting from contact with man. But again this criterion seems unnecessary; all we need do is to distinguish between those cultural traditions that result from human interference and those that develop independently of human influence.

Given that we define cultural traditions in the way suggested we can consider separately the means by which they are transmitted, whether by observational learning, imitation or verbal instruction. Just as, until recently, it was supposed that animals were incapable of using or making tools, so it has been held that they are unable to generate cultural traditions. We shall see that the latter belief is as unfounded as the former. It will become apparent that we are unique not in inheriting traditions, but in using language as a powerful means for teaching them.

SOCIAL LEARNING

We acquire much of our information and know-how from listening to the instructions of other people; but we also learn by direct observation and imitation. While animals may not speak they can and do observe the actions of their fellows.

We can best appreciate the social learning that can occur in this way by first considering what animals can learn when on their own. Psychologists have typically distinguished two sorts of information that animals and people can acquire: knowledge of the sequence of events in the outside world, and knowledge of the consequences of their own actions (Mackintosh 1974). They observe the course of events, and make predictions by using one event as a signal that another is to follow; they also note the events that follow from their own actions, and so place themselves in a position to modify their actions according to their effects. An alternative way of drawing the distinction is to contrast knowledge of two types: we may know *that* particular events are related in time or that particular objects are related in space; and we may know *how* to achieve particular ends, that is how to control the world.

A similar distinction can be drawn in regard to social learning. By watching others we can acquire information about the world and also knowledge of how to act on the world. It will be helpful to make this distinction by using different terms to refer to the two types of information. We may say that 'observational learning' occurs when knowledge of the temporal and spatial relations in the world is increased by observing the discoveries made by another individual. We can then use the word 'imitation' to refer to those instances where the actions of another individual are copied because they demonstrate how a particular end may be achieved. We need not require that the copy be exact; a child's attempts at copying the sounds of speech may be idiosyncratic, but they are nonetheless examples of imitation. Nor need we demand that the action that is copied be novel; a child may know how to raise its hand, but if it is moved to do so when it sees an adult with an arm raised we may reasonably claim that it is imitating. We have only to be confident that it would not have raised its arm at that time had it not seen the action performed by the adult. The reader should be warned that the distinction drawn here between observational learning and imitation is not made in exactly the same way as in other accounts (Hall and Goswell 1964; Mackintosh 1974).

To prove that an individual can acquire information through observational learning or imitation we must first rule out three simpler explanations. When a social animal sees another eating or frightened it may itself feel hunger or fear as if through contagion; this occurs by the process sometimes referred to as 'social facilitation' (Thorpe 1963). Though the observer might learn to find food or to avoid danger more quickly as a result, it could not be said to have *learnt* anything from its observations; what has been transmitted is not learning but a mood or state.

There is another effect of which we should be wary when claiming instances of observational learning or imitation. Social animals naturally tend to follow other members of their group, and because they belong to a group they may learn much that they would not have learnt had they led a solitary existence (Galef 1976). Many birds, for example, learn to find traditional nest sites or breeding grounds (Wilson 1975); and many primates and other mammals learn the home range of their group, the best sleeping sites and the location of the richest sources of food or water (Hall 1968). But they could do so without strictly learning *from* other members of their group. Simply by staying in the group and moving along with it they are given the opportunity to learn about their environment of their own accord. They would learn as effectively if they were pulled about on a trolley with no other animals being present.

The third effect is related to this one. Not only do social animals follow in the steps of others, they also follow their eyes. They direct their gaze towards objects at which others are looking, and may thus learn about them because their attention is drawn to them (Crawford and Spence 1939). In this case the other animal acts not as a trolley but as a pointer, without itself giving any information about the object. A good example of this is provided by the way in which great tits (*Parus major*) have learnt to open the tops of milk bottles in some areas of England (Fisher and Hinde 1949). It turns out that the birds do not need to learn how to open the top by observing how others do so.

The phenomenon can be explained simply by assuming that they are attracted to places where other birds are feeding (Hinde and Fisher 1951); and this assumption is one for which there is experimental evidence (Krebs *et al.* 1972).

Now that we have been put on our guard we can best recognize the phenomena of observational learning and imitation by citing examples of each. These are taken from the laboratory rather than from the wild, because under these conditions it is easier to analyse the type of learning involved. Observational learning is well illustrated by an experiment carried out on rhesus monkeys (Darby and Riopelle 1959). Two monkeys faced each other in separate cages, with a testing board between the two cages. They were given a series of discrimination problems in which they had to learn under which of a pair of objects food was to be found. With each pair of objects one monkey was allowed to watch the other move one of them in an attempt to find the food; and it was then given the opportunity to choose for itself. The observer monkey had much greater success on each of the problems than would be expected if it had had no opportunity to watch the other at work. The design of the experiment neatly rules out the possibility that the observer was benefiting only by having its attention drawn to the objects. It performed well irrespective of whether it had watched the other monkey move the wrong object or the right one; yet in the first case its attention would be directed towards the incorrect object. The same finding also indicates that the observer did not copy the actions it saw performed, since it did not repeat the mistakes of its companion.

We can provide an equally clear case of imitation. The demonstration is most convincing if we take some totally arbitrary act that we know to be outside the normal repertoire. A superb example is illustrated in Fig. 7.1; it shows the chimpanzee Viki which was tested by its foster parents (Hayes and Hayes 1952). They devised a series of 70 acts which they demonstrated to Viki, such as whirling on one foot, operating new toys and so on. Of those actions which she had never performed before she copied 10 the first time she saw them, including the act of stretching open her mouth as in the drawing (Fig. 7.1). There were other actions which she was known to have done before, but which were also carried out immediately she saw them performed; and when she had been through the series many times 55 of the items she learnt were

7.1 Chimpanzee Viki imitating a facial expression. From a photograph in Hayes and Hayes (1952). Drawing from Riopelle (1967).

produced in response to the appropriate demonstration.

Are monkeys and apes especially proficient in social learning as they are in the use of tools? For the present we will confine our attention to the ability to learn by watching; the capacity to imitate sounds will be discussed in the next chapter. Cases of observational learning have been reported both in birds and mammals (Davis 1973). Whether a bird eats a bit of food can be influenced by its observation of what other birds are eating. In one experiment sparrows (*Passer domesticus*) and chaffinches (*Fringilla coelebs*) were given the opportunity to watch another bird of their species eating pieces of some novel food; when themselves presented with unfamiliar food they were more likely to eat it if it was the same type of food they had seen eaten, rather than food of some different type (Turner 1964). In a similar experiment fork-tailed flycatchers (*Muscivora tyrannus*) have been shown to be more ready to peck at butterflies they would normally assume to be distasteful, if they have previously seen other birds do so (Alcock 1969). Observational learning has also been investigated in rats and cats. Rats will learn to base their choice between two patterns on the selection made by another rat (Kohn and Dennis 1972), and to avoid a candle flame to which they would otherwise be attracted if they see another rat discovering its dangers (Lore *et al.* 1971). Cats will similarly learn that a flashing light signals impending electric shock if they can observe other cats learning to avoid the shock (John *et al.* 1968).

There are more demonstrations of observational learning in monkeys and apes than in any other group of animals, though this may reflect in part the greater attention that has been paid to them by experimenters. We have already seen that rhesus monkeys can learn under which of two objects food is to be found by watching another monkey uncover it (Darby and Riopelle 1959). In the same way they can tell whether food is to be hidden to their right or left if they see another monkey finding food there (Riopelle 1960).

Monkeys can also learn where danger lies by observing a companion in the dangerous situation. Like cats rhesus monkeys will realize that an electric shock follows a warning signal if they can observe another monkey experiencing the shock and learning to avoid it (Presley and Riopelle 1959). A captive patas monkey was reported to avoid a box containing a snake after it had seen its mother being startled on opening it (Hall 1968). In a similar experiment a vervet monkey was taught to avoid touching a cup, bowl or sieve by blowing air at it when it made contact (Stephenson 1973). A second vervet monkey was then shown these objects together with others; it noted the reluctance of the first monkey, and refused to touch the three forbidden items. When finally the second monkey dared to touch one of the objects without unpleasant consequences the trained monkey also lost its fear of them.

Like other mammals, monkeys and apes are typically nervous in novel situations, as when they come across a new object or are presented with the opportunity to eat strange food (Menzel et al. 1961; Menzel 1965). If, however, they see other monkeys behaving more boldly they can overcome their initial suspicion. In one study rhesus monkeys that initially refused to drink blackcurrant juice were induced to do so on seeing other monkeys drink it (Weiskrantz and Cowey 1963). In another chimpanzees were presented with two new objects, a swing and a toy that moved and made loud 'beeping' noises; though timid at first they soon learnt to play with them when they saw their companions doing so (Menzel et al. 1972).

It is clear that the ability to learn about the world by watching others is widespread in birds and mammals. In so far as monkeys and apes are in general intelligent and inquisitive we might expect them to be efficient at observational learning. Indeed the degree to which captive monkeys watch each other and constantly learn from their observations is most impressive (Hall and Goswell 1964).

The ability to imitate actions may be very much less common in animals. There is only one report in a bird, the blue jay (Jones and Kamil 1973). As described in Chapter 5 a blue jay was seen to use bits of paper to agitate pellets of food outside its cage and thus bring them closer.

Surprisingly it was found that of the eight other birds kept in the same room five did the same. It could be that they each independently learnt how to retrieve the pellets once their attention was drawn to the paper by another bird; but it is more likely that they copied the way in which the tool could be used.

In mammals other than primates there are a few isolated examples of imitation. In the laboratory cats have been given problems in which to obtain food they had to operate simple devices such as a pedal or turntable; they learnt to do so more quickly if they had previously seen another cat learning the same trick (Herbert and Harsh 1944). In a similar experiment cats have also been shown to benefit from watching other cats pressing levers for food (John *et al.* 1968). In both studies, however, it is possible that the observers were helped only because their attention was drawn to the relevant mechansim, and that they did not actually copy the actions used in operating it. The only reported case where we can be certain that true imitation occurred is in the dolphin (*Tursiops aduncus*) in captivity; one was seen to copy the swimming and grooming postures of a seal (*Arctocephalus pusillus*), and to use a tile to scrape the bottom of the tank after seeing a diver clean it with a steel scraper (Tayler and Saayman 1973). Other well-authenticated accounts of imitation in mammals are hard to find.

There are more reports of imitation in monkeys and apes. Cebus and rhesus monkeys learn to solve simple mechanical puzzles, such as opening latches, more rapidly if they have previously watched other monkeys working on them successfully (Warden *et al.* 1940). The observers often opened the puzzles quickly and with little fumbling. Guinea baboons (*Papio papio*) kept in a zoo have been studied to see if they can learn how to take in food from a pan, using a hook on a rod (Beck 1973). One baboon learnt to do this of its own accord; of the seven others which repeatedly saw it at work none solved the problem, but one did appear to copy some of the movements, such as touching a pan with the tool.

We have already cited the demonstration of imitation of movements in the chimpanzee Viki. She was also set six problems to solve, and when she had failed on each was shown the solution by demonstration (Hayes and Hayes 1952). One was the stick-and-tunnel problem already illustrated in Fig. 5.11; food is placed in a wire tunnel and can be removed only by pushing it out with a stick. After two demonstrations she solved the problem. Another task is shown in Fig. 7.2; the door of a box containing food could be opened only by reaching with a stick and displacing a short length of string which was stretched between two posts. She solved this in 35 seconds after only one demonstration; there was little chance of her solving it so quickly had she not been shown how to do it. She performed as well on the six problems as four children aged between 26 and 36 months.

7.2 Chimpanzee Viki solving the rod-and-string test. From a photograph in Hayes and Hayes (1952). Drawing from Riopelle (1967).

A further and delightful example of the chimpanzee's propensity to imitate comes from a study of a group of chimpanzees kept in a large enclosure surrounded by high walls (Menzel 1973). As already described in Chapter 5 one chimpanzee learnt to place large branches against the walls, and then to use them as ladders for climbing into an observation house set into the wall (Figs 7.3 and 7.4). The next day four other chimpanzees broke in by using the branches as ladders in the same way. A year later one chimpanzee managed to escape over the perimeter wall by scaling it with a very long branch, and the next day the other chimpanzees followed suit.

7.3 Far left: Chimpanzee placing a branch against a wall. From Menzel (1973).

7.4 Left: Chimpanzee climbing branch to reach the observation tower. From Menzel (1973).

The full extent of the capacity of the chimpanzee to imitate can best be appreciated from the accounts of chimpanzees reared in a novel and complex environment, the human home. The chimpanzee Gua learnt by imitation such activities as brushing her hair and sitting at a typewriter and pressing the keys (Kellogg and Kellogg 1933). Viki carried out some routine household tasks such as dusting furniture and washing clothes and dishes; and she even took lipstick, and while looking in a mirror applied it to her mouth and pressed her lips together (Hayes and Hayes 1952). Circus trainers could teach chimpanzees to do such tasks, but chimpanzees brought up in a home spontaneously try out the activities they see their caretakers perform.

Though not the only animal capable of imitation the chimpanzee outstrips all others in the extent to which it spontaneously imitates and the number of novel actions that it can copy. Nonetheless it is surpassed by the human child; comparing Gua with their young son the Kelloggs concluded that their child was the more imitative (Kellogg and Kellogg 1933). Imitation can be convincingly demonstrated in children as young as 12 to 21 days of age (Meltzoff and Moore 1977); they will copy such movements as extension of the tongue, opening of the mouth and protrusion of the lips, as illustrated in Fig. 7.5. There is no need to document further here the extraordinary ability of children to imitate, nor the crucial role it plays in their socialization and education (Aronfreed 1969; Bandura 1977).

CULTURAL TRADITIONS

We have established that in the laboratory some monkeys and apes can acquire information and skills by observing their fellows. To what use do they put these abilities in the wild? Do they actually inherit cultural traditions and hand them down across the generations? To prove that they do we must establish two facts: that within a species groups of animals behave differently according to the areas in which they live; and that they do so, not because each individual learns to adapt of its own accord, but because individuals learn from each other.

Let us consider first whether they learn by observation which foods are to be eaten. A list of the foods eaten by members of different monkey groups shows that the diet may vary (Miyadi 1964). But the reason for this could as

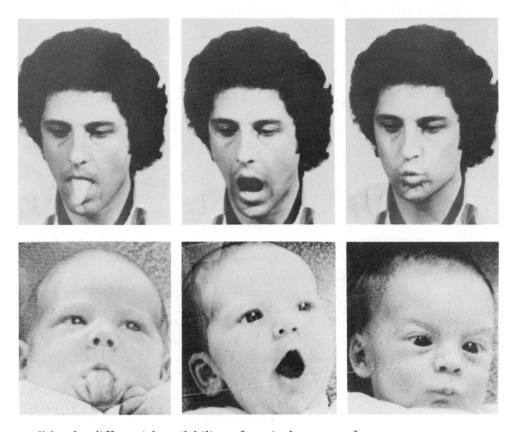

well be the differential availability of particular types of food in some areas compared with others. Baboons at the Cape Peninsula in South Africa, for example, have learnt to eat shellfish (Hall 1963a); and it is not surprising to hear that baboons inland have not. We need cases where the same foods are available in two areas but the preferences of groups in these areas differ. One such instance is provided by a study of the Nilgiri langur (*Presbytis johnii*) (Poirier 1969): 12 foods were identified which were readily available to each of four troops living in different habitats; but of these some were eaten only in one troop, others in two and so on. A similar analysis has been carried out of the diet of the mountain gorilla *G. gorilla beringei* (Schaller 1963); again foods could be listed which are eaten by one group but not by another even though they were present in the region.

The best way to investigate how food preferences can be transmitted is to provide new foods ourselves and observe the ways in which the animals come to accept them. Japanese monkeys, for instance, have been given caramels; each individual in a troop was offered one on six occasions spread over a year and two months (Itani 1965).

7.5 Imitation of facial expression in babies. From Meltzoff and Moore (1977).

On the first occasion only 11 per cent of the monkeys accepted the caramels, but on the last occasion 64 per cent of them did so, including all the 43 infants born after the first two tests were carried out. Some of the monkeys accepted the caramels of their own accord, but it was observed that others were encouraged by seeing their fellows eating them. The infants were the boldest, and those adults which were in closest contact with them were more likely to come to accept the food than those on the periphery of the group.

There is another report of the development of a food preference, in this case for meat. A troop of olive baboons (*Papio anubis*) was studied over two successive periods of a year or so during which they were observed for roughly similar times; hunting was twice as frequent in the second period as in the first (Strum 1975). In the earlier study hunting was almost entirely a male concern; females were responsible for only 6 per cent of the kills, and were present on only 2 per cent of occasions when meat was eaten. In the later study the interest of the females was greater; they were now responsible for 15 per cent of the kills, and ate meat at 52 per cent of the kills made by the group. During the second period juvenile animals also started to take part in hunting and meat eating. Of course, these facts alone do not prove that the baboons changed their behaviour because of the dissemination of a tradition; it is possible that prey became more available or that the baboons had more time to hunt (Gaulin and Kurland 1976). But cases were observed in which the influence of animals on each other was clearly apparent (Strum 1976). This is not to say that we need to suppose that the monkeys learnt *how* to hunt by watching others, only that their interest in meat was fired by the sight of others hunting and devouring prey.

Chimpanzees also eat meat, and while we know nothing of the historical development of this habit, we can compare different populations of chimpanzees and note the frequency with which they hunt and the prey they prefer to catch. A formal comparison has been made between chimpanzees living in four areas: three are in Tanzania—the Gombe National Park, the Kasakati Basin and Kasoje in the Mahale Mountains; the fourth, Mount Assirik, is in Senegal (McGrew *et al.* 1979a; McGrew in press). Many of the differences between these populations can be accounted for without invoking cultural traditions. For example, the chimpanzees at Gombe hunt very much more often than those in the Kasakati Basin; over a 3-year period two communities of chimpanzees at Gombe made roughly 60 kills a year, averaging a kill for every 55 hours of observation (Wrangham 1975). But unlike the chimpanzee in the Kasakati Basin they are artificially provided with bananas by the human observers; for some time they competed with baboons for this prize, and were thus liable to attack them (Wrangham 1974). The chimpanzees at Gombe also take a wider variety of species than other populations; but there are few carnivores there which are serious competitors (McGrew in press). However, there are some differences that remain to be explained: at Kasoje, but not at Gombe, the chimpanzees ignore the bush pig (*Potamochoerus porcus*) though they hunt another ungulate; and at Mount Assirik the chimpanzees only hunt two animals, both prosimians, and they ignore the vervet monkey though it is hunted at Kasoje. It is possible that young chimpanzees are influenced to some extent by the preferences shown by the adults, and thus that tradition plays some part in guiding their interests.

Chimpanzees also eat insects, and there is variation in the insects that are taken in different areas. Reports have been compared from five areas, and several instances have come to light in which insects that are eaten in one area are ignored in another although they are available (McGrew in press). Thus, the ant *Megaponera*, which stings, is caught by the chimpanzees of Mount Assirik, but there are no reports of it being eaten by the chimpanzees at Gombe. Similarly bees' nests are raided for the comb and honey both at Gombe and at Mount Assirik, but they are left alone by the chimpanzees at Kasoje. In such cases we may suspect that the different preferences reflect different traditions.

The cases considered so far are examples of observational learning; the animals learn what is acceptable by watching the choices made by others. Imitation, on the other hand, can best be illustrated by taking instances in which a new skill is invented and subsequently adopted by others. An example that has become justly famous is provided by a study of a group of Japanese macaques on Koshima Island (Kawamura 1963). To bring the monkeys into the open, so that they would be easier to observe, the experimenters fed them sweet potatoes on a beach. One day in 1953 Imo, a 16-month-old female, took her potatoes and washed the sand off them in a stream, and thereafter she continued to do this regularly. Other monkeys started doing the same; within 4 years roughly half the animals were washing their potatoes in this way;

and by now most of the monkeys do so. The main change was that by 1958 or so the potatoes were washed in the sea rather than in the stream, perhaps because of the salty taste of the sea water (Frisch 1968) (Fig. 7.6).

How did the tradition catch on? They did not have to learn the rubbing movements used in washing, since these are the same as those used by monkeys when cleaning dirty food; what was new was the use of water as an aid. Imo's behaviour was first imitated by her playmates, who were those most likely to see her at work, and then the mothers took over the invention from their infants (Kawamura 1963; Itani and Nishimura 1973). Later, infants were born into the group, and these were taken into the sea by their mothers. The infants had the opportunity to learn to wash potatoes by watching their mothers doing so; but it must be admitted that they could also learn to do so of their own accord, given that they were taken to the water and could pick up pieces of potato dropped by their mothers.

The invention of potato washing led Imo to a further discovery when she was 4 years old. By now the monkeys were being fed wheat as well as potatoes on the beach, and the wheat was difficult to separate from the sand. Imo took her wheat to the water, just as she did with the potatoes; she found that if the wheat was then dropped on the water the sand would sink, and the wheat could then be picked out again clean. This practice was also adopted by some of the other monkeys, and with the years more and more animals learnt the trick (Itani and Nishimura 1973). Both potato washing and wheat sifting were most readily adopted by the young; the adults, and especially the males, were more conservative (Kawai 1965a).

7.6 Japanese macaque washing a sweet potato. Courtesy of B. B. Beck.

In captivity chimpanzees are more imitative than monkeys and more competent with tools; and in wild chimpanzee populations we know of several traditions which do not result from human interference (van Lawick-Goodall 1973; Teleki 1974). One example that is well documented is the use of sticks and grasses for probing the nests of termites and ants. There are seven areas in East and West Africa in which chimpanzees are known to fish for termites (*Macrotermes*); in some they have been seen to do so, and in others tools have been found by the termite mounds (McGrew *et al.* 1979b). At Kasoje in Tanzania *Macrotermes* is rare, but the chimpanzees fish for another termite, *Pseudacanthotermes*, and also for ants (McGrew in press). Chimpanzees in Gabon ignore *Macrotermes* and use tools to obtain ants instead (McGrew *et al.* 1979b). There are, however, two areas where the chimpanzees are not known to fish for insects even though they are available: Mount Alen in Rio Muni and the Budongo Forest in Uganda (McGrew *et al.* 1979b). The use of sticks to probe honey has been observed in only three areas, at Gombe and Kasakati in Tanzania, and in Zaire (Teleki 1974).

A comparison has been made between the methods used for obtaining termites by three chimpanzee populations: these are at Gombe in East Africa, Okorobiko in Rio Muni in Central Africa, and Mount Assirik in Senegal in West Africa (McGrew *et al.* 1979b). The chimpanzees at Okorobiko do not fish for termites in the same way as the others; instead they use relatively large sticks to make holes in the termite mound and then they pick out the termites by hand. This is the more effective technique in that area given the structure of the mounds (McGrew *et al.* 1979b); but it is unlikely that each individual adopts it independently and without observing the practice of others. There are other differences in the use of tools by chimpanzees in the three areas: the chimpanzees at Gombe do not peel the bark off twigs before using them, and they often use both ends of the probe in turn; whereas the chimpanzees at Mount Assirik usually peel twigs and use only one end. In such cases we may suspect differences in cultural tradition.

In some areas chimpanzees use objects other than sticks and grasses as tools (Teleki 1974). As yet only the chimpanzees at Gombe have been seen to wipe faeces, blood or dirt off their bodies with leaves (van Lawick-Goodall 1973). These chimpanzees also crush leaves and use them as sponges to soak up water for drinking; this technique has only been reported in one other population of chimpanzees, a semi-captive group in Gambia (van Lawick-Goodall 1973). There are a few reports of chimpanzees using stones to pound nuts or hard-shelled fruit; these are from Liberia and the Ivory Coast (Teleki 1974). Of course, in the future more systematic studies of chimpanzee populations may reveal other instances of these practices. But for the present it is reasonable to appeal to local tradition when explaining why some but not other chimpanzees use tools in these ways.

Human cultures differ not only in their technology but also in their social customs. We know of one such custom which is thought to be peculiar to chimpanzees in one area. Members of the Kajabala group at Kasoje in Tanzania sometimes take up an unusual posture when grooming: the active partner clasps one hand of its mate and holds it up in the air so as to groom the underarm area (McGrew and Tutin 1978) (Fig. 7.7). This method has never been observed in the chimpanzees at Gombe,

7.7 Chimpanzee holding the arm of its grooming partner so as to reach the under-arm. From McGrew and Tutin (1978).

although chimpanzees there sometimes achieve the same end by putting up an arm to grasp a branch overhead. There are no variations in habitat which could plausibly be invoked to explain this striking difference, and we may therefore take it as evidence for social custom.

It has been assumed throughout that the variation in practice between different groups of chimpanzees is the product of learning and not genetic variation. But we need further to be convinced that individuals learn not of their own accord but by watching others who are experienced. In few cases do we have direct evidence that this is so, although indirect evidence may persuade us that it is. Observation of the chimpanzees at Gombe show that the young have many opportunities to see their mother at work fishing for termites; they often watch intently and sometimes pick up the tools that she discards and play with them or attempt to use them (van Lawick-Goodall 1968a, 1970). There are two reports of immediate imitation. The first is of a 3-year-old chimpanzee which on two occasions watched its mother using leaves to clean herself of faeces; the young chimpanzee then did exactly the same, wiping her bottom with leaves even though it was clean (van Lawick-Goodall 1970). The second report also comes from Gombe where the chimpanzees were for a long time routinely fed bananas from boxes; they tried to prize open the lids of the boxes with sticks from which they had stripped the leaves (Fig. 7.8). One female which had not previously seen the boxes observed the others at work from a distance, and then at the first attempt applied a stick to a box (van Lawick-Goodall 1970).

7.8 Chimpanzee using a stick so as to prize open the lid of a box containing bananas. From a photograph in van Lawick-Goodall (1970).

The evidence reviewed here establishes that man is not alone in possessing cultural traditions. Indeed monkeys and apes are not the only animals that transmit such traditions. It was mentioned in Chapter 4 that some songbirds learn the flourishes in their songs by hearing the songs of other birds, and in different areas birds of the same species may sing slightly different songs (Nottebohm 1972) (see Chapter 8). These dialects are the product of local tradition.

For the present, however, let us confine our interest to traditions passed on by visual observation in birds and non-primate mammals. There are already in the literature some examples of such traditions (Bonner 1980). Some concern the variation in diet between groups of mammals other than primates (Galef 1976). Some clans of rat (*Rattus norvegicus*) that live on the River Po dive to the bottom to collect bivalve molluscs, whereas others do not, even though the molluscs are available (Gandolfi and Parisi 1973). In the Ngorongoro Crater on Serengeti different clans of hyenas differ in whether they prey more on wildebeest or on zebra, and their preferences cannot be explained in terms of the relative abundance of these animals (Kruuk 1972). Preferences such as these are presumably to be explained in the same way as the similar preferences documented for primates. The young will tend at first to eat near adults, and are thus likely to pick the same food; this has been demonstrated, for instance, for rat pups (Galef 1976). They may also learn whether the food is palatable by observing the reactions of adults; the previous section showed that observational learning of this sort is not confined to primates.

On the other hand it is much harder to find examples of cultural traditions that are passed on by imitation. Oyster-catchers (*Haematopus ostralogus*) have two methods of opening edible mussels: either they hammer them open or they prize them open with their bills. It has been reported that the birds in different areas specialize in one or the other method, but do not use both; and that the young develop the technique practised in their area (Norton-Griffiths 1967). Hammering is the best method in areas where the mussels are exposed at low tide and are tightly shut, and stabbing works best in other areas where the mussels are always covered with water and less tightly closed. Experiments are needed to find out whether young birds learn of their own accord which method is best suited to the local conditions or whether they must observe others at work. Another case which requires investigation is the use of stones by sea otters in cracking shellfish; we do not know whether the pups learn to do this by watching their mothers, or whether they are able to learn this technique without having seen it used (Beck 1980). But we may reasonably conclude that, even if there are animals other than primates that transmit traditions by imitation, none rivals the chimpanzee in the variety of actions which are acquired in this way.

TEACHING

Monkeys and apes can learn from each other; but do they teach? The question is both intriguing and important. It is not answered simply by pointing to the fact that people speak and apes do not, because teaching can be practised by silent demonstration without a word being spoken.

To say that a mother teaches an infant is not simply to say that the infant learns by observing and imitating the mother. It carries the implication that the mother plays an active role and means or intends her infant to learn. But the intentions of animals are difficult to assess, because we cannot ask the individuals to give an account of them; if one animal hits another I can only point to indirect evidence if I wish to maintain that the blow was not accidental but deliberately aimed. There are several questions we might ask when considering the role played by the mother. Does she alter her normal routine, and go out of her way to provide opportunities for her infant to learn? Does she encourage her infant? Does she demonstrate the relevant actions, all the while paying attention to her infant's progress as it copies them? Does she actually take her infant's hand and physically guide her infant's actions? In principle these questions could be answered. Consider the last one: as we shall see in Chapter 8, chimpanzees have been taught to make some of the gestures of Ameslan, a sign language used by the deaf and dumb. The most effective method for teaching has proved to be to take the ape's arms and hands and physically mould them into the required postures (Fouts 1972). It would not be difficult to find out whether a chimpanzee would attempt to teach another by the same method, however ineffectively. That is not to say that the chimpanzee would be likely to do so; only that it is practical to investigate whether a chimpanzee can play an active role in teaching.

In fact we have little evidence that any animal does teach. In almost all instances there is a more parsimonious description of what the animal is doing. Take the way in which young lions learn to hunt: certainly they go out hunting with their mothers and may well benefit from the practice they get on these expeditions (Schenkel 1966); but that does not demonstrate that the purpose of the exercise must have been to train the young. Just because the mother creates an opportunity to hunt we are not forced to conclude that she does so for their sakes. Furthermore there is no indication that she demonstrates the relevent strategies and techniques. The simplest statement is just that the mother allows her infants to come out with her on a hunt.

A similar analysis can be made of most of the cases where teaching is claimed (Barnett 1968). Some monkey mothers hit and even bite their infants when they wean them (Rosenblum and Kaufman 1967); but although this does indeed deter the infants we need suppose only that the mother punishes them so as to ward them off at the time. The leader of a Japanese monkey group may prevent the members of the troop from picking up novel foods such as wheat (Frisch 1968); female Japanese monkeys have been seen pulling their offspring away from novel objects of which they are themselves afraid (Menzel 1965); and gorilla mothers sometimes take food out of the mouths of their young (Schaller 1963). But in all cases the action may be regarded as that of protecting rather than teaching.

There are cases where the mother may reasonably be said to encourage her infant. In one study a gorilla in a zoo was watched as she reared her infant (Whiten, unpublished manuscript). She supported its head with her hand as it tried to crawl at 6 weeks. A week or two later she was seen repeatedly to back away from her infant and then to entice it to her by bending her head down and facing it. Rhesus monkey mothers in captivity have been seen playing with their infants in the same way (Hinde *et al.* 1964). The gorilla also placed her infant against the bars of the cage around the time it was ready to climb, and when the infant fell off a platform she repeatedly placed it up again. Here we have a mother monitoring the success of her infant as it learns to walk and climb, and helping it in its efforts. Though she did not show her infant how it should be done she encouraged its progress.

Even if we were to accept that apes could teach we must admit that they rarely do so. Yet education of some form is universal in human cultures, and without it children would not grow up competent in the ways of the adult society. Instruction is given either by word of mouth or by demonstration. Even before language had been invented it would have been possible to teach the manufacture of simple stone tools by demonstrating the process (Washburn 1969).

But although language may not be essential it has revolutionized teaching by providing a new means of instruction. Knowledge can be formulated in words and skills in verbal instructions, and these can then be transmitted to the child. By using the symbols of language the teacher can refer to events in the past or happenings elsewhere in the world. With the invention of writing the traditional wisdom can be passed on to the child without the teacher being present. In this way the accumulation of knowledge is very greatly facilitated.

We are now in a position to see more clearly the relative abilities and achievements of man and the apes. They share with us the ability to transmit traditions across the generations. But there is also, as Tylor (1881) observed, a 'great mental gap between us and animals'. The result has been that 'upon this lower framework of animal life is raised the wondrous edifice of human language, science, art and law' (Tylor 1881). It is language which accounts for the mental gap; and it is to language that we should attribute our science, art and law.

8 Language

'The one great barrier between brute and man is language . . . Language is our Rubicon, and no brute will dare cross it' (Miller 1871). One hundred years later chimpanzees are having a brave try. The achievements of three pioneering animals, Washoe, Sarah and Lana, are enough to at least unsettle the complacent. Washoe makes comments with gestures of the hand, Sarah by writing with plastic symbols, and Lana by typing on a keyboard.

It is perhaps understandable that a rearguard action should be mounted to ensure that chimpanzees never succeed in crossing the Rubicon. This is easily done, by redefining language each time they threaten to be in sight of mastering it. There will always be some aspect of human language that is beyond the competence of a chimpanzee, if only for want of intelligence. Apes are not children; so it should not prove too difficult to find new criteria by which to set man apart.

Human language is not the only language of which we could conceive. It might, therefore, be more profitable if we set out the minimum requirements that a system of communication must meet if it is to be a language, without requiring that it share all the features of human language. Hockett and Altmann (1968) have drawn up a list of the characteristics of all known systems of communication. They call these characteristics 'design features', and they list 16 of them, all of which apply to human language. They include such features as the use of sounds for communication, and the combination of elements such as phonemes to make meaningful units.

Of these features one is crucial. There is nobody who would accept as a language a system of communication which could not be used to communicate about the outside world. A language must have symbols which can be used as names to refer to things and events; in human language these symbols are nouns and verbs. When very young children have reached the stage where they can identify items by naming them, we accept that they have learnt a language, if a very limited one (Brown 1973). The

most important limitation is that until words are combined there is no means of unambiguously distinguishing
between different states of the world. Let us take a simple
example: a dog is seen to bite a cat. To describe this
situation it is not enough to know the names for dog and
cat and the word for biting; some rule is also needed which
allows us to state whether the cat is biting the dog or the
dog is biting the cat (Brown 1970). In some languages case
grammar is used to distinguish subject and object, and in
others, as in English, the same distinction is marked by
word order. Though human languages have many other
subtleties their essential characteristic is the possession of
symbols with which the world may be described. Human
languages carry out this function in a sophisticated way,
by means of grammatical rules which allow refined and
detailed descriptions to be made.

We can best appreciate this point if language is
contrasted with the systems of communication used by
non-human primates and other animals in their natural
habitat. By recognizing the limitations of their signals we
will appreciate how revolutionary was the invention of
language.

COMMUNICATION IN ANIMALS

In any society of animals individuals are better able to
behave appropriately towards each other if they have
some means of knowing what state their fellows are in and
what they are likely to do. The moods and intentions of
others may be gauged by interpreting outward signs
(Andrew 1972). When a monkey is alarmed its hair stands
on end; and other monkeys can use this external sign as
evidence of its internal state. When a dog or a monkey is
about to bite it opens its mouth; thus other animals can tell
what it is going to do by watching for the signs that it is
preparing to do so. In general it benefits each individual
that others should be aware of its state, because in this way
fights will be avoided, group movements will be co-
ordinated, and mating will occur when the female is most
receptive.

All social animals, invertebrate and vertebrate, have
some system of signals to regulate social interactions
(Wilson 1975). These range from odour trails to calls to
facial expressions; and in vertebrates each species uses
between 10 and 37 such signals (Moynihan 1970). For our
purposes it is convenient to illustrate the principle of

animal communication by referring to examples from mammals. We will confine our interest to signals received by the distance receptors of smell, sight and hearing, because these can convey information about what is to come.

What can animals communicate? First, they can reveal their presence. Both smells and sounds can be located, even if less accurately than sights. On hearing a call an animal knows roughly where the caller is, even if the caller cannot be seen because it is dark or because there are obstacles such as trees in the way. On detecting a scent mark an animal learns that another animal has been there, and it might estimate roughly when this was, by the freshness of the mark.

Signals may also carry information about the identity of the sender. The smells left by different individuals are clearly not the same. An experiment has been conducted with lemurs (*Lemur fulvus*) in which the animal is allowed to sniff at a scent mark of one individual until its interest wanes; if it is now presented with the mark of another individual it sniffs it with renewed interest, indicating that it can tell the difference between the two marks (Harrington 1976). Using the same technique it can be demonstrated that lemurs can tell males from females, even when the female is not in oestrus (Harrington 1977). The calls made by different individuals also have their distinctive characteristics. One example will suffice to demonstrate that individuals may be recognized by their calls alone. Tape recordings of the cries of infants in distress were played to adult female vervet monkeys. These monkeys showed more concern when they heard the calls of their own infants rather than the calls of the infants belonging to other mothers (Cheney and Seyfarth 1980).

Both scent marks and calls may therefore convey information not only about the location of another individual but also about the sex and even the identity of the animal. The receiver can then take the appropriate action. In those species which defend territories an intruder is warned by the scent mark of the owner that it is on the home ground of another individual. A laboratory experiment illustrates this neatly (Charles-Dominique 1974b). Individual dwarf bushbabies (*Galago demidovii*) were allowed to explore an empty compartment next to the one they usually occupied, and they readily did so. But if this compartment had already been marked by another bushbaby, they showed great hesitation in entering; this hesitation was most obvious in the males when they smelt the scent of another male. Calls can serve a similar purpose: witness the howl of the wolf and the roar of the lion (Mech 1970; Schaller 1972). The hearer knows that other animals are present, and can take avoiding action if they are strangers. Several primates also have calls that carry far; the howler monkey howls, and the gibbon hoots (Marler 1978).

There are also situations where, on learning of the presence of another animal or group of animals, it is appropriate to seek them out. If baboons are feeding on grasses out of sight of other members of the group they sometimes grunt, and in this way inform others of where they are and ensure that they keep in contact (Andrew 1963). When an infant monkey or ape is lost it cries to summon its mother. Rhesus monkey infants, for instance, give a 'whoo' call which informs their mother of their plight and tells her where to look (Hinde and Spencer-Booth 1971). Chimpanzee infants produce a whimper like a 'hoo', and gorilla infants whine (Marler 1976b).

Thus signals serve to locate and identify an individual; but they also provide information about the state of the sender, as with the infant's cry which conveys distress. There are three states about which it is useful for animals to have information: sexual receptivity, the emotional excitement of fear or aggression, and moods such as the high spirits of play. Females typically advertise the fact that they are in oestrus by means of scent. Dogs can tell that a bitch is on heat by sniffing her urine, and prosimians scent mark more actively during courtship (Doyle 1974; Graf and Meyer-Holzapfel 1974). Male rhesus monkeys in the laboratory will work harder to gain access to females if the females are in oestrus, but will not do so if their nostrils are blocked or the olfactory nerve is cut (Michael and Keverne 1968). Indeed, even in women there is an increase in volatile fatty acids in the vagina at the middle of the menstrual cycle (Michael et al. 1974); smell may play a more important role in human sexual relations than we have generally supposed (Comfort 1971).

Whereas each scent gland can produce only one type of chemical marker both the voice and the face are capable of expressing a wide range of emotional states. Like birds and other mammals primates produce different sounds when alarmed, submissive or aggressive (Andrew 1962). Though in many species these calls are discrete, in some they grade into each other, so that not only is the intensity of the state conveyed, but also the degree to which the caller is in conflict between different states. This occurs in some, but not all, monkeys and apes (Marler 1976b). It can be best illustrated with reference to the rhesus monkey. The sound spectrographs in Fig. 8.1 show the frequencies which can be recorded in particular calls such as the roar, the bark and the scream; those on the upper row are the more aggressive and those on the lower row the more defensive (Rowell 1962). A very confident monkey threatens by roaring, a less confident one by use of the jerky sounds of the 'pant-threat'; a defensive animal may produce a geckering screech, whereas it screams if it is

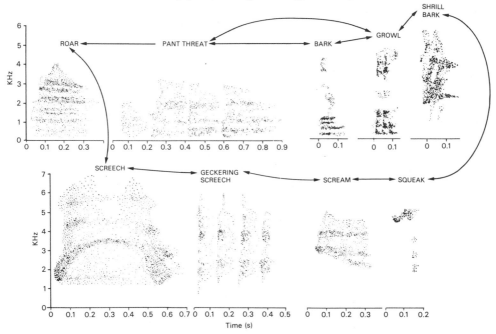

8.1 Sound spectrographs showing a graded series of rhesus monkey calls. After Rowell (1962).

losing. The transitions from sound to sound reflect the confidence of the animal. Chimpanzees and gorillas have a repertoire of 13 to 15 sounds, but can enrich the information they convey by use of subtle gradations (Table 8.1, see page 196).

When animals are in close contact both their gross and fine movements provide a rich source of information about their emotional state and likely intentions. The expressions of the face are especially informative. In those primates which are active during the daytime the facial musculature is particularly well differentiated, allowing a wide range of expressive movements (Chevalier-Skolnikoff 1973). Indeed, the facial muscles of the chimpanzee differ from our own in only one important respect: the chimpanzee lacks the risorius muscle which

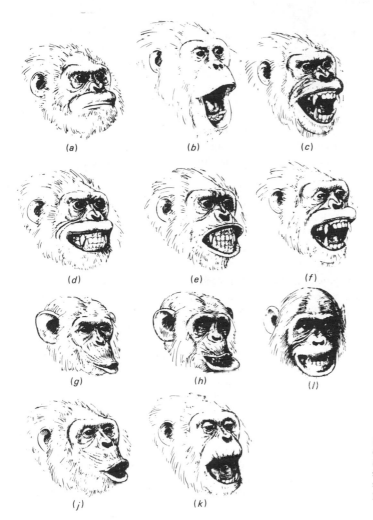

8.2 Chimpanzee facial
expressions. Expressions *a*, *b*,
c indicate aggression, *d*, *e*, *f*
submission, *g*, *h*, *i* frustration,
sadness, *j* excitement and *k*
playfulness. From Chevalier-
Skolnikoff (1973).

pulls the mouth at the corners (Huber 1931). The facial
expressions of monkeys and apes can convey subtle detail
by gradations in intensity. Fig. 8.2 portrays some of the
facial expressions seen in the chimpanzee, and the general
similarity between some of these can be readily
appreciated. Take submissive expressions as shown in the
second row: each of these has slightly different conno-
tations reflecting the degree to which the animal is
defensive or trying to reassure (van Hooff 1972). The basic
expressions of threat, submission and play are similar to
those seen in other social mammals such as dogs and lions
(Fox 1971; Schaller 1972).

One common description will apply to all the examples
of communication reviewed. In all cases the information
which is communicated provides knowledge about the

Table 8.1 The calls of chimpanzees*

Vocalization	Circumstances
1. Pant-hoot	Hearing distant group; rejoining group; meat eating in nest at night; general arousal
2. Pant-grunt	Subordinate approaching or being approached by dominant
3. Laughter	Playing, especially being tickled
4. Squeak	Being threatened, submission, close to dominant
5. Scream	Fleeing attack, submission, when lost, while attacking dominant; copulating female
6. Whimper	Begging, infant–parent separation, strange sound or object
7. Bark	Vigorous threat
8. Waa bark	Threat to other, often dominant, at distance
9. Rough grunt	Approaching and eating preferred food
10. Pant	Copulating male, grooming, meeting another as prelude to kissing, etc.
11. Grunt	Feeding, mild general arousal, social excitement
12. Cough	Mild, confident threat to subordinate chimpanzee, baboon
13. Wraa	Detection of human or other predator, also dead chimpanzee; may be threat component

* Adapted from Marler (1976b).

sender: its identity, location, state and probable intentions. But can animals communicate about the outside world? People talk about the world by using the symbols of language. Is there any equivalent system by which animals too can describe their world?

There are a few instances where it is tempting to say that animals are indeed referring to things in the world outside them. Although the facts were disputed for some time, it seems certain that, as von Frisch (1950) first claimed, honeybees returning to the hive from a source of nectar can communicate to other bees the direction and distance of the food source (Gould 1976). This they do by engaging in the 'waggle dance' in which they run through a figure of eight as illustrated in Fig. 8.3. The further the distance of the food the slower the bee dances, the less quickly it waggles its abdomen, and the lower the frequency of the bursts of sound that it produces (von Frisch 1967). The distance, therefore, is signalled by the animation with which the bee dances. If the dance takes place on a horizontal surface the direction of the food source is indicated by the straight part of the run which is directed towards the food (Fig. 8.3*a*). But if the dance is performed on a vertical surface the code is more subtle. The position of the sun is given by the line which runs vertically with respect to gravity; the angle between the position of the sun and the location of the food source is

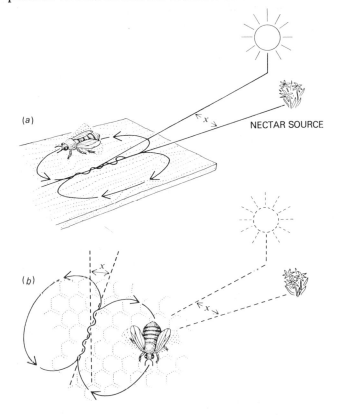

NECTAR SOURCE

8.3 Dance of honeybees. *a*, the waggle dance as performed on a horizontal surface: the orientation of the straight run indicates the direction in which nectar is to be found; *b*, the dance as performed on a vertical surface. The angle between vertical and the orientation of the straight run indicates the angle between the sun and the source of nectar. After Alcock (1979).

translated into the angle as measured from that vertical line (Fig. 8.3*b*). If, let us say, the bee orients its straight run 5° reading in a clockwise direction, the followers will search for food at a spot 5° to the right of the position of the sun. In this case the code is an arbitrary one, since the bee is not actually pointing towards the source. Does the bee's dance constitute a language? The bees certainly transmit information about the world, but they do not learn the basic code, and do not say anything else with it. For our purposes it is not essential that we decide whether to call the dance a language or not; it is enough just to note that the bee can indeed refer to the outside world.

The other cases in which animals appear to communicate directly about their environment all concern alarm calls. There are several reports that a particular species gives different alarm calls according to the predator or danger that threatens; this has been claimed for some birds and also for one or two mammals such as the ground squirrel (*Spermophilus beecheyi*) (Seyfarth *et al.* 1980). But there is only one such case in which experiments have been carried out to document fully the claim that the calls do indeed carry specific meanings. Adult vervet monkeys (*Cercopithecus aethiops*) give a different alarm call depending on which of three predators they have sighted—a python (*Python sebae*), a martial eagle (*Polemaetus bellicosus*) or a leopard (*Panthera pardus*) (Struhsaker 1967; Marler 1977). A simple experiment has shown that when they hear one of the calls the monkeys know what action it is appropriate to take (Seyfarth *et al.* 1980). If tape recordings of each of the calls are played to them the adults when on the ground are likely to respond to a 'snake' call by looking down, to an 'eagle' call by looking up, and to a 'leopard' call by running into the trees.

It might be said that the calls could simply reflect differences in the intensity of fear felt by the monkeys when in the presence of the different predators. In other words the monkeys might be communicating about their own emotional states rather than about the external stimuli to which they react. But it is not likely that in this case the monkeys are communicating degree of alarm, since all three predators are known to be a danger to vervet monkeys. A more plausible suggestion is that the calls are associated not with degree of emotion but with different emotional states; the monkeys may respond to eagles with surprise and to snakes with an aggressive mobbing call. However, we cannot be sure exactly what information the calls convey, nor how they came to carry their particular meanings.

There are three laboratory experiments which address the issue of whether animals can communicate about the world. In one, rhesus monkeys were studied two at a time (Miller 1967). Each monkey was first trained to press one lever to obtain food when one signal was presented, and to press another lever to avoid electric shock on seeing another signal. The situation was then changed, so that the first monkey could see the signals but had no levers to press, whereas the second monkey had the levers but could not see the signals. However, the second monkey was allowed to see the face of the first on a television screen. If it could correctly judge what signal was being shown from the reactions of the first, it could press the relevant lever and so obtain food and avoid shocks on both their behalfs.

In fact monkeys proved able to do this. But we should not, perhaps, be surprised, as these results probably indicate only that the observer can distinguish fear and confident expectation on the faces of their companions. In other words the communication is not directly about the state of the world, but rather the internal emotional state of the animal.

A formally similar experiment has been set up with dolphins (Bastian 1967). Two dolphins, a male and a female, were taught to press a paddle on the left for food if shown a steady light, and a paddle on the right for food if presented with an intermittent light. Conditions were then altered so that the dolphins were in separate compartments, able to hear but not to see each other. Only the female was shown the lights; but she was required to wait before pressing the appropriate paddle, until the male had been given the chance to press one of the paddles in its compartment. It was found that so long as the male could hear the female he could continue to make the correct choices. In this experiment, therefore, it is not the emotional state of one animal that is transmitted, but rather the response that it was correct to make. But how did the male dolphin know which paddle to press? Certainly he needed to hear the female, because he could no longer succeed if a soundproof shield was interposed between their two tanks. It is also true that the trains of acoustic pulses that the female emitted were shorter and slightly delayed when the steady light came on, compared with the pulses she produced when the intermittent light appeared. The male could, perhaps, have made use of this difference. But it is quite as likely that he based his choice on the sounds made by the female as she prepared to press her paddles; she swam on a very different path when waiting before approaching the left paddle compared with the right. Further experiments must be done if we are to be convinced that the dolphin can communicate the location of food with acoustical signals.

Previous chapters have repeatedly pointed to the superior abilities of the chimpanzee. Is there any hint that chimpanzees naturally possess a system of communication that enables them to pass messages about the outside world? Menzel (1974, 1979) set up tests for six chimpanzees kept in a 1-acre field. He would take one of the chimpanzees out with him while he hid food somewhere in the field, and then allowed this animal to go out in search of the food with the rest of the group. It turned out that the group made off in the direction of the food and found it very quickly, even though the chimpanzee that had previously been shown the location did not necessarily lead the procession. If one chimpanzee was shown one pile of food and another was shown a second, the group of chimpanzees would tend to go to the better of the two sources of food, where there was more food or more desirable food, fruit rather than vegetables. If objects were hidden of which they were frightened, such as a snake, the group approached cautiously and with evident signs of fear.

From this it is evident that chimpanzees can deduce facts about the world from the behaviour of an informed companion. If one chimpanzee sets out confidently in one direction they can estimate the probable location of food. If the chimpanzee is keen they assume that the food is plentiful or desirable; if it is hesitant they assume that there are grounds for caution. Indeed, chimpanzees may be able to glean a great variety of information about the world by studying the actions of others (Menzel and Johnson 1976). Both the actions and the emotional state of one individual give clues as to external conditions for which those particular actions and emotions are appropriate. It requires only intelligence to make these deductions. People continually make similar inferences, using both past history and the present context to explain the actions of their fellows. But we might reasonably distinguish a direct communication from indirect inferences that may be drawn. While these chimpanzees reach conclusions about the world from their observations of the behaviour of other chimpanzees, they do not state outright that such and such is the case.

This is not to claim that chimpanzees could not be taught to indicate directly the location of food. If a person points in the direction of the hidden food a chimpanzee can use this hint and find it (Menzel 1979). In captivity chimpanzees have been reported to be able to draw attention to objects by pointing to them (Terrace 1979b; Woodruff and Premack 1979). It might well prove possible to teach a chimpanzee to point out to its fellows where food has been hidden, given that it was allowed to share the food when they returned with it. It is, perhaps, surprising that in their natural lives chimpanzees have not hit on this relatively simple means of conveying a message.

Our review only confirms what mankind has long suspected, that with only one or two possible exceptions animals lack the means for communicating directly about the outside world. Even in the case of these exceptions we may acknowledge that the animals make reference to things while still refusing to accept that they possess a language. The bees can only specify the location of food and the vervet monkeys can only notify others of the presence of a particular predator. They may be said to use names which refer to location or animals, but they have no grammar with which to describe the state of the world in more detail. No animal uses in nature a system of communication that is equivalent to human language. Secure in this knowledge we have, until recently, been complacent, supposing that an animal that lacked a language in the wild could not be taught one in captivity. We are now much less confident that this is so.

The issue will be clarified if, at the outset, we remind ourselves of two simple points. First, we should remember that speech is only one form of language; to take the most obvious example, language can be written as well as spoken. An ape could have the capacity for language without ever being able to master speech. Secondly, we should remember that a language user has not only to be able to produce symbols so as to make a statement; he also has to be able to appreciate the meaning of the symbols when used by others. It is understandable that people are intrigued by the possibility of teaching an ape to speak, but if we are to investigate the language capacities of apes it is quite as crucial that we discover whether they can learn to comprehend speech (Lenneberg 1971). If we were faced with a mute child who nonetheless understood speech, we would have no hesitation in attributing to the child the capacity for language.

Comprehension

There are three basic abilities that must be present if speech is to be understood: the sounds of speech must be recognized as the same even when spoken by different people; these sounds must then be classified or categorized; and finally they must be associated with the things to which they refer. Of these abilities the first and second have already been discussed in Chapter 2. No conclusive evidence could be found indicating any important differences between the way in which monkeys and people recognized and classified the speech sounds they heard.

Even if speech is correctly perceived that is no guarantee that it is also understood. To appreciate the meaning of, let us say, a simple noun the listener must be able to form an association between the sound of the word and the object to which it refers, that is its referent. The word 'book' must be recognized as being associated with a book as it is usually seen or felt. In other words names can be understood only if their links with objects can be appreciated. Geschwind (1967) emphasized the fact that in speech naming requires the ability to associate sounds and sights, and raised the question of whether this ability is one that other primates possess. Chapter 2 has already mentioned that there have been investigations into the ability of macaques and great apes to form associations between the feel of an object and its appearance to the eye. We found evidence that they could indeed recognize an object as being the same when felt or seen.

But it is an independent question whether they can learn to connect the sounds they hear with the things they see. There is a genuine correspondence between the feel and the look of an object; but a name is linked with an object in an arbitrary fashion, so that usually the sound of the word gives no clue as to the appearance of the thing named.

How might we test an animal to see if it could learn the arbitrary associations between sounds and sights that are required for naming? In one experiment rhesus monkeys were taught to press a green panel on hearing a hissing noise and a red panel on hearing a tone (Dewson and Burlingame 1975). The monkeys learnt to do this; but it is not clear that this is an adequate demonstration. The monkeys need learn only that in the presence of A they should do X; to put it another way, the sounds A and B simply provide the conditions which determine the correct choice. But a name is more than a condition that dictates what should be done; a name evokes its referent.

The most direct way to settle the issue would be to establish whether animals that have been exposed to human speech can learn the meanings of spoken words. Clearly if they can do this they must be able to form the relevant associations between sounds and sights. There has been one such experiment on a dog; the other observations all refer to great apes. The dog was an Alsatian called Fellow that had received no specific training in the interpretation of speech, although its master had talked to it from birth (Warden and Warner 1928). It obeyed many different commands even when it could hear but not see its master; but, although the commands were often detailed, no tests were carried out to see how many of the words in the command were genuinely understood. The dog's comprehension of the names of objects was investigated by commanding it to pick out one of three objects; on any occasion three out of a collection of five objects were presented. Had the dog responded at random it would have chosen correctly on 33 per cent of the tests it was given; in fact it did so on 53 per cent of the tests, suggesting some rudimentary ability to understand the meanings of simple words. It might be that with specific training dogs could achieve a greater degree of comprehension than was demonstrated in Fellow.

Comprehension of speech has also been studied in two chimpanzees and one gorilla. Gua, a chimpanzee, was exposed to speech for the 9 months during which she was reared in their home by the Kelloggs (Kellogg and Kellogg 1933). They claim that she learnt to understand 95 words and phrases, which compares favourably with the 107 that were understood at the time by their son Donald, who was 3 months older. The list of words she was thought to understand included the names of people, objects and actions; and she appeared to know their meaning irrespective of which person spoke to her or the intonation used. As with Fellow we must not suppose that she grasped the meaning of all the words in a phrase, but the same may also have been true of Donald. She was given only one formal test: she was shown a card with four pictures on it, and was able to point to the picture of the dog or shoe when told to do so.

Another chimpanzee, called Ally, was also reared in a human household and he showed some understanding of speech. Again only one formal experiment was devised (Fouts et al. 1976). In this ten names of objects were chosen which he understood, and he was then taught the gestures that correspond to these words in Ameslan, the American Sign Language devised for use by the deaf. The experimenter said the word, and then demonstrated the appropriate gesture and helped Ally to make it. Although the objects were not present when he was taught the gestures Ally was then able to give the correct gestures when shown each of the objects. He could not have done this had he not genuinely understood to which of the objects the spoken names referred.

The only extensive investigation of the ability of apes to make sense of speech is that carried out on a gorilla called

Koko (Patterson 1978). This animal was trained for several years in the use of the sign language Ameslan; but at the same time her tutors deliberately spoke in her presence and also spoke to her. Her progress was assessed by giving her a standard test used by psychologists for measuring speech comprehension in children. The test consists of 40 large cards on each of which there are four or five drawings; speech comprehension is tested by requiring that one picture of the five be selected in response to a particular word or phrase. The test has four levels of difficulty, and there are 10 cards at each level. The first level tests understanding of single words, the second of two words, such as 'happy lady', the third of three words, for example, 'happy lady sleeping', and the fourth of four words, as in 'happy little girl jumping'. At the first level only one isolated word need be understood to choose correctly, but at the higher levels each of the words in the phrase must be grasped. Koko's abilities were assessed by testing her on all levels, and on two-, three- and four-word phrases she chose the correct picture more frequently than she could have done had she simply been guessing.

Here, then, is a demonstration that an ape can understand all four words in a phrase. But to do this there was no need for Koko to pay any attention to the order of the words, since the meaning of the adjectival phrase would be the same whatever the order. It is crucial that apes now be tested to see if they can also learn grammatical rules, such as those governing word order. If Koko were asked to pick out a picture of a cat biting a dog would she be as likely to choose the one of a dog biting a cat?

We can conclude that apes, and perhaps dogs, are able to form the associations between sounds and sights that are required for understanding the referents of words. When Ally heard a word it appears to have reminded him of the object as seen. In Koko this ability has been shown to extend to the understanding of simple adjectival phrases. Apes possess the elementary capacities for making sense of the individual symbols of speech.

Production

But apes do not speak. Why not? Could they do so if we acted as speech therapists? There have been two serious attempts to teach an ape to pronounce simple words, and both gave very little return for the effort expended. In 1916 Furness reported that after several years of training he had only succeeded in teaching an orang-utan to produce a very poor approximation to the words 'papa' and 'cup', both of which include the plosive sound [p] (Hewes 1977). A prolonged attempt to train the chimpanzee Viki gave similarly meagre returns: she could be persuaded only to enunciate, very badly, the words 'mama', 'papa', 'cup' and 'up', of which the last three are similar in including plosives (Hayes and Nissen 1971).

There are several reasons why apes might be so handicapped. Their vocal tract might be incapable of producing many of the sounds of speech, they might be unable to produce sounds at will, or they might have difficulty in imitating the sounds they hear. Let us consider each of these possibilities in turn.

There are a variety of respects in which the human vocal tract differs from the tract in other primates; we need not list them here as they have been fully described elsewhere (Kelemen 1948; Negus 1949; Jordan 1971a). Of these differences the crucial one is in the position of the back of the tongue with respect to the vocal tract (Lieberman 1975). The issue can best be explained by referring to Fig. 8.4, which illustrates the vocal tracts of man and chimpanzee, and labels the most important structures. The larynx, or voice box, produces a source of sound which is then modified by its passage through two cavities, the pharynx and mouth, both of which can be altered in shape so as to articulate different sounds; the rear wall of the pharyngeal cavity for the human adult is labelled in the diagram. In people the area of the pharynx can be altered by movement of the tongue because, as shown in the diagram, the back of the tongue forms the front wall of the pharyngeal cavity. But in chimpanzees, and also in the human foetus, the larynx is positioned much higher in the vocal tract, and the tongue is not shaped so as to form the

8.4 Head and neck of adult human (*a*) and adult chimpanzee (*b*). The rear wall of the pharynx is labelled in the diagram of the human adult. After Lieberman (1975).

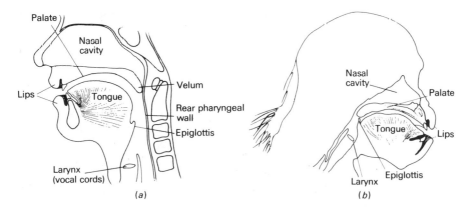

(a)   (b)

front wall of the air passage above the larynx. The consequence is that the shape of the pharynx cannot be readily modified by the movements of the tongue.

There is, therefore, a limitation on the number of different sounds that chimpanzees can produce: it has been calculated that the vocal tracts of the chimpanzee and human baby are probably incapable of articulating the human vowel sounds [i], [a] and [u] (Lieberman 1975). This is not to say that chimpanzees can produce no vowel sounds; chimpanzee sounds have been recorded bearing at least some resemblance to the five vowels (Jordan 1971b). The vocal tracts of babies and chimpanzees can, by various strategies, produce approximations of related vowel sounds (Lieberman 1975). If so, although the shape of the vocal tract might limit the chimpanzee repertoire, there is no reason why the animal should not produce some of the elementary sounds of speech. Its failure to do so at all cannot be blamed on the construction of its vocal tract.

Could it be that the chimpanzee has no voluntary control over the sounds that it makes? The issue can be settled. We attempt to teach an ape or monkey to produce calls from its repertoire, but to do so only when we give the signal. But there is a catch. If we give the animal food when it calls, it will soon learn that when the signal is given food is in the offing, and it might call not because it knows that it must call to get food, but because it is excited in expectation of the food. We might try to surmount this problem by training the animal to call if given one signal, and not to call if an alternative signal is given (Yamaguchi and Myers 1972; Sutton et al. 1973). But, even if we succeeded in teaching this to the animal, the critic could argue that the animal expects food in the one situation and not in the other; and that the call reflects the animal's state of anticipation, rather than knowledge of the results it can achieve by calling. What we need, therefore, are conditions where to achieve the same end the animal must produce one call when given one signal and a different call when given another.

Three experiments have been carried out which satisfy these conditions; one on rhesus monkeys, one on a chimpanzee, and one on an orang-utan. The monkeys were required to produce a 'coo' when a red light came on, and a 'bark' when a green one came on (Sutton 1979). If they called correctly they won themselves food. The monkeys learnt to do this, thus demonstrating that they had some voluntary control over their calls. Since in both cases they were working for the same prize, food, their production of the different calls as appropriate indicates their ability to produce them at will.

A chimpanzee has been trained to produce a bark to persuade a human companion to play (Randolph and Brooks 1967). To see if it was barking just because it was in a playful mood, the chimpanzee was also trained to initiate play by touching its human companion. If the person stood with her back to the chimpanzee only a bark would succeed in getting her to play; if she stood facing the chimpanzee the animal was required to touch her hand to achieve the same end. In the latter condition the chimpanzee barked less than in the former, which suggests that it appreciated that barks were effective in the one situation but not in the other.

In the final experiment an orang-utan was patiently trained to produce a 'kuh' noise to obtain a drink, a 'fuh' noise for food and a 'puh' noise to initiate contact (Laidler 1978). These sounds were already in the ape's repertoire, and each sound was arbitrarily associated with a particular situation. It is not clear whether the animal appreciated that the call had been assigned a meaning, or whether it simply learnt by rote that if it was to get what it wanted it would have to make the appropriate noise. What is clear is that the animal had some control over the sounds it made, although the difficulty experienced in training the monkeys and apes suggests that the degree of voluntary control may be limited.

It seems that apes can understand some speech sounds and that they can call at will. But if they are to learn to speak in the same way as children they require one further ability. They must be able to modify the sounds they make according to the sounds they hear, that is to imitate sounds. Babies babble and as they grow up they come to incorporate in their repertoire the sounds they hear around them (Lenneberg 1967). But chimpanzees brought up in homes remain relatively silent, and pick up none of the speech sounds made by their foster parents (Kellogg 1968). They do not parrot the speech they hear although they ape the actions they observe.

Yet parrots do and so do mynah birds. And considering the fact that their vocal tracts are quite unlike ours it is all the more remarkable that these birds are such accomplished mimics (Nottebohm 1976). The accuracy of their imitations can be appreciated by looking at the two spectrographs in Fig. 8.5: these show the sounds made by a parrot (*Amazona amazonica*) and by a person when saying 'praise God'.

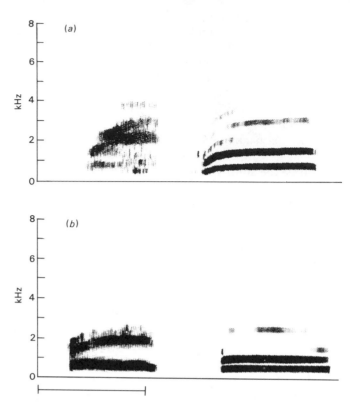

8.5 Sound spectrographs of parrot (*Amazona amazonica*) (*a*) and person (*b*) saying 'praise God'. After Nottebohm (1976). Scale bar, 1 second.

These are not the only birds that can imitate sounds. Roughly half of all species of birds learn parts of their song by listening to the songs of other birds (Nottebohm 1972). However, unlike such talented mimics such as mynah birds and parrots, many birds can only learn to produce a restricted set of sounds; the birds can learn the song of their own but not of other species. That they do indeed learn snatches of their song is easily demonstrated; we may take chaffinches as an example (Thorpe 1961). The spectrograph shown in Fig. 8.6*a* represents the typical song of an adult chaffinch. But if a chaffinch is hand-reared in isolation from other chaffinches it acquires a simpler song which lacks the flourish at the end, as in Fig. 8.6*b*. That this is not due to the deleterious effects of isolation itself we can show by rearing young chaffinches in a group; Fig. 8.6*c* demonstrates that their song is also poorly phrased and lacking in the variety of the normal version. Alternatively we can rear birds in isolation and play them the adult song through a loudspeaker; and under these circumstances they learn the full song. Indeed if we play them tapes which we have doctored so as to re-order the song the young chaffinches will learn that too; in Fig. 8.6*d*

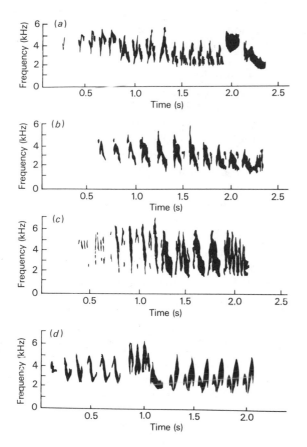

8.6 Sound spectrographs of chaffinch song. *a*, Normal song; *b*, song of bird reared in isolation; *c*, song of bird raised in group with no opportunity to hear adult song; *d*, song of a bird reared in isolation exposed to re-articulated chaffinch song with the ending in the middle. After Thorpe (1961) and Hinde (1974).

the flourish has been placed in the middle, and the spectrograph shows that this has been duly copied by the young birds. Similar experiments have been performed on other songbirds such as the white-crowned sparrow (*Zonatrichia leucophrys*) (Marler 1970). These too will imitate the songs of adults of their species, but not those of other birds such as song sparrows (*Melospiza melodia*). They lack the catholic taste of the parrot.

Why can so many birds copy sounds? The answer is that, though we may speculate, we do not actually know. If we compare the songs of the same species of songbird in different regions we often find variations between regions, the equivalent of dialects. Clearly the dialect of a bird's song provides a clue to its origins, that is to the area in which it learnt its song. This information could be used for several purposes. Reproductive isolation could be achieved by ensuring that birds avoid strangers which can be identified as such by their alien song (Nottebohm 1972). Alternatively outbreeding could be promoted, as in saddlebacks (*Philesturnus carunculatus*), if the birds leave their natal group and then learn the songs of the region into which they move (Jenkins 1978).

There are two sea mammals that also have some ability to copy sounds, the dolphin and the elephant seal. In one experiment two bottlenose dolphins (*Tursiops truncatus*) were played human speech (Lilly *et al.* 1968). They were required to produce the same number of 'clicks' as there were syllables in the words they heard, and they proved to be able to do this with remarkable accuracy. The evidence that elephant seals can imitate sounds is less direct: recordings have been made of the threat calls of adult elephant seals (*Mirounga angustirostris*) off the coasts of California and Mexico, and different dialects have been identified in four different populations (Le Boeuf and Peterson 1969). The calls vary in the rate and duration of the pulses. It seems likely, though it has not been proved, that immigrant males adopt the dialect of the breeding males already in residence.

What of monkeys and apes? There is one report which suggests that Japanese macaques may imitate sounds in the wild (Green 1975). Three groups of monkeys living in separate areas were found to produce slightly different 'coo' sounds when being fed. But it was not proved that the monkeys had copied each other. It could be that in the three groups the monkeys differed in their state of excitement when being fed, and that the variation in calls reflected differences in their motivation.

Laboratory experiments are needed, and it is remarkable that none has been mounted. It is as if everyone simply assumes that monkeys and apes cannot copy sounds. But until further investigations are conducted we will remain ignorant concerning the reasons for the failure of the chimpanzee to parrot sounds. It may be that the chimpanzee can produce a call in its repertoire to match one that it hears, but that it is unable to copy a novel sound not already in its repertoire. But speculation is a poor substitute for research.

We have considered the abilities required for producing speech; but it is still not obvious why the apes should be so handicapped. The limitations of their vocal tract do not preclude speech of any sort, and they have some voluntary control over their calls. They may well be unable to modify the sounds they produce according to novel sounds they hear, but this has to be firmly established.

One further suggestion has already been made in Chapter 4. It was there pointed out that the calls of monkeys and apes are discrete, whereas many birds produce a sequential song. Compare the crude barks and screams of the rhesus monkey shown in Fig. 8.1 with the series of notes and glissandi of the robin (*Erithacus rubecula*) illustrated in Fig. 8.7. Yet to copy human speech it is necessary not only to learn the elements or phonemes but also to learn to order them in the correct sequential pattern. We know that the young chaffinch can learn to incorporate a flourish in the middle of its song, whereas it would normally go at the end (Fig. 8.6*d*); and parrots can learn to sequence phonemes in the correct order, as in 'praise God' (Fig. 8.5). Perhaps in the chimpanzee there is an inadequate development of the brain areas necessary for the production of sequences of sound (see Chapter 4).

One thing is certain: as the next section will show it is not because they have nothing to say that apes fail to speak.

8.7 Three consecutive snatches of robin song. After Brémond (1968) and Jellis (1977).

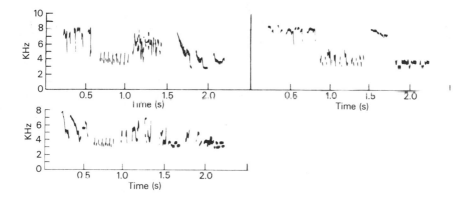

LANGUAGE

The failure of apes to learn speech was for a long time taken as convincing proof that they lack the capacity for language. But although there are people who are mute owing to deafness, they are not barred from using language. The deaf can use a system of spelling by means of their fingers, and there are also various gestural systems such as Ameslan, the American Sign Language. They can also communicate by writing. Clearly we should not conclude that apes have no capacity for language until we have tried to teach them to express themselves in some medium for language other than speech.

This point may seem obvious with hindsight; but it was not widely appreciated when the Gardners (Gardner and Gardner 1969) and Premack (1970) started their pioneering projects to try to teach apes some form of language.

The Gardners set out to train a chimpanzee called Washoe to use and understand Ameslan. In Ameslan words are replaced by gestures of the hand and arm; and meaning is further conveyed by where the gestures are made on the body and in what directions the movements occur (Klima and Bellugi 1979). In Fig. 8.8 Washoe is shown with Mrs Gardner making the sign for 'drink'. Many of the gestures are iconic, that is they bear some resemblance to the things to which they refer: thus in the sign for 'drink' the thumb is brought to the mouth (Fig. 8.8) and in the sign for 'toothbrush' the forefinger is brushed against the teeth. But others are not iconic, such as colour words.

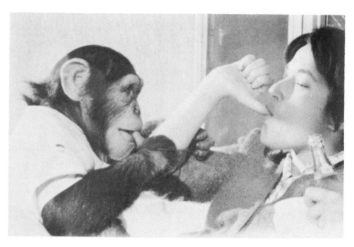

8.8 Chimpanzee Washoe signing 'drink' with B. T. Gardner. From Gardner and Gardner (1971).

Premack's (1970) study is complementary, since he set out to teach a chimpanzee called Sarah to read and write. Just as the Gardners opted for a gestural system rather than for finger spelling, so Premack used shapes which were lexigrams, that is they represented not letters but words. These shapes are like pictograms, except that they in no way resemble the things to which they refer. The shapes were placed on a vertical magnetic board which the chimpanzee could reach so as to answer questions by moving the appropriate shapes (Fig. 8.9). Examples of the shapes are provided in Fig. 8.10.

The use of a magnetic board for assessing reading and writing is clumsy, and it has therefore been modified in two ways. First, Sarah has been given sheets of paper on which questions are asked by use of visual symbols (Premack et al. 1978). Two possible answers are provided on the sheet, and she has to mark the correct one by placing a piece of masking tape on it. A more radical modification of the procedure was made by Rumbaugh

8.9 Chimpanzee Elizabeth obeying the command 'Elizabeth give apple Amy'. From Premack (1976).

(1977) for use with a chimpanzee called Lana. The chimpanzee faces a keyboard and gives answers and makes requests by pressing the keys. Lexigrams can be projected on to the keys and on to panels above, and the chimpanzee is required to press the keys with the appropriate designs in answer to questions posed on the panels (Fig. 8.11). The lexigrams were chosen arbitrarily (Fig. 8.12), and the correct syntactical use of them is defined according to the rules of 'Yerkish', a grammar invented for the project (von Glasersfeld 1977).

Washoe, Sarah and Lana have all made impressive progress, and so have other apes taught by each of these methods. The gestural system turns out to be relatively easy to teach. Fouts (1973) took four chimpanzees which had had no previous training, and was able to teach them

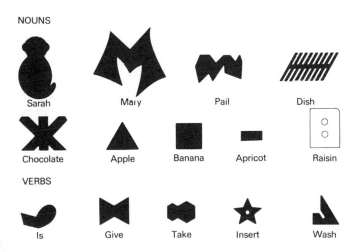

8.10 Some of the plastic symbols used by Premack (1976). After Premack and Premack (1972).

213

8.11 Chimpanzee Lana facing keyboard. From Rumbaugh (1977).

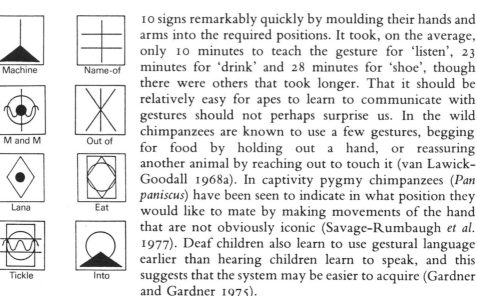

Machine

Name-of

M and M

Out of

Lana

Eat

Tickle

Into

8.12 Some of the lexigrams used by Rumbaugh. After Rumbaugh (1977).

10 signs remarkably quickly by moulding their hands and arms into the required positions. It took, on the average, only 10 minutes to teach the gesture for 'listen', 23 minutes for 'drink' and 28 minutes for 'shoe', though there were others that took longer. That it should be relatively easy for apes to learn to communicate with gestures should not perhaps surprise us. In the wild chimpanzees are known to use a few gestures, begging for food by holding out a hand, or reassuring another animal by reaching out to touch it (van Lawick-Goodall 1968a). In captivity pygmy chimpanzees (*Pan paniscus*) have been seen to indicate in what position they would like to mate by making movements of the hand that are not obviously iconic (Savage-Rumbaugh *et al.* 1977). Deaf children also learn to use gestural language earlier than hearing children learn to speak, and this suggests that the system may be easier to acquire (Gardner and Gardner 1975).

It would be churlish to deny that the apes have done better than might have been expected in learning sign language. Washoe was 11 months old when she started her training; within 51 months she had acquired a vocabulary of 132 signs, and by 1975 she had over 160 (Fouts 1975; Gardner and Gardner 1978). A detailed list of the first 132 of these has been published (Gardner and Gardner 1975). But Washoe took one further step: she spontaneously learnt to combine signs into strings of between two and five signs. She started to do this when she had been taught for 10 months, first signing 'gimme sweet' and 'come open' (Gardner and Gardner 1971). Other examples of her sequences are 'comb black', 'baby mine', 'Roger tickle' and 'more fruit' (Gardner and Gardner 1971). Washoe used the gestural system to communicate her wants and needs in everyday life, and was seen to sign to herself when playing on her own.

Washoe's achievements have since been matched by other apes. Two chimpanzees, Moja and Pili, have been trained by the Gardners from birth and they have made more rapid progress than did Washoe in the first year of training (Gardner and Gardner 1975, 1978). Several chimpanzees, including Ally and Lucy, have been successfully taught by Fouts (1975). A gorilla called Koko has also been coached by Patterson (1978, 1979). Koko's progress has been compared with that of Washoe by listing the number of signs that she reliably used. The Gardners only listed signs that had been spontaneously used for a period of 15 consecutive days (Gardner and Gardner 1971). By a similar strict criterion Koko was judged to have mastered 112 signs after 36 months of training; she was thus learning at much the same rate as Washoe, who had acquired 85 signs by this stage (Patterson 1979).

The most systematic study of ape sign language has been conducted by Terrace (1979b) who supervised the tuition of a chimpanzee called Nim for just under 4 years. With his co-workers he kept a complete transcript of every sign that Nim ever made, and many of the sessions were also videotaped. The most important contribution made by this study was that a complete record was also made of every single combination of signs that Nim was seen to produce; we shall discuss later what these data on combining signs tell us about the chimpanzee's ability to learn grammar. The conditions under which Nim was trained were, unfortunately, far from optimal; he had more than 60 different teachers, and most of them were unskilled and were recruited only for very short periods. Nonetheless Nim acquired a vocabulary of 125 signs in the first 44 months (Fig. 8.13), and he could understand 200 signs as made by his human companions (Terrace 1979b).

Chimpanzees taught to read and write have also made considerable progress. Sarah had learnt to use around 120 plastic symbols by the time of Premack's report in 1976 (Premack 1976), and could no doubt have learnt more if the trainers had attempted to teach a larger vocabulary. She was also trained to carry out commands or answer questions which were given by several symbols in combination. Two other chimpanzees have been coached, Elizabeth and Peony; in Fig. 8.9 Elizabeth is shown giving

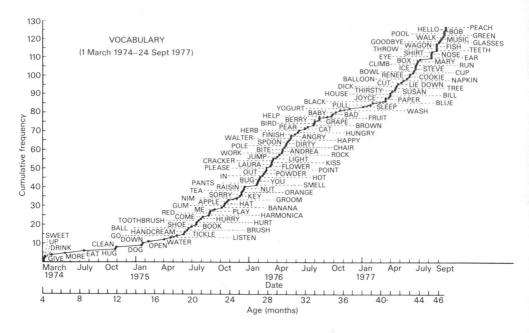

130
120 VOCABULARY
110 (1 March 1974–24 Sept 1977)

Cumulative frequency

POOL HELLO BOB PEACH
GOODBYE WALK GREEN
THROW WAGON MUSIC GLASSES
EYE SHIRT FISH TEETH
CLIMB BOX NOSE EAR
RENEE ICE MARY RUN
BOWL BALLOON CUT STEVE CUP
DICK THIRSTY COOKIE NAPKIN
HOUSE JOYCE LIE DOWN TREE
BLACK PULL SUSAN BILL
YOGURT BABY SLEEP PAPER BLUE
HELP BERRY BAD WASH
BIRD PEAR GRAPE FRUIT
HERB FINISH CAT BROWN
WALTER SPOON ANGRY HUNGRY
POLE DIRTY HAPPY
WORK BITE ANDREA CHAIR
CRACKER JUMP LIGHT ROCK
PLEASE LAURA FLOWER KISS
IN OUT POWDER POINT
PANTS BUG YOU HOT
TEA RAISIN NUT SMELL
SORRY KEY ORANGE
NIM APPLE HAT GROOM
GUM ME PLAY BANANA
RED COME HURRY HARMONICA
TOOTHBRUSH SHOE BOOK HURT
BALL HANDCREAM TICKLE BRUSH
GO DOWN OPEN WATER LISTEN
SWEET
UP
DRINK CLEAN
GIVE MORE EAT HUG DOG

March July Oct Jan Apr July Oct Jan Apr July Oct Jan Apr July Sept
1974 1975 1976 1977
Date

4 8 12 16 20 24 28 32 36 40 44 46
Age (months)

8.13 Chimpanzee Nim's vocabulary. The graph shows the order in which Nim learnt new signs. The steeper the slope of the curve the faster the rate of acquisition. After Terrace (1979b).

an apple to her trainer in response to the command 'Elizabeth give apple Amy'.

The use of a magnetic board limits the exploration of the use of language by chimpanzees to formal sessions in which the animal is tested. By using a computer to run the experiment it is possible to give constant access to a typewriter, so that it can make requests and answer questions throughout the day (Rumbaugh 1977). The chimpanzee Lana has learnt to use the keyboard to ask for such things as food and drink, to request that the window be opened, or to beg the company of her trainer (Rumbaugh and Gill 1977). She acts in response to combinations of lexigrams projected on to her panels, and herself types out signs in combination. The computer is programmed to recognize correct and incorrect usage according to the artificial grammar 'Yerkish' (von Glasersfeld 1977). Two other chimpanzees, Austin and Sherman, have also been trained to use the keyboard, but no attempt has been made to teach them to type signs in strings (Savage-Rumbaugh et al. 1980a). Instead they have been trained to use individual signs to request things such as tools or food of each other (Savage-Rumbaugh et al. 1978a,b).

There is no question that the achievement of these apes is impressive. But so are the tricks of circus animals: bears ride bicycles, chimpanzees have tea parties, and seals play tunes by pressing the rubber bulbs of horns. Perhaps it is

216

not the animals that should impress us but the ingenuity of their trainers? Do the animals understand what they are doing, or are they simply going through their paces without appreciating the point of it all? Have these apes mastered language, or have they only learnt that they can achieve their ends if they go through a rote performance, the meaning of which they do not understand?

Consider the famous horse 'Clever Hans'. It was proudly demonstrated on the stage by its owner, who claimed that it had learnt to count; and indeed it could give the answer to a simple addition by tapping its foot the correct number of times. But in fact the horse knew no arithmetic at all. It got its cue from its master's reaction when it reached the correct number, even though the master was unaware of this fact.

Are the apes also being given hints by their trainers? The way to find out is simple. Clever Hans could only give the right answer if his master was present. Thus the apes must also be tested under conditions where either there is no person in the room, or where the person does not know the correct answers and would therefore be unable to give clues to the ape. Washoe's vocabulary has been assessed under just such conditions (Gardner and Gardner 1978). She had to look at slides and name the objects shown on them by making the appropriate gesture to a person nearby. A second person was out of sight but able to watch Washoe's signs. Neither person could see what picture was showing, and both had to write down the name that they thought Washoe had given. Under these rigorous conditions Washoe was given 32 items to name, a different example of each one being shown on four occasions; she gave the correct answer for 92 out of the 128 slides. The gorilla Koko has been tested in much the same way. In one series of tests she was shown objects from a pool of 30; she gave the correct name on 31 out of 50 occasions (Patterson 1979).

Two methods have been used to check whether Sarah derives cues from her trainers. In the first, Sarah was tested by a person who did not know the meanings of the symbols or the rules for combining them (Premack 1976). Sarah's performance was slightly worse than usual, but she still performed reasonably well. The second method has already been mentioned; this was to present Sarah with questions on paper to which she had to respond by marking one of two answers with a piece of tape (Premack et al. 1978). She was able to suceed in this task even though no trainer was present at the time she marked her answers. In the case of Lana the issue is as clear–cut, since she can type her requests or answers even though it is the computer that runs her training, and no person need be present (Rumbaugh 1977).

Even if the apes are not cheating as they go through their paces, is there any evidence that they understand the point of their performance? Chimpanzees are quick to learn and they have an impressive rote memory. In one experiment chimpanzees learnt without difficulty a list of 24 sequences of designs, each sequence consisting of four designs; for each sequence they had to make an arbitrary response, pressing one of four levers (Farrer 1967). In other words chimpanzees can learn what to do when they are shown sequences of designs, even when these designs are not names or meaningful symbols. How, then, can we be sure that their use of symbols indicates a real appreciation of their meaning, rather than rote memory for the action to be taken in response to each set of symbols? If Clever Hans knew no arithmetic, perhaps these apes know no language.

The issue can be resolved. If the animal has learnt the correct response by rote its knowledge will stand it in good stead only in the original training situation. It will not know how to cope with new though related situations, and will need further experience if it is to learn what is required of it. On the other hand if the animal really appreciates the meaning of a symbol or the point of a rule it should be able to transfer that knowledge to new instances where the symbol or the rule can be applied, and it should not be in need of any further prompting or training. We can therefore test whether the animal has learnt to perform by rote by facing it with new tests which it could pass on the first occasion only if it had truly understood in the first place. The crucial information is how the animal performs on the first trial of such a test, since chimpanzees are quick on the uptake and could rapidly learn by rote alone what is demanded of them in the transfer test (Gardner and Gardner 1978).

With this point in mind let us reconsider the achievements claimed for the apes and assess how genuine they are. It is convenient to discuss first whether they understand the meaning of individual symbols and then whether they appreciate the grammatical rules for combining symbols.

No one disputes that apes can learn to use individual signs correctly, to apply, let us say, the sign for apple in the presence of an apple. The issue is whether they appreciate the nature of the true relation between a symbol and its referent. Perhaps they have just learnt a rote drill, that the way to get an apple is to make a particular gesture or to choose a particular sign. The ape could put in a correct performance without realizing that the sign *means* apple. In fact there is reason to believe that the animals do not understand the meanings of all the signs they have been taught to use (Petitto and Seidenberg 1979; Seidenberg and Petitto 1979; Terrace 1979b). It is particularly difficult to assess claims that an ape can understand words with no concrete reference such as 'please' and 'of' (Mistler-Lachman and Lachman 1974; Terrace 1979b); but to be fair it is no easy task to establish what meaning young children attribute to such words.

There is anecdotal evidence that apes taught Ameslan apply the signs in new contexts outside the strict training situation. Most of them have been brought up in the human household or other rich surroundings. There are therefore many opportunities to find out what meaning the ape attaches to a sign, since there are many examples of the items to which the signs refer—books, chairs, birds and so on. Thus Nim would gesture 'dog' on seeing a dog, looking at a picture of a dog in a book, or even on hearing the bark of a dog (Terrace 1979b).

But a more formal demonstration is needed to check that the apes properly understand that the sign refers to the thing signified. The relevant experiment has been carried out on three chimpanzees—Austin, Sherman and Lana (Savage-Rumbaugh et al. 1980b). They were set to the task of sorting objects into two piles according to whether they were foods or tools and then to carry out the same exercise with photographs of the items. There were lexigrams for each of the items in the artificial system 'Yerkish', and the chimpanzees had previously been taught to use these symbols correctly. The final test required them to sort the symbols themselves, with no objects present, and to say whether a particular lexigram referred to a food or a tool. On the first run through Austin sorted all 17 items correctly and Sherman all but one of the items; Lana failed to pass an earlier stage. Success on this test requires that the animal recall some representation of the actual object when considering a lexigram so as to decide how to categorize the symbol. The symbol conjures up a mental representation of the thing to which it refers.

On present evidence there are apes that can name. But they must be able to do more than this if they are to give unambiguous descriptions of situations and events. It has already been pointed out that rules are needed for combining symbols if accurate accounts are to be given. The example we used was that suggested by Brown (1970) when he asked if the apes could state that a dog was biting a cat or that a cat was biting a dog depending on which picture the animal was shown. All human languages have grammatical rules which allow the subject and object to be distinguished, although the means by which the distinction is drawn differ from language to language. Inflected language marks the difference by the use of case grammar. Others do so by the convention of word order; in some the correct usage is 'John cut apple', in others 'John apple cut', and in a few 'Apple John cut' (Greenberg 1966). In the version of Ameslan taught to apes the first of these orders is used.

In assessing the apes' progress it is essential that we should clearly distinguish between two claims that might be made. The first is that apes spontaneously pick up the rules of sign order; the second is that they can be taught to do so. We shall consider the evidence for each claim in turn.

An examination of the spontaneous productions of Washoe and Nim shows that their sequences were not random. On 87 out of 96 occasions Washoe put the sign for 'you' or for her companions first when addressing them (Gardner and Gardner 1975). The chimpanzees that the Gardners trained after Washoe tend to use the order agent—action and action—object in the same way as their teachers (Gardner and Gardner 1978). The analysis of Nim's sequences confirms that there is regularity (Terrace et al. 1979, 1981). In his two sign combinations it was much more common for him to place 'more' before an object such as 'banana' or an action such as 'tickle' than it was for him to place it in the second position. The same was true for the sign 'give'. When making requests he typically, though not always, put the action word before 'me' or 'Nim', as in 'tickle me' or 'hug Nim'.

But the fact that a chimpanzee tends to prefer one order to another does not prove that it appreciates that sign order carries meaning. Indeed in the two or three sign sequences produced by Washoe and Nim the meaning would be the same whatever the order of the signs; 'gimme flower' and 'flower gimme' are equivalent. Furthermore many of Nim's sequences of three or more signs contained repetitions of redundant signs, as in 'play me Nim', and thus they carried no more meaning than two sign sequences (Terrace et al. 1979). Test cases are needed where it does matter in what order the signs are put if the correct meaning is to be expressed.

Chimpanzees can be taught to put symbols in a particular order. Sarah learnt to use her plastic pieces to write such things as 'Mary give Sarah grape' (Premack 1976); and Lana could press her panels to write 'Please Roger tickle Lana' (Rumbaugh 1977). But pigeons can be trained to peck four colours in a required order, green, white, red and blue; yet in this case the colours carry no meaning and the order is purely arbitrary (Straub *et al.* 1979). Are the chimpanzees also learning nothing other than a rote drill? They are certainly doing more than the pigeons: they can decide which of many sequences a situation demands and they can fill in different symbols in particular positions. Thus Sarah might ask to be given an orange or banana or apple, and Lana might ask to be groomed or carried. But this does not prove that they appreciated that word order carried meaning (Terrace 1979a; Thompson and Church 1980). To demonstrate that they did it would be necessary to train them on a series of sentences where the situation that is described depends on the order in which the words are placed; if they could then handle new sentences of the same sort we could credit them with an understanding of the grammatical rule underlying both the old and the new sentences. There is no record of Sarah or Lana being tested on sentences which are sufficiently different from those used in training to inspire confidence that the chimpanzees do appreciate the point of word order. This is not to deny that they might pass if they were given the relevant tests.

Formal tests have been carried out on chimpanzees trained in Ameslan. Word order is used in describing the relative positions of objects; thus 'the box is in the bag' does not mean the same thing as 'the bag is in the box'. The chimpanzee Ally was given two types of test to see if he could appreciate the relevant rule: in the first he was asked to put the objects in particular places, and in the second to describe the location of objects (Fouts *et al.* 1978). For example, he might be told to put an object in a box or a purse, or he might be asked where the flower was when shown a flower on a box. The experimenters were careful to train Ally with one set of objects and locations, and then to test him out with a new set of commands and questions. Ally performed well on the transfer tests, and always used the order subject—preposition—location.

But this experiment is not decisive, because in asking where an object was the testers signed 'Where is X?', and it might be objected that they therefore cued Ally as to the subject of the sentence. The experiment has therefore been repeated in a different laboratory on a chimpanzee called Jane, and in this case care was taken to ensure that no prompting occurred (Muncer and Ettlinger 1981). Nonetheless the chimpanzee performed well on the single transfer trials. This is suggestive evidence that chimpanzees can be taught to appreciate a simple rule of word order.

This is not to say that chimpanzees can master other than the very basic elements of human language. Their competence is at best only that of a very young child (Brown 1973; Terrace *et al.* 1981). If by language we mean to include all the complexities of human language we need have no fears of competition from apes since they are so much less intelligent. Perhaps the most striking contrast is that the ape does not pick up either symbols or rules unless it is given careful tuition, whereas the child need only be exposed to language to acquire it. There is, as yet, no compelling evidence that chimpanzees can grasp any grammatical rule just by observing its use in ordinary conversation; they must be taught the rule step by step. Yet children have a thirst for language, and will learn whether their parents take trouble or not. If apes can cross the Rubicon it is only because we have built the raft.

INTELLIGENCE AND LANGUAGE

If our analysis is correct we have set ourselves an intriguing problem. How could it be that chimpanzees and gorillas have evolved the ability to learn a form of language in the laboratory when this ability lies dormant in the wild? Evolution could not supply an animal with mental or physical equipment of which it has no need, because there can be no selection pressure if the equipment is of no value in promoting survival.

Of course, there is no mystery in the failure of apes to learn a language in the wild. They have not succeeded of their own accord; it was we who taught them. To take a similar case already discussed in Chapter 5: Abang, the orang-utan, mastered the skill of making a stone tool by use of another, but achieved this only with the patient guidance of a human coach (Wright 1972). Nobody is surprised that orang-utans fail to do this in the wild, and by the same reasoning we should not be surprised that chimpanzees and gorillas fail to acquire a language when left to their own devices. The invention of language or of the art of making stone tools requires, no doubt, a greater degree of intelligence than we usually attribute to apes.

But the issue is not why apes fail in the wild, but why they succeed in the home. The problem can be raised in relation to other achievements of which apes are capable in captivity. Gorillas solve problems in the laboratory as effectively as chimpanzees (Rumbaugh 1970), yet their life in the wild is leisurely and simple, and appears to make few demands on their intelligence. Great apes can recognize themselves in mirrors, but are not required to do so in their normal lives (Gallup 1977). The problem has been elegantly discussed by Humphrey (1976), who tells the story of Henry Ford who, so it is said, ordered the kingpins of the Model T Ford to be made to an inferior specification when he discovered that they were too good for their job. 'Nature is surely at least as careful an economist as Henry Ford. It is not her habit to tolerate needless extravagance in the animals on her production lines; superfluous capacity is trimmed back, new capacity added only as and when it is needed. We do not expect therefore to find that animals possess abilities which far exceed the calls that natural living makes on them.'

There are several ways out of the impasse. The abilities might once have been used though no longer needed; demands might be made on them only occasionally, perhaps in times of crisis; or they might be used constantly, but in ways we had not suspected.

The first of these suggestions was put forward by Kortlandt and Kooij (1963), who were impressed by the variety of ways in which apes used tools in captivity. They proposed that chimpanzees had become 'dehumanized', that is abilities they had once needed had now fallen into disuse. This, they thought, might have happened if chimpanzees had once lived in a more demanding environment than the forests in which many of them now dwell. It was suggested that chimpanzees once lived in woodland and even on the savannah, and had then been forced back into forest (Kortlandt and van Zon 1969).

There would be no need to resort to such a hypothesis if we could show that the intelligence shown by the apes in our laboratories was indeed exercised in their daily life in the wild. Humphrey (1976) argued that the problems that tax them are not economic but social. Coping with their fellows may be more demanding than dealing with their physical environment, and nobody disputes the intelligence with which chimpanzees conduct their social affairs.

The intelligence required for negotiating social interactions would also enable the chimpanzee to cope with other problems, such as those set them by people.

These issues can be resolved only by more field studies of the problems that apes face in their normal surroundings. But let us suppose that these studies have been done, and that we know the answer to the general question of how apes use their intelligence in the wild; the specific question still remains. How could they have evolved the ability to learn a language when they never use one in their normal lives? We could ask the same question of the human ability to play chess or understand complex mathematics. Our hominid ancestors neither played chess nor did calculations; how then did these abilities evolve? The answer is presumably that we owe our ability to indulge in these pastimes not to specific abilities but to our general intelligence. The logical apparatus that enabled our forebears to comprehend and subdue the physical world can be used for a variety of other purposes, as in playing chess. Perhaps, then, the abilities required to fathom language may be the same ones that a chimpanzee uses to solve other problems that it does meet in its daily life.

Symbols

What abilities? Let us start by examining the capacity of the chimpanzee or gorilla to comprehend and make use of symbols, and let us agree that they communicate via signs but not symbols in the wild. A symbol is strictly a substitute for its referent whereas a sign is not. The word 'lion' refers to the animal, and can be used in talking about it in the absence of the real lion. The lion's roar, on the other hand, signals the approach of a lion; it is a sign that something is about to happen rather than a token of that event. Similarly, the chimpanzee signals that it is to attack by glaring and opening its mouth (Fig. 8.2); the facial expression is a sign but not a symbol. The distinction between sign and symbol is a logical one, and it appears sound.

But it is not so obvious that the distinction is important in understanding how signs and symbols can be learnt. Both the sign and symbol evoke some mental representation of the thing that is signified. In both cases there must be some mechanism in the brain for retrieving the stored representation of the object or event that is predicted by the signal or to which reference is made by the symbol. In principle this retrieval could be done in the same way for both. If so, a mechanism that evolved to allow animals to make predictions on the basis of spatial or temporal conjunctions of objects and events could also allow them to learn symbolic relations. Whether this would be possible for any particular species might depend on their level of general intelligence.

We said that a symbol acts as a substitute for its referent. Chimpanzees can be shown to be able to appreciate the relation in which one thing is a token or substitute for another. Chimpanzees have been trained to pull a bar against a heavy weight in order to bring grapes within reach (Wolfe 1936). They would do this even if they were paid with tokens which they could later substitute for grapes by inserting them into a slot machine. The same animals would also work to solve problems when rewarded with tokens to be exchanged at the end of the daily session (Cowles 1937). The notion that a token is convertible into something else is one that makes sense to chimpanzees.

Symbols may be iconic or not, that is they may or may not resemble the things to which they refer. The simplest symbols are parts of the thing represented or pictures of the original, as in a pictogram. Chimpanzees can be taught to pick out the appropriate fruit when shown parts of it, for example its seed or stalk (Premack 1976). They can also interpret pictures, as we noted in Chapter 2. If chimpanzees are allowed to feel an object they can pick out from two pictures the one that represents that object, and they can do so even when they are shown small photographs or line drawings (Davenport et al. 1975). Line drawings are degraded pictures, not so very different from pictograms. Though chimpanzees can draw and paint, they scribble and do not produce representational art (Morris 1962). But their problem is in making the appropriate movements rather than in making perceptual judgements. If they are given pieces to move in the manner of a jigsaw puzzle they can create a representational picture. As shown in Fig. 8.14 the chimpanzee Sarah could move the eyes, nose and mouth into appropriate positions on a blank face of a chimpanzee (Premack 1975). On one occasion she even used a piece of banana to represent a hat, after she had viewed herself in a mirror while wearing a hat (Fig. 8.14). We have good evidence, then, that chimpanzees can appreciate the similarity between pictures and the things depicted. But can they learn to use them as substitutes for the real thing? Observations on the chimpanzee Viki show that they can

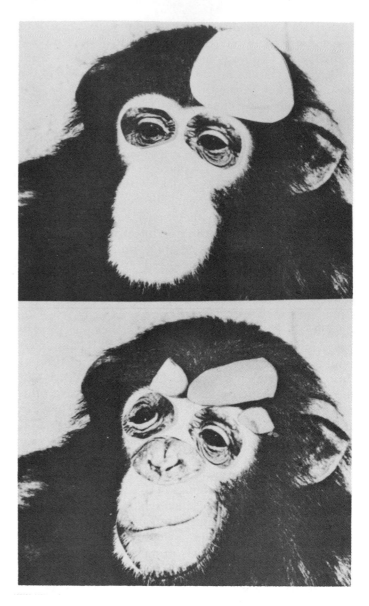

8.14 Jigsaw of chimpanzee face as reconstructed by chimpanzee Sarah. In the upper photograph she has put the eyes in place and positioned one of the other pieces as a hat; in the lower photograph all the pieces are in place and a piece of banana has been added as a hat. From Premack (1975).

(Hayes and Nissen 1971). One day Viki brought a magazine picture of a glass of iced tea to a friend as a way of asking for a drink, and she later learnt to use pictures of cars to demand car rides. These pictures were elementary symbols.

Two studies have already been quoted that suggest that chimpanzees can handle symbols. In the first Ally was taught the manual gestures that correspond in Ameslan to ten words of spoken English that he understood (Fouts *et al.* 1976). When he was then shown the objects themselves he could give the appropriate sign, even though the objects were not present when the gestures were taught. It looks as if Ally has access to some mental representation of the objects when he heared their names spoken in English.

In the second study chimpanzees Austin and Sherman succeeded in sorting symbols according to whether they referred to foods or tools. The lexigrams had not been present earlier when they had run through the sorting with the foods and tools themselves. It seems that the symbols reminded the animals of the real objects to which they referred.

In their normal life chimpanzees are not required to mentally retrieve the items referred to in any symbolic system. These mental operations must be ones which the chimpanzee calls upon for other reasons in its natural habitat. The most obvious situations are those in which the animal must make a prediction about future events. Consider a classic experiment carried out on both monkeys and chimpanzees (Tinklepaugh 1928, 1932). The animal was shown a banana and watched while it was placed in one of two containers; a few seconds later it was allowed to take the banana from the container in which it remembered the fruit being placed. The experiment was repeated with food which the animal preferred much less, a lettuce or a carrot, and again the animal found the food and ate it. Then the animal was tricked: a banana was hidden in the box while the animal watched, but a lettuce or carrot was then substituted unbeknown to the animal. When it found the less preferred food it refused to eat it, searching for the banana and finally leaving in puzzlement. How are we to explain this? Clearly the animal predicted that a banana would be in the box and was disappointed and frustrated to find that it was not. When looking in the box the animal must have been able to summon up a mental representation of the banana it confidently expected to be there. To return to the example used earlier, we may suppose that when the roar of the lion signals the approach of a lion the roar serves to evoke a mental representation of the lion before the lion arrives. Both signal and symbol give access to the representations of objects and events that are stored in the brain.

Rules

If it is true that chimpanzees can be taught an elementary rule of language, this achievement must reflect their general intelligence. That they can learn non-linguistic rules we saw in Chapter 5; we may take as an example the rule on which the oddity problem is based. The animal is faced on each trial with three objects of which two are identical, and to obtain food it must choose the object which is the odd man out (Fig. 5.7*d*). If the same set of objects is presented to the animal on many trials it can solve the problem by rote, that is it can learn which object to choose without appreciating the reason for the choice. But if it is given a series of such problems, each with a new set of objects, it has the opportunity to grasp the rule that is obeyed by all the problems, namely that the correct object is always the odd one. We can test whether the animal has understood the principle by then presenting it with new problems each for a single trial only, and if it continues to perform above a chance level we know that it has learnt the rule. Great apes can be shown in this way to appreciate the oddity concept and to apply the rule to new problems (Rumbaugh and McCormak 1967; Rumbaugh 1970, 1971).

Nonetheless there are linguists who argue that the rules of language are not like other rules and that intelligence on its own is not enough to decipher them. Chomsky (1972), for instance, asserts that 'as far as we know, possession of human language is associated with a specific type of mental organization, not simply with a higher degree of intelligence'. His evidence is that there are rules common to all languages which, as he thinks, a child could not appreciate unless it possessed special brain mechanisms for learning language. Lenneberg (1967) reviewed the empirical evidence on how children learn language, and was led to suppose that human infants possess some special 'language acquisition device'. He also concluded that there was a constraint on when this device could operate, and that if language was not learnt in the years before maturity it became less and less likely that it would be learnt at all.

But chimpanzees and gorillas cannot be supposed to possess the 'specific type of mental organization' needed for learning language, or to have evolved a special 'language acquisition device'. No such special device could evolve if it were not put to use. We face a dilemma. If such a device is indeed to be found in the brains of people, then how could chimpanzees acquire any language without it? One answer would be to claim, as Chomsky does, that the chimpanzees have not in fact learnt a language. The alternative would be to deny that people possess a language acquisition device, and to attribute our linguistic achievements to our intellectual pre-eminence.

How are we to decide between these views? The crux is whether we can demonstrate empirically that a specific language acquisition device is required if children are to learn language. It has been argued that unless children had such a device they could never learn language, as adult speech is much too complex in its grammatical organization for children to work out the rules. But this argument supposes that it is adult language from which the children learn, and ignores the fact that parents simplify their speech considerably when talking to their children. On average the language an adult uses is only six months in advance of the language of which the child is capable (Moskowitz 1978). The children can learn the rules because they are only presented with ones that they are capable of grasping at that stage.

Nor is it so certain that children can only learn language before they reach maturity. A girl called Genie was brought up under conditions of terrible privation; she was locked in her bedroom from the age of 20 months until she was $13\frac{1}{2}$ years old, and in this time her parents did not speak to her at all (Fromkin *et al.* 1974). Yet, when discovered and thus exposed to human speech she made considerable progress in learning to talk, and was able to use word order correctly in simple spoken sentences (Curtiss 1977). This is not to say that her speech was normal, and it has been suggested that the abnormalities might reflect the fact that it is Genie's right hemisphere that appears to be dominant for speech, even though she is right-handed (Curtiss 1977). But it is quite as possible that the inadequacies of her speech are to be attributed, at least in part, to the intellectual retardation caused by her impoverished childhood. Language acquisition is slowed down in retarded children and there are limits to the complexities of language that can be mastered by children of low intelligence (Lenneberg 1967).

No one pretends that chimpanzees can match children in the speed with which they learn language or the level of competence they can attain. It is, of course, possible that their inferiority reflects the lack of specialized mechanisms for learning language. But, without denying that such mechanisms may exist, it is important not to overlook the contribution made by general intelligence to our ability to acquire language.

Unlike mankind the apes have not invented language, perhaps through want of sufficient intelligence. How did our ancestors come to invent language as a tool for communication and thought? The question is one on which it is easy to speculate and almost impossible to produce any facts. Such was the controversy in the nineteenth century that in 1866 the Société de Linguistique de Paris banned all communications to the society on the history of language (Hewes 1977). Given the dearth of knowledge on the subject we may sympathize with the ban, since it probably saved reams of wasted paper. In breaking the ban here we will confine ourselves to saying only that little that is worth saying.

To discover how something evolved one must know when it evolved, and to discover how an invention was made one must know when it was made. The explanation must refer to the environmental conditions at the time, and say why it was that at that moment the time was ripe. But estimates of when language was invented vary from the coming of modern man around 35 000 years ago to the time of *Homo erectus* who first evolved around 1.5 million years ago. The accounts given of the conditions which led to the invention of language will clearly differ greatly depending on the time at which the breakthrough is supposed to have occurred.

There are three types of evidence that have been used in arriving at estimates of the time when the crucial step was taken. These are the structure of the vocal tracts of our ancestors, the relative size of their brains, and the artifacts they made. None of this evidence is decisive.

Consider the vocal tract: although the soft parts are not preserved we can nonetheless attempt a reconstruction based on the bones of the jaw and skull. Lieberman (1975) has examined reconstructions of the position of the vocal tract in a series of fossil hominids. He argues that the vocal tract was similar to that of the chimpanzee in the australopithecines and Neanderthal man; but that it was essentially modern in its construction in the more advanced hominids found near Mount Carmel in Israel from 45 000 years ago. But the accuracy of the reconstructions has been called into question; the claim concerning Neanderthal man depends on an examination of a skull from La Chapelle-aux-Saints in France, and other authorities dispute the findings (Falk 1975; LeMay 1975). But even if it were agreed that the vocal tract was similar in

Neanderthal man and chimpanzee, this would not provide a sound basis for claims that Neanderthal man lacked any form of speech. The range of sounds of which the chimpanzee vocal tract is capable is quite sufficient to permit some elementary version of spoken language.

Do casts of the brain provide better evidence? There are two ways in which they might do so. There could be a critical mass which must be surpassed if the invention of language is to prove possible. Alternatively the cast of the brain might betray structural features suggestive of specialization for speech.

The notion that there might be a critical mass is unhelpful unless it is specified exactly what that mass is critical for. Is it for speech, for language, or for the invention of language? In Chapter 4 it was argued that the ability to speak depends on specialized neural mechanisms and that it is not expensive in the neural tissue that it requires; microcephalic people can speak (Holloway 1968). If it is accepted that chimpanzees can be taught some of the elements of language then their brain has already reached the critical mass necessary for language. But they fail to pick up language unless they are carefully tutored; and they have not invented a language system of their own. However, neither fact gives us any clue as to the amount of tissue that might be needed to invent or to pick up language. In other words the relative size of the brain provides no hint as to when the hominids first invented language and when first they spoke.

The cast of a brain reproduces its size, shape, and the indentations of some of its fissures. It is tempting to look for evidence of the capacity for speech by examining the casts of the brains of our ancestors. Asymmetries between the two hemispheres have been reported in several hominids (LeMay 1976). It has been claimed, for example, that in a cast taken from a Neanderthal skull the back of the sylvian fissure runs higher on the right than on the left, just as in right-handed people (LeMay and Culebras 1972), but it has also been denied that the impression of the sylvian fissure is well enough formed at this point for such a judgement to be made (Holloway 1976). There is stronger evidence that the two hemispheres are not symmetrical in fossil hominids. In modern human populations there is a tendency for the right frontal lobe to be wider and to extend further forwards than the left, and for the left occipital lobe to be wider and to extend further backwards than the right (LeMay 1976). In fossil hominids the same pattern can be discerned; in modern apes there are asymmetries, but the pattern is different (Holloway and LaCoste-Larymondic in press). But what conclusion follows? If the hominid pattern of asymmetries is taken as a mark of language we would be forced to concede that the australopithecines used language; and this would be a bold assertion in the absence of any other evidence of any sort. For the present we should admit that the functional relevance of these asymmetries is unknown.

It might seem that there is a better prospect of making a judgement on the basis of the development of specialized regions within each hemisphere. Holloway (1976, 1978, 1980) has examined the casts of the brains of fossil hominids in great detail, and points to an expansion of parietal cortex. But this information can give us no clue as to when this tissue first assumed a role in processing language. Holloway (1972, 1974) claims to be able to identify the presence of Broca's area in some fossil hominids, but we cannot take this as firm evidence of speech. Even a microscopic examination of brain tissue reveals no very striking differences in the cellular organization of Broca's area in man and related areas in chimpanzees (von Bonin and Bailey 1961; Galaburda 1980). It is a vain hope to suppose that we could diagnose the presence of language just by looking at the brain, much less at a cast of the brain.

If neither the vocal tract nor the size and shape of the brain provides reliable clues as to the capacity for speech we must resort to evidence that is even less direct, the technological achievements of which the hominids were capable. The archaeological record has already been reviewed in Chapter 6. For this record to prove decisive we need to know what technical advances could only be made with the assistance of spoken language. The elementary techniques required for producing chopper tools or hand axes can readily be learnt by copying a teacher. But what of more complicated methods of manufacture? It has been pointed out that students today need a course of more than one semester if they are to learn how to produce standardized flakes by the Levallois technique; and this with the benefit of verbal instructions (Washburn 1969). But we cannot be confident that this settles the issue, as our ancestors had a long youth in which to watch and practice, and were studying not for a hobby but for a profession. We must remain unconvinced until told what aspects of this technique could be grasped only if described by word of mouth.

Of course stone tools are not the only evidence that

might be relevant. Marshack (1976) has argued that designs, engravings or figures are suggestive evidence of a maker who possessed a symbolic language. Some of the designs Marshack cites are non-representational; for example an engraving on an ox rib of roughly 300 000 years ago, or a molar from a mammoth carved by Neanderthal man around 50 000 years ago. If chimpanzees can scribble non-representational designs (Morris 1962), such designs cannot be proof of the capacity for speech. What then of the representational designs? The first such drawings and paintings were done by modern man (*Homo sapiens sapiens*), and they date from the Upper Palaeolithic period. The famous paintings in the caves at Lascaux in France and Altamira in Sapin come from the period of the Magdalenian culture, around 15 000 years ago (Ucko and Rosenfield 1967). The earliest representational art dates from around 30 000 years ago; a particularly fine example is a horse carved of mammoth ivory, which was excavated from an Aurignacian site at Vogelherd in Germany (Marshack 1976). It could be argued with reason that people capable of one form of symbolic representation might have been capable of speech, another form of symbolic representation. And, although this inference does not constitute proof, if modern man did not speak by that time one is at a loss to know when he did; he possessed the same brain that we do today.

The search for the origins of spoken language has been fruitless. There is no clear indication of the time at which man made his greatest invention. It is perhaps worth adding one footnote. It is not known what size of brain is essential for speech, but it is reasonable to assume that the capacity for understanding and producing speech makes great demands on the brain. Given the extraordinary size of the human brain it is inconceivable that its growth in our ancestors is unrelated to the development of the capacity to invent and use language. Our greatest invention is surely to be attributed in part to our most distinctive anatomical feature.

Given ignorance of the timing there can be little to say about the conditions that led to the breakthrough. The position is made worse by the fact that there are a great variety of advantages which would be won by the development of the capacity to speak. At any time, whatever the environmental conditions, a hominid that could speak would outdo one that could not. The location could be given of plant food or game; the hunting strategy could be planned and directed; the manufacture of tools could be taught not only by example but also by verbal instruction. It is idle to speculate on the reasons which proved decisive.

Is it possible to reconstruct the steps by which spoken language was invented? We ourselves inherit language, and are not faced with the awesome task of creating it. How, then, did our ancestors make the breakthrough? Many theories have been proposed (Hewes 1977); and two solutions are worth considering.

The first draws attention to the information about the world that a clever animal such as a chimpanzee can glean by careful observation of the actions of its companions. This was documented earlier in the chapter (Menzel 1974; Menzel and Johnson 1976). An animal hearing a particularly excited call might infer that this state could have been induced only if a particular predator were at hand. Gestures or sounds could thus be associated with particular states of the world (Premack 1976). The vervet monkey appears to have taken this step, since it has different alarm calls for predators that are equally feared (Seyfarth *et al.* 1980).

There is an alternative view. Spoken language represents the world by means of a non-iconic relation between a word and its referent; but it can also be done by gestural mime or vocal imitation. An animal could be described by imitating its posture and movements or by copying the calls that it makes. We know chimpanzees to be good mimics of what they see, and we need only suppose that our ancestors were as good. The prey could be identified and the hunt re-enacted by the use of mime, perhaps backed up by the appropriate sounds. In acting a scene the actor tells a story. The suggestion is that the invention of language might have occurred in the same way as the invention of writing. At first a drawing represents the scene; later the pictogram becomes stylized until its final form may reveal little of its origins. It is not difficult to invent iconic signs. There is a report of the manual signs spontaneously invented by six young deaf children, aged 17 to 49 months, who had no formal tuition in sign language (Feldman *et al.* 1978). All the gestures were iconic: one child hammered to denote a hammer, and another indicated a jar by pretending to unscrew the lid. Many of the signs of modern sign language are also iconic in origin (Brown 1981).

Both views give a plausible account of how names might be invented. Sounds could refer to things and events either because they are associated with the reactions of individuals or because they mimic their referents. But it is one thing to put forward an idea and quite another to show it to be correct. Since we cannot listen in to the past we would do better to observe the plea for silence on the subject of the origins of human language.

LANGUAGE AND THOUGHT

Though invented for communication language is as powerful a tool for thought. The symbols devised for talking to others can as well be used for talking to oneself. The language that describes the world in conversation also provides a means for thinking about it.

We do not know how animals think, that is in what sort of code they form a mental representation or model of the world. When a monkey expects a banana it must have some means of representing the banana to itself. When the chimpanzee decides to use a stick to rake in the banana we must suppose that it has ways of coding the relevant action and predicting the likely consequences. This code might be iconic.

It might be objected that there is no point in idle speculation, and that such subjective phenomena as mental imagery are outside the scope of science. But, in fact, psychologists have had some success in devising experiments to investigate imagery in human subjects (Paivio 1971; Cohen 1977).

For example, people were shown pairs of figures as illustrated in Fig. 8.15; and they were asked whether the two figures would prove to be identical if viewed from the same angle (Shepard and Metzler 1971). It was found that the speed with which they made their judgements was directly related to the time which would be required to turn one figure until it was oriented in the same way as the other. The greater the rotation the longer the time in which the subjects had to think, as if they were rotating in their heads a visual representation of the figures. This and similar experiments suggest that people can operate on iconic representations of objects.

But people recode much of their recorded experience in words (Baddeley 1976). It must be the case that language greatly facilitates thought. However, it has not proved easy to demonstrate this in formal experiments on children or adults (Cohen 1977).

It might be supposed that we could discover the limits of non-linguistic codes by measuring the achievements of the deaf. The profoundly deaf may never learn a spoken

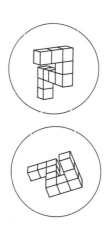

8.15 Two figures in different orientations. The subject must decide whether they are identical when in the same orientation. After Shepard and Metzler (1971).

language; but in spite of this they can rival the hearing on intelligence tests such as the Raven's Matrices, tests which were designed to measure abstract reasoning (Furth 1971). But it would be wrong to assume that this intellectual level is being achieved without any form of linguistic code at all. We need some way of discovering the code that is being used. A simple test has been devised to measure the degree to which speech coding is used (Conrad 1973). The subject is shown sequences of letters to remember that either sound alike, as in B, C, D, P, T, V, or look alike, as in K, N, V, W, X, Y. The rationale is as follows: those people who translate the letters into speech sounds and articulate them will find the first list the more difficult to learn, because they will be prone to acoustic confusions; those unable to use a speech code will find the second list the more difficult, because they will be prone to visual confusions. In fact, many of the less profoundly deaf turn out to be capable of speech coding and their good performance on cognitive tasks is thus easily explained.

Those with the greatest hearing loss still perform well on intelligence tests though they do not have access to speech codes. But there are other linguistic codes they might use; they are taught to spell words on their fingers, to read and to make gestures in Ameslan. Unlike hearing subjects the deaf do not recode the signs of Ameslan into sounds when they remember them (Bellugi *et al.* 1975). It is possible for them to recode their experience into signs so as to aid memory or thought. It is wrong to assume that the deaf think without language.

But could a chimpanzee benefit from language? In principle the relevant experiments could be done. A chimpanzee could be taught a symbolic system such as Ameslan and then assessed on problem-solving tasks. In Premack's laboratory the chimpanzee Sarah has been set difficult cognitive tasks of the sort used by psychologists interested in the intellectual development of children. Thus Sarah has been asked to judge whether the amount of liquid remains the same when poured from a jar into another jar differing in shape and size; this is the conservation problem (Woodruff *et al.* 1978). She has also been assessed for the ability to reason by analogy (Gillan *et al.* 1981). The problem is to see that if A goes with A' then B must go with B' and not C if the same relationship is to hold. For example, if lock goes with key then paint tin goes with can opener and not with paint brush. Tasks of this sort would be ideal for a study of the value of symbols in aiding thought. We could compare the performance of chimpanzees that had or had not been taught a symbolic system, whether gestural or pictorial. Would it help to have a symbol for such relations as 'same', 'different', 'greater than', 'not' and so on? Premack (1976) has already begun to tackle the issue by comparing Sarah's performance on problems posed either in the form of plastic symbols or with the real objects.

The advantages of language for thought are obvious. The world is represented in language by attaching arbitrary symbols to each of its constituent parts and to the relations between them. This description or representation of the world can be stored in the head as a working model on which operations may be performed. To use an expression coined by physicists a 'thought experiment' can be tried by mentally manipulating the model. Let us return to the chimpanzee raking in the food. A person in the same situation can formulate various plans in words, and without actually experimenting with the equipment can test out the various suggestions and discover which one works. While the chimpanzee may have some way of representing possibilities to itself it must be very much more cumbersome than the verbal solutions with which the person can experiment. It is not that chimpanzees do not think; only that they lack the symbolic system with which Rodin's 'Thinker' can operate. Their code must be clumsy at handling the more abstract concepts. Consider only the delightful example provided by Bertrand Russell, who commented that 'no matter how eloquent a dog may be he cannot tell me that his father is poor, but honest'. I defy a chimpanzee to formulate this thought in visual imagery.

One abstract concept that has proved to be of fundamental importance in the development of human technology is that of number. The concept that animals have of quantity must be crude. We know that birds and primates can estimate numbers of the order of one to seven, and we may suppose that non-primate mammals may be able to do the same. A jackdaw has been taught to choose the lid on which there were the same number of spots as on a card; and it could do this even when the spots on the lids and card differed in size, shape or distribution (Thorpe 1974). In the same way, a rhesus monkey can learn to choose the card bearing a particular number of symbols, even if the size, shape or distribution of these is altered (Hicks 1956). The ability of these animals extends to estimating the number of movements they themselves make. A grey parrot has been trained to take the number of pieces of food that corresponded to the number of notes played on a flute (Thorpe 1974). Baboons have been shown to be capable of pressing a lever the number of times that matches the number of plus signs they are shown (Levison and Findley 1967). But in all these cases the numbers have been small, less than seven. This is significant because people can form accurate estimates of a number of items up to seven, even if they are presented so quickly that there is no time to count or enumerate them. This ability is referred to as the ability to 'subitize', and it is an ability that these animals appear to share. These experiments do not, therefore, demonstrate that animals can enumerate, and indeed there is no good evidence that they can (Premack 1976).

There have been attempts to teach chimpanzees symbols for the crude concepts of number that they can handle. In one experiment chimpanzees were trained to write numbers in binary notation; the animals could turn on up to three lights, and thus write the binary versions of the numbers up to seven (Ferster 1964). When shown a number of triangles on a slide the chimpanzee could form an estimate, presumably by subitizing, and then write the correct binary number. Unfortunately it was not convincingly shown that this was other than a rote performance, since they were not tried out with other related tasks, such as estimating the number of oranges or bananas. In a different experiment the chimpanzee Lana has been taught to use symbols for 'more' and 'less' for stating whether there are more or less washers on one side of a board than the other; but again the use of the symbols was not tested in situations involving the same judgements for new materials (Dooley and Gill 1977). A final experiment has examined the ability of the chimpanzee to learn symbols for 'all', 'none', 'one' and 'some'. Of these the concept 'some' proves difficult for chimpanzees to handle. If presented with five objects, chimpanzees will learn to push some of them, that is two, three or four of them; but they perform poorly when required to repeat the exercise with a new set of objects (Brown *et al.* 1978). Nonetheless, the chimpanzee Sarah has been taught to use symbols for 'all', 'none', 'one' and 'some' and she is said to use them appropriately when given new objects about which she must make judgements (Premack 1976).

Now contrast the chimpanzee with the child. The child can enumerate, counting one by one; and the child has symbols for each number and also for a variety of arithmetic operations and concepts. Later it learns symbols for yet more abstract concepts as with the symbols x and y in algebra, which denote a number no matter which particular one. That intelligence is required to handle such ideas is not in doubt; but the ideas could not be entertained without language. Where would Einstein be without his symbols?

CONSCIOUSNESS

It is hardly controversial to claim that language is the most important contributor to our intellectual pre-eminence. But does our possession of language explain the mental characteristic that is most often cited as distinguishing man and beast, that is consciousness? Everyone lays claim to consciousness, although there are many who doubt whether a thing so insubstantial could be the object of serious scientific investigation. The main problem in such a study is not the elusiveness of the phenomenon but the vagueness of the language in which the issue is discussed. It is useful to distinguish four different notions of consciousness.

The first concept is that of the self-awareness that gives a sense of identity. People have a self-concept, an image of themselves; but so, it would seem, do chimpanzees. As we saw in Chapter 2, chimpanzees will react to their image in a mirror as if they recognized that it was themselves and not another chimpanzee (Gallup 1977). Language would not seem to be essential for the concept of self.

We are aware of ourselves in another way. At any time I know what posture I am adopting and what action I am taking. I am aware, that is, not only of events occurring in the world outside my body, but also of what my own body is doing. Do animals know what they are doing? It would be strange if they did not, since sensory information from their joints and muscles is transmitted to the brain. But we can directly show that animals are indeed aware of their activities by setting up a task on which they can succeed only if they know what they are doing. Such a task has been devised for rats, in which they are trained to press one of several levers when they hear a bleep. Which lever they must press depends on what they were doing at the time the bleep sounded; if they were rearing up they must press one lever, if they were grooming themselves another, and if they were walking yet a third (Beninger *et al.* 1974). Rats can do this, that is they can effectively report on which of several possible actions they were carrying out at the time the signal was given (Morgan and Nicholas 1979). Like us they are aware of their own actions, as indeed they must be if they are to be able to modify them according to the consequences that ensue.

The third notion is that which people most commonly have in mind when they talk of consciousness. If I open my eyes I see and am conscious that I see. If I were unconscious but with my eyes open I would not be aware of the visual impression of the world around. We commonly talk of perception as if we were watching a film and pictures were going through our head. Are we alone privileged to watch such shows, or do animals share these experiences? Until recently scientists whispered guiltily about such questions, because they had not thought of any way of investigating such private matters; but recently observations on patients with brain damage have brought matters into the open. Because of strokes or tumours some patients suffer damage to the areas of their brain that process visual information, and as a result they find themselves either blind or partially blind with a restricted view of the world. The blindness may take the form in which, if the patient gazes ahead, he can see things, let us say, to his right, but not to his left; in such a case he would be described as having a 'field defect' for his left field of view. In one such patient it was found that the blindness for the left field of view was of a peculiar sort (Weiskrantz et al. 1974). When asked whether he saw a light presented to his left he denied seeing it; but when asked to point at the light he could do so with accuracy. The patient could even guess accurately whether he was being shown a horizontal or diagonal line, while remaining totally unaware that he was seeing anything. It is as if he was seeing though blind, and this phenomenon of 'blind-sight' has since been demonstrated in other patients (Weiskrantz 1980).

How are we to explain this extraordinary effect, that a person should know the location and even form of things which he does not consciously see? Information from the eye travels to many brain centres, and destruction of one does not prevent sensory messages arriving at others. If the visual areas of the neocortex are damaged the brain still has access to information from other areas, and presumably this is how the patients are able to make correct judgements. What is missing is the visual sensation we call 'seeing', and we might speculate that this depends on an intact neocortex. There is no reason to think that possession of language is critical for conscious perception, since in these patients what matters is not whether they give a verbal report, but whether they go by what they are aware of seeing or by what their informed guesses tell them (Weiskrantz 1980). If so, why suppose that animals lack conscious perceptions? Monkeys have been studied with similar damage to the neocortex (Humphrey 1974b; Pasik and Pasik 1971); perhaps experiments might demonstrate that for them too there is a divorce between what they 'see' and what they can 'guess'. The same methods by which we train them to tell us whether or not they see could be adapted to teach them to distinguish between what they are aware of seeing and what they can tell only from guesswork. It would not be surprising if it was discovered that in animals, as in people, there is a distinction between those workings of the mind of which the owner is or is not aware.

In patients with 'blind-sight' there is a dissociation between conscious and unconscious perception. It is not that the patient sees but cannot find words to describe the perception. This point may be appreciated by contrasting these patients with others who have undergone surgery for the relief of epilepsy. In a few patients in America the fibres or commissures linking the two hemispheres have been cut, so as to confine epileptic discharges to a single hemisphere and thus mitigate the severity of the fits (Gazzaniga 1970). In such patients it is possible to present material to a single hemisphere, the left or the right. If the patient is asked to gaze at a central point visual information presented to the left of that point will reach the right hemisphere (see Fig. 2.12). Similarly, tactile information about objects in the left hand will travel to the right hemisphere, and vice versa for objects held in the right hand. Since the commissures are cut, the two hemispheres are isolated and information from one can no longer be transferred to the other. The two hemispheres now function relatively independently and in ignorance of the activity of the opposite hemisphere.

In such patients the following dramatic phenomenon can be demonstrated (Sperry and Gazzaniga 1967). The patient sits in front of the apparatus illustrated in Fig. 8.16 and gazes at a central point. A picture of an object is flashed up to the left of this point, so that information about it only reaches the right hemisphere. The patient is now asked to use his left hand, the hand controlled by the right hemisphere, to pick out the one of several objects that matches the picture shown. It turns out that he can do this, but at the same time the patient is quite unable to say what

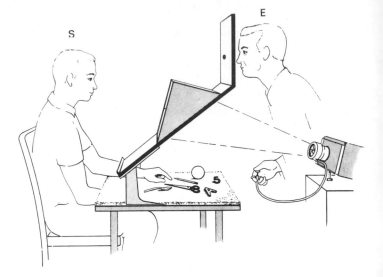

8.16 Experimental set-up for presentation of visual and tactual stimuli to patients after section of the corpus callosum. S, subject; E, experimenter. From Sperry and Gazzaniga (1967).

it was that he saw or felt, that is to name it. The reason is that the language mechanisms of the left hemisphere have no access to what is going on in the right hemisphere. In these cases, then, the patients can both see and feel while being unable to describe their perceptions in words.

The final sense in which consciousness is used is perhaps the most important, although there is no relevant experimental literature. Language is used in reporting on events in the world, describing what is seen, heard or felt. But it can also be used to report on those mental operations we call thoughts. Not only do we think in words, we can also monitor and commentate on those thoughts. It is as if we hear ourselves thinking, and listen in to our internal conversations. We have reached a peak of self-awareness unparallelled in animals. We can describe what we think in language.

We are now in a position to take stock. The first chapter posed a problem: how is it that people are so different from animals when our bodily structure is so similar? True, the human brain is prodigious in its relative size, opening up a gap between man and chimpanzee that is larger than the gap separating chimpanzee from shrew (Chapter 4). But how could that account for the sense we have of being totally unlike any animal at all? Three suggestions can be offered as to how this mental gap is to be explained.

The first might be called a 'threshold' effect. Some accomplishments, such as the invention of speech, may require a brain which surpasses a critical mass, a cerebral Rubicon. A large general-purpose computer is capable of handling types of operation for which a smaller computer may be totally inadequate.

The second possible influence might be the efficiency with which specialized functions are apportioned between the two hemispheres. As argued in Chapter 4, the specialization of function as between the two hemispheres in man may greatly increase the processing capacity as compared with brains in which there is duplication in the functions performed by the two hemispheres.

The final point is that the invention of spoken language has revolutionized thought. The use of language for thought vastly amplifies the level of intelligence that can be achieved. Animals think, but people can think in a totally new way, with a completely different code. It is as if the code used for storing and processing information in a computer were radically altered; the results of such a change might well be dramatic. Unlike animals people have ways of representing to themselves hypothetical and highly abstract situations. It is only because we possess spoken language that our technology and culture are so advanced. It is language, not manners, that maketh man.

9 Family

The previous chapters have documented man's essential characteristics. The human primate differs from other primates in several crucial respects. He is built for upright walking, and has hands which are capable of considerable skill and dexterity. His brain is three times as large as that appropriate for a non-human primate of his build; and he lives correspondingly much longer than we would predict for such a primate. As a result he is pre-eminent in intelligence as his science and technology testify. Finally, he has spoken language as his most important invention, and this serves as a tool for thought, communication and education.

These features have made possible the peculiarly human way of life. The task of this and the final chapter is to demonstrate how man's special characteristics affect his social and emotional life. Man is indeed a primate, but one that is set apart from any other animal by the degree to which he is specialized for intelligence. Observations of the social life of animals may throw some light on human society, but we should never underestimate the formative influence of human intelligence on that society. We may remind ourselves that the gap in relative brain size is greater between man and chimpanzee than between chimpanzee and shrew; and that the mental gap is widened much further as a consequence of man's use of language for thought. Yet, what would studying the solitary shrew tell us about the complex social interactions of the chimpanzee?

In examining the origins of human social life we would do well to keep in mind the difficulties of tracing the origins of *any* pattern of behaviour. It was argued in Chapter 1 that the task of accounting for something as simple as the human smile proves daunting when we face the various questions that must be answered. Any attempt to provide a historical account is likely to be thwarted by a failure to overcome one crucial obstacle. The same characteristic may be shared by two species, and yet may originate in different ways in the two of them. Similarity in anatomy or behaviour does not necessarily reflect a similar derivation.

Nature has devised two ways in which patterns of behaviour may originate (see Chapter 5). Where aspects of the environment are stable and predictable knowledge of the appropriate adaptive behaviour may be inherited, being coded in the genetic material. In development, circuits can be built into the brain according to genetic instructions, and these are programmed to run off sequences of behaviour in the relevant circumstances. So long as external conditions allow and the development of the animal is normal, it grows up with prior knowledge of how to survive, knowledge that it has not had to acquire by learning. But genetic foresight of this sort cannot occur where the environment is unpredictable, because the best strategies cannot be foretold. Under such circumstances the animal must perforce learn during its lifetime how best to respond, and the relevant information must be stored in the brain in the form of memories for future use. The difference between the two strategies might be characterized by using a distinction drawn in the jargon of computer engineers. A computer is built with circuits which are described as being 'hard wired'; but during the lifetime of the computer the programmers write in instructions which they refer to as 'soft-wired', these being modifiable and often temporary. In the same way we may distinguish between those circuits in the brain that are part of the basic design and those that are programmed by learning.

In fact almost all animals must acquire at least part of their repertoire by learning. The genes could never have foreknowledge of, say, the position of a home base or the appearance of the animal's parents. There will usually be some knowledge that can only be attained through experience. Animals differ only in the degree to which they depend on learning for their survival.

The bias towards a reliance on experience is shown most notably by those birds and mammals with highly developed brains; and of these it is man that shows this bias to the greatest extreme. When comparing different animals or comparing animals with people we must therefore be careful to assess the role of learning before making claims that a similarity in behaviour indicates a common evolutionary origin.

Recently there have been great advances made in the application of the theory of evolution to the understanding of social behaviour in animals. The new science has been christened sociobiology (Wilson 1975). It has achieved particular success in accounting for phenomena that might at first sight appear difficult to explain in terms of selection between the genetic complements of individuals. In particular much attention has been paid to how apparently 'altruistic' behaviour could have evolved (Dawkins 1976). We shall have something to say about this later.

A quaint conceit occurs throughout the literature on sociobiology: individual animals or their genes are spoken of as if they were for ever calculating their own advantage and working out their best strategies (Ruse 1979). The authors are always at pains to remind their readers that they do not actually mean to imply that conscious decisions are being made by the genes, any more than textbooks of evolutionary biology intend to suggest that the function or 'purpose' of an organ is appreciated by its owner. In both cases these phrases act as a convenient shorthand; the anthropomorphic terminology helps in avoiding long periphrases. The 'purpose' of an organ, for example, refers to the adaptive advantage that the organ gives, such that its bearers are more likely to survive to reproduce successfully. In sociobiology it is common to compare the relative costs and pay-offs of the different 'strategies' that an animal might adopt, for example in reacting to threat (Maynard Smith 1978, 1979). Here the full statement is that the reproductive success of animals behaving in particular ways can be computed, and predictions made about what genetic changes would occur in such populations over time, given a particular genetic composition at the outset.

An analysis of this sort uses 'game theory', the theory first devised to deal with human decision making, as in 'war games'. In the case of people terms such as 'strategy', 'decision', 'foresight', 'purpose', and so on are no longer metaphor. People *do* work out what would best pay. It is not implied that animals never deliberate nor foresee consequences; only that we possess language as a powerful means for doing so.

What, then, should we make of attempts to apply the theories and findings of sociobiology to man (Wilson 1975, 1978)? Forewarned, we should tread carefully. Let us suppose that some human activity pays. The sociobiologist will look to the advantage in terms of reproductive success, and may speculate about evolutionary selection pressures; the psychologist or social scientist may conclude that people appreciate the benefits of the practice, and have thus instituted it as a custom. From the armchair it is easy to invent 'Just So' stories (Gould 1978). What is needed is not so much evidence consistent with a particular story, but rather empirical data which can be explained by the one but not by the other.

There is, one might suspect, an unspoken assumption in some of the literature on human sociobiology. This is that an explanation in terms of genetics is to be preferred where it seems plausible, as if this would represent yet another victory for the respectable science of biology. Biology has indeed had very great successes, and the theory of evolution has proved a solid foundation. But there is more to biology than genes, since, as we have stressed, nature has allowed two ways, not one, in which animals can adapt. Learning is not 'unbiological'. It depends on mechanisms built into the brain under genetic instruction, according to the process of evolution. But when an animal adapts to its environment by learning, the information so acquired is stored in the brain and not in the genetic material which the animal will transmit to its successors.

MARRIAGE

It is the custom in all societies that people marry. Three patterns of association are prevalent. The most common is a partnership between a man and a woman which lasts for their lifetime. Strict monogamy has usually been promoted as the ideal in Western societies, but in practice it is not always achieved. Separation or divorce leave both partners free to form new liaisons, and thus one person may be married to several partners in succession. The third pattern is polygamy, most usually the association of several wives with one man; in Muslim society the women are said to live in a harem. When we enquire about the proportion of societies in which each pattern is to be found we find that roughly half of them practise some form of monogamy, and that in roughly half of them some at least of the inhabitants practise polygamy (Murdock 1949). But, of course, some societies are more densely populated than others and it is safe to say that for the majority of people, though not societies, the custom is for a husband to have only one wife at any one time.

What are the most important features of the organization of human families? It is not necessary to dwell on the obvious fact that people, unlike animals, form ties which they formalize through some form of marriage ceremony; formal agreements of this sort can be drawn up only with the aid of a language. In comparing social organization in animals and man it is quite as important to stress three other characteristics of human marriage. The father usually stays with the mother while the child is immature, he frequently stays with the same mother for the birth and development of more than one of their children, and he actively contributes not only to the economy of the household but also more directly to the welfare of the children. The role of the father is not restricted to the procreation of children.

Now contrast this situation with the type of organization in other mammals. Only a small number of mammals live in monogamous pairs, such as foxes, jackals and beavers (Wilson 1975). There are at least 14 or more primates that form such pairs (Clutton-Brock and Harvey 1977b); but their distribution across the primate groups does not form any obvious pattern. Monogamy occurs in two of the five apes, the gibbon and the siamang, but in few of the monkeys of the Old World. There are 15 genera of New World monkey, and of these 5 include species that are monogamous, the titi monkey (*Callicebus*) (Fig. 9.1), and some of the marmosets and tamarins. Of the prosimians the indris (*Indri*) is certainly monogamous, and there may be others. In all these cases the ties between male and female are assumed to last for many years, and perhaps for their lifetime; in some cases we know this to be true.

Like other mammals primates more typically form polygamous groups in which a male mates with more than one female (Eisenberg *et al.* 1972; Wilson 1975). When a male has relatively exclusive access to a group of females it is usual to refer to the basic unit as being a harem. If comparisons are to be made with polygamy in man it is crucial that we know for how long any particular male is associated with the same females. Though this question is easy to ask it can be answered only by mounting detailed and lengthy field studies, in which the individual members of a group must be identified and their associations followed over many years. In fact there are not many primates or other mammals on which adequate studies have been made so as to allow us to comment on the permanency of the social ties.

Long-term bonds have been convincingly demonstrated in two non-human primates that live in harems, and may be presumed in some others. Mountain gorillas

9.1 Pair of titi monkeys.
Courtesy of San Diego Zoo.

live in groups in which it is typical for several adult females to be associated with one fully adult male, although there are groups in which two or even three such males can be found (Schaller 1963; Fossey 1974). The fully adult males can easily be identified because they develop a silver rather than a black coat on their back. Gorillas living in Rwanda and Zaire have been studied continously from 1967 (Fossey 1974; Fossey and Harcourt 1977); and we know that the adult females consort with the same silverback males for many years (Harcourt 1979).

The harem is also the basic unit of the hamadryas baboons of Ethiopia; one and sometimes two adult males herd a small group of adult females (Kummer 1968) (Fig. 9.2). The males guard their females jealously from the advances of other males. When the males are juvenile they come to acquire their females by kidnapping infants and then looking after them in a maternal fashion. It is thought that these females then remain with their males until the males reach old age (Kummer 1968).

9.2 Hamadryas baboons. The picture shows three harem groups consisting of one male and several females. From Kummer and Kurt (1963).

There are other primates organized in harems, but in which the leadership of the harems changes every few years. An Old World monkey, the hanamum langur (*Presbytis entellus*), will serve as an example. In some but not all areas of India these monkeys most typically live in groups with one adult male and several females, but the adult males are replaced every two or three years (Sugiyama 1967). The new leaders drive out the old, often killing some of the infants (Hrdy 1974). This is much the same process as occurs in lions, where males lead a pride of lionesses for only two years or so before being forcibly ejected by incoming males, who take over the pride and may kill cubs in doing so (Bertram 1976).

In the harem groups mentioned so far an adult male has relatively exclusive access to a set of females, although it may sometimes tolerate the presence of one or two younger and subordinate adult males (Eisenberg *et al.* 1972). But there are also primates in which no male enjoys such exclusive rights, such as the macaques, baboons and chimpanzees. These live in 'multi-male' groups including many adult males and females. In theory in such a troop each male could have an equal chance of mating with any particular females. But the males in multi-male troops can often be ranked in an order of dominance which determines their priority to resources, and may also grant to the most dominant males prior access to the females in oestrus (Jolly 1972). In savannah baboons, for example, lower ranking males are able to copulate with females, but higher ranking animals have priority, and the first ranking male may have exclusive access on the days when the females are most fertile (Hausfater 1975; Packer 1979b).

It is also possible to detect short- and even long-term associations between particular males and females in such groups. Observation of one troop of baboons showed that it was very common for males to form short 'consortships' with females in oestrus, during which the female mated only with a particular male (Seyfarth 1978a). The associations lasted from one to eight days. In the same troop there were two pairs in which male and female showed a preference for each other's company which lasted many months, and similar persistent bonds have been noted in macaque groups (Seyfarth 1978b). Male and female chimpanzees are also known to form temporary consortships during the period when the females are most receptive, going off on their own for days or even weeks (McGinnis 1979).

But while in multi-male groups mating is not as randomly promiscuous as might appear at first sight, it is still true that in the course of a year any female may mate with many different males. The difference between a multi-male troop and a harem system can be highlighted by comparing the hamadryas baboons with groups of olive baboons also living in semi-desert in Ethiopia (Kummer 1971). At night the hamadryas baboons gather into large troops, as there is limited space on cliffs for the animals to sleep in safety, but during the day the troops split up into bands and then into their constituent harems. Resources are limited and patchily distributed, and can best be exploited by small groups. The olive baboons here form large troops as they do in more lush regions, but in this habitat they also divide into small groups during the day to search for food. But these groups are not harems, that is they do not consist of one male and a small number of associated females (Aldrich-Blake et al. 1971). Furthermore if male olive baboons are transferred into troops of hamadryas baboons they show no sign of actively herding females (Kummer 1971).

The multi-male system is quite unlike any human society. It has attracted much attention in the literature mainly because the baboons and macaques are highly successful, and are easy to observe because they spend much time on the ground. If we are to compare our human family with the social units adopted by other primates, we might feel more justified in paying attention to our closest relatives, the apes. But it comes as a shock to discover that all the main types of social organization are demonstrated by one or other of the apes.

The orang-utan lives a relatively solitary existence. In the forests of Borneo and Sumatra it is most common to find animals on their own or females with their young, although males are occasionally seen with females (MacKinnon 1974). Though many nocturnal prosimians live solitary lives when they are active (Charles-Dominique 1977), there are no species of monkey that do so. Why orang-utan society should be organized in so loose a way we do not know.

The gibbon, on the other hand, lives in tight family groups (Ellefson 1968), and so does the closely related siamang (Chivers 1974). These are the lesser apes, the apes with the least resemblance to man in anatomy and biochemistry. The gibbon and siamang both live in pairs of adult male and female, actively defending a small area against intruders. Adolescent animals leave their natal group to form their own pairs, and the pairs are probably stable for life. Here we have a system which resembles human monogamy in certain respects. But it is not easy to understand why these two apes should have adopted a pattern that is rare in primates, nor is it obvious what are the environmental conditions that promote pair-living.

The gorilla, as already noted, lives in harem groups, and females are to be found with the same males over a long period. The adolescent females usually leave their natal groups, and then become attached to the large silver-backed males, who father their infants and protect them from danger (Harcourt 1979). There is at least a superficial resemblance between this social organization and human polygamy.

But the chimpanzee, the other African ape, behaves quite differently. Chimpanzees live in large regional populations of 50 to 100 or so animals (Sugiyama 1972; Nishida 1979). The organization within the population is very flexible. The chimpanzees go around in small temporary subgroups, with only three to five or so members; and they frequently change their companions. The only stable subgroup is the association of mother with her young. The young stay with the mother until the age of 5 or 6 years, but may return to her later on visits (van Lawick-Goodall 1968a). In some cases the bonds may last for many years. But the lack of any close association between particular males and females renders chimpanzee society quite unlike the human pattern.

This survey of primates has not brought to light the conditions that might favour the long-term or even permanent association of male with female. To identify them we need to turn further afield, and it is to birds that we should look. Consider this extraordinary fact: while monogamy is rare in mammals it is practised in some form or other by roughly 92 per cent of birds (Lack 1968). Why, then, do birds behave in a way so untypical of mammals? The answer probably lies in the different reproductive patterns of the two groups: birds lay eggs, while mammals give birth to live young which they suckle.

When the eggs are laid they must be warmed and protected from predators. It is difficult for one bird to find food for itself while at the same time sitting on the eggs; but two birds can share the task, for example, by taking turns. After the nestlings are hatched much the same problem continues, since they must be supplied with food, sheltered and guarded from danger. Again one bird can stay on the nest while the other searches for food for the young. In such a situation the male bird does not necessarily achieve maximum reproductive success by inseminating a large number of females. It does better if it concentrates its efforts on ensuring the success of a single brood in any one season.

In mammals, on the other hand, the female can nourish the embryo and find herself food at the same time. When the young are born she requires no help from the male in feeding them. Even if the male could contribute to the survival of the young by remaining with the female, this does not prevent him from mating with several females and protecting them as a group or harem. If the male is not needed at all, he can best further his interests by copulating with as many females as possible without forming any lasting ties with any of them.

If this argument is correct we should be able to demonstrate that in monogamous pairs the male helps in the rearing of the young; and this is what we find in the few primates that form such pairs. It is true of most non-human primates that the males take little direct part in the care and rearing of infants, although they defend mothers and young in times of danger. It is the mother that feeds, holds and protects her young, and it is with her that they spend most of their time. When the mother moves off the infant either clings to her belly or, when it is older, rides on her back in the style of a jockey. There are a few species in which males show a more active interest (Mitchell and Brandt 1972). We have already noted that young adult male hamadryas baboons form close relationships with infant females, but this is in the interests of collecting a harem. Male Japanese macaques sometimes temporarily take over the protection of infants when their mothers give birth to new offspring. But there are only two species of Old World monkey in which the male devotes much time to the care of young infants. When infant black mangabeys (*Cercocebus aterrimus*) are a few months old they spend more time with adult males than with their mothers (Chalmers 1968). Infant Barbary apes (*Macaca sylvana*) are also often carried around by adult males, which are remarkably protective towards them. But, with these exceptions, it is fair to say that in Old World monkeys the role played by adult males is very limited.

In family pairs, paternity can be determined with relative certainty, and it is in such groups that we find the most dramatic examples of the assistance of the male in the rearing of the young (Mitchell and Brandt 1972). The marmosets and tamarins normally produce twins. These are usually carried about by the male, not the female, and are returned to the mother only for nursing (Fig. 9.3). Male titi monkeys are also responsible for holding and transporting the infants, and in the night monkey, believed to live in pairs, the male behaves in the same way. In all these primates the male probably spends more time with the infant than does the mother. However, it is not the case that the males carry the young in all pair-living primates; male gibbons do not do so, although they do show an interest in their infants by playing with them (Schaller 1965).

In human families, whether monogamous or polygamous, the father plays an important role in the upbringing of the children. This fact has rightly been stressed by anthropologists (Wilson 1980). What has led to the close association between father, mother and child that is characteristic of human society but not of most other primate communities? As is the case with birds there must be some reason why the rearing of the offspring would be unlikely to be successful without the aid of both parents.

That reason can best be appreciated by considering the reproductive strategy pursued by man in common with monkeys and apes. As described in Chapter 5 the strategy adopted is to give birth to only one infant at a time, although marmosets have twins and so occasionally do

9.3 Marmoset father carrying twins. Courtesy of San Diego Zoo.

people. The infants are slow to grow up, and are dependent on their mother for milk for at least a year. Accordingly the mother gives birth at most once a year, and in larger primates less frequently; the breastfeeding of babies helps to postpone the time of the next conception (Daly and Wilson 1978). A mother will not have very many offspring in her life, and this means that those few that she has must be cherished. A chimpanzee mother, as we have seen, will nurture her infants for several years, and may maintain ties with them over many more. The human mother must devote much of her time to the care of her children, who will not be sexually mature until they are 12 or more years old.

But there is nothing in what we have said so far that must force the human father any more than the chimpanzee father to stay and help with rearing the young. Why, then, is the human mother unable to cope on her own in the way that the chimpanzee mother does? The crucial difference between man and chimpanzee lies in the state of the infant when born. As discussed in Chapter 4 the time at which the human baby can be safely delivered is con-strained by the size of the brain. The human baby is brought to term at a time when the brain is less mature than in other primates. The consequence is that the baby is born more helpless than any other primate infant, as is shown by comparisons based on the various milestones (Schaller 1963). A baby lying in a supine position can only raise its head briefly by the age of 28 weeks or so; yet this achievement is matched by the gorilla and chimpanzee in the first 4 weeks of life. It takes the baby over twice as long as these apes before it can sit up steadily, stand up with the aid of support, and crawl by pushing the legs.

But there is a further respect in which a baby is peculiarly helpless, and this is not a simple consequence of its marked immaturity. A baby must keep near its mother; but how is it to do this? An infant chimpanzee or gorilla can cling to its mother's belly when she moves. In the first few weeks it can support its weight only for short periods, but from then on it is rarely in need of assistance (van Lawick-Goodall 1968a; Fossey 1979). Newborn babies can also support their weight by hanging from a rod, but after 4 weeks or so this ability declines (McGraw 1945). If touched on the hand babies of 4 weeks or more close their fingers in a grasp (Twitchell 1965). Babies also clench their hands and extend their arms and legs if they are suddenly shaken or tilted, the so-called 'Moro response' (Prechtl 1965). This is just what one would expect of a primate that clings to its mother to ensure a better hold as she moves off. But to what avail is this response to the baby? There is no hair to which it can cling and the big toe is so aligned that the foot is useless for grasping (Chapter 3).

The mother is forced to cradle her child, to hold it and carry it in her arms. Even though the child may learn to walk at around 1 year of age it is not capable of keeping up with adults until a year or two later, and so the mother is still called upon to transport it when distances are long (Rheingold and Keene 1965). Her activity must be restricted, and if the mother has children at intervals of 2 or 3 years she will be encumbered for an appreciable part of her life. At times she will be nursing, at others pregnant, and over a span of years she will, as one might say, 'have her hands full'.

Here, perhaps, we have the need for the father to help. The human mother is restricted in a way that is true of no other primate mother. A chimpanzee mother has little difficulty in finding food or in keeping up with other animals; she has all four limbs free for foraging, running and climbing, since she can rely on her infant to hang on. But a human mother cradling her baby must be very much less efficient at gathering food than a male or female without a baby; and she would certainly make a poor hunter. In fact, as we know, human societies take note of this situation, and assign different roles to men and women; the women do most of the gathering and the men are usually the hunters (Lee and DeVore 1968). A pregnant or nursing mother would be reliant on males if she was to secure a high-protein diet. It would be in the interests of the father to stay with the mother, forming an economic unit in which plant food and meat were shared, and in which the young were adequately fed. Having stayed to provide for one child the father would have reason to stay longer, because of the arrival of further children. But we should be clear that there is nothing in this that dictates monogamy; if a male can provide adequately for more than one female polygamy would be to his advantage. The only constraint is that in either system the male should stay to form a relatively permanent economic unit, the family.

In a human family the male partly or wholly restricts his sexual activity to intercourse with his consort. But this need not imply a reduction in sexual activity, since people are able to copulate at any time during the menstrual cycle, as can the other primates with a menstrual cycle— the apes and most of the monkeys (Butler 1974; Daly and Wilson 1978). A few New World monkeys exhibit only an oestrous cycle, like the prosimians and all other mammals. Females with an oestrous cycle only come on heat around the time of ovulation, and are not sexually receptive at other times. The female rat, for example, rejects the male on all but a half day in her cycle of 4 to 5 days, and in squirrel monkeys copulation is restricted to 2 days in the cycle (Daly and Wilson 1978) (Fig. 9.4). This is unlike the situation found in those primates with menstrual cycles, that is with cycles which terminate in bleeding due to the sloughing off of the uterine lining. In the abnormal conditions of captivity a rhesus monkey copulates most frequently around the time of ovulation in the middle of the cycle but it also does so frequently at other times in the cycle (Michael 1975) (Fig. 9.4). A similar pattern is seen in captive gorillas and chimpanzees (Nadler 1975; Lemmon and Allen 1978). People differ only in showing less obvious peaks in sexual activity during the cycle (Udry and Morris 1968) (Fig. 9.4).

People also engage in intercourse at all times of the year,

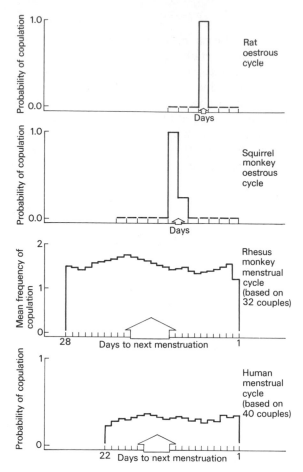

9.4 Probability or frequency of copulation at different times during the cycle in rat, squirrel monkey (a New World species), rhesus monkey (an Old World species) and man. After Daly and Wilson (1978).

and though proper information is lacking they probably do so with greater regularity throughout the year than do other primates. We know that in the wild and in captivity adult Japanese macaques mate very much more frequently at some times of the year than others, and that in many though not all monkeys there are breeding seasons during which most of the fertile matings take place (Lancaster and Lee 1965; Hinde 1974). It is true that chimpanzees may give birth at any season (van Lawick-Goodall 1968a), but it has still to be established whether matings are distributed fairly evenly over the year as in man.

There are no clear external signs of the time during the cycle when a woman ovulates. In almost all other mammals ovulation is well advertised, although it is difficult to detect in gibbons and gorillas (Alexander and Noonan 1979). The concealment of the time of ovulation has the consequence that it encourages the male to consort with the same female for some time so as to ensure fertilization (Lovejoy 1981).

We have been enquiring into the origins of the human family. The key factor, so we have suggested, was the burden of a helpless baby on the mother, such that it paid the father to stay and assist rather than to leave and thus put the survival of his offspring at risk. But nothing has yet been said of the mechanism by which any change in social organization occurred. That it came to pay individuals to behave in a particular way speaks no more of genetic than of cultural change. A situation that could give rise to selection pressures on genes could as well be assessed by individuals who are then responsible for alterations in custom.

How, then, could we distinguish between these possibilities? It is not in principle difficult to find out whether or not particular behaviour is learned. Take the titi monkey which lives in family groups. In the laboratory adult titi monkeys can be shown to differ markedly from squirrel monkeys in their social preferences and dispositions (Mason 1978). Titi monkeys that have been kept in pairs show little attraction towards other animals when given the opportunity to mix; squirrel monkeys that have been kept in the same way are more attracted to strangers and less attached to their companions (Mason 1978). The influence of learning could be studied by rearing titi monkeys either on their own or with companions of their own sex. If, as seems likely, they nonetheless formed pairs when given the opportunity, we could conclude that we must look to factors other than learning in accounting for their disposition to form pair bonds.

But how are we to use the same experimental strategy on man? Of course there are a few children who have been isolated from significant human contact in early life; Genie, who was mentioned in Chapter 8, is one such child. But when they are returned to contact with society these children are subjected to the ordinary social pressures and forces of education. Their social preferences as adults will in no way reveal the social dispositions that mankind inherits. Nor is there any use in our appealing to the universality of the family, because that may speak only of universal advantage. In hard fact we have no way of discovering whether there is any genetic basis for a social disposition such as the tendency to form family ties. And, in that case, we must be content to leave open the question of whether any significant genetic change was required for our hominid ancestors to adopt the family as the basic unit of society.

There is one rule governing marriage that some anthropologists have regarded as the distinguishing feature of human society (Lévi-Strauss 1969). In all cultures sexual relations are forbidden between mother and son, father and daughter, and brother and sister, and in no society are these relatives allowed to marry (Murdock 1949). There are some societies that restrict marriage between more distant relatives such as first cousins, but cousin marriage is permitted in some and even encouraged in others (Daly and Wilson 1978). That these rules are sometimes broken is not relevant; it is their existence that needs explaining.

There is a price to pay for incest. Each person carries recessive genes which are deleterious or lethal in the homozygous state; and close relatives are more similar in their genetic make-up than unrelated people. The children of incestuous unions are therefore more likely to carry these genes in the homozygous condition. One study looked at the children born from sexual relations between father and daughter and brother and sister. Thirty-three per cent of these children either died or suffered from such conditions as mental deficiency or a cleft lip (Adams and Neel 1967). Sexual relations between mother and son carry a similar penalty, as shown by a survey of women in Czechoslovakia referred to by Wilson (1978). Of 161 children born of incest 15 were stillborn or died early in life; and 40 per cent in all suffered from physical and mental defects. But for the 95 children born to the same women from non-incestuous relations the risk of such complications was no higher than for the population at large.

The children of incest, then, are biologically less fit. It would be tempting to suppose that the incest taboo reflects evolutionary pressures towards the elimination of inbreeding. On this view the reasons given by people for perpetuating this taboo may be regarded as rationalizations, put forward in ignorance of the evolutionary forces shaping our attitudes. But an alternative view must at least be considered: that the risk of producing handicapped children is appreciated, and it is for this reason that society forbids incestuous relations. The demonstration that a course of action pays in evolutionary terms does not prove genetic as opposed to intellectual foresight.

That evolution may indeed select against incest is known, because inbreeding is rare in animal populations.

In social mammals it is usually prevented by the emigration of sub-adult males from their natal group; these males then join other groups and mate with females to which they are not closely related (Packer 1979a). It is less common for the females to transfer between groups, although this is the pattern exemplified by the two African apes, the chimpanzee and the gorilla (Harcourt *et al.* 1976; Nishida 1979). In some cases animals are physically expelled from their natal group. Gibbons, for example, drive out their sons and daughters when they reach puberty, thus preventing any permanent increase in the size of the family group. More usually the males leave of their own accord. This pattern is typical for monkeys living in multi-male troops, such as the macaques and baboons (Itani 1972; Sade 1972; Packer 1979a).

The transfer of animals of one sex from their natal groups provides a reliable mechanism for the prevention of inbreeding, since it ensures that closely related adults of the opposite sex are unlikely to meet. An alternative arrangement would be to permit relatives to meet but to inculcate inhibitions preventing mating. There is no good evidence, however, that the mating of monkeys is restricted in this way. One survey of rhesus monkeys on Cayo Santiago found that most males left their natal groups; but of the males that stayed and so could mate with their mothers 31 per cent did so; and mating was also observed in 12 per cent of the brother – sister pairs (Missakian 1973).

In chimpanzees it is the females and not the males that transfer to other communities (Pusey 1979). The females typically alter their range after their first oestrus and are thus no longer associated with their male siblings (Pusey 1980). However, since the males stay they may sometimes meet their mothers, and four such adult males have been observed in the company of their mothers when the mothers were in oestrus (Pusey 1980). None was seen to copulate with their mother, suggesting that there may indeed be an inhibition preventing such liaisons in chimpanzees.

These observations on animals indicate that there are evolutionary pressures favouring outbreeding. But anthropologists such as Lévi-Strauss (1969) have long maintained that human beings acquire the incest taboo by cultural tradition. They point to advantages other than those of eugenics. For many of their activities families must co-operate with each other, let us say in hunting. Alliances between families can be cemented by intermarriage, fathers giving away their daughters. In very many societies the groom has to pay a bride price, in some the groom has to buy his wife by working for her kin, and in others gifts are exchanged between the families (Murdock 1957). If such a system is to be workable it is essential that incest be prevented; daughters must be married into other families and sons must be free to look for brides outside their immediate family. On this view the incest taboo is universal because there is a universal need for families to form alliances.

But how are we to tell whether the incest taboo is indeed the product of our cultural inheritance alone? Can we find any instance of the existence of a taboo which is not inculcated by cultural tradition? One case which has often been cited is the situation that is reported to occur in Israeli Kibbutzim (Shepher 1971). In many Kibbutzim the children are brought up from birth in groups consisting only of children of their own age. There is nothing to prevent adolescents from engaging in hetero-sexual activity with their peers, and no one suggests to them that this would be wrong. Yet, such activity is said not to occur. Furthermore, of 2769 marriages surveyed only 14 were between partners raised in the same age-group and none of these was between people consistently reared together from an early age.

Here is a case in which a taboo is adhered to though it is not passed on by teaching. The most plausible explanation is that it reflects a lack of sexual attraction between people who have known each other intimately for a very long time. In seeking sexual partners people may be enticed by novelty, thus preferring people of other ages or from other groups. On this interpretation it is not that incest is avoided because we harbour inhibitions, but rather be-cause we are positively attracted to those with whom we are less familiar. In the absence of empirical evidence it is uncertain to what extent this preference is learned; but it is not implausible that such a preference could be influenced by genetic factors (Lumsden and Wilson 1981).

SOCIAL TIES

It is the responsibility of parents to look after their children and bring them up until they are ready to leave the family as independent members of adult society. This involves several duties. Parents must give the baby the physical contact it needs to be secure and contented. They must provide an emotionally warm environment in which their children can grow up to be stable in temperament. It is the parents who must socialize their children and teach them what behaviour is acceptable, and it is the parents who must ensure that their children acquire the social skills they must exercise in their interactions with others.

As we shall see, there are important similarities between the ways in which the child and ape are socialized. Both need close physical contact with their mothers when young, and both are greatly distressed by separation from their mothers. But the differences are as striking. Children are brought up in a language environment. There is no risk that we would ignore this if we were considering the ways in which children are educated and taught information and skills. In considering the socialization of children we will find language to make as decisive a contribution, determining the ways in which social events are perceived and the ways in which social behaviour is regulated.

Contact

Like the infants of other social mammals, human babies find social contact reassuring. It is vital that infant mammals keep near to their mother as it is she who provides them with food and warmth; and nature has therefore arranged that physical contact is rewarding. There are two ways this might be done. The infant could be given the opportunity to learn that contact with the mother leads to consequences it desires—food and so on. In this way it will come to seek contact because of the gains it achieves. Alternatively the infant could be built such that, without the need for learning, it searches for contact in the same way that it searches for food and other necessities. We can distinguish between these two possibilities by setting up a situation in which the animal is not fed for making physical contact. This was done in a famous experiment in which rhesus monkeys were brought up away from their mothers; instead they were given two dummies as substitutes, one covered with cloth and the other made of bare wire (Harlow and Zimmerman 1959). Even if they were fed milk from the wire model they chose nonetheless to spend most of their time clinging to the soft cloth model, leaving it only for feeding (Fig. 9.5). They spent very little time on the wire model even though it provided them with their food. It is fair to conclude that in this case the animals had not learned to

9.5 Baby rhesus monkey drinking from a 'wire' surrogate mother while remaining in contact with a 'soft' surrogate mother. Courtesy of Wisconsin Regional Primate Center

seek contact as a means to some further end, but clung to the cloth model for the warmth and comfort it provided.

The features that make a mother attractive are easily demonstrated. Monkeys can be provided with model mothers differing in varying respects and their preferences measured by the time they spend clinging to each (Harlow and Suomi 1970). Faced with a choice between two cloth-covered mothers a rhesus monkey chooses the one that feeds it rather than one that is dry. A warm mother is preferred to a cold one, and a rocking mother is more attractive than one that remains still. The real mother, of course, possesses all these qualities: she suckles her infant, she provides warmth and she moves around. Deprived of its mother the infant will cling to anything that provides some of the necessary comforts: another infant, a soft, model mother, or even a piece of cloth (Harlow and Harlow 1965) (Fig. 9.6).

That substitutes of this kind provide security can be shown by placing the animal in a situation that provokes

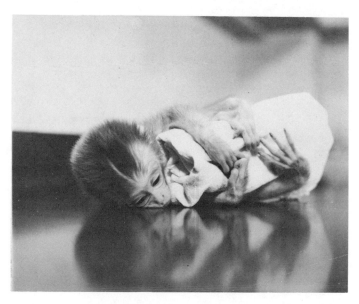

9.6 Baby rhesus monkey clinging to soft blanket. Courtesy of Wisconsin Regional Primate Center.

anxiety. Infants are typically wary of novel objects and novel situations. But if they have been reared with a substitute mother rhesus monkeys are confident and will explore so long as the mother is present (Fig. 9.7). If, on the other hand, their familiar model is not there they are terror-struck, and will huddle pitiably with their faces in their hands (Harlow and Harlow 1965; Mason 1971) (Fig. 9.8). The same phenomenon has been demonstrated in experiments on chimpanzees (Mason 1965). Young chimpanzees call in distress if placed in an unfamiliar situation;

9.7 Baby rhesus monkey exploring a novel environment in the presence of its surrogate cloth mother. Courtesy of Wisconsin Regional Primate Center.

265

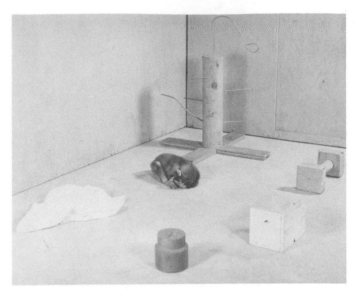

9.8 Baby rhesus monkey freezing in terror in novel environment in absence of its surrogate cloth mother. Courtesy of Wisconsin Regional Primate Center.

but they call very little if they are able to cling on to a person that they know. They will even tolerate pain better if they are held; if given mild electric shocks to their feet they whimper less if they can clutch on to a familiar person. If substitute mothers inspire such feelings of security we may be sure that the real mother has a yet more potent effect.

Human babies have as great a need for physical contact. If the mother holds the baby in such a way that it can cling to her the baby tightens its grasp when she suddenly moves (Prechtl 1965). If an adult tries to put down a baby of 9 months or so she will find it very difficult to peel it off if the baby is in a strange setting (Bowlby 1969). Like monkeys babies are reassured by being rocked; they cry less and given the optimal type of stimulation they will usually stop crying within 15 seconds (Gordon and Foss 1965; Ambrose 1969). Even though brought up with their mothers children often seek other sources of comfort. In one study of children of 18 months a third were given to thumb sucking or had been in the past (Schaffer and Emerson 1964a). Baby monkeys deprived of their mothers also have a tendency to suck their fingers or thumb for comfort (Berkson 1968). Human babies also use other substitutes—blankets, cuddly toys and so on. Over a third of the children in one survey had by the age of 18 months adopted some particular cuddly object to which they were attached (Schaffer and Emerson 1964a). That other primates sometimes seek solace in the same way is documented by the pathetic photograph (Fig. 9.9) of a chimpanzee in captivity clutching a mop as a comfort blanket.

9.9 Chimpanzee in captivity clutching mop for comfort. From Mason (1967).

The mother provides a secure base from which the baby can explore the world around. In one experiment babies of 10 months of age were quite happy to leave their mother in one room and explore a large room which they had never previously entered, and they did so willingly if the room contained novel toys (Rheingold and Eckerman 1970). Throughout they kept contact with their mother by repeatedly returning to the room in which she sat, as if for reassurance. Yet if infants were placed on their own in the same room in the absence of their mother they were greatly distressed, since they now lacked a secure base to which they could return. Much the same pattern is seen if children are watched out of doors. Children of 15 to 30 months have been observed with their mothers in parks (Anderson 1972). The children wandered away from their mother, though not straying more than 200 feet or so, but they often returned to her side of their own accord. This is strikingly reminiscent of the behaviour of a rhesus monkey left in a novel environment with a soft model as a substitute mother: it ventures out to play and returns occasionally for reassurance (Harlow and Mears 1979) (Fig. 9.10). For any mammal such a policy is a sound one, since the mother is both provider and defender, and safety is to be found in her presence.

Physical contact continues to be reassuring even in adults. This is evident from the time that some social mammals spend in grooming one another, and from the rituals they perform in greeting. Most mammals groom with their mouth, licking or combing with their teeth.

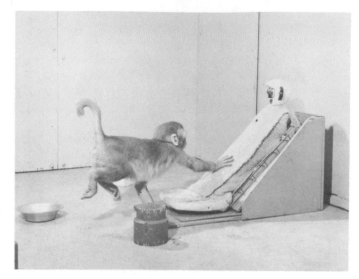

9.10 Baby rhesus monkey in novel environment returning to its surrogate mother for comfort. Courtesy of Wisconsin Regional Primate Center.

The prosimians also use their teeth, although some of them part the fur with their hands. But the monkeys use their hands not only to separate the fur but also to remove particles from the skin. Some will spend long periods of the day contentedly picking over each other's fur, and they sometimes resolve conflicts with the two parties settling down to a grooming session (Sparks 1967) (Fig. 3.5). Since people wear clothes and lack a thick coat of fur grooming is not an appropriate way of maintaining contact, but there are still hints that grooming may be pleasurable. In some peoples it is not unusual for one person to search through the hair of a companion for parasites; this practice has been reported for Polynesians, South American Indians and others (Yerkes 1933; Eibl-Eibesfeldt 1971). Even in Western societies the hairdresser appears to provide intimate contact that is pleasurable to the customer (Morris 1971). And people seem to enjoy stroking dogs and other pets, quite apart from any satisfaction given to the animal. It would be worth trying to back anecdotal evidence of this sort with a proper investigation of the comfort that people may derive from such activities.

When greeting social mammals often make bodily contact. Lions rub their heads and wolves rub muzzles (Schaller 1972; Mech 1970). The most complex set of gestures has been described in the chimpanzee (van Lawick-Goodall 1968a,b). A chimpanzee may put out a hand towards a companion for reassurance, as in the drawing (Fig. 9.11) where a female returns to her group

after giving birth to a baby. Or a dominant animal can help a submissive one to relax simply by reaching out and touching it with the hand. Chimpanzees sometimes even embrace when meeting. We can assume that they are reassured in this way, since they may also put their arms round each other when facing a common danger. Perhaps most striking to the human observer is the fact that in greeting chimpanzees have been seen touching lips or putting their lips to the hand of their companion.

To us these actions are, perhaps, slightly unnerving. That an ape might look like us is no matter: that it should behave in such human ways is uncanny. It is little wonder that chimpanzees are so popular for spectators at zoos and circuses. But the similarities between man and ape should not be exaggerated. Chimpanzees touch hands, but do not shake them; they press lips together but do not kiss. The hand shake is certainly a gesture universal amongst mankind. The Waika Indians of South America, the Balinese, the Papuans and the people of Sumatra all shake hands (Eibl-Eibesfeldt 1972). But the exact pattern and the conventional meaning of the gesture may vary between different cultures from East to West (Firth 1973). In the same way the kiss may be seen in all human lovers, but it is not a universal practice as a form of greeting (Firth 1973). How then are we to view the matter? There is little doubt that people react to contact in the same way as apes; they are reassured, and particularly so if contact is made between highly sensitive areas such as the palm of the hand or the lips. Thus we would expect to find that the hand and the lips were used in those situations where there was a need to give or secure reassurance; and meetings provide just such conditions of uncertainty. But we should not be surprised to find that different peoples adopted their own conventional ways of communicating, just as they have their own languages. Hence the variations in the rituals found appropriate in different cultures.

Separation

Separation from the mother is traumatic for any mammalian infant. On its own the infant is exposed to predation and other dangers. The only way in which the infant can secure protection is by calling, that is by informing the parents of where it is and alerting them to its distress. If the parents are out of sight or out of reach calling is the most effective way of ensuring that contact is regained.

We should distinguish between two fates that may befall such an infant (Mineka and Suomi 1978). It may lose its mother, either temporarily or permanently, while still remaining in the company of its siblings and other members of the group; the mother might, for example, die. Alternatively the infant might get separated from the group as well as from its parents, perhaps by getting lost. Of these two situations the first involves loss of contact with the mother, and the second loss of social contact of any kind through isolation. It is with the first of these that we are primarily concerned, in so far as it serves to illustrate the special contribution made by the immediate family to the infant's sense of security.

The effects of temporary separations have been particularly studied in monkeys in captivity. If a rhesus or pig-tailed macaque (*Macaca nemestrina*) is left with its familiar companions but its mother is removed from the group the monkey's immediate response is one of evident distress and agitation (Kaufman and Rosenblum 1969; Hinde and Spencer Booth 1971). The infant screams at the time of separation and later makes pathetic cooing calls usually described as 'woo calls'. Chimpanzees also whimper with 'hoo' like calls when separated from their mother in the wild (Marler 1976b); and their face may take on the expression of a weeping child (van Hooff 1976).

From the early months human babies react to separation in much the same way. They protest and cry when temporarily separated from their mothers in the ordinary course of life, when put down or left with other adults, and so on (Schaffer and Emerson 1964a). Understandably the intensity of the reaction is greater if the child is not only separated from its mother but also moved into a new and strange environment with new caretakers, whether in a residential nursery, foster home or hospital (Rutter 1972, 1981; Bowlby 1973). But although separation elicits protest in monkey and man, the human baby is better able to register that protest. The baby does not simply cry; it weeps tears. And it does not simply whimper; it roars. It is perhaps not fanciful to suppose that an infant as helpless as a human baby would especially benefit from the ability to cry so loudly as to be certain of capturing the attention of adults. For many months if the baby is on its own it must be retrieved, and the baby's loud cry is necessary if this is to be achieved.

But what happens if contact is not regained? Protest turns to despair. After a day or so after its mother is removed a rhesus or pig-tailed macaque typically gives up the struggle, and sits hunched with its head held low (Kaufman and Rosenblum 1969; Hinde 1974) (Fig. 9.12). It sits alone, no longer playing or interacting with other members of the group. After a few days it usually recovers, becomes more active, and starts to show some interest in its surroundings. To the human observer it seems tempting to attribute to the animal the state of depression: inactivity, apathy and avoidance of social contact are all symptoms of depression in man (Beck 1967). But the most persuasive feature is the facial expression. In the drawing of a chimpanzee (Fig. 9.13) the drooping face betrays the animal's reaction to the death of

9.12 Baby pig-tailed monkey depressed after its mother has been removed from the group. From Kaufman and Rosenblum (1969).

its mother. In the same way children of 2 or 3 sometimes respond with despair when first placed in a residential nursery or hospital, withdrawing, becoming less active, and taking on the posture and features of grief (Bowlby 1969).

The severity of this emotional reaction depends on the conditions after the separation from the mother, and in particular whether the infant is moved into a strange environment, and whether it is provided with adequate maternal care by some other person. The importance of the first factor can be demonstrated in rhesus monkeys by comparing their reaction under two conditions. In the first the mother is taken away but the infant remains in its home cage; in the second it is the infant that is removed to an unfamiliar cage. Even though the infants left in their familiar surroundings are not adopted by their other cage-mates they call very much less than infants placed in a new cage (Hinde and Davies 1972); yet infants show little disturbance if placed in a new cage with their mothers (Hinde and McGinnis 1977). There is reason to think that young children can also be strongly affected by the shock of entry into some novel environment such as a hospital (Rutter 1981).

9.13 Chimpanzee Merlin depressed after losing his mother. From a photograph in van Lawick-Goodall (1971).

But the quality of substitute care is probably the greater influence. In the examples of separation in monkeys that we have quoted so far the infants were not adopted by any other member of their group. Bonnet macaques (*Macaca radiata*) behave quite differently: they tend to show much more interest in infants, and adult females will adopt and care for infants whose mothers have been temporarily removed from the group (Kaufman and Rosenblum 1969). The infant bonnet macaques usually show nothing resembling the severe reaction to separation that is seen in other macaques when their mother is removed from the group. It could, of course, be that bonnet macaques are temperamentally less prone to emotional disturbance, but this seems unlikely to be the whole story. In one experiment a pig-tailed macaque received some comfort from other adults, and did not go through a phase of depression (Kaufman and Rosenblum 1969); and in another a bonnet macaque did become depressed when left in its own cage with pig-tailed monkeys which showed no concern (Kaufman and Stynes 1978). There are two cases reported in which chimpanzees in the wild have adopted their young siblings after the death of their mother (van Lawick-Goodall 1968a, 1975). Although the infants showed marked signs of depression at first, attachment to their siblings seems to have provided them with some comfort.

There is suggestive evidence that in children separated from their mothers the distress may be less marked if they are put in the care of good foster-parents (Bowlby 1973; Rutter 1981). In one detailed study four children were observed while in the temporary care of a foster-mother whom they knew before their mothers had been admitted to hospital (Robertson and Robertson 1971). Though all showed signs of strain the quality of the care provided prevented any very strong emotional reaction.

But how adequate can substitute care be? It has been suggested in the past that separation from mother in the early years may result in a difficulty in forming emotional attachments (Bowlby 1952). The strongest version of this view holds that early experiences with the mother are critical for the development of emotional maturity, and that the damage done by maternal deprivation may be irreversible. Few would now defend the thesis in so extreme a form (Bowlby 1969, 1973); but it is worth identifying the sources of confusion in the animal and human literature that once led to its ready acceptance.

If a rhesus monkey is taken from its mother at birth and

reared in isolation for many months it becomes, not surprisingly, an emotional cripple (Harlow and Harlow 1965). The severity of the effects depends on the conditions of isolation and the length of time for which it is imposed (Sackett 1968, 1969). The monkey is more disturbed if caged out of sight of other animals than if able to see them through the netting; and isolation for 6 months or a year is more devastating than isolation for 3 months. These monkeys are terrified, withdrawn and apparently unable to make social contacts. The severity of the symptoms and the fact that they may last for years makes it tempting to suppose that the lack of early contact with a mother results in permanent handicap.

But this conclusion is unsound, and for two reasons. In the first place more has been done to the monkeys than simply to separate them from their mothers. They have been placed in a novel cage and then isolated from all contact with any other animal. Monkeys brought up away from the mother but with their peers grow up to be more normal than monkeys isolated on their own (Chamove 1966; Chamove *et al.* 1973). The crucial factor, so it appears, is not the maternal deprivation but the isolation.

And then, to take the second point, what right have we to conclude that the effects cannot be reversed unless we have made strenuous attempts to reverse them? Monkeys isolated for the first year of their life are indeed very damaged emotionally, but they are not beyond help. If such a monkey is gradually introduced to a much younger monkey, as the months pass by it comes to lose its terror and to appear much less threatened, and it even learns to play with its new partner (Suomi and Harlow 1972). Attachment made early in life can also be changed. In one study rhesus monkeys were reared for some months with their mother, or with another infant, or with a model mother substitute. In spite of making these early attachments the monkeys could be induced to form new bonds after separation; when they were gradually introduced to docile dogs they came to adopt them as substitutes (Mason and Kenney 1974) (Fig. 9.14). Yet it should not have proved possible to manipulate the attachments of the monkeys in this way if attachments must be formed early in life if they are to be formed at all.

The belief that maternal deprivation early in life has irreversible ill-effects is no better supported by the human literature (Rutter 1972). We have to ask whether the emotional effects result from the separation itself or from other events associated with the loss of the mother. What

9.14 Young rhesus monkey clinging to a dog to which it has become attached. From Mason and Kenney (1974).

of the marital discord that may lead to the breaking up of the home, of the lack of physical and social stimulation in some hospitals, or the inadequacy of the care provided in some of our institutions for children (Rutter 1981)? Nobody disputes that children need at least one person with whom they can form a close and affectionate relationship, nor that the lack of such bonds may result in distortions of personality. There are children who grow up 'affectionless', apparently unwilling to commit themselves to any real friendships, and it is true that some of these have lost their mothers in childhood (Bowlby 1952). But it has yet to be shown that it is this that is the cause of their problem, rather than the constant disappointment and let-down as one caretaker succeeds another in the institutions in which they are reared (Rutter 1972). To prove that separation itself has a long-lasting effect we would need evidence of the fates of children who, after the death of their mother, were brought up in their own home or in a good adoptive family. And there is no good published evidence that such children are unable to form adequate emotional ties.

Our first impression must be that the reaction to

separation is remarkably similar in children and infant monkeys and apes: agitation and protest, then despondency and inaction, and finally recovery and the formation of new attachments. Clearly we are alike in our need for contact and affiliation, and in the way in which loss disrupts our emotional stability. Like many other mammals man is a 'contact' species (Hediger 1950).

But what of the contribution of language to our emotional and mental life? In the previous chapter (Chapter 8) we reminded ourselves of the way in which language promoted the intelligent solution of problems regarding the physical world. It is as powerful as an aid in solving psychological problems. Language provides a set of symbols for representing to ourselves the state of the world and the course of events within it. Problems can be solved in the head by recourse to internal speech, that is by the silent manipulation of these symbols in the head. The difficulty can be formulated and the various possible solutions tried out, and this can be done by operating not on the real world but on a symbolic model of the world which is coded in verbal terms.

Now consider the child reacting to some crisis such as temporary separation from the mother. A child that has learned to speak has a language with which to ask why this disaster has occurred and with which to search for possible explanations. It may decide that the parents are to blame, and may appear sullen and untrusting when first it returns home. Indeed clinicians have sometimes detected signs of such a reaction, and described children as 'detached' when first reunited with their parents (Bowlby 1969). Monkeys show no such difficulty in re-establishing close relations (Hinde and Spencer-Booth 1971). But then they lack a language in which to formulate explanations for the distressing events they have experienced; even were their parents to blame for the separation infant monkeys have no means of telling themselves that this is so.

The ability to think with the aid of language can also be responsible for prolonging the misery caused by events such as separation. Events can be constantly kept in mind by brooding on them, since the symbols that refer to them can be recalled at any time, and the events thus represented without end. The mind can go over the problem rehearsing it again and again, in just the same way as it can think over an intellectual problem. But constantly reminding oneself of the issue and its implications may in the end do more harm than good, leading to an exaggeration in the mind of the true proportions of the problem. It is very common for patients suffering from depression to brood incessantly about their situation (Beck 1967). That monkeys and apes can recall events is not in doubt; but they lack the language with which to brood on them.

This being so we would expect to find that events such as separation could have a more lasting impact on people than on other primates. It is true that even in rhesus monkeys it is possible to pick up effects one and even two years later after only very brief separations (Hinde and Spencer-Booth 1971). But these effects are very minor; the monkeys are slightly less active and are more cautious when confronted with novel objects in a strange cage. The ill-effects might be expected to be more severe and long-lasting the greater the duration of separation and the more often it was experienced. But in people, who can so easily mentally relive the experience, the symptoms may persist for a very long time indeed. It is partly because man has language that he can make himself so miserable. Perhaps this is why he is 'gifted with that superior power of misery which distinguishes the human being and places him at a proud distance from the most melancholy chimpanzee . . .' (George Eliot).

SOCIALIZATION

Both man and ape enjoy a long youth (see Chapter 5). This allows an extended period of education, not only in the laws of the physical world but also in the ways of their fellow beings. Adult chimpanzees, for example, have a very sophisticated knowledge of the behaviour of other chimpanzees and of how they may be manipulated (Humphrey 1976). Interactions between chimpanzees are highly complex and give evidence of a high degree of social skill. Such skills are as important to the animal as manual skills, and they can be acquired only through extensive practice while the animal is young.

This learning takes place in a protected environment under the eye of the mother. Chimpanzee mothers permit their infants more social contact as they grow older, but are ready to intervene if their infants are in physical danger or become embroiled in play that is too rough (van Lawick-Goodall 1968a). The role of the mother is to provide the opportunity to learn how to interact with others, only stepping in when necessary so as to prevent harm.

What does the infant have to learn? If it is to interact smoothly with other animals it must be able to gauge their moods and intentions, and it can only do this by correctly interpreting the outward signs as shown by the expressions of the face and by the posture and movements of the body. There is no reason why the infant should have to learn the meanings of the basic expressions. Baby rhesus monkeys are disturbed by photographs of monkeys threatening, even if they have been reared on their own and have never seen another monkey (Sackett 1966). Nonetheless it may well be that the more subtle nuances must be learned through experience, and it is quite certain that any idiosyncratic usages by particular individuals can be interpreted only by acquiring familiarity with the individuals concerned.

Only by interacting with another animal is it possible to assess features such as strength and temperament, and thus to predict how the individual would behave in a dispute or friendly encounter. Social play provides the relevant experience. Young male baboons, for example, spend much of their time in rough and tumble play, sparring and wrestling with each other (Owens 1975a). But the aggression is rarely serious, and there are frequent reversals of fortune (Owens 1975b). By taking first the active then the passive role the animal can keep his partner in play, and thus gain extensive experience of his temperament and reactions. In this way he can work out where he stands with respect to his fellows and how it would best pay him to respond when in competition with them for some desired resource. The animals can learn their position in the group only by learning the relative strength and determination of others. The strong insist on precedence because they learn that they can enforce it, and the weak give way because they learn this to be the most prudent course (Rowell 1974). Each individual learns what he can get away with, that is what others will allow him to do. The parents contribute little to the process of socialization; their offspring must learn to make their own way and to fend for themselves.

Human children must also learn what others will tolerate. But they are not simply left to find out on their own; their parents play a much more active role. The parents specifically teach them how to behave and pass on to them the norms prescribed by a particular culture. The children learn not only how others react but also what is expected of them; in other words they learn the rules laid down by society to govern social interactions. And these rules can exist only because there is language in which they can be formulated.

Human parents socialize their children by active intervention when they transgress and by laying down the rules they must obey. No monkey trains its infant in the way a person does. Certainly pig-tailed monkey mothers hit and even bite their infants at the time of weaning so as to repel their advances and prevent them from pestering (Jensen *et al.* 1969); and in the same way human parents may be punitive when their children are a nuisance. But parents also use punishment to enforce conduct they believe to be correct and not simply of immediate convenience to themselves. The deliberate moulding of behaviour by reward and punishment is to be found only in human society. Furthermore parents need not rely simply on physical means of control: they allocate praise and blame, and give verbal explanations of why they approve and disapprove.

The difference between human and animal may be simply stated: a monkey may control its offspring by inducing fear, but a man can do so by instilling a conscience. Consider an experiment carried out on dogs to study the effects of punishment (Solomon 1960). Young puppies were presented with two bowls, one containing their favourite meat and another with a commercial dog food they liked much less. They were then taught to restrain themselves from eating their preferred meat and to take the tinned food. In some animals this was done by swatting them on the rump as they approached the taboo food, and in others by swatting them after they had eaten some of the meat. Resistance to temptation was stronger in the first group than the second, but the animals in the second group showed much more emotional disturbance if they gave way to temptation. On the face of it one might suppose that immediate punishment produced fear and delayed punishment produced 'guilt' (Eysenck 1977); but this conclusion is unwarranted. The dogs punished after they had taken some food had every reason to be frightened while eating, as they could not be sure that punishment would not follow. There is no good reason to re-describe their justifiable fears as reactions of guilt.

But in children a distinction may very reasonably be drawn between fear and guilt. A person may refrain from an act either because he is afraid of being detected and punished or because he would feel guilty even if he knew that the act would go unnoticed and unpunished. Behaviour may be controlled by fear of external punishment or by guilt owing to the threat of internal or self-punishment (Bandura and Walters 1959). The first is only effective when there is a risk of external sanctions, but the second works even when there are no such sanctions.

People are self-governing in a way that is true of no animal (Bandura 1977). During socialization the young come to accept ideals, that is ideas of how they themselves think they should be. Often they acquire these by taking them from other people they admire, that is by imitation of models (Bandura 1977). People regulate their behaviour such that they correct any deviations from the ideals they have set themselves. They feel guilty, that is they punish themselves, when they act in ways other than those of which they themselves approve. In the language of social psychologists they 'internalize' the moral values of the people with whom they identify, adopting them as their own (Bandura and Walters 1963;Argyle 1964; Aronfreed 1968). In this way they become their own judge of the actions that they perform. The role of the parents and other teachers is to state the values that they recommend for adoption, and themselves to set an example to be followed.

How has it come about that people should regulate their behaviour in this way? A moment's thought will reveal that we owe this capacity to the possession of language. It is yet one more benefit that derived from the invention of language. Ideals, rules and values can only be formulated in words. Though devised for communicating with others language can be used for communicating with oneself, that is for commenting on one's own behaviour. It is the task of human parents to turn their children into responsible adults capable of directing their own lives according to principles in which they believe. An ape has no words with which to put forward recommendations or prescribe a course of action; nor can it taunt itself for behaving in a way it thinks to be improper. It is unable to teach its offspring what it expects of them, and can only give them the opportunity to learn for themselves what other members of the group will tolerate. Without language an ape must remain forever an unsocialized child devoid of conscience.

The importance of ideals in human society is best illustrated by taking the case of altruism. It was mentioned earlier in the chapter that the understanding of altruism has been a central concern of the science of sociobiology (Ruse 1979). Altruism poses a problem for evolutionary theory because if animals were to behave in a genuinely altruistic manner it would be difficult to explain how the genes predisposing towards altruism could be handed down the generations in spite of the selective forces operating against them. We may call an act altruistic if the animal benefits others at cost to itself. But individuals that act against their own self-interest would be less likely to pass on their genetic complement to future generations than would individuals that act to serve their own selfish interests. The result would be that 'selfish' individuals would be more likely to pass on their genes to the next generations; and the genes controlling altruistic behaviour would be less well represented in future generations. The problem would be solved if we could demonstrate that the behaviour was not a case of true altruism at all; in other words that the act carried hidden advantages.

How are we to show that the relevant genes could confer selective advantage? Various answers have been given, and we may briefly rehearse two of them (Dawkins 1976). The first is simply that the individual may be acting in a way that promotes his long-term, though not his immediate, welfare. To take one example, male baboons (*Papio anubis*) have been observed to form temporary partnerships, assisting each other in wresting oestrous females from another male (Packer 1977). Though on any occasion only one of the partners mated with the female, over many occasions each could take his turn. The term 'reciprocal altruism' has been suggested for cases such as this where one good turn is repaid by another (Trivers 1971). There is no problem in appreciating how in principle genes promoting reciprocal altruism could confer selective advantage.

A second answer suggests a way in which behaviour that is genuinely to the disadvantage of the individual could nonetheless persist. It simply states the consequences of an elementary fact of genetics: related animals have a similar complement of genes, the degrees of similarity varying as a function of the closeness of the relationship. If an animal acts so as to benefit its relative there is an above average chance that it will be acting to the advantage of individuals that carry the same genes that predispose towards altruism. If these individuals survive the genes will be transmitted to the next generation, even though the altruist may not itself survive. This process is referred to as 'kin selection', since the genes are passed on indirectly via the kin (Maynard Smith 1964). It provides an explanation of some altruistic acts which are of no obvious advantage to the individual. Lionesses, for instance, will feed the cubs of other mothers; that they should do so is less surprising when we discover that the lionesses in a pride are related roughly as cousins, and thus that the lionesses are helping cubs which share many of their own genes (Bertram 1976).

What relevance has this discussion to our understanding of altruistic behaviour in people? It can only contribute if we make the assumption that there are genes which either promote altruism or do so indirectly by biasing what is learnt during socialization. Thus in discussing reciprocal altruism in animals and man Trivers (1971) argues that it is reasonable to assume that 'the underlying emotional dispositions affecting altruistic behavior have important genetic components'. The notion that the genes might be able to influence the content of learning has been used by Alexander (1979), Durham (1979) and Lumsden and Wilson (1981) in trying to apply evolutionary principles to human behaviour. It is not implausible that our genes might have some influence on what goals we seek, although it is difficult to think of a way of demonstrating the fact empirically.

But, while not denying that animal studies may be of some relevance to human altruism, we should not be so blinkered that we fail to acknowledge the far-reaching consequences of the fact that people can cultivate ideals. Take the case where a man dives into a river to save someone who is drowning. He may do so knowing full well that the person is not a relative, and that the chances of them ever meeting again are very small indeed. Of course we can always accuse the altruist of harbouring hidden motives, a desire for glory whether now or in heaven; but there is no reason why we should not accept that such an act could be carried out from genuine altruism with no hope of personal return. People can learn to regulate their lives according to any ideal they choose, and thus can sincerely adopt the principle of helping others. Parents attempt to inculcate altruistic ideals in their children, and sometimes they succeed. It is for the social psychologists to assess how easy it is to inculcate in people the ideals of co-operation (Wispé 1978; Rushton 1980).

It is not being claimed that a situation could arise in which most people adopt practices that reduce their biological fitness. To some extent our genetic inheritance must constrain what is learnt. But any account of human altruism must highlight the extraordinary capacity of the human brain for consciously comparing different goals and calculating how particular ends would best be achieved (Alexander 1979).

As children grow up they are trained to take on some role in adult society. Each individual contributes to the co-operative enterprise by performing a particular task and is rewarded accordingly. In human society there is division of labour not only between the sexes but also within the sexes.

It is true that division of labour is not to be found only in human society; there are insect societies in which the members of the various castes carry out different duties (Wilson 1971). To take ants as an example; there are three basic castes within the females—the queen, the worker and the soldier. The queen produces the brood, the workers care for it and gather food, and the soldiers defend the nest. But although these societies are very impressive in the complexity of their social organization, nonetheless they differ from human society in a fundamental way. Ants are born physically equipped for the tasks they will perform; the workers are sterile, the soldiers are built for combat. But people either take on tasks that are assigned to them or choose the jobs they find attractive. The qualifications result from training, and there is a great variety of tasks which people can be trained to perform.

In the social vertebrates other than man division of labour is usually only found between the sexes. It is common for the males to be larger than the females and, being more strongly built, they are better able to defend the young. In some primates the difference between male and female is extreme: the male olive baboon is twice the size of the female, and the male gorilla is 1.72 times as large (Clutton-Brock and Harvey 1977a). It is in the interest of the females to mate with the male that will prove to be the best stud, and the female must be sure that he will prove capable in defence of her and her young. To some extent the female can estimate these qualities from his size.

In monogamous species the male and female tend to be of a more similar build (Alexander et al. 1979). The male marmoset is only 1.08 times the weight of the female, and for the gibbon the corresponding figure is 1.11 (Clutton-Brock and Harvey 1977b). The difference between the human male and female is as small: the man is only around 1.08 times as tall as the woman (Alexander et al. 1979). Though societies often lay down the tasks thought appropriate for men and women members of either sex are capable of tackling all tasks.

There is no clear division of labour within the sexes in

mammals other than man. It has been suggested that it is possible to distinguish different roles taken by adult males in some primates (Gartlan 1968). In vervet monkeys, for example, different males can be seen maintaining a vigilant survey at different times, as if on watch. But this fact is not enough to convince us that there is indeed a 'vigilance role' which is shared between the members of the troop. The animals on vigil may be watching on behalf of themselves and their young, and they may look out when they have time to spare from feeding and other tasks. To show that the animals keep watch at different times is not necessarily to show that they take it in turns.

Another role suggested is that of leader. It is certainly true that the most dominant male may do more than his share of protecting the troop. Both in the wild and in captivity the most dominant male in groups of macaques is the most ready to challenge strangers and chase them away (Bernstein 1964, 1966; Lindburg 1971). These same animals are also the most likely to intervene in squabbles within the group, springing to the defence of the less able members (Bernstein 1970). There are also primates in which the leading male determines the direction of travel; in hamadryas baboons, for instance, even if there are two adult males in the harem it is the older one that decides when the group should move and in what direction (Kummer 1968). But none of these observations proves true division of labour. The most dominant male may be the most confident animal by reason of greater strength or more robust temperament. Such an animal would naturally be the most plucky in defence, the most ready to rescue and protect, and the most willing to assert itself and impose its will on others. In other words it is not that the animal assumes a role; its actions reflect its capacities and its knowledge of what it will get away with. It has yet to be shown that the term 'role' has any useful application in discussing the social organization of animals other than insects.

Co-operation in animals

Do animals ever co-operate towards a common end, granted that the contribution of each individual is much the same? They do, but much less than we might suppose. Of course many birds and mammals seek protection in numbers and also look for food together. In this way individuals increase their chances of evading predators and can cash in on discoveries of food made by others (Wilson

1975). But animals cannot be said to be co-operating with others simply because they move around in a group.

There are some birds and mammals that co-operate in defence. Musk oxen (*Ovibos maschatus*) stand and face wolves in a phalanx (Mech 1970). When a baboon troop is in danger the adult males retreat last, and they sometimes turn and face the predator together (Altmann and Altmann 1970), and buffalo (*Syncerus caffer*) will even launch a joint attack against lions (Jarman 1974). By acting in unison the males can offer greater resistance than can any individual on its own. But though these are indeed examples of co-operation no sophisticated strategy is required; each animal simply does much what it would do on its own, but does it in concert with others.

Some mammals also co-operate when hunting. Members of the cat family stalk prey on their own, although the lion also stalks in groups; but the canids such as the wolf and hunting dog stalk, chase and bring down their prey in packs (Kleiman and Eisenberg 1973). The canids are in general smaller than the cats, and can only master prey that are larger than themselves by joining forces. We can show that groups can sometimes hunt more effectively than individuals by comparing the success of different hunts according to the number of animals taking part. Lions are roughly twice as likely to make a kill if they hunt in pairs than on their own, and if they are hunting large animals such as wildebeest and zebra they do best if they go out in groups of six or more (Schaller 1972). Hyenas can roughly double their success in attacking wildebeest calves if they hunt in groups of three or more rather than on their own (Kruuk 1972). The reason is that a single individual cannot cope with both the calf and the wildebeest cow defending it; whereas in a group one hyena can deal with the calf while the others ward off the attacks made by the mother. In this case different animals do indeed carry out different tasks.

Do the animals co-ordinate their movements when stalking prey so as to carry out some joint strategy? The evidence is slight and difficult to interpret (Peters and Mech 1975). Animals can hunt efficiently in groups without adopting any joint strategy. Wild dogs usually pursue their prey in headlong chase, each individual doing its best to reach the animal they are hunting (Schaller 1972). This is not to say that they are unaware of the presence of other members of the group, nor that they act with complete independence. But in general the animals in the pack take up the chase in much the way they would if hunting on their own.

But there are other cases where the movements of the animals are well co-ordinated. It has been reported that wolves and lions will sometimes fan out and encircle their prey (Schaller 1972; Peters and Mech 1975). Here each individual takes a different route, and these routes are not those that they would have chosen had they been stalking on their own. In taking a circuitous route an animal is clearly aware of the direction in which the other members of the group are approaching, and it adjusts its actions accordingly. But there is no reason to suppose that there is a group strategy. Each individual simply adopts the same tactic; the animals differ only in the direction from which they approach. The most parsimonious explanation is that when stalking it pays an animal to keep well away from others so as to minimize the chances that it will be noticed. If they are to space themselves out each individual must of necessity take a different route towards the prey.

There are rare instances which such an explanation is clearly inadequate. There are one or two reports of wolves and lions apparently driving prey into an ambush (Mech 1970; Schaller 1972; Peters and Mech 1975). Here animals differ in the tactics they use, some moving towards the prey, others lying in wait. Clearly the animals that are lying low are aware of the actions of the others and are taking into account their likely effects on the prey.

But the reports do not testify unambiguously to the degree of co-operation that is involved. We should distinguish two cases. In the first each animal adopts the tactic that it calculates to be to its own direct advantage; that is it attempts to maximize its own chances of making a kill. In the second case an individual gives up its claim to be the first to catch the prey, and acts so as to ensure that a kill will be made by others. In this way it benefits indirectly, because it can then be assured of some meat from the kill. That individuals adopt different tactics during a hunt is not sufficient evidence to decide between these two accounts. With people we need be in no doubt: roles can be assigned and tactics discussed. The function of the beater is to drive the quarry in the required direction so that others can catch it. But we cannot ask animals why they are adopting the tactics that they are, and the issue is difficult to settle.

Social carnivores typically share the meat from a kill, but it is very rare for there to be sharing between animals that live off plant foods. There are only a few reports for primates other than man. In evaluating these we must draw a distinction between food passing hands because it is stolen and food being positively offered to others to take. There are of course a variety of intervening cases: an animal might take the left-overs, or the 'donor' might simply relinquish its possession without putting up any resistance. We should also distinguish whether it is parents offering food to their offspring or adults voluntarily sharing it between themselves. People engage in both types of sharing, but it is the distribution of resources amongst adults that might be thought to be one mark of human society.

Sharing of plant food between adults and young has been claimed to occur in titi monkeys and chimpanzees in the wild. A study of one family of titi monkeys reported that occasionally the infant tried to get fruit from the adult male or female, usually by touching the fruit or the hands or mouth of the adult eating it (Starin 1978). The male allowed it to remove small pieces on three occasions and dropped the remaining fruit on four others. That the male should be so tolerant of the infant may reflect the greater 'paternal' interest that is typically displayed by male primates living in family groups.

Food transfer between chimpanzees has been found to be relatively common in the population living in the Gombe National Park in Tanzania (McGrew 1975). These animals are fed bananas from boxes, and there is considerable competition for this highly prized fruit. In 21 months bananas changed hands on 457 occasions; on 85 per cent of these the bananas passed between mothers and offspring. Infants were also seen to cadge pieces of other fruit where the shells were too hard for them to open. But the report gives too little detail for us to assess how often the mother actually proffered food, and how often she simply tolerated scrounging on the part of her offspring. In the same population the transfer of bananas has occasionally been seen from adult males to adult females (McGrew 1975). But again the exact nature of the transaction has not been documented. We may suppose that it is the competition for bananas that encourages animals to attempt to cadge them off others.

In the laboratory juvenile gibbons have been faced with much the same situation: different pairs of animals have each been presented with one piece of banana to see how they would react given the limited supply of this delicacy (Berkson and Schusterman 1964). Certainly bits of banana changed hands, but the initiative was taken by the partners who were beaten to the prize; they simply took hold of the food and wrested it away. In captivity douc langurs

(*Pygathrix nemaeus*) have also been observed competing over leafy *Eugenia* branches with which they were supplied (Kavanagh 1972). On four occasions one animal was actually seen to pass part of a branch to another animal that was attempting to feed off the same branch. But in two of these instances females appeared to be attempting to placate more dominant males, and in the other two the donors benefited by preventing further competition.

We should not be surprised to find that it is more common for hunters to share meat than it is for animals to share the vegetable food they collect. Carnivore infants are too weak and unskilled to be able to hunt for themselves; and of necessity any meat that they eat must be supplied by others. Some carnivores feed their young by disgorging meat that they have predigested; this is true, for example, of wolves, jackals (*Canis aureus*) and wild dogs (*Lycaon pictus*) (van Lawick and van Lawick-Goodall 1970; Mech 1970). It is of particular interest that in all three species it is not only the parents that will provide for the pups in this way. Other adult members of the pack will sometimes regurgitate for the young, and some will even stay behind with them when others go out on a hunt. Without doubt the pups benefit from the 'parental' care shown by these helpers; it has been shown that more jackal pups survive in groups in which there are adults who provide this assistance (Moehlman 1979). But why should animals other than the parents care for the pups in this way? The reason for this apparent altruism is to be found in the nature of relationship between the helpers and the pups. Jackals live in family groups, and the basic unit of the wolf pack is probably also the family (Mech 1970; Moehlman 1979); we can be less sure of the basic composition of a pack of wild dogs. Let us take jackals to illustrate the point. The animals seen helping the pups are in fact their elder siblings, and are thus as closely related to them genetically as they will be to any offspring they produce in the future (Moehlman 1979). Thus it pays them to care for their siblings in a parental fashion.

If we turn our attention to sharing between adults it is certainly true that in carnivores that hunt in groups the meat from a large kill is consumed by many adults. However, there is no evidence that they actively share it out; each animal simply tears off a piece for itself. But, as we have already noted, wolves, jackals and wild dogs regurgitate for the young on return from the kill; and they do the same for any adults that remained behind to guard the pups (Kuhme 1965; Mech 1970; Moehlman 1979).

This is perhaps the most convincing example of co-operation and of division of labour in any mammal other than man.

As has been mentioned chimpanzees also hunt on occasion, usually just grabbing some small animal when a suitable opportunity arises (Teleki 1973a). Lone animals do most of the hunting, but occasionally between two and five chimpanzees may take part. In such cases the animals have sometimes been seen to co-ordinate their actions, and even to fan out and then turn inwards on the prey (Teleki 1975). The meat is highly prized (Fig. 9.15). If there are other chimpanzees present at the time they will often grab at the carcass, and they are usually free to take some of the meat without risk of retaliation. The animals with a major share of the meat then move off to consume it elsewhere, but it is typical for small groups of other chimpanzees to gather round them in the hope of obtaining a morsel. They attempt to wrench pieces off and pick up any left-overs; but they also try less direct methods, holding out their hands in the gesture of begging (Teleki 1973b). Slightly under a third of these requests is granted, occasionally by dropping a piece of meat into the hand. Roughly 80 per cent of the requests are made of adults by other adults; females tend to make more requests than males, no doubt because it is the males that are responsible for the hunting (Teleki 1975). It is certainly surprising that the exchanges occur in a relaxed atmosphere and with

9.15 Chimpanzees feeding off a carcass. Courtesy of G. Teleki.

little of the overt aggression that is manifested at a kill made by lions or hyenas (Teleki 1973b). But this should not lead us to ignore the essential point, which is that chimpanzees do not so much actively share meat as tolerate scrounging.

Could we persuade them to co-operate to a greater extent? In the laboratory we have the means, because situations can be set up in which communal success in obtaining some prized item can be guaranteed only if two animals pool their efforts. Suppose that food can only be obtained by the use of a tool; and that one animal has the tool but lacks access to the food container, but the other is near the container but lacks the relevant implement. In just such conditions hamadryas baboons have been seen to co-operate, the female fetching a rake for the male to pull in a tray of food (Beck 1973). A similar situation has been arranged for chimpanzees. Food could only be obtained from a vending machine, and a poker chip had to be inserted to operate the mechanism; one chimpanzee had the tokens but only its partner had access to the dispenser (Nissen and Crawford 1936). Under these circumstances the first animal handed over tokens even when they had not been solicited, since only in this way could it get the food.

But what if there were several things that might be passed, and the chimpanzee was required to specify which one it wanted? We can help the animal by first teaching it a system of symbols. The experiment has been done with two chimpanzees taught to type on a keyboard in Yerkish (Savage-Rumbaugh et al. 1978a) (see Chapter 8). One had access to the keyboard, and the other could see a display of the symbols that were operated. The first was given one of six containers but lacked the implements with which to open them to get at food; the second had the implements, each one appropriate for one of the six containers, but it could not itself reach the containers. Under these circumstances the first animal learnt to request the relevant implement, and the second to supply it on reading the request on its display. The same two chimpanzees have also been taught to specify which of several foods they wanted the other to pass to them (Savage-Rumbaugh et al. 1978b).One typed on the keyboard and the other was encouraged to attend to the symbol on the projector and to comply with the request.

It has been objected that the chimpanzees might be going through a rote performance, not comprehending that the lexigrams are symbols for the various tools or foods. Pigeons can be trained to press a key of one colour depending on the position of the key pecked by another pigeon, even though the keys carry no meaning (Epstein *et al.* 1980). But there is independent evidence that these two chimpanzees appreciate that symbols refer to things (Savage-Rumbaugh *et al.* 1980b) (see Chapter 8); and there is no evidence that pigeons can be trained to make genuine requests of each other by whatever means (Savage-Rumbaugh and Rumbaugh 1980).

A different approach is to require not that something be passed but that two animals pool their combined efforts to obtain food. For example, it can be arranged that a box containing food must be dragged in by ropes, but that it is too heavy for one animal to succeed unaided (Crawford 1937). In this situation one chimpanzee will solicit help from its partner, putting out its hand, touching or even pushing the other animal, until at last they both put their hands to the ropes and pull in the box.

In all these cases the animals are under pressure to co-operate because neither will get food unless they do so. Wild dogs hunt in groups because no individual could fell a zebra by itself; and in the same way co-operation can be forced in the laboratory if it is the only way in which individuals can achieve their ends.

Hominids

In turning our attention back to man it is now obvious what questions we must ask. What were the tasks that the early hominids could accomplish only if they acted with common purpose? And why did the enterprise demand that the various individuals play different roles?

The answer to the first question is that hunting is one such task, though of course not the only one. If the prey is much larger than the predator co-operation of some sort is essential if a kill is to be made at all; and, as we have seen, this is why wolves and wild dogs hunt in packs. Chimpanzees kill nothing larger than a colobus monkey of 10 kilograms or so (Teleki 1975). Yet, although the early hominids were of slighter build than chimpanzees, in East Africa they appear to have hunted larger animals such as pigs and antelopes (Isaac 1978a,b) (see Chapter 6). Like chimpanzees the hominids were not naturally equipped with the lethal weapons of a large carnivore such as a lion; but their use of manufactured weapons would partly account for their success. We may reasonably assume that two hunters might be more effective than one when attempting to catch animals of this size. If we look to the people still making a living from hunting and gathering in Africa we find that they often go out looking for small prey on their own; but they also hunt in pairs, and the Mbuti pygmies and G/wi bushmen occasionally hunt in bands of 10 or more (Teleki 1975). It is not implausible that the early hominids might sometimes have formed pairs when hunting.

We can be more certain that in later times in Europe co-operative hunting was essential; for now we find the hominids hunting large ungulates such as horses and reindeer (Chapter 6). At Torralba and Ambrona in Spain the remains of many large mammals have been found in association with the tools of *Homo erectus*; and remarkably there are the bones of many elephants (*Elephas antiquus*) (Howell 1972). It seems likely that these beasts were driven into the bog by groups of hominids; and the traces of fire suggest that flames might have been deliberately used to scare the elephants, and thus to drive them in the desired direction (Howell 1972). In recent times a similar tactic was used by groups of Netsilik Eskimos, who would drive herds of caribou (*Rangifer trandus*) on to thin ice and thus trap them (Balikci 1970). We may reasonably conclude that, at least during the Ice Ages in Europe, the survival of the hominids depended on achieving the co-operation necessary if they were to hunt herds of large animals successfully.

The second question is how it came about that human society is organized around the principle of division of labour. Even when hunting demands co-operation it does not necessarily require that different individuals use different tactics, as the example of the wild dogs shows. There are two separate issues; division of labour between the sexes and the assigning of different tasks to individuals of the same sex.

In hunter—gatherer societies today it is the men who do most of the hunting and the women who gather the plant food (Lee and DeVore 1968). In chimpanzee societies meat forms only a very small proportion of the diet; but surprisingly hunting is almost exclusively a male activity (McGrew 1979). In contrast the females work termite mounds about three times as frequently as the males, and are twice as likely to devote over an hour to the task (McGrew 1979). What is it about these tasks that one engages the interest of males and the other of the females? The most obvious difference is that hunting demands a willingness to roam far in search of prey and to engage in active pursuits, whereas probing for ants is a sedentary pastime which requires little physical exertion. Females are often constrained in what they can do; if they have infants they are unable to run fast and far, and even if they have older offspring they are better able to keep watch over them if they are sedentary than if they are off on a chase. The males can afford to go after prey in the hope of securing large chunks of meat; the females are better advised to search for their meat in the form of many small insects, in the hope of scrounging larger pieces off the males when possible.

Women are faced with a situation much worse than that facing female chimpanzees. Their young are more helpless, require more constant care, and are carried in the arms. Even if the baby is strapped to the back women are hampered when running, and it is much easier for women so burdened to wander at their own pace gathering fruit or nuts. There is no need to suppose that it is temperament which determines the choice of activities pursued by the two sexes; the division of labour is adequately accounted for by the consequences of childbirth for the female. Hunter − gatherer society simply formalizes the arrangement by encouraging women to collect plant foods whether they have children or not.

If women do little hunting themselves most of their meat must come from the men. When they are lactating women require roughly 1000 more calories in their diet than usual (Gunther 1971); and therefore at this time especially they stand to benefit if they can obtain high-protein meat. But why must the meat be actively shared? Why do the women not simply scrounge what they can get? The answer lies again in the extent to which women are restricted when they have young children, such that they find it difficult to move far from the base. Female chimpanzees can take meat from the males because they are often near the site of a kill; but female wild dogs must remain with their pups at the den and are thus dependent on the males returning with meat. If men are to ensure that their women and young are provided for, they must bring back to base at least some of the game they kill. This is not to claim that meat need always form a high proportion of the diet, or to suggest that women are necessarily always supplied with a high proportion of the game that is taken (Woodburn 1968; Teleki 1975). The need for active sharing of food must be greater the more the group is dependent on meat; and that dependence increases in the more northerly climes (Lee 1968).

293

There is archaeological evidence suggesting that in East Africa the social life of the early hominids was organized around a home base by around 1.5 million years ago (Isaac 1976a). At Lake Turkana, for example, there are sites at which tools have been found together with a large number of bones. It seems unlikely that so many animals of different species would all be killed at the one spot; and we may reasonably assume that instead the carcasses were carried to the site for butchering (Isaac 1976a, 1981). Whatever the basic social unit at that time we must suppose that the two sexes were more dependent on each other in their economic life than is true of chimpanzees today.

The division of labour within the sexes could have resulted partly from the increasing dependence of the hominids on big game hunting in difficult times. We have already noted that the hominids relied not just on their weapons and their numbers but also on cunning. At Ambrona they drove elephants into a trap; today the Mbuti pygmies divide, one man stopping the elephant from the front and the others slicing one tendon and then the other from behind (Turnbull 1966). The simplest of joint strategies can be carried out without a word being spoken; directions can be given by pointing and by gesture. Indeed most living hunters deliberately make use of gestures rather than words so as to remain unnoticed by the prey (Teleki 1975).

But consider the sophistication of the strategies that become possible if language is used, at least in the planning of the hunt. Now individuals can directly say where the prey is to be found, what the species is, and how many animals there might be. The strategy can be formulated in words, plans laid and the likely movements of the prey anticipated. And most important of all instructions can be given, and different instructions to different individuals or sub-groups.

This is not to say that because animals lack language they could in no circumstances adopt hunting strategies in which different contributions are made by different individuals. Indeed in the earlier discussion it was left undecided whether the reported cases of ambush illustrate such strategies in operation. If they do it is possible to explain the origin of such strategies only by supposing that the animals independently learnt by experience that their success was greater if they carried out the relevant manoeuvres. There is no way in which they could instruct each other as to what to do, except perhaps by making vague indications of the direction to be taken. Chimpanzees could, for example, point with their hands and so guide the movements of another animal. In captivity chimpanzees are quite capable of following the direction in which a person points and thus locating food (Menzel 1978). But without language animals have no way of giving more detailed instructions, for instance to move round the back and then lie in wait until other members of the group succeed in driving the prey in the required direction.

To put it plainly an animal may behave differently from other members of the group, but that does not necessarily entitle us to state that it has a particular 'role'. We use the word 'role' when referring to the part that is assigned to them and which they are expected to play. But only people assign functions and formulate such expectations; and this is because only people have language with which to do so, Certainly it would be reasonable to say that soldier ants play a role, but here the instructions are given to them not by other ants but by their genes. A soldier ant may know what to do; but only human soldiers do what they are told.

10 Competition

People may co-operate more than animals, but we have yet to learn to maintain a harmonious social order. Our failure to do so might be explained by laying the blame either on society or on our animal heritage. On the one view we should look to inadequate socialization and to matters of politics, and on the other to the problem of controlling the emotional reactions with which we have been equipped by nature. This bald statement is a caricature of the opposing claims made in popular accounts such as those of Montagu (1976, 1978) on the one hand and Ardrey (1961, 1967) on the other. But it is reasonable to assert that the one party believes that to get to the root of the problem we must achieve a better understanding of society, whereas the other party holds that it is a matter of higher priority that we come to understand human nature.

FUNCTIONS OF AGGRESSION

Aggression poses problems for mankind, and it has therefore been common to regard it as a sign of maladjustment. But students of animal behaviour look at the issue from a different perspective. They observe that fighting is widespread amongst the vertebrates, and assume that it can be so only because it is to the advantage of the animals that fight (Lorenz 1963; Wilson 1975). If it does not pay individuals to behave in this way it is not obvious how evolution could have equipped them with weapons and with the knowledge of how to use them.

If we consider the situations that provoke animals to fight it will quickly become apparent how aggression can pay. It will be helpful to list the things over which animals dispute.

1. Animals are often in competition for resources such as food, water and shelter. The more severe the competition the more likely that fighting will break out. We can illustrate this best by examining the effects of the

artificial provision of food to animals. In India many rhesus monkeys live in villages and towns, where they are fed by the local people. It has been shown that they are more likely to threaten at times of feeding than at other times, and in one group in Calcutta actual fights occur very much more frequently when the animals are being fed (Southwick *et al.* 1976). This effect has also been studied in rhesus monkeys in captivity; the amount of aggression was greatly increased if the monkeys were fed from a single basket rather than from eight set in different places (Southwick 1967). For some years the chimpanzees in the Gombe National Park have also been provided with bananas so as to attract them to the study area. At the times when bananas are available in boxes the chimpanzees engage in more disputes than they do when the boxes are empty; and this is true even when the same number of animals are present in the two cases (Wrangham 1974).

2. Animals may compete for mates. In many monkeys conflicts are especially intense during mating periods (Nagel and Kummer 1974). For example, in the rhesus monkeys on Cayo Santiago the incidence of wounds and of deaths from fighting is much higher during the season in which mating is most frequent (Wilson and Boelkins 1970). Some monkeys, such as hamadryas baboons, live in harems (see Chapter 9), and the adult males guard their females and prevent them from straying too far. In a field experiment on four occasions corn was placed in a pile near a troop of hamadryas baboons; this resulted in fights between individuals and finally in battles between the bands (Kummer 1968) (Fig. 10.14). As the harem groups converged the males became insecure and tried to ensure that their females did not approach other males. The ensuing fights were not so much over food as the need to guard females from the advances of competing males.

3. Strangers may be attacked. Xenophobia has been observed in monkeys both in the wild and in captivity. In one experiment four groups of rhesus monkeys living either in villages or in towns were selected; an attempt was then made to introduce other monkeys either singly or in pairs into each of the groups (Southwick *et al.* 1974). All were ejected except for infants, which were presumably not taken to pose any threat. In a related experiment a group of 17 rhesus monkeys was kept in a large cage; these animals threatened and attacked any pair of monkeys the experimenters tried to introduce, even though at the same time two monkeys were removed so as to keep the

total number constant (Southwick 1967). A large series of such introductions has been conducted with rhesus monkeys housed in groups of various sizes and composition (Bernstein *et al.* 1974). Whether introduced singly or with others the newcomers usually met with a hostile reception; they received many more threats or attacks than they themselves directed at others.

4. Animals will fight to protect their own lives. This is true whether they are threatened by a member of their own species or by a predator, and is sufficiently well known for there to be no need to document it here.

5. Animals will fight to protect the lives of their young. Again we need little persuading that this is so, since we are already aware that mothers will defend their young (Fig. 10.1). Rhesus monkey mothers will come to the aid of their offspring even when they are juveniles (Lindburg 1971).

These are the main situations in which non–human primates and other mammals can be provoked to fight. What do they have in common? In each case the reproductive fitness of the animal is at risk. It cannot reproduce unless it continues to live; and to protect its own life it must defend itself and also ensure that it gains the resources that it needs for survival. Given that it lives it must reproduce, and to do so it must win access to mates. Strangers are potential rivals for resources and for mates, and thus they may pose a threat to an individual's reproductive success. Finally, if the animal succeeds in breeding any threat to its offspring makes it less likely that the parent's genes will be represented in future generations.

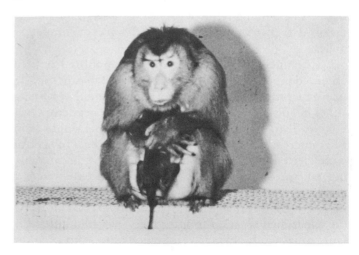

10.1 Pig–tailed monkey mother threatening the camera and protecting her infant. From Kaufman and Rosenblum (1969).

Animals fight to ensure that they have viable offspring which will survive to reproduce; in other words they fight when the replication of their own genes is at risk. It is no more difficult to see how the ability to fight might be promoted by natural selection than the ability to eat or to mate.

CONTROLS

If fighting pays why do animals not fight more, and why do they not fight to the death? At first sight one would think that the best way of dealing with competitors, whether for food or mates, would be to eliminate them. In fact we know that animals rarely kill each other, and that they more usually engage in ritual combat (Lorenz 1963). To take one example, the oryx (*Oryx*) antelope has long pointed horns, but when two bulls fight over females they clash horns and push with their heads but rarely stab each other with the points (Eibl-Eibesfeldt 1975) (Fig. 10.2). This is not to say that animals never deliver fatal injuries to members of their own species: there are reports of deaths

10.2 Oryx antelopes sparring. Courtesy of San Diego Zoo.

299

from fights in lions, hyenas and rhesus monkeys (Lindburg 1971; Schaller 1972; Kruuk 1972); and there are cases in other animals. But it is still true that in the main animals fail to press home the advantage when they have a competitor cornered, even when they have the weapons with which to deal a lethal blow.

This can only be because the benefits of doing so are outweighed by the costs. There must be disadvantages to the individual of engaging in full-scale combat, and these are not hard to seek. The animal risks personal injury and it is in danger of wasting time that could be better spent by engaging in other activities. An animal cannot afford to concentrate on any one task to the exclusion of others; it must eat, drink, mate and so on. There would be no point in an animal fighting if it failed to devote adequate time to these concerns and thus failed either to survive or to reproduce.

The costs and values of fighting can be incorporated into a formal model by assigning arbitrary values to each. By using a computer we can then simulate the process of evolution, and so discover which of the possible strategies that animals might adopt would prove the most successful in the long run. More precisely we can establish which is the 'evolutionarily stable strategy', where that is defined as the strategy which, if most members of a population adopt it, cannot be bettered by an alternative strategy (Maynard Smith and Price 1973; Dawkins 1976). It turns out that the evolutionarily stable strategy is not that of escalating fighting without provocation; in a population in which this strategy was commonly adopted individuals would frequently be confronted by other individuals that behaved in the same way. The stable strategy is that of escalating the fight only when the opponent does so (Maynard Smith and Price 1973; Maynard Smith 1978). In other words we would expect animals to retaliate in general but not to force more severe confrontations than are necessary. Ritual or conventional fighting is what we should predict.

There are, however, certain conditions which favour the escalation of disputes. These conditions are sometimes met when animals live in captivity. We noted earlier that rhesus monkeys kept in a large cage were provoked to fight when their food was supplied from a single container (Southwick 1967). Animals that failed to force their way to the food would necessarily go without, whereas in the wild they could give way to the stronger in the knowledge that there was food to be found elsewhere. In captivity the stakes were high; they were in danger of starvation. In zoos there may also be limited access to females. The most famous example concerns the hamadryas baboons kept on 'monkey hill' in London Zoo: in five years 8 males and 30 females were killed (Zuckerman 1932). The setting up of the colony was badly mismanaged; 94 males and 6 females were put together, and at a later date a further 30 adult females and 5 immature males were added. Yet, as we now know, hamadryas baboon males herd harems in the wild (Kummer 1968); in the zoo there were very many too few females, and the result was savage fighting as the males tried to establish their harems. As in the previous example, therefore, the penalty for not fighting was severe.

Under natural conditions it is usually less critical for the animal that it wins any particular dispute. It often pays individuals to give way rather than to take up the challenge. Precedence may be established in two ways: some animals set up territories which they defend against intruders; others win a position in a rank order or dominance hierarchy. Both systems are common in vertebrates (Wilson 1975).

In a territorial system space is divided up between individuals or groups such that the owners have priority in their areas. In general territory owners win on their home ground and intruders lose. This is easily demonstrated with small animals over which the experimenter has some control. Sticklebacks (*Gasterosteus aculeatus*) can be moved about in glass tubes in an aquarium: if both are moved into the territory owned by one of them the intruder attempts to flee; but if they are now moved to the territory of the second the roles are reversed and it is the first stickleback that now flees (Tinbergen 1953). To take another example, male speckled wood butterflies (*Pararge aegeria*) compete for a position on the sun spots on the forest floor where they attract and court females; the owner is usually successful in challenging intruders, but if netted and removed it is later unsuccessful in attempting to win back the same spot from a new owner (Davies 1978a). In such a system it is not so much an individual's personal characteristics that determine the outcome of a dispute but where the individual happens to be.

In a dominance system it is the qualities of the animal that determine its position in the hierarchy. Each individual learns the strengths and weaknesses of its companions, and it is therefore able to judge which animals it would be foolish to challenge (Rowell 1974). We may contrast the two systems as follows: in a territorial system the animal's chances depend on *where* it is, not *who* it is; in a hierarchical system its chances depend on *who* it is, not *where* it is. This formulation is over-simple, since the characteristics of an individual may determine the size of its territory; but nonetheless this rule of thumb will be of help to us in deciding whether or not to classify particular species as being territorial.

Territory

It was in birds that the territorial system was first described in detail (Howard 1920). The classical description applies in the case of many birds, such as the robin. In spring the male robin defends an area in which it feeds, attracts a mate, rears its young and supplies them with food; and it often returns to the same site the next year (Lack 1953). But not all birds occupy territories of this sort: some feed outside their territories, and gulls nesting in colonies defend only the nest site itself (Hinde 1956; Crook 1965).

The term 'territorial' has also been used in describing the behaviour of some mammals (Bates 1970). There are small solitary mammals that live in a confined area which they defend and in which they both feed and mate. But many mammals live in groups all the year round and these may range over large areas. To identify group territories it is necessary to be convinced that the groups are prepared to defend either the whole of the area in which they range or some core area within it. That two groups display at each other when they meet is not of itself adequate proof of territoriality, since it may reflect only an intolerance of strangers rather than the defence of a particular boundary. That two groups avoid each other is no better proof, since they may be attached to their home area and unwilling to roam. In principle we would require evidence that a group won on its home ground and lost disputes elsewhere; in practice we must be content with indirect evidence that this is so.

In discussions of mammals the concept of 'territory' has been extended in two ways. It has been suggested that some mammals have 'moving territories' and that others may have 'time territories'. Howler monkeys, for example, may move from area to area during the year, although at all times different groups keep their distance (Chivers 1969). But while it might be claimed that the groups occupy mobile territories it would be more parsimonious to state simply that they avoid contact with other groups, since there is no evidence that at any one time they would win in the one area but not in another. Ring-tailed lemurs, on the other hand, have been reported in one study to make temporary use of a system by which territories are allocated not in space but in time (Jolly 1972). The groups were observed to make use of the same areas but at different times. But again it is not clear that concept of territory applies at all. No evidence was provided that one group wins at one particular time and loses at another, and we may therefore describe the situation in simpler terms by stating that the groups avoided each other, and they did this by avoiding an area at the time at which they knew it would be used by other groups. This is not to say that the concepts of a moving territory or a time territory have no application, only that we should be clear as to the criteria which would have to be satisfied.

Some non-human primates defend territories which fit the same description as many of the territories reported in birds. It has been relatively easy to demonstrate territoriality in some of the small nocturnal prosimians that lead solitary lives by day—animals such as the mouse-lemur, the sportive lemur (*Lepilemur mustelinus*) and bushbabies (Martin 1972; Charles-Dominique 1974b). The males do not enter the territory of other males, and in the laboratory it has been shown that dwarf bushbabies will refuse to enter a compartment which another male has inhabited and which it has marked with its scent (Charles-Dominique 1974b). If in the wild bushbabies are transplanted into an unknown area they fail to challenge the occupants of territories and instead they flee down the tree (Charles-Dominique 1974b).

All the non-human primates that live in pairs also defend territories (Clutton-Brock and Harvey 1977a). Our best evidence for this is the nature of the ritual confrontations that take place at the boundaries between two territories. Titi monkeys (Fig. 8.1), for example, usually meet neighbouring pairs in the early morning and engage in excited displays in which they call loudly and chase each other vigorously (Mason 1971). Similarly the lesser apes, the gibbons and siamangs, often engage in a chorus of calls after dawn, and threaten their neighbours across the borders chasing them off when they intrude (Ellefson 1968; Chivers 1974) (Fig. 10.3).

Of those monkeys that live in harems or in multi-male groups only some defend territories (Jolly 1972). The most significant fact is that there is great variation: one species may be territorial and a closely related species may

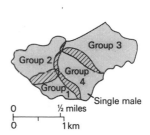

10.3 Territories of three gibbon pairs and one single male. The stippled areas are those used by only one group; areas of overlap are shown by hatching. The territory of group 3 borders on the coast. After Ellefson (1968) and Jolly (1972).

not; and there are even instances where a species occupies territories in one area but not in another. Thus, the Nilgiri langur (*Presbytis johnii*) in South India defends territorial borders, and it has been reported that males pursuing intruders turn back and flee when they reach the core area of the intruder's territory (Poirier 1970, 1974). The grey langur (*Presbytis entellus*) in Ceylon engages in chases across territorial borders (Ripley 1967); yet in North India they have not been seen to do this (Jay 1965). Again, the black and white colobus monkey (*Colobus badius*) lives in one-male harems which occupy defended territories; yet the red colobus monkey (*Colobus guereza*), though living in the same region, is organized into multi-male groups which have a more extensive range which they do not defend (Clutton-Brock 1974).

There is also variation in the practices of monkeys living in multi-male groups. There is some evidence that vervet monkeys, which spend much of the day on the gound, may occupy defended territories which have little overlap (Struhsaker 1967). But in macaques and baboons the ranges of different groups often overlap extensively (DeVore and Hall 1965; Altmann and Altmann 1970; Lindburg 1971) (Fig. 10.4). When groups meet their interactions may be peaceable, though they are not always so (Lindburg 1971; Deag 1973). Even when fighting occurs we should be careful not to assume that these fights are territorial, since to draw that conclusion we require further evidence that the outcome of the incident is determined by *where* the groups happen to meet. Intolerance of others is not in itself proof of territoriality.

Even the two African apes, our nearest living relatives, appear to differ in the way in which relations between groups are organized. The ranges of gorillas may overlap

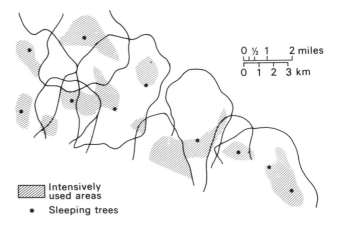

10.4 Home ranges of olive baboons. The dots indicate sleeping trees, and the hatched areas show the core areas within the range. After DeVore and Hall (1965) and Jolly (1972).

0 ½ 1   2 miles
0 1 2 3 km

▨ Intensively used areas
• Sleeping trees

extensively, although the core areas are rarely visited by members of other groups (Schaller 1963; Fossey and Harcourt 1977). The gorillas do not overtly defend any parts of their range, although groups may show excitement on meeting (Fossey 1974; Fossey and Harcourt 1977). In chimpanzees also the ranges of regional populations sometimes overlap, though each community has a core area for its exclusive use (Nishida 1979). But chimpanzees differ from gorillas in that there is good evidence that the males sometimes go out on safari to patrol the boundaries, and that they search for neighbours or strangers and display when they see them (van Lawick-Goodall *et al.* 1979) (Fig. 10.5). It is true that lone gorilla males occasionally harass and even attack animals they meet (Fossey 1979); but there is no compelling evidence that they are patrolling boundaries.

This review suggests that it only pays animals to defend territories under certain environmental conditions. Animals of the same species may occupy territories in one

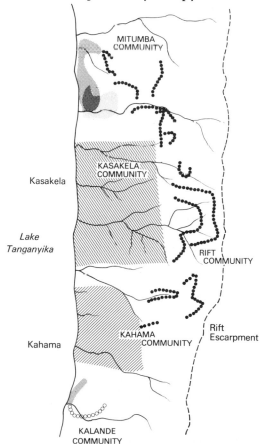

10.5 Core areas of two chimpanzee communities in Gombe National Park, Tanzania. ●, The peripheral boundaries patrolled by male chimpanzees in the Kasakela community; ○, the boundaries patrolled by the Kahama chimpanzees. Hatching, core areas; stippling, three safaris in peripheral areas. After van Lawick-Goodall *et al.* (1979).

ecological niche and not in another. The sifaka (*Propithecus verreauxi*), which is a diurnal prosimian, provides an informative example. In southern Madagascar there is food enough in a home range to feed just one group during the dry season, whereas in the north there is much more food available but particular food types are widely scattered; the sifakas defend territories in the south but not in the north (Sussman and Richard 1974). For an animal to defend a territory it is necessary that there be an adequate supply of food in one place to support potential territory owners, and that the area be small enough to be defensible without an uneconomic expenditure of energy (Davies 1978b).

The mechanism by which territoriality is established is probably a simple one. Consider individual territories: we need suppose only that the animal becomes attached to a particular site, and that it is intolerant of the presence of other animals (Tinbergen 1957). It wins on its home ground where the familiar surroundings inspire confidence and loses elsewhere because it lacks confidence. We can speculate that it might prove possible to manipulate the environment so that an animal, such as a macaque, which is not normally territorial might be induced to defend a territory. If macaques are housed in cages on their own they become familiar with the site where they live and get their food. If we tried to introduce monkeys into the cages of other animals we would probably find that each animal was more successful in disputes that took place in its home cage than in those that took place elsewhere.

Dominance hierarchies

Dominance hierarchies are sometimes referred to as 'pecking orders' because they were first well described in domestic chickens (Schjelderup-Ebbe 1935). If grain is available in a trough a pecking order soon becomes evident in hens that have been reared together; high rank brings prior access to the trough as well as to the roost (Guhl 1956). A linear hierarchy is usually formed; if A pecks B and B pecks C then A will peck C (Fig. 10.6).

Both simple and more complex hierarchies have been reported in many mammals (Wilson 1975). It is of especial interest to know whether the more dominant animals have the greater reproductive fitness, that is whether they produce more viable offspring than the less dominant members of the group. That they may do so has been demonstrated in an elegant experiment conducted on

10.6 (*opposite*) Pecking order in domestic hens. The hens with bowed heads (black) indicate the number of hens submissive to the hen in that column. The number of hens with upright heads (white) indicate the number of hens that are dominant over the hen in that column. The number of times that a hen pecks each of the other hens is indicated by the numbers in the column. Example: hen BB is dominated by six hens and is dominant over five hens. Hen Y is top in the hierarchy and hen BR bottom. After Guhl (1956).

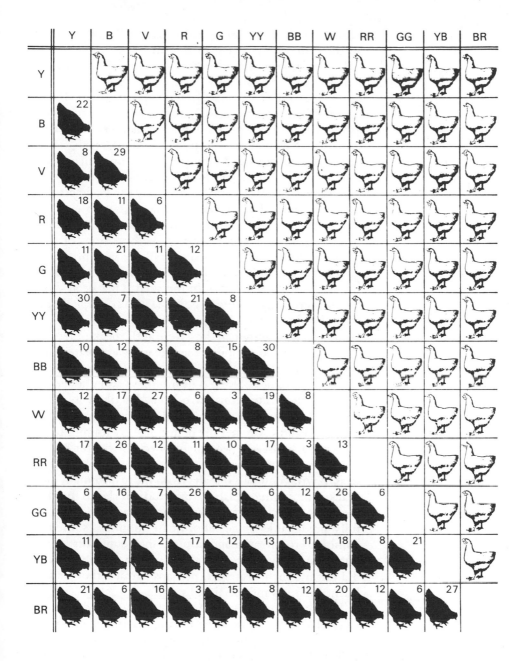

mice (DeFries and McClearn 1970). Male mice of three different strains were used so that the paternity of the offspring could be established by the colour of their coat. Twenty-two groups were set up of three males from the different strains and three females. In each group the males established a dominance hierarchy by fighting; in 18 of the groups the most dominant males sired all the litters, and in all they sired 92 per cent of the offspring.

In most non-human primates males are dominant over females (Jolly 1972). However, adult males can only be dominant over adult males in those groups in which there is more than one adult male; and many primates live in groups with only one adult male (Chapter 9). In those primates that live in multimale groups, such as the macaques, baboons and chimpanzees, dominance hierarchies are very common (Jolly 1972).

An animal's position in the hierarchy can be determined in several ways. For example, we can see who gets food first, we can observe who gives ground when animals meet, and we can keep count of the outcomes of fights between individuals. In rhesus monkeys in captivity the rank order established in each of these three ways is much the same (Richards 1974). In the wild it has been shown that in a group of yellow baboons (*Papio cynocephalus*) the most dominant male had priority of access to females in oestrus on the days when they were at the peak of fertility, and that the male second in the hierarchy copulated more than did other males in the group (Hausfater 1975).

The hierarchies observed in monkeys and apes are not always linear. Situations have been described in which, though A is dominant over B and B is dominant over C, animals B and C can get the better of A by joining forces. One case has already been mentioned in Chapter 8. Male olive baboons were seen to form temporary partnerships so as to wrest oestrous females from more dominant males (Packer 1977). In one laboratory study of rhesus monkeys the order of access to a drinking spout was found not to be fully predictable, since subordinate monkeys sometimes combined to threaten and displace their superiors (Mason 1978). Monkeys reared on their own in their early years did not use such strategies, perhaps because they had not learnt the relevant social skills.

There is no mystery about the working of a dominance hierarchy. There is no need to suppose that some species are born with a genetic make-up that predisposes them to form hierarchies whereas others are not. For animals to establish a hierarchy it is necessary only that they be able to recognize each other and to learn to challenge others only when they are likely to win. In other words the animals need be capable only of learning to whom it pays them to submit (Rowell 1974). Animals that do not form dominance hierarchies in natural conditions can be induced to do so in captivity if they compete for resources in a confined space. House mice (*Mus*), for instance, defend individual territories in the wild; but if they are kept in groups in small cages they will establish a rank order (Archer 1970). Animals in captivity must obtain their food from containers, and there is generally competition for access to these. Dominance hierarchies are especially promoted by such conditions (Rowell 1967, 1974).

This account has stressed that whether animals defend territories or set up hierarchies depends on the conditions in which they live. For this reason it is not helpful, when comparing man with animals, to conduct the discussion in terms of whether or not we share an 'instinct' for territoriality or dominance.

THE HUMAN HERITAGE

Genetics

Now consider human disputes. To what extent does our genetic endowment predispose us to behave in the same way as other primates? This question is deliberately formulated in terms which make no mention of any 'instincts' or 'innate behaviour'. It is important that we understand at the outset why these terms only serve to confuse the issue.

Darwin was an excellent naturalist, and in *The Origin of Species* he included a chapter on instinct (Darwin 1859); in this he explained how species inherit their various instincts in the same way that they acquire their physical characteristics. Biology is firmly based on Darwin's theory of evolution by natural selection, and for the first half of this century zoologists interested in the behaviour of animals took their science to be the study of instinct (Tinbergen 1951). But ethologists now regard the terms 'instinct' and 'innate' as unhelpful and potentially misleading (Lehrman 1953, 1970; Tinbergen 1963).

Both terms suggest that the behaviour in question is set on a rigid course, and that it will occur irrespective of environmental conditions. The animal is regarded as a robot which will go inexorably through its paces under whatever circumstances it is reared. Take a concrete example: it is true that even if squirrels (*Sciurus vulgaris*) are reared without access to hard objects they will make furrows in nuts when first provided with them, and will attempt to split them by inserting their incisors and twisting (Eibl-Eibesfeldt 1975). But that is not to say that squirrels could not be reared in so abnormal an environment that they failed to do this; nor that the squirrels have nothing to learn about how nuts can be opened. Indeed we know that they learn by experience the most economical ways of preparing the nut for splitting. We need a way of describing such situations which acknowledges the contribution of both genetic instructions and environmental circumstances and allows us to weigh up the relative contribution of each.

It has been suggested that the most fruitful way of formulating questions about the influence of the genes on behaviour is to ask to what extent differences in behaviour between species can be attributed to genetic differences between them (Hinde 1970). In an ideal experiment we might rear animals of two species in identical environments, and if we find behavioural differences we could justifiably conclude that they reflect the different composition of the two groups. This conclusion leaves open the possibility that evidence might be found of environmental influences if a study was made of the effects of different rearing conditions, by bringing up some animals in each species in one way and some in another.

But it is cumbersome to talk always of attributing differences to differences, and when we discuss experiments on environmental factors we typically use a more convenient shorthand. Let us say that we are interested in the effects of abnormal rearing conditions. We take rhesus monkeys and rear them either in isolation or with their mothers; we later note that the monkeys in the two groups differ markedly in temperament, and that in particular the isolated animals are unusually fearful (Sackett 1969). We, therefore, attribute the differences in fear to the different conditions of rearing; but we conclude that isolation produces or causes the abnormal state. In saying this we are not claiming that this is the *sole* influence on the development of stability; it is the only one that we looked at in our experiment. Had we done other experiments we might have demonstrated other effects; we might, for example, have found that if a monkey is reared with a fearful mother it is more prone to fear than a monkey reared with a stable mother.

If it is proper to conclude that isolation influences temperament there is no reason why it should be improper to conclude from our genetic experiments that particular behaviour patterns are influenced by the genes. It is necessary only that the reader be aware that in science such statements carry the proviso that the experimenter is only making claims about the conditions he studied. In asserting that an action is to some extent under the control of the genes nothing need be implied about the degree to which it is also controlled by other factors.

This point can best be illustrated by considering an actual genetic experiment. The experimenters wanted to know whether the aggressiveness of an animal could be influenced in any way by its genetic complement, and they studied this issue in mice by a selective breeding experiment (Lagerspetz 1964). Mice were classified as more or less aggressive on the basis of tests in which two animals of the same sex were put together for a standard time and ratings were made of their aggressive behaviour. Breeding pairs were then set up so that a mouse which scored highly on aggression mated with another mouse that scored highly, and a mouse that was low on aggression mated with another mouse with a low score. The offspring were then all tested for aggressiveness and again like were paired with like to breed the next generation; the process was then repeated in succeeding generations. The results are given in Fig. 10.7 which plots the scores on the aggression test for the succeeding generations of the two lines of mice. It is established that it is possible to breed mice selectively for high or low aggressiveness, and thus that aggressiveness is to some extent under the influence of genetic factors.

But as described so far this experiment says nothing about possible environmental influences, and it would be a misunderstanding to take the results as denying the operation of any environmental effects. These factors can be looked at only by experimentally manipulating the external conditions, for example by rearing some mice of the aggressive strain with non-aggressive mothers and

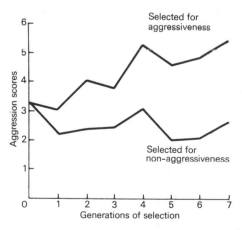

10.7 Results of an experiment on selective breeding for aggressiveness in mice. The aggression scores increase in successive generations in the line selected for aggressiveness. After Lagerspetz (1964) and Barash (1977).

some mice of the non-aggressive strain with aggressive mothers. This has been done and it was found that the mice of the high-aggressive strain are less aggressive when fostered with mothers of the low-aggressive strain (Lagerspetz 1969). This finding in no way invalidates the original statement, which was that the level of aggressiveness is to some extent determined by the genes.

Can we be more specific and actually put a figure on the relative contribution made by genetic as opposed to environmental factors? In principle we could, though in practice it would be difficult to arrive at a reliable estimate. We would have to investigate each of the sorts of experience that might have some influence; and the final figure for the genetic contribution would hold only for the range of environmental variation that we had sampled.

This can be appreciated by examining a technique much used to investigate the degree of inheritance of traits in people (Shields 1973). This makes use of the convenient fact that identical twins come from a single ovum or egg, and therefore share much the same genetic complement; whereas non-identical twins come from separate ova which have been fertilized by different sperm, and these twins are therefore no more similar genetically than are siblings who come from separate ova fertilized at different times. If we find that identical twins are more similar than non-identical twins, whether in abilities or temperament, we will be tempted to attribute this fact to the greater genetic similarity of the identical twins. But it might be argued that the identical twins are brought up more closely and share more experiences than fraternal twins. We can try to counter this criticism by testing twins that have been separated from each other early in life and then brought up apart in different homes. We suppose that in such cases the identical twins are no closer in their experience than the non-identical twins.

The study of twins provides data on the basis of which 'heritability' indices can be calculated for the trait under examination (Jinks and Fulker 1970). These indices vary theoretically from 0.0 to 1.0, where 1.0 means wholly under genetic influence. But it is essential that we appreciate that the figure for heritability is a proportion and that it is crucially dependent on the degree to which the experiences of the twins differed, since the more similar their backgrounds the greater the proportional contribution that the genes *could* make. Only if we had examined the influence of the full range of the social and economic conditions of a society would the exact estimate of heritability be of much worth.

The method of studying twins enables us to make some assessment of the degree to which differences between people in intelligence or temperament reflect genetic differences between them (Eysenck 1973). But unfortunately it will not help us answer questions about the degree to which universal characteristics of mankind are to be attributed to our genetic heritage. Let us suppose that we gave a valid questionnaire on irritability or aggressiveness to identical and non-identical twins, and that we discovered that the trait was to some degree heritable. That would tell us nothing directly about whether man is by nature an especially aggressive species, or to what extent society teaches him to be aggressive.

In principle, of course, we can discover whether some action is learnt by depriving individuals of the opportunity to learn it and then observing whether or not they still perform it. In Chapter 1 this method was illustrated with the example of the human smile. Here it was not necessary deliberately to interfere with development, since there are children who are born blind, and who therefore lack the opportunity to witness the facial expressions used by others (Freedman 1964; Eibl-Eibesfeldt 1973). But how are we to answer the questions about the contribution of learning to complex social behaviour? It is not feasible to change the early lives of children by removing them from the influences of society in the way that has been done with monkeys (see Chapter 9). It is true that some children are taken from their homes because of parental discord or death, but they are nonetheless brought up in a social setting in which they are taught by adults. There are, of course, a few cruel parents who have deliberately reared their children in isolation: one such child was Genie who was brought up for 11 years or so in an attic room on her own (Fromkin et al. 1974). But these children could hardly provide evidence as to the extent to which people learn to be aggressive, since they have suffered a long history of frustration which may itself provoke them to aggressive outbursts. Rhesus monkeys reared on their own are very aggressive, but this may be because they are terrified of other animals when they first meet them and are poor at judging their intentions (Sackett 1969). Neither in animals nor in man do isolation studies tell us much of importance about the development of aggression (Hinde 1974).

It might appear that we have reached an impasse. We

can neither examine nor tamper with the genetic instructions nor can we isolate individuals from the instruction given by social experience. But there is still one course left open, since we can look at the effects of different regimes of socialization. People in different cultures use a wide variety of methods for rearing their young, and we could in principle try to relate the temperament of the adults to the ways in which they were brought up (Whiting and Child 1953). If we found peoples who were relatively peaceable we could claim either that they had failed to learn aggressive ways or that they had successfully learnt how to control their aggression (Montagu 1978). But it is going to be difficult to make out this case convincingly, because there will always be many respects in which cultures differ other than in techniques of child rearing; these include the size of the society, the methods of subsistence and technological sophistication. It may be any one of these which is responsible for the differences in the behaviour of adults.

It would be better to conduct an experiment and to compare in one society the efficacy of different strategies for training the young. Indeed since we are directly interested in minimizing aggression this is the very experiment that we need to conduct. If we found that it was relatively easy to mould youngsters so that they had an even temperament and were not prone to anger this would go some way towards convincing us that we need pay less attention than some suggest to the contribution of genetic factors. Though we cannot modify the genes we can in principle modify the environment by social engineering, and so discover the limits within which the human temperament is malleable. Until such experiments are done we would do well to admit that there is little to be gained from prolonged discussion of the contribution of the genes to aggressive behaviour in man.

Questions

It is not just that we lack the experimental evidence. The issues are often formulated in terms that are a barrier to clear thought or debate. It has already been argued that it is not helpful to talk of an 'instinct' for aggression, and that instead it would be better to discuss the relative contribution of genetic factors. But no useful enquiry can be conducted so long as we treat 'aggression' as if it were a unitary phenomenon, and thus fail to unravel the many questions that are raised in debates on aggression. Only by considering each one separately can we form sensible opinions (Hinde 1969, 1974). There are nine such questions.

1. *What stimuli provoke us to aggression? And do we learn to which stimuli to react?* Like animals we fight to protect our own lives and the lives of our offspring. Disputes also arise when people are in danger of losing their sexual partners, as through adultery. People compete for resources. Young children will quarrel over toys, and will resort to biting and hitting when toys are taken away (Blurton Jones 1972a,b). In general the frustration that occurs when a person fails to get what he wants is a potent stimulus for aggression (Berkowitz 1962).

This is not to say that we are impelled to act aggressively in such situations, only that we often do. Nor is it to deny that the provoking stimuli can be very much more subtle than they are in animals. We can be set off by verbal insults; we defend our 'honour'; and we will fight for what we believe to be 'right'. We are sophisticated in our interpretation of the actions of others, and perceptive when they threaten our interests.

Clearly we are sensitive to such subtle cues because we have learnt how to interpret them. As children we watch how adults behave and are influenced by their choice of targets to attack. If children watch an adult punching an inflated rubber doll they will attack it themselves when given the opportunity (Bandura 1973). But it is not plausible to argue that young children have to learn all the contexts in which it is appropriate to react. There is no need for them to learn that they should defend themselves or that it may help to throw temper tantrums when thwarted.

2. *What is the pattern of the aggressive response? And do we learn it?* Unarmed we have much the same repertoire at our disposal as other primates: we can wrestle, punch, kick and bite. Like monkeys and apes we stare in threat, and we tense our mouths in anger (van Hooff 1967; Chevalier-Skolnikoff 1973) (Figs 10.1, 10.8 and 10.9). The temper tantrum of the child can be matched by the contortions of the angry chimpanzee (van Hooff 1967).

We do not learn the basic expressions of anger. Even children born blind and deaf will frown, bite their lips and stamp their feet in temper (Eibl-Eibesfeldt 1973). It is hardly necessary to add that there are other displays that are learnt, such as the song duels of Eskimos (Balikci 1970).

10.8 Chimpanzee threatening. From a photograph by H. van Lawick.

3. *Are there differences between individuals in how aggressive they are? And, if so, can they be related in part to any genetic variation between individuals?* We can conceptualize aggressiveness as the ease with which an individual can be aroused to anger. There is some justification for treating it as a trait: individuals tend to show something of the same pattern through infancy into adolescence, and some continuity can be traced into adulthood (Kagan and Moss 1962). In adults both aggressiveness and hostility can be measured on a questionnaire filled out by the subject (Buss 1961).

There is no question that a person's irritability and aggressiveness is affected by his upbringing and life experiences (Berkowitz 1962; Bandura 1973). But is our temperament in any way affected by our genetic makeup? We know that it is possible to breed strains of rats for high or low fearfulness (Broadhurst 1969); and studies of identical and non-identical twins suggest that individual differences in anxiety reflect to some extent genetic differences between people (Shields 1973). As stated earlier mice can be bred for high or low aggressiveness (Lagerspetz 1964); and different breeds of dogs are more or less liable to threaten and attack (Scott and Fuller 1974). But no one has yet given valid questionnaires of agressiveness to a series of identical and non-identical twins. It has yet to be established whether the genes play any role in determining differences between people in aggressiveness.

10.9 Threatening face posed by a man from the Fore of New Guinea. It was posed in response to the cue 'you are angry and about to fight'. From Ekman (1973).

4. *Is man a peculiarly aggressive species? And, if so, is it the human way of life and social conditions that are to blame?* For simplicity let us ignore verbal acts of aggression and defer the discussion of warfare until a later section. Even then it is not obvious how we are to go about answering the question. If we are looking for temperamental differences we could only form a worthwhile judgement if we were able to compare species under roughly the same conditions and in much the same environment. We should also need to agree on what we are to count as acts of aggression, that is whether threats are included or whether we only rate physical contact. Finally we would have to work out the rate of aggressive acts as a proportion of the total number of interactions we observe, since the more the interactions the greater the opportunity for fighting.

The task of making such comparisons, even between two species of monkey, is daunting. If we measure the number of aggressive episodes in baboons and in patas monkeys living in the same area we can, of course, report that there are more incidents in the baboons than in the patas monkeys (Nagel and Kummer 1974). But the two species live in totally different groups, baboons in multi-male groups and patas monkeys in harems with single adult males. Baboon males are frequently interacting with other adult males, but the patas monkey leaders do not come into contact with other adult males. The opportunity for fights is in no way balanced between the groups, and we can therefore draw no firm conclusions about the different temperaments of the two species of monkey. There probably are genuine temperamental differences between monkeys as field data suggest (Nagel and Kummer 1974); but we cannot take this as proved until studies have been conducted in captivity where the experimenters can control the size and composition of the groups and the supply of resources such as food.

It takes little thought to appreciate that there is not much hope of making valid comparisons between the rates of aggression in man and other primates. If we were to attempt some count of aggressive incidents we would still need to express this as a proportion of the total number of interactions of any sort; but it would not be practicable to gather such data. Certainly we can compute without too much trouble the murder rate per thousand individuals; and we may be relieved that the rate as calculated in this way is not obviously higher than it is in lions or hyenas (Johnson 1972; Wilson 1975, 1978). But a proper comparison must take into account the number of occasions on which murder čould take place.

Even if we were convinced that people were more prone to violence than, say, a chimpanzee the task of accounting for such a difference would be formidable. It is easy to list a host of factors that are implicated by social psychologists and social anthropologists—slum conditions, social inequality, the availability of guns and alcohol, and so on. How are we to control for all these precipitating agents and thus lay bare the temperament with which man has been endowed by nature?

5. *Do people defend territories? And, if so, do they learn to do so?* Our answer will obviously depend on what we are prepared to count as a territory. Different authors have used the word territoriality to cover phenomena as disparate as military defence of a country, town or village, protection of the family home, ownership of land or goods, respect for privacy, and even the temporary claims to a chair in a hospital or a place in a library or canteen (Edney 1974).

In animals a territory is always a space. Usually it is defended for a long period, but nomadic animals may defend different areas of ground at different times; male wildebeest, for example, when on the move will take up successive positions which they will defend, and these can be properly regarded as territories (Wilson 1975). We need not therefore require of a human territory that it be permanent. Some people do indeed defend areas which must be counted as territories by the definition we have used with animals. For example, the Pygmies and the San of the Kalahari Desert claim rights to particular hunting grounds, and attempt to keep out trespassers, although members of bands with which they inter-marry may be allowed entry (Turnbull 1966; Eibl-Eibesfeldt 1974). But the Hadza in Tanzania do not divide up their hunting areas in this way (Woodburn 1968). In settled communities in which the people depend on agriculture, peasants till their own plots and pastoralists tend their herds; the land and stock are defended against trespassers and nomadic raiders. The people are dependent upon the areas of land in which their crops are planted and on which their animals are pastured. It is not unreasonable to extend the word territory to cover division of land of this sort.

Ownership of goods is quite another matter. The analogy between possession of, let us say, a car and the area which a gibbon defends is too loose to be of much value. There are two crucial differences: the things that I own are mine irrespective of *where* I happen to be; and I can transfer property in the form of a gift or through an economic transaction. The nearest analogy in the animal literature is provided by an experiment on the way in which hamadryas baboon males acquire and keep their females (Kummer *et al.* 1974). Male A was put in an enclosure with a female while male B was allowed to watch from a separate cage; when, after some time, male B was permitted to enter the enclosure it failed to challenge the rights of male A to the female. It was not that male A was simply dominant as a result of superior strength. The roles could be reversed; male A would fail to challenge male B for a female which it had been allowed to acquire. The female belongs to the 'owner' irrespective of *where* the owner happens to be, so that this is not like territoriality. There is, in fact, no reason why we need to put the word 'owner' in quotes. In this example there is, of course, no notion of exchange; we would only expect to observe genuine exchange or transfer of property in the case of food or tools. Chapter 8 cited one or two examples of food sharing and the transfer of tools in monkeys and apes, but ownership was not implied.

There is little profit to be gained from discussing territoriality in man as if we had or had not inherited some *propensity* from our primate ancestors. It was stressed earlier that animals of the same species may defend territories in some conditions and not in others. The titi monkeys, for instance, occupy small territories in the wild, and yet they may fail to set up territories in a large field cage (Mason 1971). It would be more accurate to say that we are capable of dividing up land and protecting it, and that like other animals we only do so where it would pay. What pays the hunter or the farmer may not pay the city dweller.

A territorial animal fails to challenge the owner of a

territory because it suspects that the owner will prove the more confident because it is fighting on its home ground. But in people the division of land and property does not rest just on this simple psychological principle. Because we communicate through language we devise rules governing property; we call trespassers and thieves to trial, and invoke social and legal sanctions to deter cheating. We come to agreements as to what is a satisfactory exchange when we barter and as to the worth of goods that we sell. We will learn nothing of value about these by studying animals. The only factor in common is that both animals and people make decisions as to when it will and when it will not be worth challenging another individual to secure something that is prized.

6. *Do people set up dominance hierarchies? And, if so, do they learn to do so?* It is not difficult to find examples of such hierarchies. If we observe disputes between children at a nursery school we can count the number of times each child wins or loses arguments arising over toys or other matters. One such study reported that the boys could be ranked in order on this basis (McGrew 1972). Furthermore, who hits who turns out to be a good predictor of who is the more dominant in other respects; for example who takes toys, who gives commands, and who is the more verbally aggressive (Krebs 1974). Fig. 10.10 illustrates a dominance hierarchy in children as assessed by a wide variety of such interactions. Hierarchies of this sort are reasonably analogous to the hierarchies found in animals.

But we should distinguish between power and status. In the children we have mentioned high rank reflected the ability to persuade others to do one's will; and certainly there are hierarchies of power in some adult societies, for example the formalized hierarchy of a military regiment. However, it would be an unwarranted over-simplification to extend the term dominance hierarchy to all the other inequalities that exist in many human societies, as in status and wealth. People may be ranked on the basis of many qualities—intelligence, powers of oratory, artistic talent and so on. In one study of adolescent boys at a camp it was found that the boys could indeed be ranked in status, but that status was conferred by athletic prowess (Savin-Williams 1977). Different sub-groups value different qualities, and a person's position on one scale may well not tally with his position on another.

In some human societies a person's status and wealth are

	Andrew	John	Peter	David	Eric	Karen*	Connie*	Mick	Nancy*	Sandra*	Veronica*	Richard	Tim	Harriet*	Dawn*	Fern*
Andrew																
John	D															
Peter	D	D														
David	D	D	D													
Eric	D	D	D	D												
Karen*	D	.	D	.	D											
Connie*	D	D	D	D	D	D										
Mick	D	D	D	.	D	D	D									
Nancy*	D	D	.	D	D	D	D	D								
Sandra*	.	D	D	.	.	D	.	.	D							
Veronica*	.	.	.	.	.	D	.	.	=	D						
Richard	D	.	D	D	D	D	.	D	.	D	D					
Tim	D	D	D	D	D	D	.	.	.	D	D	D				
Harriet*	.	.	.	.	D	D	.	.	.	D	.	D	D			
Dawn*	.	.	D	D	.	D	D	.	.	D	.	D	.	D		
Fern*	.	.	D	.	.	D	.	.	D	.	.	.	.	.	D	

10.10 Dominance hierarchy in young children in a nursery school. The symbol D means that the child at the bottom in the column is dominant over the child to the left in the row. The symbol • means that the two children are equal. A space means that the relationship is unknown. Example: Karen is dominant over Connie but is dominated by Eric. Andrew is top of the hierarchy and Fern is at the bottom. *, Girls. After Krebs (1974).

not acquired simply because of personal characteristics or achievements; they can be granted by virtue of the status of the parents or the social class into which the individual has been born. Nothing is to be gained from drawing loose analogies between the dominance hierarchies of monkeys and an aristocracy. Human parents have many ways of influencing the success of their offspring; they can pass on both wealth and education. Admittedly we know that in macaques the sons of high-ranking females have the advantage of associating with high-ranking males when they are young, and that they are more likely to win dominant positions for themselves in adulthood (Koford 1963; Kawai 1965b) (Fig. 10.11). But we have yet to rule out the possibility that the real advantage is that of genetic inheritance from high-ranking parents of those qualities that determine dominance.

There is no clear equivalent to class or caste in animals except in social insects (Wilson 1975). Social stratification is not a universal phenomenon in human societies. In societies that are organized into bands formal social classes are absent, although there may be distinctions of wealth (Murdock 1949). A hereditary aristocracy or class of nobles is found in 20.2 per cent of societies, and a complex stratification into three or more social classes or castes in 18.1 per cent (Murdock 1957; Coult and Habenstein 1965). These figures are for freemen only; they do not take account of slaves. Slavery has been reported in only three

Names of monkeys													
Mothers	Zuku ♀ (22–30)	Yami ♀ (12–14)			Kaede ♀ (16–20)								Buna ♀ (12–14)
Offspring	Anzu (7)♀	Lulu ♀(4)	Nobara (8)♀			Ede (4)♀	Itigo (6)♀	Momo (7)♀	Opal (3)♂	Nemu (5)♀			
Grandchild				Quack (3)♂									

	Zuku	Anzu	Yami	Lulu	Nobara	Quack	Kaede	Ede	Itigo	Momo	Opal	Nemu	Buna
Zuku		+	+	+	+	+	+	+	+	+	+	+	+
Anzu	−		+	+	+	+	+	+	+	+	+	+	+
Yami	−	−		+	+	+	+	+	+	+	+	+	+
Lulu	−	−	−		+	+	(+)	+	+	+	+	+	+
Nobara	−	−	−	−		+	+	+	+	+	+	+	+
Quack	−	−	−	−	−		(+)	+	+	+	+	+	+
Kaede	−	−	−	(+)	−	(+)		+	+	+	+	+	+
Ede	−	−	−	−	−	−	−		+	+	+	+	+
Itigo	−	−	−	−	−	−	−	−		+	+	+	+
Momo	−	−	−	−	−	−	−	−	−		(+)	+	+
Opal	−	−	−	−	−	−	−	−	−	(+)		+	+
Nemu	−	−	−	−	−	−	−	−	−	−	−		+
Buna	−	−	−	−	−	−	−	−	−	−	−	−	

10.11 Dominance hierarchy in a Japanese macaque group. The troop is unusual in having no permanent adult male. The symbol + means that the animal to the left in that row dominates the animal at the top in that column; − means that the animal to the left is dominated by the animal at the top; ± means that the relationship is equivocal. Example: Lulu dominates Quack but is dominated by Yami. Zuku is at the top of the hierarchy and Buna at the bottom. Note that the offspring typically take the rank just beneath their mother. The numbers in parentheses give the ages of the animals. After Kawai (1965b) and Jolly (1972).

of the tribes that are organized into migratory bands; it is much more common in settled villages or neighbourhoods (Murdock 1949).

In this section and in the previous one attention has been drawn to the fact that people own property, have formal systems of exchange, can influence the success of their offspring, and may be born into a particular class or caste. That none of this is true of monkeys and apes tells us only perhaps that human beings are capable of organizing their social life in a more complex way, and that they have the ability to produce the goods that form their property. The fact that in some conditions both children and adults may form hierarchies of power tells us nothing sinister about our genetic inheritance. There are no 'genes for dominance' in animals or people.

We need only suppose that we are born with the ability to calculate our best interest; where there is competition for some prize there will be winners and losers so long as people pursue their own selfish ends. This statement in no way denies that people can be persuaded through socialization or the sanctions of the law to co-operate rather than to compete. Our psychology does not forbid the setting up of co-operatives and communes in which the resources and goods are owned in common and shared equally by all.

7. *Do people actively seek out opportunities to pick fights? And, if so, do they learn to do so?* The future of the human race would be bleak if it was indeed human nature to behave in this way. But why suppose that it is? One would not have thought that it would pay people or animals to fight without cause, since as pointed out earlier there are always costs that may be incurred by fighting.

Yet, Lorenz (1963) appeared to suggest that animals may look for fights. The claim is best appreciated by reference to Fig. 10.12: the two axes represent the degree of provocation and the passage of time. At time t_0 the provoking agent must be of degree 4 to evoke an aggressive response; we may re-phrase this by saying that the threshold for successful provocation is 4. Now Lorenz (1963) states that 'there are few instinctive behaviour patterns in which threshold-lowering and appetitive behaviour are so strongly marked as they are, unfortunately, in intra-specific aggression'. He supposes that given the passage of time alone the threshold for provocation may decrease, until it has a value of, let us say, 1 at t_2. It is as if, so he maintains, animals have a 'need' for aggression just as for food and water; and the longer an animal goes without food or water the more likely it is to search for them as the physiological need becomes more pressing. Unfortunately Lorenz does not make it clear in his account whether he envisages that the threshold for aggression might reach the value of 0 at, say, time t_4 and thus that fights would spontaneously erupt without any demonstrable external provocation. Tinbergen (1968) argues that Lorenz did not mean to imply this, and there is therefore no need further to consider this extreme position. Nonetheless Lorenz (1963) does argue that aggression is so likely in human society that the 'need' for it must be discharged by channelling the emotion into other activities that are less disruptive, such as competitive games.

Why did Lorenz ever arrive at the views we have attributed to him? Partly, perhaps, he regarded aggression as a 'natural' activity and wrongly drew analogies between the mechanisms for aggression and for other 'natural' activities. But that aggressive behaviour may have adaptive value in some circumstances in no way entails that it must be regulated in the same way as eating and drinking (Crook 1968). There is probably a second reason: Lorenz is confusing two quite distinct situations. In the first an animal attacks another with little apparent provocation; in the second the animal is provoked by another but actually

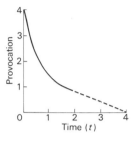

10.12 Diagram showing hypothetical change in the threshold for provocation with time. The numbers on the left show the degree of provocation required to stimulate aggression. The numbers at the bottom show the passage of time. The dotted line illustrates the possibility that with the passage of time alone the animal might indulge in aggression with no provoking stimulus at all (at t_4). See text.

attacks a third party. It is only the first of these cases which is the subject of controversy; no one disputes that animals may redirect their aggression onto a scapegoat when they are inhibited from dealing directly with the offender. To cite just one example: in a study of chacma baboons in the wild a dominant male was observed on a particular day to be roughly 10 times as aggressive to other members of the group as usual; on this day it was excited by the presence of a strange baboon, but was unable to chase it off because the stranger sheltered behind the observer (Hall 1963a). Episodes of this sort are not uncommon in monkey and ape societies (Hall and DeVore 1965; Hamburg 1971); and human beings are similarly prone to redirect their anger and vent it on innocent individuals (Yates 1962).

Experimentally it is possible to induce an animal to threaten and even to attack another by causing it to be irritable as a result of frustration or pain. This can be done by failing to give the animal food it had reason to expect or by giving it mild electric shocks. These phenomena have been well documented in pigeons and rodents (Ulrich 1966; Hinde 1974; Moyer 1976). If a pigeon has learnt to peck a button to deliver food and it then finds that pressing the button is no longer effective it will be more likely to attack a nearby pigeon or even a stuffed model (Azrin et al. 1966). Similarly if a rat receives shock to the feet through a grid floor it will threaten another rat so long as that animal is reasonably near at the time (Ulrich and Azrin 1962). A squirrel monkey will learn to pull down an object to bite if it receives a shock to its tail (Azrin et al. 1966). In all these cases the animal is unable to hit back at the cause of the insult, since it was the experimenter who indirectly arranged it and the animal has no way of fighting invisible electric shocks.

The issue can be clarified by looking at Fig. 10.13. We can describe the case of irritable redirected aggression as follows: at time t_0 the animal is provoked, and the provocation is sufficient in degree to elicit the state of readiness to attack; but, for some reason, it is either not possible or not prudent to retaliate. In this situation the threshold for provocation is temporarily lowered, so that at time t_2 the animal will respond with aggression to only a minor irritant. It will, therefore, be more likely to pick on another animal even though that animal has done nothing much to deserve it. If no suitable scapegoat exists we would predict that with the further passage of time to t_4 the animal would regain its composure and be no easier to arouse to anger than it had been in the first place. The

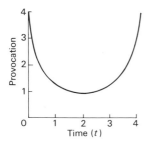

10.13 Diagram showing hypothetical change in the threshold for provocation after the animal has been provoked. The numbers on the left show the degree of provocation required to stimulate aggression. The numbers at the bottom show the passage of time. See text.

situation is therefore totally unlike that depicted in Fig. 10.12 where it was supposed that without an initial provocation at t_0 and with the passage of time alone the threshold for aggression would continue to decrease. The fact that there is a phenomenon of redirected aggression as illustrated by Fig. 10.13 has no bearing on whether animals or people ever behave as described in Fig. 10.12.

Is there any good evidence that Lorenz (1963) was correct in supposing that aggression might become more and not less likely as time passes? Several experiments have been carried out with territorial fish which have sometimes been interpreted as evidence for this view. A Siamese fighting fish (*Betta splendens*) can be taught to swim through a small hoop if by doing so it switches on a lamp so that it can see itself in a mirror or present itself with a model fish (Thompson 1963). Since the fish then displays at its reflection or at the model it could be argued that the fish is learning to swim through the hoop because in this way it can provide itself with an opportunity to threaten and display.

Are there alternative explanations of this phenomenon? Siamese fighting fish will also learn the trick in order to view a marble, and in this case we must suppose that they are motivated by curiosity (Johnson and Johnson 1973). Nonetheless the fish are more strongly motivated to confront another fighting fish than a marble. They will learn to swim down an alley and round a corner at the end in order to find and threaten another fighting fish; but if a marble is now substituted for the fish they gradually lose interest and finally stop swimming down the alley at all (Bols 1977). Damsel fish (*Microspathodon chrysurus*) will also learn to swim into a glass bottle to see another damsel fish, but enter much less frequently when there is only a silver object on view (Rasa 1971).

But further thought reveals that these findings do not settle the point at issue. The claim under examination is that animals will seek opportunities to fight without initial provocation, as illustrated in Fig. 10.12. But consider the experiments in which fighting fish swim down an alley (Bols 1977). When the fish starts swimming there is indeed no provocation *in sight*. But that does not mean that the animal is therefore acting without provocation when it swims down the alley to confront another male; it has learnt in previous trials of the presence of an intruder and is therefore reacting to a threat which it *knows* to be there. These fish patrol their territories, and will swim to any area in which there is danger from an intruder. The reason why they react less vigorously to the presence of a marble is, of course, that the marble constitutes no threat. The experiments prove not that animals seek out fights but that they chase off intruders.

There is, then, no reason to believe that it is in the nature of animals or people to search for opportunities to pick fights. But, whether they can learn to do so is quite a different matter. There are two ways in which experience could promote behaviour of this sort. First, repeated success in combat could instil self-confidence, and the individual might be the more ready to react to the slightest signs of threat by attacking before the opponent has time to make a move. Secondly, fighting could be encouraged if it leads to other consequences which are much prized. We know that both effects operate. Mice can be trained to be ready fighters by always pairing them with partners they can beat (Scott 1958). The mice learn to attack more quickly and effectively when faced with another mouse; and they will even attack females and young. The same method of training has proved effective with dogs (Kuo 1967). It has also proved possible to teach rats to attack innocent neighbours in the same compartment by the simple device of giving them access to drinking water whenever they do so (Ulrich *et al.* 1963). Here the animals are fighting because normal conditions have been altered such that fighting has a novel pay-off.

In people aggressive behaviour sometimes wins approval. In the laboratory people can be induced to behave punitively if the experimenter encourages them to do so (Bandura 1979). In some societies the men are tempted to go in search of fights because by doing so they can gain status and prove their manhood; this is true, for example, of the Xavante and the Yąnamamö of South America and the Dani of New Guinea (Maybury-Lewis 1967; Chagnon 1968; Carpenter 1974). In such societies a man values his honour and his reputation highly, and thus the social norms promote the virtues of a warrior. Like animals, people can be taught to pick fights if the rewards are high enough.

8. *Is aggression inevitable?* Nobody denies that like animals we have the capacity to defend ourselves and our interests (Montagu 1976). But we have not been convinced that either animals or people have a tendency to fight with little or no provocation. So we are left wondering whether aggression is inevitable given provocation, and whether

societies might be envisaged in which there is less provocation.

Whether an individual engages in an act of aggression is determined by several factors: past history, current internal state and present environmental conditions (Hinde 1974). It is wrong to view aggression as if it were simply triggered by some external stimulus such that the explosion must follow as in the firing of a gun. Even when there is a provoking stimulus it is not inevitable that the behaviour can be triggered. This is convincingly shown by experiments in which the stimulus that sets off the behaviour is applied directly to the brain itself. We have known for some time that direct electrical stimulation of the brain in animals can elicit particular behaviour patterns depending where the current is applied; stimulation of nuclei in the hypothalamus can induce animals to eat, drink, hoard, mate or attack (Valenstein *et al.* 1969). Behaviour can be elicited which we know to be unlearnt: cats that have been reared in isolation from other cats will nonetheless attack another cat when the current is turned on (Roberts and Berquist 1968). But it is not inevitable that the animals go through the routine. A rhesus monkey that would usually attack when the electrical stimulation is applied will fail to do so if it is faced with a monkey more dominant than itself (Delgado 1967). In other words even such a direct trigger does not cause 'unthinking' aggression.

Once we accept that aggression is not a simple reflex we remove the only remaining *a priori* reason for supposing that it could not be controlled. The extent to which people *can* control it is an issue which can be settled only by investigating the success of their attempts to do so.

There are two ways in which society can try to prevent aggression: through the socialization of the young and through social reform. The study of the behaviour of animals will tell us little about the likely success of either measure. It is for the social psychologist and the sociologist to try their hand. Anthropologists may continue the search for societies more peaceable than those of the Western world (Montagu 1978). It is better to look for the Garden of Eden rather than to refuse to set out because of theological doubts as to whether it exists. At least we will find out how far we can go.

The debate about human agression has itself been conducted with some rancour (Montagu 1976). The reason, perhaps, is that mankind is beset by the problems caused by warfare so that the issue is not merely an academic one. To the eight questions already discussed we have therefore to add a ninth. *Is warfare unique to mankind? And if so is that because of a fatal flaw in the temperament we have inherited or because of the nature of the complex society we have been able to create?*

If we define a battle as an aggressive encounter between two groups then battles may be said to occur in other species. There are ants that engage in pitched battles between colonies, and the same is true of some mammals (Wilson 1975). For instance, spotted hyenas (*Crocuta crocuta*) defend territories in the crowded conditions of the Ngorongoro Crater in Tanzania, and battles sometimes take place between clans (Kruuk 1972). In one study of grey langurs in Ceylon 30 aggressive encounters were seen, attacks were observed on 20 occasions, and actual fights on 4 (Ripley 1967; Nagel and Kummer 1974).

There are certain conditions that promote such fights: crowding, competition for food and disruption caused by human interference. Rhesus monkeys living in temple precincts in India sometimes fight viciously; two groups suddenly meet around the corner of a building, and neither has the time to withdraw or to give prior warning before contact is made (Southwick *et al.* 1965). Japanese monkeys at Takasakiyama have been observed to engage in protracted battles when they congregate in very large numbers on the grounds where they are fed (Carpenter 1974). The rhesus monkeys of Cayo Santiago, a small island off Puerto Rico, were transported there in 1940, and at first they fought fiercely and animals were killed (Carpenter 1974). Most of the 400 or so animals were strangers and they were all wholly dependent on the food with which they were now supplied from hoppers. Japanese monkeys in captivity have also been reported to engage in mob attacks on single individuals when their lives are disrupted by a drastic increase or decrease in the size of the area in which they were kept (Alexander and Roth 1971).

There is one field study of hamadryas baboons in which four battles were directly provoked by the experimenters; some of the details have already been mentioned (Kummer 1968). Fights started when corn was tipped out in a pile and several harem groups were attracted to it. As the animals came close together the adult males felt threatened by the proximity of other adult males to their females. The fights between males involved more and more animals until bands of between 20 and 90 individuals were chasing each other (Fig. 10.14). The one spontaneous fight of this sort that was observed seems to have been caused by competition for space on the cliffs the monkeys used for a sleeping; again the males perceived a threat to the integrity of their harems.

But a battle is not a war. To conduct a war over several days requires an intellectual, social and economic sophistication to which animals do not aspire.

Like most other mammals our primate relatives must spend much of each day on the search for food. Only the carnivores win enough food to sustain them over several days or to allow them to store a surplus; lions need hunt only every few days, and there are others such as the red fox (*Vulpus vulpus*) that cache meat to be eaten (Schaller 1972; MacDonald 1976).

Two economic factors make war feasible in human society: the surplus of grain and the exploitation of animal food. There are still peoples who live in an economy which is so simple as to allow only limited skirmishes. The Dani of New Guinea engage in day-long battles, but afterwards they return to their homes and their daily commitments (Gardner and Heider 1968). The Netsilik Eskimos used to send out revenge parties to kill, but the

10.14 Battle between bands of hamadryas baboons. The rear band is withdrawing up the river bank. From Kummer (1968).

parties could not be away for long (Balikci 1970). The Yąnamamö Indians of South America are noted for their fierceness at the present, and 24 per cent of adult males die in warfare; yet the raids can only last for up to a week as food has to be gathered and the vegetable gardens must be tended (Chagnon 1968). Lengthy warfare can only occur in societies that have reached a certain level of development in the cultivation of plants and the domestication of animals.

A measure of social organization is also required. We have found little if any evidence that any mammals engage in joint strategies when hunting (Chapter 9); neither do they do so in attack. In this respect their societies are less sophisticated than those of the ants with their warrior castes (Wilson 1975). But in human society the growth of cities and the division of the citizens into classes allows the creation of a soldier class, whether of slaves or free-born people. Some can till the fields while others fight.

Weapons make more destructive the wars that economic and social advance make possible. Furthermore long-range weapons relieve the user of the burden of witnessing the agony of the people he kills. It is presumably easier to press a trigger than to fight hand to hand and face to face (Lorenz 1963).

But who is it that has his finger on the trigger—a biological monster or a competent soldier? That man is more intelligent than other primates is not in doubt (Chapters 5 and 6). He is further blessed with the invention of language; and with this in his ordinary life he can communicate his ideas, plan strategies, and solve problems in his head (Chapters 7, 8 and 9). But if he chooses to go to war he can put his intelligence to more sinister use. He has the language with which to engage in propaganda and persuade others of his views. Language allows him to formulate and communicate tactical ideas. And it is because man has language that he can represent to himself the wickedness of others.

The reason why man is the only primate that conducts wars is that only man is *able* to do so. There is no cause to suspect the monstrous presence of a 'beast within'. Our trouble is that we are too clever for our own good.

Conclusion

The preface to this book held out the promise that the text would tell chimpanzees how to become men. What solid advice has the book to offer an enquiring chimpanzee?

To be of genuine help the advice will have to clarify the nature of the transformation and how it is to be accomplished. The previous pages have compared man with the other primates in order to enumerate the characteristics that ally man with the Primates and those that are uniquely his own. From this comparison it emerges that many of the distinctively human features can be derived by following the rules governing the construction of other primates.

There is no implication in this that mankind evolved from modern primates as erroneously suggested by the cartoon at the beginning of this book (frontispiece). The chimpanzee has gone its own way since diverging from the ancestors it shares with man. Only the study of the fossils themselves will establish in what order the changes occurred in the hominid line, and what were the environmental circumstances that promoted the revolution.

What is required to make a primate human? One answer is given by textbooks of physical anthropology which set out the defining features of the genus *Homo* and the species *Homo sapiens*. These rightly stress the major alterations of form, as in the shape of the foot, pelvis and vertebrae. Many separate changes were needed to adapt the skeleton for upright walking. There were also major changes in the pattern of the teeth in the hominid line—a reduction in the anterior teeth relative to the molars and a new shape for the dental arcade. But a chimpanzee with small anterior teeth and the skeletal structure for an upright gait would still fail to fool anyone into ranking it human. The cartoonist who drew the caricature shown as the frontispiece held a view to which we all subscribe, that the differences that matter are from the neck up.

The reason that man has always set himself apart from animals is that he believes himself to be unique in mental character. The case rests on language, invention, conscience, consciousness and free will. These attributes are owed to the singular development of the human brain. An account of these is to be found in textbooks not of physical anthropology but of neurology and psychology.

When described in these terms the mental gap between man and chimpanzee tends to sound mysterious. Yet mankind is the product of evolution and the transformation was completed rapidly: present estimates allow somewhere between 5 and 15 million years. The previous chapters have given an account of the change that has the virtue that it lacks mystery, however naive it may be. It attributes the peculiarly human form of mental life to relatively simple changes in the human brain.

There is no special difficulty in the belief that complex properties can emerge when biological systems are modified according to elementary principles. There are three considerations:

1. Quantitative changes in structure may permit functions that are new in kind. There is a regrettable tendency to decry 'mere' quantitative change as if it could not hold the key to qualitative innovation. As D'Arcy Thompson (1917) put it in his book *On Growth and Form*, we are apt to suppose that size makes no 'essential difference, and that Lilliput and Brobdingnag are all alike, according as we look at them through one end of the glass or the other'. But the difference between big and little brains, relative to body size, is not simply that the former tackle the same range of problems but with greater efficiency. The smaller brains may be inadequate to tackle certain *kinds* of task at all. It is not just the type of program that determines whether a computer can play chess well or even at all; the quality of its play is limited by the storage capacity of the machine.

2. Relatively simple changes in the genetic control of growth can have far-reaching effects on form. The human brain differs from the chimpanzee brain in its extreme development of cortical structures, in particular the cerebellar cortex and the association areas of the neocortex. But the proportions of the different areas are predictable from the rules governing the construction of primate brains of differing size (see Chapter 4). Furthermore there appears to be a basic uniformity in the number and types of cells used in the building of the different neocortical areas; and the human brain follows the general pattern for mammals. Even in the case of the two speech areas we believe we can detect regions in the monkey

brain which are alike in their basic cellular organization. The evolution of the human brain appears to have been characterized more by an expansion of existing areas than any more radical reconstruction.

3. The adoption of a new code for handling information can have revolutionary results. In appreciating the importance of language for communicating with others it is easy to underplay its importance for communicating with oneself. Language allows the formulation of propositions, whether about the physical or social world, and these propositions can be transmitted in conversation or in teaching. Without doubt this ability has led to the transformation of human society: rules can be issued, strategies can be discussed, roles can be laid down, traditions can be passed on. But at the same time the mental life of the individual is altered beyond recognition. The same language that describes the outside world can report on the current mental activity of the language user so that a conscious record can be kept. With the aid of language alternative courses of action can be stated and compared, and thus deliberate choice made. The language that describes reality also serves to formulate ideals, so that individuals can regulate their own behaviour according to their convictions or conscience.

None of these human attributes would have been possible without a code that articulates propositions. It must be admitted that this speculative claim is difficult to test. Chimpanzees can be taught to use labels for items or simple relationships. It is, therefore, feasible to assess the effects of using these symbols on their ability to remember items or to perceive relationships on cognitive problems (Chapter 8). But, even if it were agreed that chimpanzees could construct sentences, it is not practicable to investigate in chimpanzees the advantages of language for complex propositional thought.

We have set the chimpanzees a clearcut task. They must expand their brains according to the primate pattern until they have the capacity to think with the aid of language. Of course it is possible that, when faced with the option of becoming a man, a rational chimpanzee would take one look at human society and turn down the offer.

References

Adams, M. S. and Neel, J. V. (1967). Children of incest. *Pediatrics* **40**, 55–62.

Aiello, L. C. (1981). Locomotion in the Miocene Hominoidea. *Symp. Soc. Study hum. Biol.* **21**, 63–69.

Aiello, L. C. and M. D. Day (in press). The evolution of locomotion in the Hominidae. In *Progress in Anatomy* (eds R. J. Harrison and V. Navaratnam). Cambridge University Press, Cambridge.

Alcock, J. (1969). Observational learning in three species of birds. *Ibis* **111**, 308–321.

Alcock, J. (1972). The evolution of the use of tools by feeding animals. *Evolution* **26**, 464–473.

Alcock, J. (1979). *Animal Behavior: an Evolutionary Approach*, 2nd edn. Sinauer, Sunderland, Mass.

Aldrich-Blake, F. P. G., Bunn, T. K., Dunbar, R. I. M. and Headley, P. M. (1971). Observations on baboons, *Papio anubis*, in an arid region in Ethiopia. *Folia primatol.* **15**, 1–35.

Alexander, B. K. and Roth, E. M. (1971). The effects of acute crowding on aggressive behavior of Japanese monkeys. *Behaviour* **39**, 73–90.

Alexander, R. D. (1979). *Darwinism and Human Affairs*. University of Washington Press, Washington.

Alexander, R. D. and Noonan, K. M. (1979). Concealment of ovulation, parental care, and human social evolution. In *Evolutionary Biology and Human Social Behavior* (eds N. A. Chagnon and W. Irons), pp. 436–461. Duxbury, North Scituate, Mass.

Alexander, R. D., Hoogland, J. L., Howard, R. D., Noonan, K. M. and Sherman, P. W. (1979). Sexual dimorphism and breeding systems in pinnepeds, ungulates, primates and humans. In *Evolutionary Biology and Human Social Behavior* (eds N. A. Chagnon and W. Irons), pp. 402–435. Duxbury, North Scituate, Mass.

Altmann, S. A. ed. (1967). *Social Communication among Primates*. University of Chicago Press, Chicago.

Altmann, S. A. and Altmann, J. (1970). *Baboon Ecology*. University of Chicago Press, Chicago.

Ambrose, J. A. (1969). Discussion. In *Stimulation in Early Infancy* (ed. J. A. Ambrose), pp. 103–105. Academic Press, New York.

Ames, L. B. (1949). Development of interpersonal smiling responses in the pre-school years. *J. genet. Psychol.* **74**, 273–291.

Amsterdam, B. (1972). Mirror self-image reactions before age two. *Devl Psychobiol.* **5**, 297–305.

Anderson, J. W. (1972). Attachment behaviour out of doors. In *Ethological Studies of Child Behaviour* (ed. N. Blurton Jones), pp. 199–215. Cambridge University Press, Cambridge.

Andrew, R. J. (1962). The situations producing vocalization in the Primates. *Ann. N. Y. Acad. Sci.* **102**, 296–315.

Andrew, R. J. (1963). The origin and evolution of the calls and facial expressions of the Primates. *Behaviour* **20**, 1–109.

Andrew, R. J. (1972). The information potentially available in mammal displays. In *Non-Verbal Communication* (ed. R. A. Hinde), pp. 179–204. Cambridge University Press, Cambridge.

Annett, M. (1972). The distribution of manual asymmetry. *Br. J. Psychol.* **63**, 343–358.

Annett, M. (1973). Handedness in families. *Ann. hum. Gen.* **37**, 93–105.

Archer, J. (1970). Effects of population density on behaviour in rodents. In *Social Behaviour of Birds and Mammals* (ed. J. H. Crook), pp. 169–210. Academic Press, London.

Ardrey, R. (1961). *African Genesis*. Collins, London.

Ardrey, R. (1967). *The Territorial Imperative*. Collins, London.

Argyle, M. (1964). Introjection: a form of social learning. *Br. J. Psychol.* **55**, 391–402.

Aronfreed, J. (1968). *Conduct and Conscience*. Academic Press, New York.

Aronfreed, J. (1969). The problem of imitation. In *Advances in Child Development and Behavior* (ed. L. P. Lipsitt and H. W. Reese), pp. 209–319. Academic Press, New York.

Azrin, N. H., Hutchinson, R. R. and Hake, D. F. (1966). Extinction-induced aggression. *J. exp. Anal. Behav.* **9**, 191–204.

Baddeley, A. D. (1976). *The Psychology of Memory*. Harper and Row, New York.

Bailey, P. and von Bonin, G. (1951). *The Isocortex of Man*. University of Illinois Press, Urbana.

Bailey, P., von Bonin, G. and McCullogh, W. S. (1950). *The Isocortex of the Chimpanzee*. University of Illinois Press, Urbana.

Balikci, A. (1970). *The Netsilik Eskimo*. Natural History Press, New York.

Bandura, A. (1973). *Aggression: a Social Learning Analysis*. Prentice-Hall, Englewood Cliffs, NJ.

Bandura, A. (1977). *Social Learning Theory*. Prentice-Hall, Englewood Cliffs, NJ.

Bandura, A. (1979). Psychological mechanisms of aggression. In *Human Ethology* (eds M. von Cranach, K. Foppa, W. Lepenies and D. Ploog), pp. 316–356. Cambridge University Press, Cambridge.

Bandura, A. and Walters, R. H. (1959). *Adolescent Aggression*. Ronald Press, New York.

Bandura, A. and Walters, R. H. (1963). *Social Learning and Personality Development*. Holt, Rinehart and Winston, New York.

Barash, D. P. (1977). *Sociobiology and Behavior*. Elsevier, New York.

Barnett, S. A. (1968). The "instinct to teach". *Nature* **220**, 747–749.

Barnsley, R. H. and Rabinovitch, M. B. (1970). Handedness: proficiency versus stated preference. *Percept. Motor Skills* **30**, 343–362.

Basser, L. S. (1962). Hemiplegia of early onset and the faculty of speech, with special reference to the effects of hemispherectomy. *Brain* **85**, 427–460.

REFERENCES   Bastian, J. (1967). The transmission of arbitrary environmental information between bottlenose dolphins. In *Les Systèmes Sonars Animaux, Biologic et Bionique* (ed. R. G. Busnel), pp. 803–873. Laboratoire de Physiologie Acoustique, Jouy-en-Josas.

Bates, B. C. (1970). Territorial behavior in primates: a review of recent field studies. *Primates* 11, 271–284.

Bauer, K. (1974). Comparative analysis of protein determinants in primatological research. In *Prosimian Biology* (eds R. D. Martin, G. A. Doyle and A. C. Walker), pp. 915–936. Duckworth, London.

Beck, A. (1967). *Depression: Clinical, Experimental and Theoretical Aspects.* University of Pennsylvania Press, Philadelphia.

Beck, B. B. (1973). Cooperative tool use by captive hamadryas baboons. *Science* 182, 594–597.

Beck, B. B. (1975). Primate tool behavior. In *Socioecology and Psychology of Primates* (ed. R. H. Tuttle), pp. 413–447. Mouton, The Hague.

Beck, B. B. (1980). *Animal Tool Behavior.* Garland, New York.

Beck, C. H. M. and Barton, R. L. (1972). Deviation and laterality of hand preference in monkeys. *Cortex* 8, 339–363.

Beecher, M. D., Petersen, M. R., Zoloth, S. R., Moody, D. B. and Stebbins, W. C. (1979). Perception of conspecific vocalizations by Japanese macaques. *Brain Behav. Evol.* 16, 443–460.

Bellugi, U., Klima, E. S. and Siple, P. (1975). Remembering in signs. *Cognition* 3, 93–125.

Beninger, R. J., Kendall, S. B. and Vanderwolf, C. H. (1974). The ability of rats to discriminate their own behaviors. *Can. J. Psychol.* 28, 79–91.

Berkowitz, L. (1962). *Aggression: a Social Psychological Analysis.* McGraw-Hill, New York.

Berkson, G. (1968). Development of abnormal stereotyped behaviors. *Devl Psychobiol.* 1, 118–132.

Berkson, G. and Schusterman, R. J. (1964). Reciprocal food sharing of gibbons. *Primates* 5, 1–10.

Bernstein, I. S. (1964). The role of dominant male rhesus in response to external challenges to the group. *J. comp. Physiol. Psychol.* 57, 404–406.

Bernstein, I. S. (1966). An investigation of the organization of pigtail monkey groups through the use of challenges. *Primates* 7, 471–480.

Bernstein, I. S. (1970). Primate status hierarchies. In *Primate Behavior* (ed. L. A. Rosenblum), Vol. 1, pp. 71–109. Academic Press, New York.

Bernstein, I. S., Gordon, T. P. and Rose, R. M. (1974). Factors influencing the expression of aggression during introductions to rhesus monkey groups. In *Primate Aggression, Territoriality and Xenophobia* (ed. R. L. Holloway), pp. 211–240. Academic Press, New York.

Bertram, B. C. R. (1976). Kin selection in lions and evolution. In *Growing Points in Ethology* (eds P. P. G. Bateson and R. A. Hinde), pp. 281–301. Cambridge University Press, Cambridge.

Bielicki, T. (1969). Deviation-amplifying cybernetic systems and hominid evolution. *Materialy i prace Anthropologiczne* 77, 57–60.

Bilsborough, A. (1973). A multivariate study of evolutionary change in the hominid cranial vault and some evolution rates. *J. hum. Evol.* 2, 387–404.

Binford, S. R. (1968). Early Upper Pleistocene adaptations in the Levant. *Am. Anthropol.* 70, 707–717.

336

Bingham, H. C. (1929). Chimpanzee translocation by means of boxes.
Comp. Psychol. Mon. **5**, 1–91.

Birch, H. G. (1945). The relation of previous experience to insightful problem solving. *J. comp. Psychol.* **38**, 367–383.

Bishop, A. (1964). Use of hand in lower primates. In *Evolutionary and Genetic Biology of Primates* (ed. J. Buettner-Janusch), Vol. 2, pp. 133–225. Academic Press, New York.

Blackfan, K. D. (1933). Growth and development of the child: part II, anatomy and physiology. In *White House Conference on Child Health and Protection*, pp. 176–190. Appleton Century Crofts, New York.

Blinkov, S. M. and Gleser, I. I. (1968). *The Human Brain in Figures and Tables: a Quantitative Handbook.* Plenum Press, New York.

Blumenberg, B. (1978). Hominid ECV versus time: available data does not permit a choice of model. *J. hum. Evol.* **7**, 425–436.

Blurton Jones, N. G. (1972a). Non-verbal communication in children. In *Non-Verbal Communication* (ed. R. A. Hinde), pp. 271–296. Cambridge University Press, Cambridge.

Blurton Jones, N. G. (1972b). Categories of child – child interaction. In *Ethological Studies of Child Behaviour* (ed. N. G. Blurton Jones), pp. 97–127. Cambridge University Press, Cambridge.

Bogen, J. and Bogen, G. M. (1976). Wernicke's region: where is it? *Ann. N. Y. Acad. Sci.* **280**, 834–843.

Bok, S. T. (1959). *Histonomy of the Cerebral Cortex.* Van Nostrand, Princeton.

Bols, R. J. (1977). Display reinforcement in the Siamese fighting fish, *Betta splendens*: aggression motivation or curiosity? *J. comp. Physiol. Psychol.* **91**, 233–244.

Bonin, G. von (1944). Architectonics of the precentral motor cortex and some adjacent areas. In *The Precentral Motor Cortex* (ed. P. Bucy), pp. 7–82. University of Illinois Press, Urbana.

Bonin, G. von (1963). *The Evolution of the Human Brain.* Chicago University Press, Chicago.

Bonin, G. von and Bailey, P. (1947). *The Neocortex of Macaca mulatta.* University of Illinois Press, Urbana.

Bonin, G. von and Bailey, P. (1961). Pattern of the cerebral isocortex. *Primatologia*, II 2 Lief. 10, 1–42.

Bonner, J. T. (1980). *The Evolution of Culture in Animals.* Princeton University Press, Princeton.

Bordes, F. (1968). *The Old Stone Age.* Weidenfeld and Nicolson, London.

Bowlby, J. (1952). *Maternal Care and Mental Health*, 2nd edn. WHO monograph, Geneva.

Bowlby, J. (1969). *Attachment and Loss.* Hogarth Press, London.

Bowlby, J. (1973). *Separation: Anxiety and Anger.* Hogarth Press, London.

Bowman, R. I. (1961). Morphological differentiation and adaptation in the Galapagos finches. *Univ. Calif. Berkeley Publ. Zool.* **58**, 1–326.

Braak, H. (1978). On magnopyramidal temporal fields in the human brain: probable morphological counterpart of Wernicke's sensory speech region. *Anat. Embryol.* **152**, 141–169.

Brain, C. K. (1978). Some aspects of the South African australopithecine sites and their bone accumulations. In *Early Hominids in Africa* (ed. C. J. Jolly), pp. 131–161. Duckworth, London.

Brémond, J. C. (1968). Rechèrches sur la semantique et les elements vecteurs d'information dans les signaux acoustiques du rouge-gorge (*Erithacus rubecula* L.). *La Terre et la Vie* **22**, 109–220.

Broadhurst, P. L. (1969). Psychogenetics of emotionality in the rat. *Ann. N. Y. Acad. Sci.* **159**, 806–824.

Brodal, A. (1981). *Neurological Anatomy in Relation to Clinical Medicine*, 3rd edn. Oxford University Press, Oxford.

Brodmann, K. (1912). Neue Ergebnisse über die Vergleichende histologische Localisation der Grosshirnrinde mit besonderer Berücksichtigung des Stirnhirns. *Anat. Anz.*, Suppl. **41**, 157–216.

Brody, H. (1970). Structural changes in the ageing nervous system. *Interdisc. Topics Geront.* **7**, 9–21.

Brown, D. P. F., Lenneberg, E. H. and Ettlinger, G. (1978). Ability of chimpanzees to respond to symbols of quantity in comparison with that of children and of monkeys. *J. comp. Physiol. Psychol.* **92**, 815–820.

Brown, R. (1970). The first sentences of child and chimpanzee. In *Psycholinguistics* (ed. R. Brown), pp. 208–231. MacMillan, New York.

Brown, R. (1973). *A First Language: the Early Stages.* Allen and Unwin, London.

Brown, R. (1981). Symbolic and syntactic capacities. *Phil. Trans. R. Soc. Lond.* B**292**, 197–204.

Bruce, E. J. and Ayala, F. J. (1978). Humans and apes are genetically very similar. *Nature* **276**, 264–265.

Bryant, P. E., Jones, P., Claxton, V. and Perkins, G. M. (1972). Recognition of shapes across modalities by infants. *Nature* **240**, 303–304.

Buettner-Janusch, J. (1966). *Origins of Man: Physical Anthropology.* Wiley, New York.

Buettner-Janusch, J. and Andrew, R. J. (1962). The use of the incisors by primates in grooming. *Am. J. phys. Anthrop.* **20**, 127–129.

Bunn, H. T. (1981). Archaeological evidence for meat-eating by Plio-Pleistocene hominids from Koobi Fora and Olduvai Gorge. *Nature* **291**, 574–577.

Burdick, C. K. and Miller, J. D. (1975). Speech perception by the chinchilla: discrimination of sustained [a] and [i]. *J. acoust. Soc. Am.* **58**, 415–427.

Buss, A. H. (1961). *The Psychology of Aggression.* Wiley, New York.

Butler, H. (1974). Evolutionary trends in primate sex cycles. *Contr. Primat.* **3**, 2–35.

Butler, R. A. (1965). Investigative behavior. In *Behavior of Non-Human Primates* (eds A. M. Schrier, H. F. Harlow and F. Stollnitz), pp. 463–493. Academic Press, New York.

Butter, C. (1968). *Neuropsychology: the Study of Brain and Behavior.* Brooks/Cole, Belmont, California.

Butzer, K. (1972). *Environment and Archeology.* Aldine, Chicago.

Campbell, B. (1964). Quantitative taxonomy and human evolution. In *Classification and Human Evolution* (ed. S. L. Washburn), pp. 50–74. Methuen, London.

Campbell, B. (1972). Man for all seasons. In *Sexual Selection and the Descent of Man* (ed. B. Campbell), pp. 40–58. Aldine-Atherton, Chicago.

Campbell, B. (1974). *Human Evolution*, 2nd edn. Heinemann, London.

Carpenter, C. R. (1974). Aggressive behavioral systems. In *Primate Aggression, Territoriality and Xenophobia* (ed. R. L. Holloway), pp. 459–496. Academic Press, New York.

Cartmill, M. (1974). Rethinking primate origins. *Science* **184**, 436–443.

Chagnon, N. A. (1968). *Yąnomamö: the Fierce People*. Holt, Rinehart and Winston, New York.

Chalmers, N. R. (1968). The social behaviour of free-living mangabeys in Uganda. *Folia primat.* **8**, 263–281.

Chamove, A. S. (1966). The effect of varying peer experience on social behavior in the rhesus monkey. Unpubl. MA thesis, University of Wisconsin.

Chamove, A. S., Rosenblum, L. A. and Harlow, H. F. (1973). Monkeys (*Macaca mulatta*) raised only with peers: a pilot study. *Anim. Behav.* **21**, 316–325.

Charles-Dominique, P. (1972). Ecologie et vie sociale de *Galago demidovii* (Fischer: 1808; Prosimii). *Z. Tierpsychol.*, Suppl. **9**, 1–41.

Charles-Dominique, P. (1974a) Ecology and feeding behavior of five sympatric lorisids in Gabon. In *Prosimian Biology* (eds R. D. Martin, G. A. Doyle and A. C. Walker), pp. 131–150. Duckworth, London.

Charles-Dominique, P. (1974b). Aggression and territoriality in nocturnal prosimians. In *Primate Aggression, Territoriality and Xenophobia* (ed. R. L. Holloway), pp. 31–48. Academic Press, New York.

Charles-Dominique, P. (1975). Nocturnality and diurnality. In *Phylogeny of the Primates* (eds W. P. Luckett and F. S. Szalay), pp. 69–87. Plenum Press, New York.

Charles-Dominique, P. (1977) *Ecology and Behaviour of Nocturnal Prosimians*. Duckworth, London.

Cheney, D. L. and Seyfarth, R. M. (1980). Vocal recognition in free-ranging vervets. *Anim. Behav.* **28**, 362–367.

Cherry, C. M., Case, S. M. and Wilson, A. C. (1978). Frog perspective on the morphological difference between humans and chimpanzees. *Science* **200**, 209–211.

Chevalier-Skolnikoff, S. (1973). Facial expression of emotion in non-human primates. In *Darwin and Facial Expression* (ed. P. Ekman), pp. 11–89. Academic Press, New York.

Chiang, M. (1967). Use of tools by wild macaque monkeys in Singapore. *Nature* **214**, 1258–1259.

Chivers, D. J. (1969). On the daily behaviour and spacing of howling monkey groups. *Folia primat.* **10**, 48–102.

Chivers, D. J. (1974). *The Siamang in Malaya*. (Contr. Primat. **4**.) Karger, Basel.

Chomsky, N. (1972). *Language and Mind*. Harcourt Brace and Jovanovich, New York.

Clarke, P. G. H., Donaldson, I. M. L. and Whitteridge, D. (1976). Binocular visual mechanisms in cortical areas I and II of the sheep. *J. Physiol., Lond.* **256**, 509–526.

Clutton-Brock, T. H. (1974). Primate social organization and ecology. *Nature* **250**, 539–542.

REFERENCES

Clutton-Brock, T. H. and Harvey, P. H. (1977a). Primate ecology and social organization. *J. Zool.* **183**, 1−39.

Clutton-Brock, T. H. and Harvey, P. H. (1977b). Species differences in feeding and ranging behaviour in primates. In *Primate Ecology* (ed. T. H. Clutton-Brock), pp. 557−584. Academic Press, New York.

Clutton-Brock, T. H. and Harvey, P. H. (1980). Primate brains and ecology. *J. Zool.* **190**, 309−323.

Cobb, S. (1960). A note on the size of the avian olfactory bulb. *Epilepsy* **1**, 394−402.

Cobb, S. (1965). Brain size. *Archs Neurol., Chicago* **12**, 555−561.

Cohen, G. (1977). *The Psychology of Cognition.* Academic Press, London.

Comfort, A. (1971). Likelihood of human pheromones. *Nature* **230**, 432−433.

Conrad, R. (1973). Some correlates of speech coding in the short-term memory of the deaf. *J. Speech Hearing Res.* **16**, 375−384.

Corballis, M. C. and Morgan, M. J. (1978). On the biological basis of human laterality. I. Evidence for a maturation left−right gradient. *Behav. Brain Sci.* **2**, 261−269.

Coult, A. D. R. and Habenstein, R. W. (1965). *Cross Tabulations of Murdock's World Ethnographic Sample.* University of Missouri, Columbia.

Cowey, A. (1968). Discrimination. In *Analysis of Behavioral Change* (ed. L. Weiskrantz), pp. 189−238. Harper, New York.

Cowey, A., Parkinson, A. M. and Warnick, L. (1975). Global stereopsis in rhesus monkeys. *Q. Jl exp. Psychol.* **27**, 93−109.

Cowey, A. and Weiskrantz, L. (1975). Demonstration of cross-modal matching in rhesus monkeys, *Macaca mulatta. Neuropsychologia* **13**, 117−120.

Cowey, A. and Weiskrantz, L. (1976). Auditory sequence discrimination in *Macaca mulatta*: the role of the superior temporal cortex. *Neuropsychologia* **14**, 1−10.

Cowles, J. T. (1937). Food tokens as incentives for learning by chimpanzees. *Comp. Psychol. Mon.* **14**, 1−96.

Crawford, M. P. (1937). The cooperative solving of problems by young chimpanzees. *Comp. Psychol. Mon.* **14**, 1−88.

Crawford, M. P. and Spence, K. W. (1939). Observational learning of discrimination problems by chimpanzees. *J. comp. Psychol.* **27**, 133−147.

Crompton, A. W., Taylor, C. R. and Jagger, J. A. (1978). Evolution of homeothermy in mammals. *Nature* **272**, 333−336.

Crook, J. H. (1965). The adaptive significance of avian organizations. *Symp. zool. Soc. Lond.* **14**, 181−218.

Crook, J. H. (1968). The nature and function of territorial aggression. In *Man and Aggression* (ed. J. H. Crook), pp. 141−178. Oxford University Press, Oxford.

Curtis, G. H. (1981). Establishing a relevant time scale in anthropological and archaeological research. *Phil. Trans. R. Soc. Land.* B**292**, 7−19.

Curtiss, S. (1977). *Genie: a Psycholinguistic Study of a Modern "Wild Child".* Academic Press, New York.

Daly, M. and Wilson, M. (1978). *Sex, Evolution and Behavior.* Duxbury, North Scituate, Mass.

Darby, C. L. and Riopelle, A. J. (1959). Observational learning in the rhesus monkey. *J. comp. Physiol. Psychol.* **52**, 94–98.

Darlington, C. D. (1964). *Genetics and Man.* Allen and Unwin, London.

Darlington, C. D. (1969). *The Evolution of Man and Society.* Allen and Unwin, London.

Dart, R. A. (1956). The relationship of brain size and brain patterns to human status. *S. Afr. J. med. Sci.* **21**, 23–45.

Dart, R. (1957). *The Osteodontokeratic Culture of Australopithecus prometheus.* Transvaal Museum, Pretoria.

Darwin, C. (1859). *The Origin of Species.* John Murray, London.

Darwin, C. (1871). *The Descent of Man and Selection in Relation to Sex,* 1st edn. John Murray, London.

Darwin, C. (1872). *The Expression of the Emotions in Man and Animals.* John Murray, London.

Davenport, R. K. and Rogers, C. M. (1970). Intermodal equivalence of stimuli in apes. *Science* **168**, 279–281.

Davenport, R. K. and Rogers, C. M. (1971). Perception of photographs by apes. *Behaviour* **39**, 318–320.

Davenport, R. K., Rogers, C. M. and Russell, I. S. (1973). Cross-modal perception in apes. *Neuropsychologia* **11**, 21–28.

Davenport, R. K., Rogers, C. M. and Russell, I. S. (1975). Cross-modal perception in apes: altered visual cues and delay. *Neuropsychologia* **13**, 229–235.

Davies, N. B. (1978a). Territorial defence in the speckled wood butterfly (*Pararge aegeria*): the resident always wins. *Anim. Behav.* **26**, 138–147.

Davies, N. B. (1978b). Ecological questions and territorial behaviour. In *Behavioural Ecology* (eds J. R. Krebs and N. B. Davies), pp. 317–350. Blackwell, Oxford.

Davis, J. M. (1973). Imitation: a review and critique. In *Perspectives in Ethology* (eds P. P. G. Bateson and P. H. Klopfer), pp. 43–72. Plenum Press, New York.

Davis, R. T. (1974). *Monkeys as Perceivers. Primate Behaviour* (ed. L. A. Rosenblum), Vol. 3. Academic Press, New York.

Davis, R. T. and Leary, R. W. (1968). Learning of detour problems by lemurs and seven species of monkeys. *Percept. Motor Skills* **27**, 1031–1034.

Davis, R. T., Leary, R. W., Stevens, D. A. and Thompson, R. (1967). Learning and perception of oddity problems by lemurs and seven species of monkeys. *Primates* **8**, 311–322.

Dawkins, R. (1976). *The Selfish Gene.* Oxford University Press, Oxford.

Day, M. H. (1977). *Guide to Fossil Man,* 3rd edn. Cassell, London.

Day, M. H. and Wickens, E. H. (1980). Laetoli Pliocene hominid footprints and bipedalism. *Nature* **286**, 385–387.

Day, M. H., Leakey, R. E. F., Walker, A. C. and Wood, B. A. (1975). New hominids from East Rudolf, Kenya. I. *Am. J. phys. Anthrop.* **42**, 461–478.

Deag, J. M. (1973). Intergroup encounters in the wild Barbary macaque *Macaca sylvana* L. In *Comparative Behaviour and Ecology of Primates* (eds R. P. Michael and J. H. Crook), pp. 315–374. Academic Press, London.

REFERENCES

Decker, R. L. and Szalay, F. S. (1974). Origins and function of the apes in the Eocene Adapidae (Lemuriformes, Primates). In *Primate Locomotion* (ed. F. A. Jenkins), pp. 261–292. Academic Press, New York.

Deevey, E. S. (1950). The probability of death. *Scient. Am.* **182** (April), 58–60.

DeFries, J. C. and McClearn, G. E. (1970). Social dominance and Darwinian fitness in the laboratory mouse. *Am. Nat.* **104**, 408–411.

Delgado, J. M. R. (1967). Social rank and radio-stimulated aggressiveness in monkeys. *J. nerv. ment. Dis.* **144**, 383–390.

Delson, E. and Andrews, P. (1975). Evolution and interrelationships of the catarrhine primates. In *Phylogeny of the Primates* (ed. P. Luckett), pp. 405–446. Plenum Press, New York.

Deregowski, J. B. (1972). Pictorial perception and culture. *Scient. Am.* **227** (Nov.), 82–88.

Deuel, R. K. (1977). Loss of motor habits after cortical lesions. *Neuropsychologia* **15**, 205–215.

DeValois, R. L. and Jacobs, G. H. (1968). Primate color vision. *Science* **162**, 533–540.

DeValois, R. L. and Jacobs, G. H. (1971). Vision. In *Behavior of Nonhuman Primates* (eds A. M. Schrier and F. Stollnitz), Vol. 3, pp. 107–157. Academic Press, New York.

DeVore, I. ed. (1965). *Primate Behavior.* Holt, Rinehart and Winston, New York.

DeVore, I. and Hall, K. R. L. (1965). Baboon ecology. In *Primate Behavior* (ed. I. DeVore), pp. 20–52. Holt, Rinehart and Winston, New York.

Dewson, J. M. (1964). Speech sound discrimination by cats. *Science* **144**, 555–556.

Dewson, J. H. (1977). Preliminary evidence of hemispheric asymmetry of auditory function in monkeys. In *Lateralization in the Nervous System* (eds S. Hårnad, R. W. Doty, L. Goldstein, J. Jaynes and G. Krauthamer), pp. 63–71. Academic Press, New York.

Dewson, J. H. and Burlingame, A. C. (1975). Auditory discrimination and recall in monkeys. *Science* **187**, 267–268.

Dewson, J. H., Pribram, K. H. and Lynch, J. C. (1969). Effects of ablations of temporal cortex upon speech sound discrimination in the monkey. *Expl Neurol.* **24**, 579–591.

Dewson, J. H., Cowey, A. and Weiskrantz, L. (1970). Disruption of auditory sequence discrimination by unilateral and bilateral cortical ablations of superior temporal gyrus in the monkey. *Expl Neurol.* **28**, 529–548.

Dooley, G. B. and Gill, T. V. (1977). Acquisition and use of mathematical skills by a linguistic chimpanzee. In *Language Learning by a Chimpanzee* (ed. D. M. Rumbaugh), pp. 247–260. Academic Press, New York.

Doyle, G. A. (1974). Behavior of prosimians. In *Behavior of Nonhuman Primates* (eds A. M. Schrier and F. Stollnitz), Vol. 5, pp. 155–353. Academic Press, New York.

Dumond, D. E. (1980). The archeology of Alaska and the peopling of America. *Science* **209**, 984–991.

Dunbar, R. I. M (1976). Australopithecine diet based on a baboon analogy. *J. hum. Evol.* **5**, 161–167.

Durham, W. H. (1979). Towards a coevolutionary theory of human biology and culture. In *Evolutionary Biology and Human Social Behavior* (eds N. A. Chagnon and W. Irons), pp. 39–59. Duxbury, North Scituate, Mass.

Eccles, J. C. (1973). *The Understanding of the Brain*. McGraw-Hill, New York.

Economo, C. von (1929). *The Cytoarchitectonics of the Human Cerebral Cortex*. Oxford University Press, London.

Edney, J. J. (1974). Human territoriality. *Psychol. Bull.* **81**, 959–975.

Ehrlich, A. and Calvin, W. H. (1967). Visual discrimination behavior in *Galago* and owl monkey. *Psychonom. Sci.* **9**, 509–510.

Eibl-Eibesfeldt, I. (1967). Concepts of ethology and their significance in the study of human behavior. In *Early Behavior* (eds H. W. Stevenson, E. H. Hess and H. L. Rheingold), pp. 127–146. Wiley, New York.

Eibl-Eibesfeldt, I. (1971). *Love and Hate*. Methuen, London.

Eibl-Eibesfeldt, I. (1972). Similarities and differences between cultures in expressive movements. In *Non-Verbal Communication* (ed. R. A. Hinde), pp. 297–312. Cambridge University Press, Cambridge.

Eibl-Eibesfeldt, I. (1973). The expressive behavior of the deaf-and-blind born. In *Social Communication and Movement* (eds M. von Cranach and I. Vine), pp. 163–194. Academic Press, London.

Eibl-Eibesfeldt, I. (1974). The myth of the aggression-free hunter and gatherer society. In *Primate Aggression, Territoriality and Xenophobia* (ed. R. L. Holloway), pp. 435–457. Academic Press, New York.

Eibl-Eibesfeldt, I. (1975). *Ethology: the Biology of Behavior*, 2nd edn. Holt, Rinehart and Winston, New York.

Eisenberg, J. F. (1975). Phylogeny, behavior, and ecology in the Mammalia. In *Phylogeny of the Primates* (eds W. P. Luckett and F. S. Szalay), pp. 47–68. Plenum Press, New York.

Eisenberg, J. F., Muckenhirn, N. A. and Rudran, R. (1972). The relation between ecology and social structure in primates. *Science* **176**, 863–874.

Ekman, P. (1973). Cross-cultural studies of facial expression. In *Darwin and Facial Expression* (ed. P. Ekman), pp. 169–222. Academic Press, New York.

Ellefson, J. O. (1968). Territorial behavior in the common white-handed gibbon, *Hylobates lar*. In *Primates* (ed. P. C. Jay), pp. 180–199. Holt, Rinehart and Winston, New York.

Elliott, R. C. (1976). Problem solving in cebus and rhesus monkeys. *Bull. psychonom. Sci.* **7**, 319–320.

Elliott, R. C. (1977). Cross-modal recognition in three primates. *Neuropsychologia* **15**, 183–186.

Epstein, R., Lanza, R. and Skinner, B. F. (1980). Symbolic communication between two pigeons (*Columba livia domestica*). *Science* **207**, 543–545.

Ettlinger, G. (1977). Cross-modal equivalence in non-human primates. In *Behavioral Primatology I* (ed. A. M. Schrier), pp. 71–104. Erlbaum, Hillsdale, NJ.

Ettlinger, G. and Gautrin, D. (1971). Visual discrimination performance in the monkey: the effect of unilateral removal of temporal cortex. *Cortex* **7**, 317–331.

Eysenck, H. J. (1973). *The Inequality of Man*. Temple Smith, London.
Eysenck, H. J. (1977). *Crime and Personality*, 3rd edn. Routledge and Kegan Paul, London.

Falk, D. (1975). Comparative anatomy of the larynx in man and chimpanzee: implication for language in Neanderthal man. *Am. J. phys. Anthrop.* **43**, 123−132.
Falk, D. (1980). Hominid brain evolution: the approach from paleoneurology *Yb. phys. Anthrop.* **23**, 93 107.
Farrer, D. N. (1967). Picture memory in the chimpanzee. *Percept. Motor Skills* **25**, 305−315.
Feldman, H., Goldin-Meadow, S. and Gleitman, L. (1978). Beyond Herodotus: the creation of language by linguistically deprived deaf children. In *Action Gesture and Symbol* (ed. A. Lock), pp. 351−414. Academic Press, New York.
Ferster, C. B. (1964). Arithmetic behavior in chimpanzees. *Scient. Am.* **210** (May), 98−106.
Finch, G. (1941). Chimpanzee handedness. *Science* **94**, 117−118.
Firth, R. (1973). *Symbols: Public and Private*. Allen and Unwin, London.
Fisher, J. and Hinde, R. A. (1949). The opening of milk bottles by birds. *Br. Birds* **42**, 347−357.
Fleagle, J. G. and Simons, E. L. (1978). Humeral morphology of the earliest apes. *Nature* **276**, 705−707.
Fleming, J. D. (1974). The state of the apes. *Psychol. Today* (Jan.), 31−46.
Forge, A. (1970). Learning to see in New Guinea. In *Socialization: the Approach from Social Anthropology* (ed. P. Mayer), pp. 269−291. Tavistock, London.
Fossey, D. (1974). Observation on the home range of one group of mountain gorillas (*Gorilla gorilla beringei*). *Anim. Behav.* **22**, 568−581.
Fossey, D. (1979). Development of the mountain gorilla (*Gorilla gorilla beringei*): the first thirty-six months. In *The Great Apes* (eds D. A. Hamburg and E. R. McCown), pp. 139−184. Benjamin/Cummings, Menlo Park, California.
Fossey, D. and Harcourt, A. H. (1977). Feeding ecology of free-ranging mountain gorilla (*Gorilla gorilla beringei*). In *Primate Ecology* (ed. T. Clutton-Brock), pp. 415−447. Academic Press, London.
Fouts, R. S. (1972). Use of guidance in teaching sign language to a chimpanzee. *J. comp. Physiol. Psychol.* **80**, 515−522.
Fouts, R. S. (1973). Acquisition and testing of gestural signs in four young chimpanzees. *Science* **180**, 970−980.
Fouts, R. S. (1975). Capacities for language in great apes. In *Socioecology and Psychology of Primates* (ed. R. H. Tuttle), pp. 371−390. Mouton, The Hague.
Fouts, R. S., Chown, B. and Goodwin, L. (1976). Transfer of signed responses in American Sign Language from vocal English stimuli to physical object stimuli by a chimpanzee (*Pan*). *Learn. and Motiv.* **7**, 458−475.
Fouts, R., Shapiro, G. and O'Neill, C. (1978). Studies of linguistic behavior in apes and children. In *Understanding Language through Sign Language* (ed. P. Siple), pp. 163−185. Academic Press, New York.

Fox, M. W. (1971). *Behavior of Wolves, Dogs, and Related Canids.* Cape, London.

Fox, R. and Blake, R. R. (1971). Stereoscopic vision in the cat. *Nature* **233**, 55–56.

Fox, R., Lehmkuhle, S. W. and Bush, R. C. (1977). Stereopsis in the falcon. *Science* **197**, 79–81.

Freedman, D. G. (1964). Smiling in blind infants and the issue of innate versus acquired. *J. Child Psychol. Psychiat.* **5**, 171–184.

Frisch, J. E. (1968). Individual behavior and intertroop variability in Japanese macaques. In *Primates* (ed. P. C. Jay), pp. 243–252. Holt, Rinehart and Winston, New York.

Frisch, K. von. (1950). *Bees: their Vision, Chemical Senses and Language.* Oxford University Press, London.

Frisch, K. von. (1967). *The Dance Language and Orientation of Bees.* Harvard University Press, Cambridge, Mass.

Fromkin, V., Krashen, S., Curtis, S., Rigler, D. and Rigler, M. (1974). The development of language in Genie: a case of language acquisition beyond the "critical period". *Brain and Lang.* **1**, 81–107.

Frost, G. T. (1980). Tool behavior and the origins of laterality. *J. hum. Evol.* **9**, 447–459.

Furth, H. G. (1971). Linguistic deficiency and thinking: research with deaf subjects. *Psychol. Bull.* **76**, 1964–1969.

Fuster, J. M. (1980). *The Prefrontal Cortex.* Raven Press, New York.

Galaburda, A. M. (1980). La région de Broca. *Revue Neurol., Paris* **136**, 609–616.

Galaburda, A. M. and Pandya, D. N. (1981). Role of architectonics and connections in the study of primate brain evolution. *Am. J. Phys. Anthropol.* (in the press).

Galaburda, A. and Sanides, F. (1980). Cytoarchitectonic organization of the human auditory cortex. *J. comp. Neurol.* **190**, 597–610.

Galaburda, A. M., Sanides, F. and Geschwind, N. (1978). Human brain: cytoarchitectonic left–right asymmetries in the temporal speech region. *Arch. Neurol.* **35**, 812–817.

Galef, B. G. (1976). Social transmission of acquired behaviour: a discussion of tradition and social learning in vertebrates. *Adv. Study Behav.* **6**, 77–100.

Gallup, G. G. (1975). Towards an operational definition of self-awareness. In *Socioecology and Psychology of Primates* (ed. R. H. Tuttle), pp. 309–341. Mouton, The Hague.

Gallup, G. G. (1977). Self recognition in primates. *Am. Psychol.* **32** (May), 329–338.

Gandolfi, C. and Parisi, V. (1973). Ethological aspects of predation by rats (*Rattus norvegicus*) on bivalves *Unio pictorum* and *Cerastoderma lamarcki.* *Bull. Zool.* **40**, 69–74.

Garcha, H. S. and Ettlinger, G. (1979). Object sorting by chimpanzees and monkeys. *Cortex* **15**, 213–224.

Gardner, B. T. and Gardner, R. A. (1971). Two-way communication with an infant chimpanzee. In *Behavior of Nonhuman Primates* (eds A. M. Schrier and F. Stollnitz), pp. 117–184. Academic Press, New York.

Gardner, R. and Heider, K. G. (1968). *Gardens of War: Life and Death in the New Guinea Stone Age*. Random House, New York.

Gardner, R. A. and Gardner, B. T. (1969). Teaching sign language to a chimpanzee. *Science* **165**, 664–672.

Gardner, R. A. and Gardner, B. T. (1975). Early signs of language in child and chimpanzee. *Science* **187**, 752–753.

Gardner, R. A. and Gardner, B. T. (1978). Comparative psychology and language acquisition. *Ann. N. Y. Acad. Sci.* **309**, 37–76.

Gartlan, J. S. (1968). Structure and function in primate society. *Folia primat.* **8**, 89–120.

Gaulin, S. J. and Kurland, J. A. (1976). Primate predation and bioenergetics. *Science* **191**, 314–315.

Gazzaniga, M. S. (1970). *The Bisected Brain*. Appleton-Century-Crofts, New York.

Gazzaniga, M. S. and Hillyard, S. A. (1971). Language and speech capacity of the right hemisphere. *Neuropsychologia* **9**, 273–280.

Geschwind, N. (1967). Neurological foundations of language. In *Progress in Learning Disabilities* (eds E. R. John and H. R. Myckulbust), pp. 182–198. Grune and Stratton, New York.

Geschwind, N. (1972). Language and the brain. *Scient. Am.* **226** (April), 76–83.

Geschwind, N. and Levitsky, W. (1968). Human brain: left–right asymmetries in temporal speech region. *Science* **161**, 186–187.

Getzels, J. W. and Jackson, P. W. (1962). *Creativity and Intelligence*. Wiley, New York.

Gidley, J. W. (1919). Significance of divergence of the first digit in the primitive mammalian foot. *J. Wash. Acad. Sci.* **9**, 273–280.

Gillan, D. J., Premack, D. and Woodruff, G. (1981). Reasoning in the chimpanzee: I. Analogical reasoning. *J. exp. Psychol., Anim. Behav. Processes* **7**, 1–17.

Gingerich, P. D. (1977). Correlation of tooth size and body size in living hominoid primates, with a note on relative brain size in *Aegyptopithecus* and *Proconsul*. *Am. J. phys. Anthrop.* **47**, 395–398.

Glasersfeld, E. von (1977). Linguistic communication: theory and definition. In *Language Learning by a Chimpanzee* (ed. D. Rumbaugh), pp. 55–71. Academic Press, New York.

Glickman, S. E. and Sroges, R. W. (1966). Curiosity in zoo animals. *Behaviour* **26**, 151–188.

Glickstein, M. (1976). The vertebrate eye. In *Evolution of Brain and Behavior in Vertebrates* (eds R. B. Masterton, M. E. Bitterman, C. B. Campbell and N. Hotton), pp. 53–71. Erlbaum, Hillsdale, NJ.

Goodman, M. (1975). Protein sequence and immunological specificity. In *Phylogeny of the Primates* (eds W. P. Luckett and F. S. Szalay), pp. 219–248. Plenum Press, New York.

Gordon, T. and Foss, B. M. (1965). The role of stimulation on the delay of onset of crying in the newborn infant. *Q. Jl exp. Psychol.* **18**, 79–81.

Gould, J. (1976). The dance-language controversy. *Q. Rev. Biol.* **51**, 211–244.

Gould, S. J. (1976). Grades and clades revisited. In *Evolution, Brain and Behavior: Persistent Problems* (eds R. B. Masterton, W. Hodos and H. Jerison), pp. 115–122. Erlbaum, Hillsdale, NJ.

Gould, S. J. (1977). *Ontogeny and Phylogeny.* Harvard University Press, Cambridge, Mass.

Gould, S. J. (1978). Sociobiology: the art of storytelling. *New Scient.* **80** (16 Nov.), 530—533.

Graf, R. von and Meyer-Holzapfel, M. (1974). Die Wirkung von Harnmarken auf Artgenossen beim Haushund. *Z. Tierpsychol.* **35**, 320—332.

Green, H. D. and Walker, A. E. (1938). The effects of ablation of the cortical face area in monkeys. *J. Neurophysiol.* **1**, 262—280.

Green, S. (1975). Dialects in Japanese monkeys; vocal learning and cultural transmission of locale-specific vocal behavior. *Z. Tierpsychol.* **38**, 309—314.

Greenberg, J. H. (1966). *Language Universals.* Mouton, The Hague.

Gregory, R. L. (1966). *Eye and Brain.* Weidenfeld and Nicolson, London.

Guhl, A. M. (1956). The social order of chickens. *Scient. Am.* **194** (Feb.), 42—46.

Gunther, R. (1971). *Infant Feeding.* Penguin, Harmondsworth, Middlesex.

Haines, R. W. (1958). Arboreal or terrestrial ancestry of the placental mammals. *Q. Rev. Biol.* **33**, 1—23.

Haldane, J. B. S. (1949). Suggestions as to quantitative measurement of rates of evolution. *Evolution* **3**, 51—56.

Haldane, J. B. S. (1956). The argument from animals to men: an examination of its validity for anthropology. *J. R. anthrop. Inst.* **86**, 1—14.

Hall, K. R. L. (1963a). Variations in the ecology of the Chacma baboon, *Papio ursinus. Symp. zool. Soc. Lond.* **10**, 1—28.

Hall, K. R. L. (1963b). Observational learning in monkeys and apes. *Br. J. Psychol.* **54**, 201—226.

Hall, K. R. L. (1965). Behaviour and ecology of the wild patas monkey, *Erythrocebus patas*, in Uganda. *J. Zool.* **148**, 15—87.

Hall, K. R. L. (1968). Social learning in monkeys. In *Primates* (ed. P. C. Jay), pp. 383—419. Holt, Rinehart and Winston, New York.

Hall, K. R. L. and DeVore, I. (1965). Baboon social behaviour. In *Primate Behavior* (ed. I. DeVore), pp. 53—110. Holt, Rinehart and Winston, New York.

Hall, K. R. L. and Goswell, M. J. (1964). Aspects of social learning in captive patas monkeys. *Primates* **5**, 59—70.

Halsband, U. and Passingham, R. E. (to be published). The role of premotor and parietal cortex in the direction of action.

Hamburg, D. A. (1971). Psychobiological studies of aggressive behaviour. *Nature* **230**, 19—23.

Hamilton, J. A. (1936). Intelligence and the human brain. *Psychol. Rev.* **43**, 308—321.

Hamilton, W. J., Buskirk, R. E. and Buskirk, W. H. (1975). Defensive stoning by baboons. *Nature* **256**, 488—489.

Harcourt, A. H. (1979). Social relationship between adult male and female mountain gorillas in the wild. *Anim. Behav.* **27**, 325—342.

REFERENCES   Harcourt, A. H., Stewart, K. S. and Fossey, D. (1976). Male emigration and female transfer in wild mountain gorilla. *Nature* **261**, 226–227.

Harding, R. S. O. (1973). Predation by a troop of olive baboons (*Papio anubis*). *Am. J. phys. Anthrop.* **38**, 587–592.

Harlow, H. F. (1949). The formation of learning sets. *Psychol. Rev.* **56**, 51–65.

Harlow, H. F. and Harlow, M. K. (1965). The affectional systems. In *Behavior of Nonhuman Primates* (eds A. M. Schrier, H. F. Harlow and F. Stollnitz), Vol. 2, pp. 287–334. Academic Press, New York.

Harlow, H. F. and Mears, C. (1979). *The Human Model: Primate Perspectives.* Wiley, New York.

Harlow, H. F. and Suomi, S. J. (1970). Nature of love—simplified. *Am. Psychol.* **25**, 161–168.

Harlow, H. F. and Zimmerman, R. R. (1959). Affectional responses in the infant monkey. *Science* **130**, 421–432.

Harman, P. J. (1947). Quantitative analysis of the brain–isocortex relationship in Mammalia. *Anat. Rec.* **97**, 342.

Harrington, J. E. (1976). Discrimination between individuals by scent in *Lemur fulvus. Anim. Behav.* **24**, 207–212.

Harrington, J. E. (1977). Discrimination between males and females by scent in *Lemur fulvus. Anim. Behav.* **25**, 147–151.

Harrison, G. A. Weiner, J. S. and Reynolds, V. (1977). Human evolution. In *Human Biology*, 2nd edn (by G. A. Harrison, J. S. Weiner, J. M. Tanner and N. A. Barnicot), pp. 3–93. Oxford University Press, Oxford.

Harter, S. (1965). Discrimination learning set in children as a function of intelligence and mental age. *J. exp. Child Psychol.* **2**, 31–43.

Harting, J. K. and Noback, C. R. (1970). Corticospinal projections from the pre- and postcentral gyri in the squirrel monkey (*Saimiri sciureus*). *Brain Res.* **24**, 322–328.

Hast, M. H., Fischer, J. M., Wetzela, B. and Thompson, V. E. (1974). Cortical motor representation of the laryngeal muscles in *Macaca mulatta. Brain Res.* **73**, 229–240.

Hausfater, G. (1975). *Dominance and Reproduction in Baboons (Papio cynocephalus).* (Contr. Primat. **7**.) Karger, Basel.

Hay, R. L. (1980). The KBS Tuff controversy may be ended. *Nature* **284**, 401.

Hayes, K. J. (1951). *The Ape in Our House.* Harper, New York.

Hayes, K. J. and Hayes, C. (1952). Imitation in a home-raised chimpanzee. *J. comp. Physiol. Psychol.* **45**, 450–459.

Hayes, K. J. and Nissen, C. H. (1971). Higher mental functions of a home-raised chimpanzee. In *Behavior of Nonhuman Primates* (eds A. M. Schrier and F. Stollnitz), Vol. 4, pp. 59–115. Academic Press, New York.

Hayes, K. J., Thompson, R. and Hayes, C. (1953). Discrimination learning set in chimpanzees. *J. comp. Physiol. Psychol.* **46**, 99–104.

Hécaen, H. and Albert, M. L. (1978). *Human Neuropsychology.* Wiley, New York.

Hediger, H. (1950). *Wild Animals in Captivity.* Butterworth, London.

Heffner, R. and Heffner, H. (1980). Hearing in the elephant (*Elephas maximus*). *Science* **208**, 518–520.

Heffner, R. and Masterton, B. (1975). Variation in form of the pyramidal tract and its relationship to digital dexterity. *Brain Behav. Evol.* **12**, 161–200.

Herbert, M. J. and Harsh, C. M. (1944). Observational learning by cats. *J. comp. Physiol. Psychol.* **37**, 81–95.

Herman, L. M. (1980). Cognitive characteristics of dolphins. In *Cetacean Behavior: Mechanisms and Functions* (ed. L. M. Herman), pp. 368–429. Wiley, New York.

Herman, L. M. and Arbett, W. R. (1973). Stimulus control and auditory discrimination learning sets in the bottlenose dolphin. *J. exp. anal. Behav.* **19**, 379–394.

Herman, L. M. and Gordon, J. A. (1974). Auditory delayed matching in the bottlenose dolphin. *J. exp. anal. Behav.* **21**, 19–26.

Hernstein, R. J. (1979). Acquisition, generalization, and discrimination reversal of a natural concept. *J. exp. Psychol., Anim. Behav. Processes* **5**, 116–129.

Hernstein, R. J. and Loveland, D. H. (1964). Complex visual concept in the pigeon. *Science* **146**, 549–551.

Hernstein, R. J., Loveland, D. H. and Cable, C. (1976). Natural concepts in pigeons. *J. exp. Psychol., Anim. Behav. Processes* **2**, 285–302.

Hershkovitz, P. (1974). A new genus of late Oligocene monkey (Cebidae, Platyrrhini) with notes on postorbital closure and platyrrhine evolution. *Folia primat.* **21**, 1–35.

Hess, E. H. (1973). Comparative sensory processes. In *Comparative Psychology: a Modern Survey* (eds D. A. Dewsbury and D. A. Rethlingshafer), pp. 344–394. McGraw-Hill, New York.

Hewes, G. W. (1964). Hominid bipedalism: independent evidence for the food carrying theory. *Science* **146**, 416–418.

Hewes, G. W. (1977). Language origin theories. In *Language Learning by a Chimpanzee* (ed. D. M. Rumbaugh), pp. 3–53. Academic Press, New York.

Hicks, L. H. (1956). An analysis of number-concept formation in the rhesus monkey. *J. comp. Physiol. Psychol.* **49**, 212–218.

Hicks, R. E. and Kinsbourne, M. (1976a). Human handedness: a partial cross-fostering study. *Science* **192**, 908–910.

Hicks, R. E. and Kinsbourne, M. (1976b). On the genesis of human handedness: a review. *J. Motor Behav.* **8**, 257–266.

Hill, W. C. O. (1953). *Primates. Vol. 1: Strepsirhini.* Edinburgh University Press, Edinburgh.

Hill, W. C. O. (1972). *Evolutionary Biology of the Primates.* Academic Press, London.

Hinde, R. A. (1956). The biological significance of the territories of birds. *Ibis* **98**, 340–369.

Hinde, R. A. (1969). The bases of aggression in animals. *J. psychosom. Res.* **13**, 213–219.

Hinde, R. A. (1970). *Animal Behaviour*, 2nd edn. McGraw-Hill, New York.

Hinde, R. A. (1974). *Biological Bases of Human Social Behaviour.* McGraw-Hill, New York.

Hinde, R. A. and Davies, C. (1972). Removing infant rhesus from mother for thirteen days compared with removing mother from infant. *J. Child Psychol. Psychiat.* **13**, 227–237.

Hinde, R. A. and Fisher, J. (1951). Further observations on the opening of milk bottles by birds. *Br. Birds* **44**, 392–396.

Hinde, R. A. and McGinnis, L. (1977). Some factors influencing the effects of temporary mother-infant separation: some experiments with rhesus monkeys. *Psychol. Med.* **7**, 197–212.

Hinde, R. A. and Spencer-Booth, Y. (1971). Effect of brief separation from mother on rhesus monkeys. *Science* **173**, 111–118.

Hinde, R. A., Rowell, T. E. and Spencer-Booth, Y. (1964). Behaviour of socially living rhesus monkeys in their first six months. *Proc. zool. Soc. Lond.* **143**, 609–649.

Hoadley, M. F. and Pearson, K. (1929). On measurement of the internal diameter of the skull in relation: I to the prediction of its capacity, II to the "pre-eminence" of the left hemisphere. *Biometrika* **21**, 85–123.

Hochberg, J. and Brooks, V. (1962). Pictorial recognition as an unlearnt ability: a study of one child's performance. *Am. J. Psychol.* **75**, 624–626.

Hockett, C. F. and Altmann, S. A. (1968). A note on design features. In *Animal Communication* (ed. T. A. Sebeok), pp. 61–72. Indiana University Press, Bloomington.

Hockett, C. F. and Ascher, R. (1964). The human revolution. *Curr. Anthrop.* **5**, 135–168.

Hodos, W. (1970). Evolutionary interpretation of neural and behavioral studies of living vertebrates. In *Neurosciences* (ed. F. O. Schmidt), Vol. 2, 26–38. Rockefeller University Press, New York.

Holloway, R. L. (1967). The evolution of the human brain: some notes towards a synthesis between neural structure and the evolution of complex behavior. *Curr. Anthrop.* **12**, 3–19.

Holloway, R. L. (1968). The evolution of the primate brain: some aspects of quantitative relations. *Brain Res.* **7**, 121–172.

Holloway, R. L. (1969). Culture: a human domain. *Curr. Anthrop.* **10**, 395–412.

Holloway, R. L. (1970). Neural parameters, hunting, and the evolution of the human brain. In *The Primate Brain* (eds C. R. Noback and W. Montagna), pp. 299–310. Appleton-Century-Crofts, New York.

Holloway, R. L. (1972). New australopithecine endocast, SK 1585, from Swartkrans, South Africa. *Am. J. phys. Anthropol.* **37**, 173–186.

Holloway, R. L. (1974). The casts of fossil hominid brains. *Scient. Am.* **231** (July), 106–115.

Holloway, R. L. (1976). Paleoneurological evidence for language origins. *Ann. N. Y. Acad. Sci.* **280**, 330–348.

Holloway, R. L. (1978). Problems of brain endocast interpretation and African hominid evolution. In *Early Hominids from Africa* (ed. C. Jolly), pp. 379–401. Duckworth, London.

Holloway, R. L. (1979). Brain size, allometry, and reorganization; towards a synthesis. In *Development and Evolution of Brain Size* (ed. M. E. Hahn), pp. 61–88. Academic Press, New York.

Holloway, R. L. (1980). The O.H.7. (Olduvai Gorge, Tanzania) hominid partial brain endocast revisited. *Am. J. phys. Anthrop.* **53**, 267–274.

Holloway, R. L. (1981). Exploring the dorsal surface of hominoid brain endocasts by stereoplotter and discriminant analysis. *Phil. Trans. R. Soc. Lond.* B**292**, 155–166.

Holloway, R. L. and LaCoste-Larymondic, M. C. de (in press). Brain endocast asymmetry in pongids and hominids: Some preliminary findings on the pàleontology of cerebral dominance. *Amer. J. phys. Anthropol.*

Holt, A. B., Cheek, D. B., Mellits, E. D. and Hill, D. E. (1975). Brain size and the relation of the primate to the nonprimate. In *Fetal and Postnatal Cellular Growth and Nutrition* (ed. D. B. Cheek), pp. 23–44. Wiley, New York.

Hooff, J. A. R. A. M. van (1967). The facial displays of the catarrhine monkeys and apes. In *Primate Ethology* (ed. D. Morris), pp. 7–68. Weidenfeld and Nicolson, London.

Hooff, J. A. R. A. M. van (1972). A comparative approach to the phylogeny of laughter and smiling. In *Non-Verbal Communication* (ed. R. A. Hinde), pp. 209–238. Cambridge University Press, Cambridge.

Hooff, J. A. R. A. M. van (1976). The comparison of facial expression in man and higher primates. In *Methods of Inference from Animal to Human Behavior* (ed. M. von Cranach), pp. 165–196. Mouton, The Hague.

Hopf, A. (1965). Volumetrische Untersuchungen zur vergleichenden Anatomie des Thalamus. *J. Hirnforsch.* **8**, 25–38.

Horn, J. C. and Donaldson, G. (1976). On the myth of intellectual decline in adulthood. *Am. Psychol.* **31**, 701–719.

Howard, H. E. (1920). *Territory in Bird Life*. John Murray, London.

Howell, F. C. (1972). Recent advances in human evolutionary studies. In *Perspectives in Human Evolution* (eds S. L. Washburn and P. Dolhinow), Vol. 2, pp. 51–128. Holt, Rinehart and Winston, New York.

Hrdy, S. B. (1974). Male–male competition and infanticide among the langurs (*Presbytis entellus*) of Abu, Rajasthan. *Folia primat.* **22**, 19–58.

Huber, E. (1931). *Evolution of Facial Musculature and Facial Expression*. Oxford University Press, London.

Hughes, A. (1977). The topography of vision in mammals of contrasting life style: comparative optics and retinal organization. In *Handbook of Sensory Physiology: The Visual System* (ed. F. Crescitelli), Vol. VII, 5, pp. 615–755. Springer-Verlag, Berlin.

Hughes, H. R. and Tobias, P. V. (1977). A fossil skull probably of the genus *Homo* from Sterkfontein, Transvaal. *Nature* **265**, 310–312.

Humphrey, N. K. (1974a). Species and individuals in the perceptual world of monkeys. *Perception* **3**, 105–114.

Humphrey, N. K. (1974b). Vision in a monkey without striate cortex: a case study. *Perception* **3**, 241–255.

Humphrey, N. K. (1976). The social function of intellect. In *Growing Points in Ethology* (eds P. P. G. Bateson and R. A. Hinde), pp. 303–317. Cambridge University Press, Cambridge.

Huxley, T. H. (1863). *Evidence as to Man's Place in Nature*. Williams and Norgate, London.

Ingram, D. (1975). Motor asymmetries in young children. *Neuropsychologia* **13**, 95–102.

Isaac, G. Ll. (1976a). Plio-Pleistocene assemblages from East Rudolf, Kenya. In *Earliest Man and Environments in the Lake Rudolf Basin* (eds Y. Coppens, F. C. Howell, G. Ll. Isaac, and R. E. F. Leakey), pp. 552–564. Chicago University Press, Chicago.

Isaac, G. Ll. (1976b). The activities of early African hominids: a review of archaeological evidence for the time span two and a half to one million years ago. In *Human Origins: Louis Leakey and the East African Evidence* (eds G. Ll. Isaac and E. R. McGown), pp. 483–514. Benjamin, Menlo Park, California.

Isaac, G. Ll. (1976c). Stages of cultural elaboration in the Pleistocene: possible archaeological indicators of the development of language capabilities. *Ann. N. Y. Acad. Sci.* **280**, 275–288.

Isaac, G. Ll. (1978a). The food-sharing behavior of protohuman hominids. *Scient. Am.* **238** (April), 90–108.

Isaac, G. Ll. (1978b). The archaeological evidence for the activities of the early African hominids. In *Early Hominids and Africa* (ed. C. J. Jolly), pp. 219–254. Duckworth, London.

Isaac, G. Ll. (1981). Emergence of human behaviour patterns: archaeological tests of alternative models of early hominid behaviour; excavation and experiments. *Phil. Trans. R. Soc. Lond.* B**292**, 177–188.

Isaac, G. Ll. and Crader, D. C. (1981). To what extent were early hominids carnivorous; an archaeological perspective. In *Omnivorous Primates* (eds R. S. O. Harding and G. Teleki), pp. 37–103. Columbia University Press, New York.

Itani, J. (1965). On the acquisition and propagation of a new food habit in the troop of Japanese monkeys at Takasakiyama. In *Japanese Monkeys* (ed. S. A. Altmann), pp. 52–65. Published by the editor.

Itani, J. (1972). A preliminary essay on the relationship between social organization and incest avoidance in non-human primates. In *Primate Socialization* (ed. F. E. Poirier), pp. 165–171. Random House, New York.

Itani, J. (1979). Distribution and adaptation of chimpanzees in an arid area. In *The Great Apes* (eds D. A. Hamburg and E. R. McGown), pp. 55–71. Benjamin/Cummings, Menlo Park, California.

Itani, J. and Nishimura, A. (1973). The study of infrahuman culture in Japan. *Proc. 4th Int. Congr. Primat.* **1**, 20–50. Karger, Basel.

Jarman, P. J. (1974). The social organization of antelope in relation to their ecology. *Behaviour* **48**, 215–267.

Jarvis, M. J. and Ettlinger, G. (1977). Cross-modal recognition in chimpanzees and monkeys. *Neuropsychologia*, **15**, 499–506.

Jay, P. C. (1965). The hanamun langur of North India. In *Primate Behavior* (ed. I. DeVore), pp. 197–249. Holt, Rinehart and Winston, New York.

Jellis, R. (1977). *Bird Songs and their Meaning*. BBC, London.

Jenkins, F. A. (1972). Chimpanzee bipedalism: cineradiographic analysis and implications for the evolution of gait. *Science* **178**, 877–879.

Jenkins, F. A. (1974). Tree shrew locomotion and the origins of primate arborealism. In *Primate Locomotion* (ed. F. A. Jenkins), pp. 85–115. Academic Press, New York.

Jenkins, P. E. (1978). Cultural transmission of song patterns and dialect development in a free-living bird population. *Anim. Behav.* **26**, 50–78.

Jensen, G. D., Bobbitt, R. A. and B. N. Gordon. (1969). Patterns and sequences of hitting behavior in mother and infant monkeys (*Macaca nemestrina*). *Psychiat. Res.* **7**, 55−61.

Jerison, H. J. (1973). *Evolution of the Brain and Intelligence.* Academic Press, New York.

Jerison, H. J. (1976a). Paleoneurology and the evolution of mind. *Scient. Am.* **234** (Jan.) 90−101.

Jerison, H. J. (1976b). The paleoneurology of language. *Ann. N. Y. Acad. Sci.* **280**, 370−382.

Jerison, H. J. (1979a). Brain, body and encephalization in early primates. *J. hum. Evol.* **8**, 615−635.

Jerison, H. J. (1979b). The evolution of diversity in brain size. In *Development and Evolution of Brain Size* (eds M. E. Hahn, C. Jensen and B. C. Dudek), pp. 29−57. Academic Press, New York.

Jinks, J. L. and Fulker, D. W. (1970). Comparison of the biometrical and genetical, multivariate and classical approaches to the analysis of human behavior. *Psychol. Bull.* **73**, 311−349.

Johanson, D. C. and Edey, M. A. (1981). *Lucy: the Beginnings of Humankind.* Simon and Schuster, New York.

Johanson, D. and Taieb, M. (1976). Plio-Pleistocene hominid discoveries in Hadar, Ethiopia. *Nature* **260**, 293−297.

Johanson, D. and White, T. D. (1979). A systematic assessment of early African hominids. *Science* **203**, 321−330.

John, E. R., Chesler, I. and Bartlett, F. (1968). Observation learning in cats. *Science* **159**, 1489−1491.

Johnson, R. N. (1972). *Aggression in Man and Animals.* Saunders, Philadelphia.

Johnson, R. N. and Johnson, L. D. (1973). Intra- and interspecific social and aggressive behavior in the Siamese fighting fish, *Betta splendens*. *Anim. Behav.* **21**, 665−672.

Jolly, A. (1964). Prosimians' manipulation of simple object problems. *Anim. Behav.* **12**, 560−570.

Jolly, A. (1972). *The Evolution of Primate Behaviour.* Macmillan, London.

Jolly, C. J. (1967). The evolution of the baboons. In *The Baboon in Medical Research* (ed. H. Vagtborg), Vol. 2, pp. 23−50. University of Texas Press, Austin.

Jolly, C. J. (1970). The seed eater: a new model of hominid differentiation based on a baboon analogy. *Man* **5**, 5−26.

Jones, P. R. (1981). Experimental implement manufacture and use: a case study from Olduvai Gorge, Tanzania. *Phil. Trans. R. Soc. Lond.* B**292**, 189−195.

Jones, T. B. and Kamil, A. C. (1973). Tool-making and tool-using in the Northern blue jay. *Science* **180**, 1076−1078.

Jordan, J. (1971a) Studies on the structure of the organ of voice and vocalization in the chimpanzee. I. *Folia morphol.* **30**, 97−126.

Jordan, J. (1971b). Studies on the structure of the organ of voice and vocalization in the chimpanzee. III. *Folia morphol.* **30**, 322−340.

Julesz, B. (1971). *Foundations of Cyclopean Perception.* Chicago University Press, Chicago.

REFERENCES   Jürgens, U. (1979). Neural control of vocalization in non-human primates. In *Neurobiology of Social Communication in Primates* (eds H. D. Steklis and M. J. Raleigh), pp. 11–44. Academic Press, New York.

Kaas, J. H., Hall, W. C. and Diamond, I. T. (1970). Cortical visual areas I and II in the hedgehog: relation between evoked potential maps and architectonic subdivisions. *J. Neurophysiol.* **33**, 595–615.

Kaas, J. H., Guillery, R. W. and Allman, J. M. (1972). Some principles of organization in the dorsal lateral geniculate nucleus. *Brain Behav. Evol.* **6**, 253–299.

Kagan, J. and Moss, H. A. (1962). *Birth to Maturity: a Study in Psychological Development*. Wiley, New York.

Kaufman, I. C. and Rosenblum, L. A. (1969). Effects of separation from mother on the emotional behavior of infant monkeys. *Ann. N. Y. Acad. Sci.* **159**, 681–695.

Kaufman, I. C. and Stynes, A. J. (1978). Depression can be induced in a bonnet macaque. *Psychosom. Med.* **40**, 71–75.

Kavanagh, M. (1972). Food-sharing behavior within a group of douc monkeys (*Pygathrix nemaeus nemaeus*). *Nature* **239**, 406–407.

Kawai, M. (1965a) Newly acquired pre-cultural behavior of a natural troop of Japanese monkeys. *Primates* **6**, 1–30.

Kawai, M. (1965b). On the system of social ranks in a natural troop of Japanese monkeys. I. Basic rank and dependent rank. In *Japanese Monkeys* (ed. S. A. Altmann), pp. 66–86. Published by the editor.

Kawamura, S. (1963). The process of sub-culture propagation among Japanese macaques. In *Primate Social Behavior* (ed. C. H. Southwick), pp. 82–90. Van Nostrand, New York.

Kay, R. F. and Cartmill, M. (1974). Skull of *Palaechthon nacimienti*. *Nature* **252**, 37–38.

Kelemen, G. (1948). The anatomical basis of phonation in the chimpanzee. *J. Morphol.* **82**, 229–256.

Kellogg, W. N. (1968). Chimpanzees in experimental homes. *Psychol. Rec.* **18**, 489–498.

Kellogg, W. N. and Kellogg, I. A. (1933). *The Ape and the Child*. McGraw-Hill, New York.

Kennedy, G. (1980). *Paleoanthropology*. McGraw-Hill, New York.

Kimura, D. (1976). The neural basis of language qua gesture. In *Studies in Neurolinguistics* (eds H. Avakian-Whitaker and H. A. Whitaker), Vol. 2, pp. 145–156. Academic Press, New York.

Kimura, D. (1979). Neuromotor mechanisms in the evolution of human communication. In *Neurobiology of Social Communication in Primates*. (eds H. D. Steklis and M. J. Raleigh), pp. 197–219. Academic Press, New York.

King, M. C. and Wilson, A. C. (1975). Evolution at two levels in humans and chimpanzees. *Science* **118**, 107–116.

Kintz, B. L., Foster, M. S., Hart, J. O., O'Malley, J. J., Palmer, E. L. and Sullivan, S. L. (1969). A comparison of learning sets in humans, primates and subprimates. *J. gen. Psychol.* **80**, 189–204.

Kirk, R. L. (1981). *Aboriginal Man Adapting: the Human Biology of Australian Aborigines*. Clarendon Press, Oxford.

Kleiman, D. G. and Eisenberg, J. F. (1973). Comparison of canid and felid social systems from an evolutionary perspective. *Anim. Behav.* **21**, 637−659.

Klima, E. and Bellugi, U. (1979). *The Signs of Language.* Harvard University Press, Cambridge, Mass.

Kochetkova, V. I. (1978). *Paleoneurology.* Wiley, New York.

Koestler, A. (1964). *The Act of Creation.* Hutchinson, London.

Koford, C. B. (1963). Rank of mothers and sons in bands of rhesus monkeys. *Science* **141**, 356−357.

Köhler, W. (1925). *The Mentality of Apes,* 2nd edn. Routledge and Kegan Paul, London.

Kohn, D. and Dennis, M. (1972). Observation and discrimination learning in the rat: specific and nonspecific effects. *J. comp. Physiol. Psychol.* **78**, 292−296.

Kohne, D. E. (1975). DNA evolution data and its relevance to mammalian phylogeny. In *Phylogeny of the Primates* (eds W. P. Luckett and F. S. Szalay), pp. 249−261. Plenum Press, New York.

Kolb, B. and Milner, B. (1981). Performance of complex arm and facial movements after focal brain lesions. *Neuropsychologia.* **19**, 491−504.

Kolb, B. and Whishaw, I. Q. (1980). *Fundamentals of Human Neuropsychology.* Freeman, San Francisco.

Kortlandt, A. (1972). *New Perspectives on Ape and Human Evolution.* Preliminary edition. Stichting voor Psychobiologie, Amsterdam.

Kortlandt, A. (1980a). The ecosytem in which the incipient hominines could have evolved. In *Proceedings of the 8th Pan-African Congress of Prehistory and Quaternary Studies,* Nairobi 1977 (eds R. E. Leakey and B. A. Ogot), pp. 133−136. National Museums of Kenya, Nairobi.

Kortlandt, A. (1980b). How might early hominids have defended themselves against large predators and food competition? *J. hum. Evol.* **9**, 79−112.

Kortlandt, A. and Kooij. M. (1963). Protohominid behavior in primates (preliminary communication). *Symp. zool. Soc. Lond.* **10**, 61−88.

Kortlandt, A. and Zon J. C. J. van (1969). The present status of research on the dehumanization hypothesis of African ape evolution. *Proc. 2nd Int. Congr. Primat.* **3**, 10−13, Karger, Basel.

Krebs, J. R., MacRoberts, M. and Cullen, J. M. (1972). Flocking and feeding in great tit *Parus major*—an experimental study. *Ibis* **114**, 507−530.

Krebs, K. (1974). Children and their pecking order. *New Society* **36** (12 April), 127−129.

Kroeber, A. L. and Kluckhold, C. (1952). Culture: a critical review of concepts and definitions. *Peabody Mus. Am. Archeol. Ethnol.* **47**.

Krompecher, S. and Lipák. J. (1966). A simple method for determining cerebralization: brain weight and intelligence. *J. comp. Neurol.* **127**, 113−120.

Krustov, G. F. (1970). The problem of the origin of man. *Soviet Psychol.* **9**, 6−31.

Kruuk, H. (1972). *The Spotted Hyena.* Chicago University Press, Chicago.

Kuhl, P. K. (1979). Models and mechanism in speech perception. *Brain Behav. Evol.* **16**, 374−408.

REFERENCES   Kuhl, P. K. and Miller, J. D. (1975). Speech perception by the chinchilla: voiced—voiceless distinction in alveolar plosive consonants. *Science* **190**, 69—72.

Kuhme, W. (1965). Communal food distribution and division of labour in African hunting dogs. *Nature* **205**, 443—444.

Kummer, H. (1968). *Social Organization of Hamadryas Baboons.* University of Chicago Press, Chicago.

Kummer, H. (1971). *Primate Societies: Group Techniques of Ecological Adaptation.* University of Chicago Press, Chicago.

Kummer, H. and Kurt, F. (1963). Social units of a free-living population of hamadryas baboons. *Folia primat.* **1**, 4—19.

Kummer, H., Götz, W. and Angst, W. (1974). Triadic differentiation: an inhibitory process protecting pair bonds in baboons. *Behaviour* **49**, 62—87.

Kuo, Z. Y. (1967). *The Dynamics of Behavior Development.* Random House, New York.

Kurtén, B. (1960). Rates of evolution in fossil mammals. *Cold Spring Harb. Symp. quant. Biol.* **24**, 205—215.

Kurtén, B. (1971). *The Age of Mammals.* Weidenfeld and Nicolson, London.

Kuypers, H. G. J. M. (1964). The descending pathways to the spinal cord: their anatomy and function. In *Organization of the Spinal Cord* (eds J. C. Eccles and J. P. Schadé), Vol. 11, 178—202.

Kuypers, H. G. J. M. and Brinkman, H. (1970). Precentral projections to different parts of the spinal intermediate zone in the rhesus monkey. *Brain Res.* **24**, 29—48.

Lack, D. (1953). *The Life of the Robin.* Penguin, London.

Lack, D. (1968). *Ecological Adaptations for Breeding in Birds.* Methuen, London.

Lagerspetz, K. M. J. (1964). Studies on the aggressive behavior of mice. *Annls Acad. Sci. Fenn.*, B, **3**, 1—131.

Lagerspetz, K. M. J. (1969). Aggression and aggressiveness in laboratory mice. In *Aggressive Behavior* (eds S. Garattini and E. B. Sigg), pp. 77—85. Excerpta Medica, Amsterdam.

Laidler, K. (1978). Language in the orang-utan. In *Action, Gesture and Symbol* (ed. A. Lock), pp. 133—155. Academic Press, New York.

Lancaster, J. B. and Lee, R. B. (1965). The annual reproductive cycle in monkeys and apes. In *Primate Behavior* (ed. I. DeVore), pp. 486—513. Holt, Rinehart and Winston, New York.

Lawick, H. van and Lawick-Goodall, J. van (1970). *Innocent Killers.* Collins, London.

Lawick-Goodall, J. van (1968a). The behaviour of free-living chimpanzees in the Gombe Stream reserve. *Anim. Behav. Monogr.* **1**, 161—311.

Lawick-Goodall, J. van (1968b). A preliminary report on expressive movements and communication in the Gombe Stream chimpanzees. In *Primates* (ed. P. C. Jay), pp. 313—382. Holt, Rinehart and Winston, New York.

Lawick-Goodall, J. van (1970). Tool-using in primates and other vertebrates. *Adv. Study Behav.* **3**, 195—249.

Lawick-Goodall, J. van (1971). *In the Shadow of Man.* Collins, London.

Lawick-Goodall, J. van (1973). Cultural elements in a chimpanzee community. *Proc. 4th Int. Congr. Primat.* **1**, 144–184. Karger, Basel.

Lawick-Goodall, J. van (1975). The chimpanzee. In *The Quest for Man* (ed. V. Goodall), pp. 131–169. Praeger, New York.

Lawick-Goodall, J. van, Lawick, H. van and Packer, C. (1973). Tool-using in free-living baboons in the Gombe National Park, Tanzania. *Nature* **241**, 212–213.

Lawick-Goodall, J. van, Bandora, A., Bergmann, E., Busse, C., Matama, H., Mpongo, E. Pierce, H. and Riss, D. (1979). Intercommunity interactions in the chimpanzee population of the Gombe National Park. In *The Great Apes* (eds D. A. Hamburg and E. R. McGown), pp. 13–53. Benjamin/Cummings, Menlo Park, California.

Lawrence, D. G. and Kuypers, H. G. J. M. (1968). The functional organization of the motor system in the monkey. I. The effects of bilateral pyramidal lesions. *Brain* **91**, 1–14.

Leakey, L. S. B. (1973). Was *Homo erectus* responsible for the hand-axe culture? *J. hum. Evol.* **2**, 493–498.

Leakey, L. S. B., Tobias, P. V. and Napier, J. R. (1964). A new species of the genus *Homo* from Olduvai Gorge. *Nature* **202**, 7–9.

Leakey, M. D. (1967). Preliminary survey of the cultural material from Beds I and II, Olduvai Gorge, Tanzania. In *Background to Evolution in Africa* (eds W. W. Bishop and J. D. Clark), pp. 417–442. University of Chicago Press, Chicago.

Leakey, M. D. (1976). A summary and discussion of the archaeological evidence from Bed I and Bed II, Olduvai Gorge, Tanzania. In *Human Origins: Louis Leakey and the East African Evidence* (eds G. Ll. Isaac and E. R. McGown), pp. 431–459. Benjamin, Menlo Park, California.

Leakey, M. D. (1979). *Olduvai Gorge: My Search for Earliest Man.* Collins, London.

Leakey, M. D. (1981). Tracks and tools. *Phil. Trans. R. Soc. Lond.* B **292**, 95–102.

Leakey, M. D. and Hay, R. C. (1979). Pliocene footprints in the Laetolil Beds at Laetoli, northern Tanzania. *Nature* **278**, 317–323.

Leakey, M. D., Hay, R. L., Curtis, G. H., Drake, R. E., Jackes, M. K. and White, T. D. (1976). Fossil hominids from the Laetolil Beds. *Nature* **262**, 460–466.

Leakey, R. E. F. (1973a). Evidence for an advanced Plio-Pleistocene hominid from East Rudolf, Kenya. *Nature* **242**, 447–450.

Leakey, R. E. F. (1973b). Australopithecines and hominines: a summary of the evidence from the early Pleistocene of Eastern Africa. *Symp. zool. Soc. Lond.* **33**, 53–69.

Leakey, R. E. (1981). *The Making of Mankind.* Michael Joseph, London.

Leakey, R. E. F. and Walker, A. (1976). Australopithecines, *Homo erectus* and the single species hypothesis. *Nature* **261**, 572–574.

Le Boeuf, B. J. and Peterson, R. S. (1969). Dialects in elephant seals. *Science* **166**, 1654–1656.

Le Gros Clark, W. E. (1964). *The Fossil Evidence for Human Evolution*, 2nd edn. University of Chicago Press, Chicago.

Le Gros Clark, W. E. (1970). *History of the Primates*, 10th edn. British Museum (Natural History), London.

Le Gros Clark, W. E. (1971). *The Antecedents of Man*, 3rd edn. Edinburgh University Press, Edinburgh.

Le Gros Clark, W. E. and Leakey, L. S. B. (1951). *The Miocene Hominoidea of East Africa*. (Fossil Mammals of Africa **1**, pp. 1—117). British Museum (Natural History), London.

Lee, R. B. (1968). What hunters do for a living, or how to make out on scarce resources. In *Man the Hunter* (eds R. B. Lee and I. DeVore), pp. 30—48. Aldine Press, Chicago.

Lee, R. B. and DeVore, I. eds (1968). *Man the Hunter*. Aldine, Chicago.

Lehman, R. A. (1978). The handedness of rhesus monkeys. I. Distribution, *Neuropsychologia* **16**, 33—42.

Lehrman, D. S. (1953). Problems raised by instinct theories. *Q. Rev. Biol.* **28**, 337—365.

Lehrman, D. S. (1970). Semantic and conceptual issues in the nature—nurture problem. In *Development and Evolution of Behavior* (eds L. R. Aronson, E. Tobach, D. S. Lehrman and J. S. Rosenblatt), pp. 17—52. Freeman, San Francisco.

Leinonen, L., Hyvärinen, J. and Sovijärvi, A. R. A. (1980). Functional properties of neurons in the temporo-parietal association cortex of awake monkey. *Expl Brain Res.* **39**, 203—215.

LeMay, M. (1975). The language capability of Neanderthal man. *Am. J. phys. Anthropol.* **43**, 9—14.

LeMay, M. (1976). Morphological cerebral asymmetries of modern man, fossil man, and nonhuman primates. *Ann. N. Y. Acad. Sci.* **280**, 349—366.

LeMay, M. and Culebras, A. (1972). Human brain-morphological differences in the hemispheres demonstrable by carotid arteriography. *New Engl. J. Med.* **287**, 168—170.

Lemmon, W. B. and Allen, M. L. (1978). Continual sexual receptivity in the female chimpanzee. *Folia primat.* **30**, 80—88.

Lende, R. A. (1970). Cortical localization in the tree shrew (*Tupaia*). *Brain Res.* **18**, 61—75.

Lende, R. A. and Sadler, K. M. (1967). Sensory and motor areas in neocortex of hedgehog (*Erinaceus*). *Brain Res.* **5**, 390—405.

Lenneberg, E. H. (1967). *Biological Foundations of Language*. Wiley, New York.

Lenneberg, E. H. (1971). Of language, knowledge, apes, and brains. *J. Psycholing. Res.* **1**, 1—28.

Leutenegger, W. (1973a). Encephalization in australopithecines: a new estimate. *Folia primat.* **19**, 9—17.

Leutenegger, W. (1973b). Maternal—fetal weight relationship in primates. *Folia primat.* **20**, 280—293.

Lévi-Strauss, C. (1969). *The Elementary Structure of Kinship*. Beacon Press, Boston.

Levison, P. K. and Findley, J. D. (1967). Counting behavior in baboons: an error contingency reinforcement schedule. *Psychol. Rep.* **2(** 393—394.

Levy, J. (1977). The mammalian brain and the adaptive advantage of cerebral asymmetry. *Ann. N. Y. Acad. Sci.* **299**, 264—272.

Levy, J. and Trevarthen, C. (1977). Perceptual, semantic and phonetic aspects of elementary language processes in split-brain patients. *Brain* **100**, 105—118.

Lewin, R. (1981). Ethiopian stone tools are world's oldest. *Science* **211**, 806–807.

Lieberman, P. (1975). *On the Origins of Language*. MacMillan, New York.

Lilly, C., Miller, A. M. and Truby, H. M. (1968). Reprogramming of the sonic output of the dolphin: sonic burst count matching. *J. acoust. Soc. Am.* **43**, 1412–1424.

Lindburg, D. G. (1971). The rhesus monkey in North India. In *Primate Behavior* (ed. L. A. Rosenblum), Vol. 2, pp. 1–106. Academic Press, New York.

Lore, R., Blanc, A. and Suedfeld, P. (1971). Empathic learning of a passive-avoidance response in domesticated *Rattus norvegicus*. *Anim. Behav.* **19**, 112–114.

Lorenz, K. (1963). *On Aggression*. Methuen, London.

Lovejoy, C. O. (1981). The origin of man. *Science* **211**, 341–350.

Lovejoy, C. O., Burstein, A. H. and Heiple, K. G. (1972). Primate phylogeny and immunological distance. *Science* **176**, 803–805.

Luckett, W. P. and Szalay, F. S. (1975). *Phylogeny of the Primates*. Plenum Press, New York.

Lumley, H. de (1969). A Paleolithic camp at Nice. *Scient. Am.* **220** (May), 42–56.

Lumsden, C. J. and Wilson, E. O. (1981). *Genes, Mind and Culture: the Coevolutionary Process*. Harvard University Press, Cambridge, Mass.

Luria, A. R. (1970). *Traumatic Aphasia*. Mouton, The Hague.

MacDonald, D. W. (1976). Food caching by red foxes and some other carnivores. *Z. Tierpsychol.* **42**, 170–185.

McGinnis, P. R. (1979). Sexual behaviour in free-living chimpanzees: consort relationships. In *The Great Apes* (eds D. A. Hamburg and E. R. McGown), pp. 429–439. Benjamin/Cummings Menlo Park, California.

McGraw, M. B. (1945). *The Neuromuscular Maturation of the Human Infant*. Columbia University Press, New York.

McGrew, W. C. (1972). *An Ethological Study of Children's Behaviour*. Academic Press, London.

McGrew, W. C. (1975). Patterns of plant food sharing by wild chimpanzees. *Proc. 5th Int. Congr. Primat.* 304–309. Karger, Basel.

McGrew, W. C. (1979). Evolutionary implications of sex differences in chimpanzee predation and tool use. In *The Great Apes* (eds D. A. Hamburg and E. R. McGown), pp. 441–463. Benjamin, Menlo Park, California.

McGrew, W. C. (in press). Animal foods in the diets of wild chimpanzees: why cross-cultural variation? *Carnivore*.

McGrew, W. C. and Tutin, C. E. G. (1973). Chimpanzee tool use in dental grooming. *Nature* **241**, 477–478.

McGrew, W. C. and Tutin, C. E. G. (1978). Evidence for a social custom in wild chimpanzees? *Man* **13**, 234–251.

McGrew, W. C., Tutin, C. E. G. and Baldwin, P. J. (1979a). New data on meat eating by wild chimpanzees. *Curr. Anthrop.* **20**, 238–239.

McGrew, W. C., Tutin, C. E. G. and Baldwin, P. J. (1979b). Chimpanzees, tools and termites: cross-cultural comparison of Senegal, Tanzania and Rio Muni. *Man* **14**, 185–214.

McHenry, H. M. (1976). Early hominid body weight and encephalization. *Am. J. phys. Anthrop.* **45**, 77–83.

McHenry, H. M. and Corrucini, R. S. (1980). Late Tertiary hominoid and human origins. *Nature* **285**, 397–398.

McHenry, H. M., Andrews, P. and Corrucini, R. I. (1980). Miocene hominoid palatofacial morphology. *Folia primat.* **33**, 241–252.

McKenna, M. C. (1976). Comments on Radinsky's "Later mammal radiations". In *Evolution of the Brain and Behavior in Vertebrates* (eds R. B. Masterton, M. E. Bitterman, C. B. G. Campbell and N. Hotton), pp. 245–250. Erlbaum, Hillsdale, NJ.

MacKinnon, J. (1974). The behaviour and ecology of wild orang-utans (*Pongo pygmeaus*). *Anim. Behav.* **22**, 3–74.

Mackintosh, N. J. (1974). *Animal Learning.* Academic Press, London.

MacNeilage, P. F. (1970). Motor control of serial ordering of speech. *Psychol. Rev.* **77**, 182–196.

Mangold-Wirz, K. (1966). Cerebralisation und ontogenesmodus bei Eutherien. *Acta anat.* **63**, 449–508.

Marais, E. (1969). *The Soul of the Ape.* Blond, London.

Marler, P. (1970). A comparative approach to vocal learning: song development in white-crowned sparrows. *J. comp. Physiol. Psychol.* **71**, 1–25.

Marler, P. (1976a). An ethological theory of the origin of vocal learning. *Ann. N. Y. Acad. Sci.* **280**, 386–396.

Marler, P. (1976b). Social organization, communication and graded signals: the chimpanzee and gorilla. In *Growing Points in Ethology* (eds P. P. G. Bateson and R. A. Hinde), pp. 239–280. Cambridge University Press, Cambridge.

Marler, P. (1977). Primate vocalization: affective or symbolic? In *Progress in Ape Research* (ed. G. H. Bourne), pp. 85–96. Academic Press, New York.

Marler, P. (1978). Vocal ethology of primates: implications for psycho-physics and psychophysiology. In *Recent Advances in Primatology* (eds D. J. Chivers and J. Herbert), Vol. 1, pp. 795–801. Academic Press, London.

Marshack, A. (1976). Implications of the Paleolithic symbolic evidence for the origins of language. *Am. Scient.* **64**, 136–140.

Martin, G. (1978). Through the owl's eye. *New Scient.* **77**, 72–74.

Martin, R. D. (1972). A preliminary field-study of the lesser mouse lemur (*Microcebus murinus,* J. F. Miller 1777). *Z. Tierpsychol.*, Suppl. **9**, 43–89.

Martin, R. D. (1973). Comparative anatomy and primate systematics. *Symp. zool. Soc. Lond.* **33**, 301–337.

Martin, R. D. (1974). The biological basis of human behaviour. In *The Biology of Brains* (ed. W. B. Broughton), pp. 215–250. Blackwell, Oxford.

Maruyama, M. (1963). The second cybernetics: deviation-amplifying mutual-causal processes. *Am. Scient.* **51**, 164–179.

Mason, W. A. (1965). Determinants of social behavior in young chimpanzees. In *Behavior of Nonhuman Primates* (eds A. M. Schrier, H. F. Harlow and F. Stollnitz), Vol. 2, pp. 335–364. Academic Press, New York.

Mason, W. A. (1967). Motivational aspects of social responsiveness in young chimpanzees. In *Early Behavior: a Comparative and Developmental Approach* (eds H. W. Stevenson, E. H. Hess and H. L. Rheingold), pp. 103–126. Wiley, New York.

Mason, W. A. (1971). Field and laboratory studies of social organization in *Saimiri* and *Callicebus*. In *Primate Behavior* (ed. L. A. Rosenblum), Vol. 2, pp. 107–137. Academic Press, New York.

Mason, W. A. (1978). Ontogeny of social systems. In *Recent Advances in Primatology* (eds D. J. Chivers and J. Herbert), Vol. 1, pp. 5–14. Academic Press, London.

Mason, W. A. and Kenney, M. D. (1974). Redirection of filial attachments in rhesus monkeys: dogs as mother surrogates. *Science* **183**, 1209–1211.

Masterton, B., Heffner, H. and Ravizza, R. (1969). The evolution of human hearing. *J. acoust. Soc. Am.* **45**, 966–985.

Mateer, C. and Kimura, D. (1977). Impairment of nonverbal oral movements in aphasia. *Brain and Lang.* **4**, 262–276.

Matthew, W. D. (1904). The arboreal ancestry of the Mammalia. *Am. Nat.* **38**, 811–818.

Matthew, W. D. (1937). Paleocene fauna of the San Juan basin, New Mexico. *Trans. Am. phil. Soc.* **30**, 1–510.

Maybury-Lewis, D. (1967). *Akwẽ-Shavante Society*. Oxford University Press, Oxford.

Maynard Smith, J. (1964). Group selection and kin selection. *Nature* **201**, 1145–1147.

Maynard Smith, J. (1975). *The Theory of Evolution*, 3rd edn. Penguin, Harmondsworth, Middlesex.

Maynard Smith, J. (1978). The evolution of behaviour. *Scient. Am.* **239** (Sept.), 136–145.

Maynard Smith, J. (1979). Game theory and the evolution of behavior. *Proc. R. Soc. Lond.* **B205**, 475–488.

Maynard Smith, J. and Price, G. R. (1973). The logic of animal conflict. *Nature* **246**, 15–18.

Mech, L. D. (1970). *The Wolf*. Natural History Press, New York.

Mello, N. (1968). Color generalization in cat following discrimination training on achromatic intensity and wavelength. *Neuropsychologia* **6**, 341–354.

Meltzoff, A. N. and Borton, R. W. (1979). Intermodal matching by human neonates. *Nature* **282**, 403–404.

Meltzoff, A. N. and Moore, M. K. (1977). Imitation of facial and manual gestures by human neonates. *Science* **198**, 75–80.

Menzel, E. W. (1965). Responsiveness to objects in free-ranging Japanese monkeys. *Behaviour* **26**, 130–150.

Menzel, E. W. (1973). Further observations on the use of ladders in a group of young chimpanzees. *Folia primat.* **19**, 450–457.

Menzel, E. W. (1974). A group of young chimpanzees in a one-acre field. In *Behavior of Nonhuman Primates* (eds A. M. Schrier and F. Stollnitz), Vol. 3, pp. 83–153. Academic Press, New York.

Menzel, E. W. (1978). Cognitive mapping in chimpanzees. In *Cognitive Processes in Animal Behavior* (eds S. H. Hulse, H. Fowler and W. K. Honig), pp. 375–422. Erlbaum, Hillsdale, NJ.

REFERENCES   Menzel, E. W. (1979). Communication of object-locations in a group of young chimpanzees. In *The Great Apes* (eds D. A. Hamburg and E. R. McGown), pp. 359–371. Benjamin/Cummings, Menlo Park, California.

Menzel, E. W. and Johnson, M. K. (1976). Communication and cognitive organization in human and other animals. *Ann. N. Y. Acad. Sci.* **280**, 131–142.

Menzel, E. W., Davenport, R. K. and Rogers, C. M. (1961). Some aspects of behavior towards novelty in young chimpanzees. *J. comp. Physiol. Psychol.* **54**, 16–19.

Menzel, E. W., Davenport, R. K. and Rogers, C. M. (1970). The development of tool using in wild-born and restriction-reared chimpanzees. *Folia primat.* **12**, 273–283.

Menzel, E. W., Davenport, R. K. and Rogers, C. M. (1972). Proto-cultural aspects of chimpanzees' responsiveness to novel objects. *Folia primat.* **17**, 161–170.

Merrick, H. V. (1976). Recent archaeological research in the Plio-Pleistocene deposits of the lower Omo in Southwestern Ethiopia. In *Human Origins: Louis Leakey and the East African Evidence* (eds G. Ll. Isaac and E. R. McGown), pp. 461–481. Benjamin, Menlo Park, California.

Michael, R. P. (1975). Hormonal steroids and sexual communication in primates. *J. steroid Biochem.* **6**, 161–170.

Michael, R. P. and Keverne, E. B. (1968). Pheromones in the communication of sexual states in primates. *Nature* **218**, 746–749.

Michael, R. P., Bonshall, R. W. and Warner, P. (1974). Human vaginal secretions: volatile fatty acid content. *Science* **186**, 1217–1219.

Miles, R. C. (1965). Discrimination learning sets. In *Behavior of Nonhuman Primates* (eds A. M. Schrier, H. F. Harlow and F. Stollnitz), Vol. 1, pp. 51–95. Academic Press, New York.

Miller, F. M. (1871). *Lectures on the Science of Language*, Vol. 1, Longman and Green, London.

Miller, R. E. (1967). Experimental approaches to the physiological and behavioral concomitant of affective communication in rhesus monkeys. In *Social Communication among Primates* (ed. S. A. Altmann), pp. 125–134. Chicago University Press, Chicago.

Milner, B. (1964). Some effects of frontal lobectomy in man. In *The Frontal Granular Cortex* (eds J. M. Warren and K. Akert), pp. 313–334. McGraw-Hill, New York.

Milner, B. (1971). Interhemispheric differences in the lateralization of psychological processes in man. *Br. med. Bull.* **27**, 272–277.

Milner, B. (1973). Hemispheric specialization: scope and limits. In *Neurosciences* (ed. F. Schmidt), Vol. 3, pp. 75–89. MIT Press, Boston.

Milner, B. (1975). Psychological aspects of focal epilepsy and its neurosurgical management. In *Advances in Neurology* (eds D. P. Purpura, J. K. Penry and R. D. Walter), Vol. 8, pp. 299–321. Raven Press, New York.

Milner, B. and Teuber, H. L. (1968). Alterations of perception and memory in man: reflections on methods. In *Analysis of Behavioural Change* (ed. L. Weiskrantz), pp. 263–375. Harper, New York.

Mineka, S. and Suomi, S. J. (1978). Social separation in monkeys. *Psychol.*
Bull. **85**, 1376–1400.

Mishkin, M. (1964). Perseveration of central sets after frontal lesions in monkeys. In *The Frontal Granular Cortex and Behavior* (eds J. M. Warren and K. Akert), pp. 219–241. McGraw-Hill, New York.

Missakian, E. A. (1973). Genealogical mating activity in free-ranging groups of rhesus monkeys (*Macaca mulatta*) on Cayo Santiago. *Behaviour* **45**, 225–241.

Mistler-Lachman, J. L. and Lachman, R. (1974). Language in man, monkeys and machines. *Science* **185**, 871–872.

Mitchell, G. and Brandt, E. M. (1972). Paternal behavior in primates. In *Primate Socialization* (ed. F. E. Poirier), pp. 173–206. Random House, New York.

Miyadi, D. (1964). Social life of Japanese monkeys. *Science* **143**, 783–786.

Moehlman, P. D. (1979). Jackal helpers and pup survival. *Nature* **277**, 382–383.

Mohr, J. P. (1976) Broca's area and Broca's aphasia. In *Studies in Neurolinguistics* (eds H. Avakian-Whitaker and H. A. Whitaker), Vol. 1, pp. 202–235. Academic Press, New York.

Mohr, J. P., Pessin, M. S., Finkelstein, S., Funkenstein, H. H., Duncan, G. W. and Davis, K. R. (1978). Broca's asphasia—pathologic and clinical. *Neurologia* **28**, 311–324.

Moll, L. and Kuypers, H. G. J. M. (1975). Role of premotor cortical areas and ventrolateral nucleus in visual guidance of relatively independent hand and finger movements in monkeys. *Expl Brain Res.*, Suppl. **23**, 142.

Moll, L. and Kuypers, H. G. J. M. (1977). Premotor cortical ablations in monkeys: contralateral changes in visually guided reaching behavior. *Science* **198**, 317–319.

Montagu, A. (1976). *The Nature of Human Aggression.* Oxford University Press, Oxford.

Montagu, A. (1978). *Learning Non-Aggression.* Oxford University Press, Oxford.

Morgan, M. (1977). Embryology and inheritance of asymmetry. In *Lateralization in the Nervous System* (eds S. Harnad, R. W. Doty, L. Goldstein, J. Jaynes and G. Krauthamer), pp. 173–194. Academic Press, New York.

Morgan, M. and Corballis, M. C. (1978). On the biological basis of human laterality: II. The mechanisms of inheritance. *Brain Behav. Sci.* **2**, 270–277.

Morgan, M. and Nicholas, D. J. (1979). Discrimination between reinforced action patterns in the rat. *Learn. and Motiv.* **10**, 1–22.

Morris, D. (1962). *The Biology of Art.* Methuen, London.

Morris, D. (1967). *The Naked Ape.* Cape, London.

Morris, D. (1971). *Intimate Behaviour.* Cape, London.

Morris, D. (1977). *Manwatching.* Cape, London.

Morris, K. and Lawick-Goodall, J. van (1977). Competition for meat between chimpanzees and baboons in the Gombe National Park. *Folia primat.* **28**, 109–121.

Morse, P.A. and Snowdon, C. T. (1975). An investigation of categorical speech discrimination by rhesus monkeys. *Percept. Psychophys.* **17**, 9–16.

Moskowitz, B. A. (1978). The acquisition of language. *Scient. Am.* **239** (Nov.), 82–96.

Moulton, D. G. (1978). Olfaction. In *Handbook of Behavioral Neurobiology* (ed. R. B. Masterton), Vol. 1, pp. 91–117. Plenum Press, New York.

Moulton, D. G., Ashton, E. H. and Eayrs, J. L. (1960). Studies in olfactory acuity: IV. Relative detectability of *n*-aliphatic acids by the dog. *Anim. Behav.* **8**, 117–128.

Moyer, K. F. (1976). *The Psychobiology of Aggression*. Harper, New York.

Moynihan, M. H. (1970). Control, suppression, decay, disappearance and replacement of displays. *J. theoret. Biol.* **29**, 85–112.

Muncer, S. J. and Ettlinger, G. (1981). Communication by a chimpanzee: first-trial mastery of word order that is critical for meaning, but failure to negate conjunctions. *Neuropsychologia* **19**, 73–78.

Murdock, G. P. (1949). *Social Structure*. MacMillan, New York.

Murdock, G. P. (1957). World ethnographic sample. *Am. Anthrop.* **59**, 664–687.

Murdock, K. and Sullivan, L. R. (1923). A contribution to the study of mental and physical measurement in normal schoolchildren. *Am. phys. Educ. Rev.* **28**, 209–215, 276–280, 328–330.

Myers, R. E. (1976). Comparative neurology of vocalization and speech: proof of a dichotomy. *Ann. N. Y. Acad. Sci.* **280**, 745–757.

Nadler, R. D. (1975). Sexual cyclicity in captive lowland gorillas. *Science* **189**, 813–814.

Nagel, U. and Kummer, H. (1974). Variation in cercopithecoid aggressive behavior. In *Primate Aggression, Territoriality and Xenophobia* (ed. R. L. Holloway), pp. 159–184. Academic Press, New York.

Nakamura, R. K. and Gazzaniga, M. S. (1978). Hemispherectomy versus commissurotomy in the monkey: one hemisphere can be better than two. *Expl Neurol.* **59**, 202–208.

Napier, J. R. (1961). Prehensility and opposability in the hands of primates. *Symp. zool. Soc. Lond.* **5**, 115–132.

Napier, J. R. (1962). Fossil hand bones from Olduvai Gorge. *Nature* **196**, 409–411.

Napier, J. R. (1970). Paleoecology and catarrhine evolution. In *Old World Monkeys* (eds J. R. Napier and P. H. Napier), pp. 53–95. Academic Press, London.

Napier, J. R. (1971). *The Roots of Mankind*. Allen and Unwin, London.

Napier, J. R. and Napier, P. H. (1967). *A Handbook of Living Primates*. Academic Press, London.

Negus, V. E. (1949). *The Comparative Anatomy and Physiology of the Larynx*. Hafner, New York.

Newman, J. D. (1979). Central nervous system processing of sounds in primates. In *Neurobiology of Social Communication* (eds H. Steklis and M. J. Raleigh), pp. 69–109. Academic Press, New York.

Nishida, T. (1973). The ant-gathering behavior by the use of tools among wild chimpanzees of the Mahale mountains. *J. hum. Evol.* **2**, 357–370.

Nishida, T. (1979). The social structure of chimpanzees of the Mahale mountains. In *The Great Apes* (eds D. A. Hamburg and E. R. McGown), pp. 73–121. Benjamin/Cummings, Menlo Park, California.

Nissen, H. W. and Crawford, D. M. P. (1936). A preliminary study of food sharing behavior in young chimpanzees. *J. comp. Psychol.* **22**, 383–419.

Noback, C. R. (1975). The visual system of primates in phylogenetic studies. In *Phylogeny of the Primates* (eds W. P. Luckett and F. S. Szalay), pp. 199–218. Plenum Press, New York.

Norton-Griffiths, M. (1967). Some ecological aspects of the feeding behaviour of the oyster-catcher *Haematopus ostralogus* on the edible mussel *Mytilus edulis*. *Ibis* **109**, 412–424.

Nottebohm, F. (1972). The origin of vocal learning. *Am. Nat.* **106**, 116–140.

Nottebohm, F. (1976). Vocal tract and brain: a search for evolutionary bottlenecks. *Ann. N. Y. Acad. Sci.* **280**, 643–649.

Nottebohm, F. (1977). Asymmetries in neural control of vocalization in the canary. In *Lateralization in the Nervous System* (eds S. Harnad, R. Doty, L. Goldstein, J. Jaynes and G. Krauthamer), pp. 23–44. Academic Press, New York.

Nottebohm, F. (1979). Origin and mechanism in the establishment of cerebral dominance. In *Handbook of Behavioral Neurobiology* (ed. M. S. Gazzaniga), Vol. 2, pp. 295–344. Plenum Press, New York.

Oakley, K. P. (1969). *Frameworks for Dating Fossil Man*, 3rd edn. Weidenfeld and Nicolson, London.

Oakley, K. P. (1972). *Man the Tool-Maker*, 6th edn. British Museum (Natural History), London.

Oakley, K. P. (1980). Relative dating of the fossil hominids of Europe. *Bull. Br. Mus. nat. Hist.* (Geol.) **34**, 1–63.

Ojemann, G. A. and Mateer, C. (1979a). Human language centers: localization of memory, syntax, and sequential motor-phoneme identification system. *Science* **205**, 1401–1403.

Ojemann, G. A. and Mateer, C. (1979b). Cortical and subcortical organization of human communication: evidence from stimulation studies. In *Neurobiology of Social Communication* (eds H. D. Steklis and M. J. Raleigh), pp. 111–131. Academic Press, New York.

Olivier, G. (1973). Hominization and cranial capacity. In *Human Evolution* (ed. M. H. Day), pp. 87–101. Taylor and Francis, London.

Ordy, J. M. and Samorajski, T. (1968). Visual acuity and ERG-CFF in relation to the morphologic organization of the retina among diurnal and nocturnal primates. *Vision Res.* **8**, 1205–1225.

Owen, R. (1858). On the characters, principles of division, and primary groups of the class Mammalia. *Proc. Linn. Soc. Lond.* **2**, 1–37.

Owens, N. W. (1975a). Social play behavior in free-living baboons, *Papio anubis. Anim. Behav.* **23**, 387–408.

Owens, N. W. (1975b). A comparison of aggressive play and aggression in free-living baboons, *Papio anubis. Anim. Behav.* **23**, 757–765.

Oxnard, C. E. (1973). Some locomotor adaptation among lower primates: implications for primate evolution. *Symp. zool. Soc. Lond.* **33**, 255–299.

Packer, C. (1977). Reciprocal altruism in olive baboons. *Nature* **265**, 441−443.

Packer, C. (1979a). Intertroop transfer and inbreeding avoidance in *Papio anubis*. *Anim. Behav.* **27**, 1−36.

Packer, C. (1979b). Male dominance and reproductive activity in *Papio anubis*. *Anim. Behav.* **27**, 37−45.

Paivio, A. (1971). *Imagery and Verbal Processes*. Holt, Rinehart and Winston, New York.

Pakkenberg, H. and Voigt, J. (1964). Brain weight of the Danes: forensic material. *Acta anat.* **56**, 297−307.

Parker, C. E. (1974). Behavioral diversity in ten species of nonhuman primates. *J. comp. Physiol. Psychol.* **87**, 930−937.

Pasik, T. and Pasik, P. (1971). The visual world of monkeys deprived of striate cortex. Effective stimulus parameters and the importance of the accessory optic system. *Vision Res.*, Suppl. **3**, 419−435.

Passingham, R. E. (1973). Anatomical differences between the neocortex of man and other primates. *Brain Behav. Evol.* **7**, 337−359.

Passingham, R. E. (1975a). The brain and intelligence. *Brain Behav. Evol.* **11**, 1−15.

Passingham, R. E. (1975b). Changes in the size and organization of the brain in man and his ancestors. *Brain Behav. Evol.* **11**, 73−90.

Passingham, R. E. (1978). Brain size and intelligence in primates. In *Recent Advances in Primatology* (eds D. Chivers and K. A. Joysey), Vol. 3, pp. 85−86. Academic Press, London.

Passingham, R. E. (1979a). Specialization and the language areas. In *Neurobiology of Social Communication* (eds H. D. Steklis and M. J. Raleigh), pp. 221−256. Academic Press, New York.

Passingham, R. E. (1979b). Brain size and intelligence in man. *Brain Behav. Evol.*, **16**, 253−270.

Passingham, R. E. (1981a). Primate specializations in brain and intelligence. *Symp. zool. Soc. Lond.* **46**, 361−388.

Passingham, R. E. (1981b). Broca's area and the origins of human vocal skill. *Phil. Trans. R. Soc. Lond.* B **292**, 167−175.

Passingham, R. E. (1981c). Intelligence. In *The Oxford Companion to Animal Behaviour* (ed. D. McFarland), pp. 310−317. Oxford University Press, Oxford.

Passingham, R. E. and Ettlinger, G. (1974). A comparison of cortical function in man and other primates. *Int. Rev. Neurobiol.* **16**, 233−299.

Passingham, R. E., Perry, H. and Wilkinson, F. (1978). Failure to develop a precision grip in monkeys with unilateral cortical lesions made in infancy. *Brain Res.* **145**, 410−414.

Patterson, F. G. (1978). The gestures of a gorilla: language acquisition in another pongid. *Brain and Lang.* **5**, 72−97.

Patterson, F. G. (1979). Linguistic capabilities of a young lowland gorilla. Unpublished dissertation, Stanford University.

Pearson, R. and Pearson, L. (1976). *The Vertebrate Brain*. Academic Press, London.

Penfield, W. and Jaspar, H. (1954). *Epilepsy and the Functional Anatomy of the Human Brain*. Little Brown, Boston.

Penfield, W. and Rasmussen, T. (1950). *The Cerebral Cortex of Man*. MacMillan, New York.

Penfield, W. and Roberts, L. (1959). *Speech and Brain Mechanisms.* Princeton University Press, Princeton.

Peters, R. and Mech, C. D. (1975). Behavioral and intellectual adaptation of selected mammalian predators to the problem of hunting large animals. In *The Socioecology and Psychology of Primates* (ed. R. H. Tuttle), pp. 279–305. Mouton, The Hague.

Petersen, M. R., Beecher, M. D., Zoloth, S. R., Moody, D. B. and Stebbins, W. C. (1978). Neural lateralization of species-specific vocalization by Japanese macaques (*Macaca fuscata*). *Science* **202**, 324–327.

Petitto, L. A. and Seidenberg, M. S. (1979). On the evidence for linguistic ability: signing apes. *Brain and Lang.* **8**, 162–183.

Petras, J. M. (1969). Some efferent connections of the motor and somatosensory cortex of simian primates and felid, canid and procyonid carnivores. *Ann. N. Y. Acad. Sci.* **167**, 469–505.

Pettigrew, J. D. (1972). The neurophysiology of binocular vision. *Scient. Am.* **227** (Aug.), 84–95.

Pfeiffer, J. E. (1978). *The Emergence of Man*, 3rd edn. Harper, New York.

Philips, C. G. (1971). Evolution of the corticospinal tract in primates with special reference to the hand. *Proc. 3rd Int. Congr. Primat.* **2**, 2–23. Karger, Basel.

Philips, C. G. and Porter, R. (1977). *Corticospinal Neurones: their Role in Movement.* Academic Press, London.

Pianka, E. R. (1970). On r- and k- selection. *Am. Nat.* **104**, 592–597.

Pilbeam, D. (1970). *The Evolution of Man.* Thames and Hudson, London.

Pilbeam, D. (1972). *The Ascent of Man.* MacMillan, New York.

Pilbeam, D., Meyer, G. E., Badgley, C., Rose, M. D., Pickford, M. H. L., Behrensmeyer, A. K. and Shah, S. M. I. (1977). New hominoid primates from the Siwaliks of Pakistan and their bearing on hominoid evolution. *Nature* **270**, 689–695.

Pisoni, D. B. (1979). On the perception of speech sounds as biologically significant signals. *Brain Behav. Evol.* **16**, 330–350.

Poirier, F. E. (1969). Behavioral flexibility and intertroop variation among Nilgiri langurs (*Prebytis johnii*) of South India. *Folia primat.* **11**, 119–133.

Poirier, F. E. (1970). The Nilgiri langur (*Presbytis johnii*) of South India. In *Primate Behavior* (ed. L. A. Rosenblum), Vol. 1, pp. 254–383. Academic Press, New York.

Poirier, F. E. (1974). Colobine aggression: a review. In *Primate Aggression, Territoriality and Xenophobia* (ed. R. L. Holloway), pp. 123–157. Academic Press, New York.

Potts, R. and Shipman, P. (1981). Cutmarks made by stone tools on bones from Olduvai Gorge, Tanzania. *Nature*, **291**, 577–580.

Prechtl, H. F. R. (1965). Problems of behavioral studies in the newborn infant. In *Advances in the Study of Behavior* (eds D. S. Lehrman, R. A. Hinde and E. Shaw), Vol. 1, pp. 75–98. Academic Press, New York.

Premack, A. J. and Premack, D. (1972). Teaching language to an ape. *Scient. Am.* **227** (Oct.), 92–99.

Premack, D. (1970). A functional analysis of language. *J. exp. anal. Behav.* **14**, 107–125.

Premack, D. (1975). Putting a face together. *Science* **188**, 228–236.

Premack, D. (1976). *Intelligence in Ape and Man.* Erlbaum, Hillsdale, NJ.

Premack, D. and Woodruff, G. (1978). Chimpanzee problem solving: a test for comprehension. *Science* **202**, 532–535.

Premack, D., Woodruff, G. and Kennel, K. (1978). Paper-marking test for chimpanzee: simple control for social cues. *Science* **202**, 903–905.

Presley, W. J. and Riopelle, A. J. (1959). Observational learning of an avoidance response. *J. genet. Psychol.* **95**, 251–254.

Prestrude, A. M. (1970). Sensory capacities of the chimpanzee. *Psychol. Bull.* **74**, 47–67.

Pusey, A. E. (1979). Inter-community transfer of chimpanzees in Gombe National Park. In *The Great Apes* (eds D. A. Hamburg and E. R. McGown), pp. 465–479. Benjamin/Cummings, Menlo Park, California.

Pusey, A. E. (1980). Inbreeding avoidance in chimpanzees. *Anim. Behav.* **28**, 543–552.

Radinsky, L. (1970). The fossil evidence of prosimian evolution. In *The Primate Brain* (eds C. R. Noback and W. Montagna), pp. 209–224. Appleton-Century-Crofts, New York.

Radinsky, L. (1973). *Aegyptopithecus* endocasts: oldest record of a pongid brain. *Am. J. phys. Anthrop.* **39**, 239–248.

Radinsky, L. (1974). The fossil evidence of anthropoid brain evolution. *Am. J. phys. Anthrop.* **41**, 15–27.

Radinsky, L. (1975a). Primate brain evolution. *Am. Scient.* **63**, 656–663.

Radinsky, L. (1975b). Evolution of the felid brain. *Brain Behav. Evol.* **11**, 214–254.

Radinsky, L. (1976). The brain of *Mesonyx*, a middle Eocene mesonychid condylarth. *Fieldiana, Geol.* **33**, 323–337.

Radinsky, L. (1977). Early primate brains: fact and fiction. *J. hum. Evol.* **6**, 79–86.

Radinsky, L. (1978). Evolution of brain size in carnivores and ungulates. *Am. Nat.* **112**, 812–831.

Radinsky, L. (1979). *The fossil record of primate brain evolution.* (James Arthur Lecture.) American Museum of Natural History, New York.

Randolph, M. C. and Brooks, B. A. (1967). Conditioning of a vocal response in a chimpanzee through social reinforcement. *Folia primat.* **5**, 70–79.

Rasa, O. A. C. (1971). Appetence for aggression in juvenile damsel fish. *Z. Tierpsychol.*, Suppl. **7**, 1–70.

Rasmussen, T. and Milner, B. (1977). The role of early left-brain injury in determining lateralization of cerebral speech function. *Ann. N. Y. Acad. Sci.* **299**, 355–369.

Ratcliff, G., Dila, C., Taylor, L. and Milner, B. (1980). The morphological asymmetry of the hemispheres and cerebral dominance for speech: a possible relationship. *Brain and Lang.* **11**, 87–98.

Reynolds, V. (1975). How wild are the Gombe chimpanzees? *Man* **10**, 123–125.

Rheingold, H. L. and Eckerman, C. O. (1970). The infant separates himself from his mother. *Science* **168**, 78–83.

Rheingold, H. L. and Keene, G. C. (1965). Transport of the human
young. In *Determinants of Infant Behaviour* (ed. B. M. Foss), Vol. 3, pp. 87–107. Methuen, London.

Richards, S. M. (1974). The concept of dominance. *Anim. Behav.* **22**, 914–930.

Riddell, W. I. (1979). Cerebral indices and behavioral differences. In *Development and Evolution of Brain Size* (eds M. E. Hahn, C. Jensen and B. C. Dudek), pp. 89–109. Academic Press, New York.

Riopelle, A. J. (1960). Observational learning of a position habit by monkeys. *J. comp. Physiol. Psychol.* **53**, 426–428.

Riopelle, A. J. (1967). *Animal Problem Solving*, Penguin Books, Harmondsworth, Middlesex.

Ripley, S. (1967). Intertroop encounters among Ceylon gray langurs (*Presbytis entellus*). In *Social Communication among Primates* (ed. S. A. Altmann), pp. 237–253. Chicago University Press, Chicago.

Roberts, W. W. and Berquist, E. H. (1968). Attack elicited by hypothalamus stimulation in cats reared in social isolation. *J. comp. Physiol. Psychol.* **66**, 590–595.

Robertson, J. and Robertson, J. (1971). Young children in brief separation: a fresh look. *Psychoanal. Study Child.* **26**, 264–315.

Robinson, J. T. (1972). *Early Hominid Posture and Locomotion.* Chicago University Press, Chicago.

Roche, H. and Tiercelin, J.-J. (1980). Industries lithiques de la formation Plio-Pléistocène d'Hadar, Ethiopie (campagne 1976). In *Proceedings of the 8th Pan-African Congress of Prehistory and Quaternary Studies*, Nairobi, 1977 (eds R. E. F. Leakey and B. A. Ogot), pp. 194–199. National Museums of Kenya, Nairobi.

Rockel, A. J., Hiorns, R. W. and Powell, T. P. S. (1980). The basic uniformity in structure of the neocortex. *Brain* **133**, 221–244.

Romer, A. S. (1959). *The Vertebrate Story*, 4th edn. Chicago University Press, Chicago.

Romer, A. S. (1966). *Vertebrate Paleontology*, 3rd edn. Chicago University Press, Chicago.

Rose, M. D. (1976). Bipedal behavior of olive baboons (*Papio anubis*) and its relevance to an understanding of the evolution of human bipedalism. *Am. J. phys. Anthrop.* **44**, 247–262.

Rosen, S. (1974). *Introduction to the Primates Living and Fossil.* Prentice-Hall, Englewood Cliffs, NJ.

Rosenblum, L. A. and Kaufman, I. C. (1967). Laboratory observation of early mother-infant relations in pigtail and bonnet macaques. In *Social Communication among Primates* (ed. S. A. Altmann), pp. 33–41. Chicago University Press, Chicago.

Rosenfield, D. B. (1980). Cerebral dominance and stuttering. *J. fluency Disorders* **5**, 171–185.

Rosenfield, D. B. and Goodglass, H. (1980). Dichotic testing of cerebral dominance in stutterers. *Brain and Lang.* **11**, 170–180.

Rowell, T. E. (1962). Agonistic noises of the rhesus monkey (*Macaca mulatta*). *Symp. zool. Soc. Lond.* **8**, 91–96.

Rowell, T. E. (1967). A quantitative comparison of the behaviour of a wild and a caged baboon group. *Anim. Behav.* **15**, 499–509.

Rowell, T. E. (1974). The concept of social dominance. *Behav. Biol.* **11**, 131–154.

Rubens, A. B. (1977). Anatomical asymmetries of the human cerebral cortex. In *Lateralization in the Nervous System* (eds S. Harnad, R. W. Doty, L. Goldstein, J. Jaynes and G. Krauthamer), pp. 503–516. Academic Press, New York.

Rumbaugh, D. M. (1970). Learning skills of anthropoids. In *Primate Behavior* (ed. L. A. Rosenblum), Vol. 1, pp. 1–70. Academic Press, New York.

Rumbaugh, D. M. (1971). Chimpanzee intelligence. In *The Chimpanzee* (ed. G. H. Bourne), Vol. 4, pp. 19–45. Karger, Basel.

Rumbaugh, D. M. ed. (1977). *Language Learning by a Chimpanzee.* Academic Press, New York.

Rumbaugh, D. M. and Gill, T. V. (1977). Lana's acquisition of language skills. In *Language Learning by a Chimpanzee* (ed. D. M. Rumbaugh), pp. 165–192. Academic Press, New York.

Rumbaugh, D. M. and McCormack, C. (1967). The learning skills of primates: a comparative study of apes and monkeys. In *Progress in Primatology* (eds D. Starck, R. Schneider and H. J. Kuhn), pp. 289–306. Fischer, Stuttgart.

Ruse, M. (1979). *Sociobiology: Sense or Nonsense.* Reidel, Boston.

Rushton, J. P. (1980). *Altruism, Socialization and Society.* Prentice-Hall, Englewood Cliffs, NJ.

Rutter, M. (1972). Maternal deprivation reconsidered. *J. psychosom. Res.* **16**, 241–250.

Rutter, M. (1981). *Maternal Deprivation Reassessed*, 2nd edn. Penguin, Harmondsworth, Middlesex.

Sacher, G. A. (1972). Table of lifespans of mammals. In *Biology Data Book* (eds P. L. Altman and D. S. Dittmer), 2nd edn. FASEB, Bethesda, Md.

Sacher, G. A. (1975). Maturation and longevity in relation to cranial capacity in hominid evolution. In *Primate Functional Morphology and Evolution* (ed. R. Tuttle), pp. 417–441. Mouton, The Hague.

Sacher, G. A. (1976). Evaluation of the entropy and information terms governing mammalian longevity. *Interdiscipl. Topics Geront.* **9**, 69–82.

Sacher, G. A. and Staffeldt, E. F. (1974). Relation of gestation time to brain weight for placental mammals: implications for the theory of vertebrate growth. *Am. Nat.* **108**, 593–615.

Sackett, G. P. (1966). Monkeys reared in isolation with pictures as visual input: evidence for an innate releasing mechanism. *Science* **154**, 1468–1473.

Sackett, G. P. (1968). The persistence of abnormal behavior in monkeys following isolation rearing. In *Role of Learning in Psychotherapy* (ed. R. Porter), pp. 3–25. Churchill, London.

Sackett, G. P. (1969). Abnormal behavior in laboratory-reared rhesus monkeys. In *Abnormal Behavior in Animals* (ed. M. W. Fox), pp. 293–331. Saunders, New York.

Sade, D. S. (1972). A longitudinal study of social behavior in rhesus monkeys. In *The Functional and Evolutionary Biology of Primates* (ed. R. H. Tuttle), pp. 378–398. Aldine Press, Chicago.

Sarich, V. M. and Cronin, J. E. (1976). Molecular systematics of the REFERENCES
primates. In *Molecular Anthropology* (eds M. Goodman and R. E.
Tashian), pp. 141–170. Plenum Press, New York.

Sarmiento, R. F. (1975). The steroacuity of macaque monkey. *Vis. Res.*
15, 493–498.

Sarnat, H. B. and Netsky, M. G. (1974). *Evolution of the Nervous System.*
Oxford University Press, New York.

Savage-Rumbaugh, E. S. and Rumbaugh, D. M. (1980). Requisites of
symbolic communication—or, are words for birds? *Psychol. Rec.* **30**,
305–315.

Savage-Rumbaugh, E. S., Wilkerson, B. T. and Bakeman, R. (1977).
Spontaneous gestural communication among conspecifics in the
pygmy chimpanzee (*Pan paniscus*). In *Progress in Ape Research* (ed.
G. H. Bourne), pp. 97–116. Academic Press, New York.

Savage-Rumbaugh, E. S., Rumbaugh, D. M. and Boysen, S. (1978a).
Linguistically mediated tool use and exchange by chimpanzees (*Pan
troglodytes*). *Behav. Brain Sci.* **201**, 539–554.

Savage-Rumbaugh, E. S., Rumbaugh, D. M. and Boysen, S. (1978b).
Symbolic communication between two chimpanzees (*Pan troglodytes*).
Science **201**, 641–644.

Savage-Rumbaugh, E. S., Rumbaugh, D. M. and Boysen, S. (1980a). Do
apes use language? *Am. Scient.* **68**, 49–61.

Savage-Rumbaugh, E. S., Rumbaugh, D. M., Smith, S. T. and Lawson, J.
(1980b). Reference: the linguistic essential. *Science* **210**, 922–925.

Savin-Williams, R. C. (1977). Dominance in a human adolescent group.
Anim. Behav., **25**, 400–406.

Schaffer, H. R. and Emerson, P. E. (1964a). Patterns of response to
physical contact in early human development. *J. Child Psychol.
Psychiat.* **5**, 1–13.

Schaffer, H. R. and Emerson, P. E. (1964b). The development of social
attachments in infancy. *Mon. Soc. Res. Child Dev.* **29**(3).

Schaller, G. B. (1963). *The Mountain Gorilla: Ecology and Behavior.*
Chicago University Press, Chicago.

Schaller, G. B. (1965). Behavioral comparisons of the apes. In *Primate
Behavior* (ed. I. DeVore), pp. 474–481. Holt, Rinehart and Winston,
New York.

Schaller, G. B. (1972). *The Serengeti Lion.* Chicago University Press,
Chicago.

Schaller, G. B. and Lowther, G. (1969). The relevance of carnivore
behavior to the study of early hominids. *SW J. Anthrop.* **25**, 307–341.

Scheibel, M. E., Lindsay, R. D., Tomiyasu, U. and Scheibel, A. B.
(1975). Progressive dendritic changes in ageing human cortex. *Expl
Neurol.* **47**, 392–403.

Schenkel, R. (1966). Play, exploration and territoriality in the wild lion.
In *Play, Exploration and Territory* (eds P. A. Jewell and C. Loizos),
pp. 11–22. Academic Press, London.

Schiller, P. H. (1952). Innate constituents of complex responses in
primates. *Psychol. Rev.* **59**, 177–191.

Schjelderup-Ebbe, T. (1935). Social behavior of birds. In *Handbook of
Social Psychology* (ed. C. A. Murchison), pp. 947–972. Clark
University Press, Worcester, Mass.

Schmidt-Nielsen, K. (1972). *How Animals Work*. Cambridge University Press, Cambridge.

Schultz, A. H. (1940). Growth and development of the chimpanzee. *Contrib. Embryol.* **170**, 1—63.

Schultz, A. H. (1941). The relative size of the cranial capacity in primates. *Am. J. phys. Anthropol.* **28**, 273—287.

Schultz, A. H. (1950). The physical distinctions of man. *Proc. Am. phil. Soc.* **94**, 428—449.

Schultz, A. H. (1956). Postembryonic age changes. *Primatologia* **1**, 887—964.

Scott, J. P. (1958). *Aggression*. Chicago University Press, Chicago.

Scott, J. P. and Fuller, J. L. (1974). *Dog Behavior: the Genetic Basis*. Chicago University Press, Chicago.

Seckel, H. P. G. (1960). *Bird Headed Dwarfs*. Karger, Basel.

Segal, M., Campbell, D. T. and Herskovits, M. J. (1966). *The Influence of Culture on Visual Perception*. Bobbs-Merrill, Indianapolis.

Seidenberg, M. S. and Petitto, L. A. (1979). Signing behavior in apes: a critical review. *Cognition* **7**, 177—215.

Seyfarth, R. M. (1978a). Social relationships among adult male and female baboons. I. Behaviour during sexual consortship. *Behaviour* **44**, 204—226.

Seyfarth, R. M. (1978b). Social relationships among adult male and female baboons. II. Behaviour during the female reproductive cycle. *Behaviour* **44**, 229—247.

Seyfarth, R. M., Cheney, D. L. and Marler, P. (1980). Vervet monkeys alarm calls: semantic communication in a free ranging primate. *Anim. Behav.* **28**, 1070—1094.

Shariff, G. A. (1953). Cell counts in the primate cerebral cortex. *J. comp. Neurol.*, **98**, 381—400.

Shell, W. F. and Riopelle, A. J. (1958). Prosimian discrimination learning in platyrrhine monkeys, *J. comp. Physiol. Psychol.* **51**, 467—470.

Shepard, R. N. and Metzler, J. (1971). Mental rotation of three-dimensional objects. *Science* **171**, 701—703.

Shepher, J. (1971). Mate selection among second generation Kibbutz adolescents and adults: incest avoidance and negative imprinting. *Archs Sexual Behav.* **1**, 293—307.

Shields, J. (1973). Heredity and psychological abnormality. In *Handbook of Abnormal Psychology* (ed. H. J. Eysenck), 2nd edn, pp. 540—603. Pitman, London.

Simonds, P. E. (1974). *The Social Primates*. Harper, New York.

Simons, E. L. (1962). Fossil evidence relating to the early evolution of primate behavior. *Ann. N. Y. Acad. Sci.* **102**, 282—294.

Simons, E. L. (1969). The origin and radiation of the primates. *Ann. N. Y. Acad. Sci.* **167**, 319—331.

Simons, E. L. (1972). *Primate Evolution: an Introduction to Man's Place in Nature*. MacMillan, New York.

Simons, E. L. (1981). Man's immediate forerunners. *Phil. Trans. R. Soc. Lond.* B**292**, 21—41.

Simons, E. L. (1977). *Ramapithecus*. *Scient. Am.* **236** (May), 28—35.

Simons, E. L. and Ettel, P. C. (1970). *Gigantopithecus. Scient. Am.* **222** (Jan.) 76−85.

Simons, E. L. and Pilbeam, D. R. (1972). Hominid paleoprimatology. In *The Functional and Evolutionary Biology of Primates* (ed. R. Tuttle), pp. 36−62. Aldine, Chicago.

Simpson, G. G. (1975). Recent advances in methods of phylogenetic inference. In *Phylogeny of the Primates* (eds W. P. Luckett and F. S. Szalay), pp. 3−19. Plenum Press, New York.

Sinnott, J. M., Beecher, M. D., Moody, D. B. and Stebbins, W. C. (1976). Speech sound discrimination by monkeys and humans. *J. acoust. Soc. Am.* **60**, 687−695.

Slotnik, B. M. and Ptak, J. E. (1977). Olfactory intensity-difference thresholds in rats and humans. *Physiol. Behav.* **19**, 795−802.

Smith, A. J. (1966). Speech and other functions after left (dominant) hemispherectomy. *J. Neurol. Neurosurg. Psychiat.* **29**, 467−471.

Snowdon, C. T. (1979). Response of non-human animals to speech and to species-specific sounds. *Brain Behav. Evol.* **16**, 409−429.

Solomon, R. L. (1960). Unpublished study, cited by O. H. Mowrer in *Learning Theory and the Symbolic Process*. Wiley, New York.

Southwick, C. H. (1967). An experimental study of intragroup agonistic behavior in rhesus monkeys (*Macaca mulatta*). *Behaviour* **28**, 182−209.

Southwick, C. H., Beg, M. A. and Siddiqi, M. F. (1965). Rhesus monkeys in North India. In *Primate Behavior* (ed. I. DeVore), pp. 111−159. Holt, Rinehart and Winston, New York.

Southwick, C. H., Siddiqi, M. F., Farooqui, M. Y. and Pal, B. C. (1974). Xenophobia among free-ranging rhesus groups in India. In *Primate Aggression, Territoriality and Xenophobia* (ed. R. L. Holloway), pp. 185−209. Academic Press, New York.

Southwick, C. H., Siddiqi, M. F., Farooqui, M. Y. and Pal, B. C. (1976). Effects of artificial feeding on aggressive behavior of rhesus monkeys in India. *Anim. Behav.* **24**, 11−15.

Sparks, J. (1967). Allogrooming in primates: a review. In *Primate Ethology* (ed. D. Morris), pp. 148−175.

Sperry, R. W. (1968). Hemisphere deconnection and units in conscious awareness. *Am. Psychol.* **23**, 723−733.

Sperry, R. W. and Gazzaniga, M. S. (1967). Language following surgical disconnection of the hemispheres. In *Brain Mechanisms Underlying Speech and Language* (eds C. H. Millikan and F. L. Darley), pp. 108−115. Grune and Stratton, New York.

Staddon, J. E. R. (1980). On a possible relation between cultural transmission and anatomical evolution. In *Perspectives in Ethology* (eds P. P. G. Bateson and P. H. Klopfer), Vol. 4, pp. 135−145. Plenum Press, New York.

Stahl, W. R. G. (1965). Organ weights in primates and other mammals. *Science* **150**, 1039−1041.

Starck, D. (1975). The development of the chondrocranium in primates. In *Phylogeny of the Primates* (eds W. P. Luckett and F. S. Starck), pp. 127−155. Plenum Press, New York.

Starin, E. D. (1978). Food transfer by wild titi monkeys (*Callicebus torquatus torquatus*). *Folia primat.* **30**, 145−151.

Stebbins, W. C. (1971). Hearing. In *Behavior of Nonhuman Primates* (eds A. M. Schrier and F. Stollnitz), pp. 159–192. Academic Press, New York.

Stebbins, W. C. (1973). Hearing of old world monkeys (Cercopithinae). *Am. J. phys. Anthrop.* **38**, 357–364.

Stebbins, W. C. (1976). Comparative hearing function in the vertebrates. In *Evolution of Brain and Behavior in Vertebrates* (eds B. Masterton, M. E. Bitterman, C. B. G. Campbell and N. Hotton), pp. 107–113. Erlbaum, Hillsdale, NJ.

Stebbins, W. C. (1978). Hearing of the primates. In *Recent Advances in Primatology* (eds D. J. Chivers and J. Herbert), pp. 705–720. Academic Press, London.

Stephan, H. (1972). Evolution of primates brains: a comparative anatomical investigation. In *The Functional and Evolutionary Biology of the Primates.* (ed. R. Tuttle), pp. 155–174. Aldine, Chicago.

Stephan, H. and Andy, O. J. (1969). Quantitative comparative neuroanatomy of primates: an attempt at a phylogenetic interpretation. *Ann. N. Y. Acad. Sci.* **167**, 370–387.

Stephan, H., Bauchot, R. and Andy, O. J. (1970). Data on size of the brain and of various brain parts in insectivores and primates. In *The Primate Brain* (eds C. R. Noback and W. Montagna), pp. 289–297. Appleton-Century-Crofts, New York.

Stephenson, G. R. (1973). Biology of communication and population structure. In *Behavioral Regulation of Behavior in Primates* (ed. C. R. Carpenter), pp. 34–55. Bucknell University Press, Lewisberg.

Stern, J. T. (1971). *Functional Morphology of the Hip and Thigh of Cebid Monkeys and its Implication for the Evolution of Erect Posture.* (Biblo. Primatol., **14**.) Karger, Basel.

Straub, R. O., Seidenberg, M. S., Bever, T. G. and Terrace, H. S. (1979). Serial learning in the pigeon. *J. exp. anal. Behav.*, **32**, 137–148.

Strong, P. N. (1967). Comparative studies in oddity learning. III. Apparatus transfer in chimpanzees and children. *Psychonom. Sci.* **7**, 43.

Strong, P. N. and Hedges, M. (1966). Comparative studies on simple oddity learning. I. Cats, racoons, monkeys and chimpanzees, *Psychonom. Sci.* **5**, 13–14.

Struhsaker, T. T. (1967). Social structure among vervet monkeys (*Cercopithecus aethiops*). *Behaviour* **29**, 83–121.

Strum, S. C. (1975). Primate predation: interim report on the development of a tradition in a troop of olive baboons. *Science* **187**, 755–757.

Strum, S. C. (1976). Primate predation and bioenergetics. *Science* **191**, 315–317.

Suarez, S. D. and Gallup, G. G. (1981). Self-recognition in chimpanzees and orang-utans, but not gorillas. *J. hum. Evol.* **10**, 175–188.

Sugiyama, Y. (1967). Social organization of hanamun langurs. In *Social Communication among Primates* (ed. S. A. Altmann), pp. 221–236. Chicago University Press, Chicago.

Sugiyama, Y. (1972). Social characteristics and socialization of wild chimpanzees. In *Primate Socialization* (ed. F. E. Poirier), pp. 145–163. Random House, New York.

Suomi, S. J. and Harlow, H. F. (1972). Social rehabilitation of isolate-reared monkeys. *Devl Psychol.* **6**, 487–496.

Sussman, R. W. and Richard, A. (1974). The role of aggression among diurnal prosimians. In *Primate Aggression, Territoriality and Xenophobia* (ed. R. L. Holloway), pp. 49–76. Academic Press, New York.

Sutton, D. (1979). Mechanisms underlying vocal control in nonhuman primates. In *Neurobiology of Social Communication* (eds H. D. Steklis and M. J. Raleigh), pp. 45–67. Academic Press, New York.

Sutton, D., Larson, C., Taylor, E. M. and Lindeman, R. C. (1973). Vocalization in rhesus monkeys: conditionability. *Brain Res.* **52**, 225–231.

Sutton, D., Larson, C. and Lindeman, R. C. (1974). Neocortical and limbic lesion effects on primate phonation. *Brain Res.* **71**, 61–75.

Suzuki, A. (1975). The origin of hominid hunting: a primatological perspective. In *Socioecology and Psychology of Primates* (ed. R. H. Tuttle), pp. 259–278. Mouton, The Hague.

Szalay, F. S. and Decker, R. L. (1974). Origins, evolution and function of the tarsus in late Cretaceous Eutheria and Paleocene primates. In *Primate Locomotion* (ed. F. A. Jenkins), pp. 223–259. Academic Press, New York.

Szarski, H. (1971). The importance of deviation-amplifying circuits in evolution. *Acta biotheoret.* **20**, 168–170.

Tanner, J. M. (1961). *Growth and Adolescence*, 2nd edn. Blackwell, Oxford.

Tayler, C. K. and Saayman, G. S. (1973). Imitative behavior by Indian Ocean bottlenose dolphins (*Tursiops aduncus*) in captivity. *Behaviour* **44**, 286–298.

Teleki, G. (1973a). *The Predatory Behavior of Wild Chimpanzees*. Bucknell University Press, Lewisburg.

Teleki, G. (1973b). The omnivorous chimpanzee. *Scient. Am.* **228** (Jan.), 33–42.

Teleki, G. (1974). Chimpanzee subsistence technology: materials and skills. *J. hum. Evol.* **3**, 575–594.

Teleki, G. (1975). Primate subsistence patterns: collector predators and gatherer hunters. *J. hum. Evol.* **4**, 125–184.

Terrace, H. S. (1979a). Is problem-solving language? *J. exp. Anal. Behav.* **31**, 161–175.

Terrace, H. S. (1979b). *Nim*. Eyre Methuen, London.

Terrace, H. S., Petitto, L. A., Sanders, R. J. and Bever, T. G. (1979). Can an ape create a sentence? *Science* **206**, 891–902.

Terrace, H. S., Petitto, L. A., Sanders, R. J. and Bever, T. G. (1981). On the grammatical capacity of apes. In *Children's Language* (ed. K. Nelson), Vol. 2, pp. 371–495. Gardner Press, New York.

Thompson, C. R. and Church, R. M. (1980). An explanation of the language of a chimpanzee. *Science* **28**, 313–314.

Thompson, D'Arcy W. (1917). *On Growth and Form*. Cambridge University Press, Cambridge.

Thompson, R. F. (1967). *Foundations of Physiological Psychology*. Harper, New York.

Thompson, T. I. (1963). Visual reinforcement in Siamese fighting fish. *Science* **141**, 55–57.

Thorndike, E. L. (1911). *Animal Intelligence*. MacMillan, New York.

Thorpe, W. H. (1961). *Bird Song*. Cambridge University Press, Cambridge.

Thorpe, W. H. (1963). *Learning and Instinct in Animals*, 2nd edn. Methuen, London.

Thorpe, W. H. (1974). *Animal Nature and Human Nature*. Methuen, London.

Tiger, L and Fox, R. (1972). *The Imperial Animal*. Secker and Warburg, London.

Tinbergen, N. (1951). *The Study of Instinct*. Oxford University Press, Oxford.

Tinbergen, N. (1953). *Social Behaviour in Animals*. Methuen, London.

Tinbergen, N. (1957). The function of territory. *Bird Study* **14**, 14−27.

Tinbergen, N. (1963). On aims and methods of ethology. *Z. Tierpsychol.* **20**, 410−433.

Tinbergen, N. (1968). On war and peace in animals and man. *Science* **160**, 1411−1418.

Tinklepaugh, O. L. (1928). An experimental study of representative factors in monkeys. *J. comp. Psychol.* **8**, 197−236.

Tinklepaugh, O. L. (1932). Multiple delayed reaction with chimpanzees and monkeys. *J. comp. Psychol.* **13**, 207−243.

Tobias, P. V. (1970). Brain size, grey matter, and race—fact or fiction? *Am. J. phys. Anthropol.* **32**, 3−25.

Tobias, P. V. (1971). *The Brain in Hominid Evolution*. Columbia University Press, New York.

Tobias, P. V. (1975). Brain evolution of the Hominoidea. In *Primate Functional Morphology and Evolution* (ed. R. H. Tuttle), pp. 353−392. Mouton, The Hague.

Tobias, P. V. (1976). African hominids: dating and phylogeny. In *Human Origins: Louis Leakey and the East African Evidence* (eds G. Ll. Isaac and E. R. McGown), pp. 377−422. Benjamin, Menlo Park, California.

Tobias, P. V. (1981). The emergence of man in Africa and beyond. *Phil. Trans. R. Soc. Lond.* B**292**, 43−56.

Tokuda, K. (1969). On the handedness of Japanese monkeys. *Primates* **10**, 41−46.

Tommila, V. (1974). Stereoscopic and binocular vision. *Ophthalmology* **169**, 90−98.

Towe, A. L. (1973). Relative number of pyramidal tract neurons in mammals of different sizes. *Brain Behav. Evol.* **7**, 1−17.

Tower, D. B. (1954). Structural and functional organization of mammalian cerebral cortex: the correlation of neurone density with brain size. *J. comp. Neurol.* **101**, 19−52.

Treff, H. A. (1967). Tiefenscharfe und Sehscharfe beim Galago (*Galago senegalensis*). *Z. vergl. Physiol.* **54**, 26−57.

Trivers, R. L. (1971). The evolution of reciprocal altruism. *Q. J. Biol.* **46**, 35−57.

Turnbull, C. M. (1966). *Wayward Servants: The Two World of the African Pygmies*. Eyre and Spottiswoode, London.

Turner, E. R. A. (1964). Social feeding in birds. *Behaviour* **24**, 1−46.

Tuttle, R. H. (1975). Parallelism, brachiation and hominoid phylogeny. In *Phylogeny of the Primates* (eds W. P. Luckett and F. S. Szalay), pp. 447−480. Plenum Press, New York.

Twitchell, T. E. (1965). The automatic grasping response of infants.
Neuropsychologia **3**, 247−259.
Tylor, E. B. (1881). *Anthropology*. Macmillan, London.

Ucko, P. J. and Rosenfeld, A. (1967). *Palaeolithic Cave Art*. Weidenfeld and Nicolson, London.
Udry, J. R. and Morris, N. M. (1968). Distribution of coitus in the menstrual cycle. *Nature* **220**, 593−596.
Ulrich, R. (1966). Pain as a cause of aggression. *Am. Zool.* **6**, 643−662.
Ulrich, R. and Azrin, N. H. (1962). Reflexive fighting in response to aversive stimulation. *J. exp. Anal. Behav.* **5**, 511−520.
Ulrich, R., Johnston, M. Richardson, J. and Wolff, P. C. (1963). The operant conditioning of fighting behavior in rats. *Psychol. Rec.* **13**, 465−470.

Valen, L. Van (1974). Brain size and intelligence in man. *Am. J. phys. Anthrop.* **40**, 417−424.
Valenstein, E. S., Cox, V. C. and Kakolewski, J. W. (1969). The hypothalamus and motivated behavior. In *Reinforcement and Behavior* (ed. J. C. Tapp), pp. 242−287. Academic Press, New York.
Vernon, P. E. (1961). *The Structure of Human Abilities*. Methuen, London.

Walker, A. and Leakey, R. E. F. (1978). The hominids of East Turkana. *Scient. Am.* **239** (Aug.), 44−56.
Walker, A. E. and Green, H. D. (1938) Electrical excitability of the motor face area: a comparative study in primates. *J. Neurophysiol.* **1**, 152−165.
Walls, G. L. (1967). *The Vertebrate Eye and its Adaptive Radiation*. Hafner, New York.
Warden, C. J. and Warner, L. H. (1928). The sensory capacities and intelligence of dogs, with a report on the ability of the noted dog "Fellow" to respond to verbal stimuli. *Q. Rev. Biol.* **3**, 1−28.
Warden, C. J., Fjeld, H. A. and Koch, A. M. (1940). Imitative behaviour in cebus and rhesus monkeys. *J. genet. Psychol.* **56**, 311−322.
Warren, J. M. (1965). Primate learning in comparative perspective. In *Behavior of Nonhuman Primates* (eds A. M. Schrier, H. F. Harlow and F. Stollnitz), Vol. 1, pp. 249−281. Academic Press, New York.
Warren, J. M. (1966). Reversal learning and the formation of learning sets by cats and rhesus monkeys. *J. comp. Physiol. Psychol.* **61**, 421−428.
Warren, J. M. (1973). Learning in vertebrates. In *Comparative Psychology: a Modern Survey* (eds D. A. Dewsbury and D. A. Rethlingshafer), pp. 471−509. McGraw-Hill, New York.
Warren, J. M. (1974). Possibly unique characteristics of learning by primates. *J. hum. Evol.* **3**, 445−454.
Warren, J. M. (1976). Tool use in mammals. In *Evolution of Brain and Behavior in Vertebrates* (eds R. B. Masterton, M. E. Bitterman, C. B. G. Campbell and N. Hotton), pp. 407−424. Erlbaum, Hillsdale, NJ.
Warren, J. M. (1977). Handedness and cerebral dominance in monkeys. In *Lateralization in the Nervous System* (eds S. Harnad, R. W. Doty, L. Goldstein, J. Jaynes and G. Krauthamer), pp. 151−172. Academic Press, New York.

Warren, J. M. and Nonnemann, A. J. (1976). The search for cerebral dominance in rhesus monkeys. *Ann. N. Y. Acad. Sci.* **180**, 733–744.

Warren, J. M., Ablanalp, J. M. and Warren, H. B. (1967). The development of handedness in cats and rhesus monkeys. In *Early Behavior* (eds H. W. Stevenson, E. H. Hess and H. L. Rheingold), pp. 73–101. Wiley, New York.

Warrington, E. K. and Taylor, A. M. (1973). The contribution of the right parietal lobe to object recognition. *Cortex* **9**, 152–164.

Washburn, S. L. (1969). The evolution of human behavior. In *The Uniqueness of Man* (ed. J. D. Roslansky), pp. 167–189. North-Holland, Amsterdam.

Waters, R. S. and Wilson, W. A. (1976). Speech perception by rhesus monkeys: the voicing distinction in synthesized labial and velar stop consonants. *Percept. Psychophys.* **17**, 285–289.

Wegener, J. G. (1964). Auditory discrimination behavior of normal monkeys. *J. Audit. Res.* **4**, 81–106.

Wegener, J. G. (1976). Some variables in auditory pattern discrimination learning. *Neuropsychologia* **14**, 149–159.

Weiskrantz, L. (1980). Varieties of residual experience. *Q. Jl exp. Psychol.* **32**, 365–386.

Weiskrantz, L. and Cowey, A. (1963). The aetiology of food reward in monkeys. *Anim. Behav.* **11**, 225–234.

Weiskrantz, L. and Cowey, A. (1967). Comparison of the effects of striate cortex and retinal lesions on visual acuity in the monkey. *Science* **155**, 104–106.

Weiskrantz, L., Warrington, E. K., Sanders, M. D. and Marshall, J. (1974). Visual capacity of the hemianopic field following a restricted occipital ablation. *Brain* **97**, 709–728.

Welker, C. (1971). Microelectrode delineation of fine-grain somatotopic organization of SmI cerebral neocortex in albino rat. *Brain Res.* **26**, 259–275.

Welker, C. and Seidenstein, S. (1959). Somatic sensory representation in the cerebral cortex of the racoon (*Procyon lotor*). *J. comp. Neurol.* **111**, 469–501.

Welles, J. F. (1975). The anthropoid hand: a comparative study of prehension. *Proc. 5th Int. Congr. Primatol.* 30–33. Karger, Basel.

White, L. A. (1959). The concept of culture. *Am. Anthrop.* **61**, 227–251.

Whiten, A. Parental encouragement and teaching in the great apes and man. Unpublished manuscript.

Whiting, J. W. M. and Child, I. L. (1953). *Child Training and Personality.* Yale University Press, New Haven.

Wilson, A. P. and Boelkins, R. C. (1970). Evidence for seasonal variation in aggressive behavior in *Macaca mulatta*. *Anim. Behav.* **18**, 719–724.

Wilson, E. O. (1971). *The Insect Societies.* Harvard University Press, Cambridge, Mass.

Wilson, E. O. (1975). *Sociobiology: the New Synthesis.* Harvard University Press, Cambridge, Mass.

Wilson, E. O. (1978). *On Human Nature.* Harvard University Press, Cambridge, Mass.

Wilson, P. J. (1980). *Man, the Promising Primate.* Yale University Press, New Haven.

Winkelmann, R. N. (1963). Nerve endings in the skin of primates. In *Evolutionary and Genetic Biology of Primates* (ed. J. Buettner-Janusch), Vol. 1, pp. 229–259. Academic Press, New York.

Winner, E. and Ettlinger, G. (1979). Do chimpanzees recognize photographs as representations of objects? *Neuropsychologia* **17**, 413–420.

Wispé, L. G. ed. (1978). *Altruism, Sympathy and Helping*. Academic Press, New York.

Witelson, S. (1977). Anatomic asymmetry in the temporal lobe: its documentation, phylogenesis and relationship to functional asymmetry. *Ann. N. Y. Acad. Sci.* **299**, 328–354.

Wolberg, D. L. (1970). The hypothesized osteodontokeratic culture of the australopithecines: a look at the evidence and the opinions. *Curr. Anthrop.* **11**, 23–30.

Wolfe, J, B. (1936). Effectiveness of token rewards for chimpanzees. *Comp. Psychol. Mon.* **12**, 1–72.

Wolin, L. R. and Massopust, L. C. (1970). Morphology of the primate retina. In *The Primate Brain* (eds C. R. Noback and W. Montagna), 1–27. Appleton-Century-Crofts, New York.

Wood, B. (1978). *Human Evolution*. Chapman and Hall, London.

Woodburn, J. (1968). An introduction to Hadza ecology. In *Man the Hunter* (eds R. B. Lee and I. DeVore), pp. 49–55. Aldine, Chicago.

Woodburn, J. (1970). *Hunters and Gatherers: the Material Culture of the Nomadic Hadza*. British Museum, London.

Wood Jones. F. (1926). *The Arboreal Man*. Hafner, New York.

Woodruff, G. and Premack, D. (1979). Intentional communication in the chimpanzee: the development of deception. *Cognition* **7**, 333–362.

Woodruff, G., Premack, D. and Kennel, K. (1978). Conservation of liquid and solid quantity by the chimpanzee. *Science* **202**, 991–994.

Woolsey, C. N. (1958). Organization of somatic sensory and motor areas of the cerebral cortex. In *Biological and Biochemical Basis of Behavior* (eds H. F. Harlow and C. N. Woolsey), pp. 63–81. University of Wisconsin Press, Wisconsin.

Woolsey, C. N., Settlage, P. H., Meyer, D. R., Sencer, W., Pinto Hamuy, T. and Travis, M. (1952). Pattern of localization in precentral and "supplementary" motor areas and their relation to the concept of a premotor area. *Res. Publ. Assoc. nerv. ment. Dis.* **30**, 238–264.

Wrangham, R. W. (1974). Artificial feeding of chimpanzees and baboons in their natural habitat. *Anim. Behav.* **22**, 83–93.

Wrangham, R. (1975). The Behavioural Ecology of Chimpanzees in Gombe National Park, Tanzania, Unpubl. PhD thesis, University of Cambridge.

Wright, R. V. S. (1972). Imitative learning of a flaked-tool technology—the case of an orang-utan. *Mankind* **8**, 296–306.

Yamaguchi, S. and Myers, R. E. (1972). Failure of discriminative vocal conditioning in rhesus monkey. *Brain Res.* **37**, 109–114.

Yates, A. J. (1962). *Frustration and Conflict*. Methuen, London.

REFERENCES

Yeni-Komshian, G. H. and Benson, D. A. (1976). Anatomical study of cerebral asymmetry in the temporal lobe of humans, chimpanzees and rhesus monkeys. *Science* **192**, 387–389.

Yerkes, R. M. (1933). Genetic aspects of grooming, a socially important primate behavior pattern. *J. Soc. Psychol.* **4**, 3–25.

Yerkes, R. M. (1943). *Chimpanzees: a Laboratory Colony*. Yale University Press, New Haven.

Zaidel, E. (1977). Auditory vocabulary of the right hemisphere following brain bisection or hemispherectomy. *Cortex* **12**, 191–211.

Zuckerman, S. (1932). *The Social Life of Monkeys and Apes*. Kegan Paul, London.

Author index

Woodburn, J. 147, 159, 293, 319
Wood Jones, F. 54
Woodruff, G. 131, 200, 236
Woolsey, C. N. 34, 35, 68
Wrangham, R. W. 181, 297

Wright, R. V. S. 136, 137, 138, 222

Yamaguchi, S. 206
Yates, A. 324
Yeni-Komshian, G. H. 95

Yerkes, R. M. 130, 268

Zaidel, E. 93
Zuckerman, S. 301

Subject index